THE SPIRITS

OF AMERICA

THE SPIRITS
OF AMERICA

A SOCIAL
HISTORY OF
ALCOHOL

Eric Burns

Temple University Press
PHILADELPHIA

Temple University Press, Philadelphia 19122
Copyright © 2004 by Temple University
All rights reserved
Published 2004
Printed in the United States of America

Library of Congress Cataloging-in-Publication Data

Burns, Eric.
    The spirits of America : a social history of alcohol / Eric Burns.
       p. cm.
    Includes bibliographical references and index.
    ISBN 1-59213-214-6 (cloth : alk. paper)
    1. Drinking of alcoholic beverages—United States—History.   2 Drinking customs—
United States—History.   3. Temperance—United States—History.   I. Title.
HV5292.B87   2004
394.1'3'0973—dc21   2003050790

2 4 6 8 9 7 5 3

To Toby
with love and respect
for what has passed
and all that will come

Contents

Introduction:
The Spirits of the World

Thousands of years ago, before Christ or Buddha or Muhammad, before democracy or industry or technology as we know the terms today, before the Roman Empire rose or the Colossus of Rhodes fell, before water wheels or paddle wheel boats, before decimals or compasses, before the first dice were rolled or the first sheet music was carved into a cuneiform tablet, before sundials were invented or silver coins minted or stone bridges built across rivers—before any of this happened and before most of it was even a flash in the minds of madmen, there were people in Asia Minor drinking beer. They were drinking it after they ate and after they worked their fields. They were drinking it to warm their chills and to cool their fevers and to produce sensations that they could produce in no other way, with no other food or beverage or plant of the age. They were drinking it when they conversed with one another and when they conversed with their gods and sometimes, especially when they had gotten carried away and imbibed too much of the stuff, gulping it like water and paying no attention to the consequences, they were drinking it when they conversed with themselves.

And, thousands of years ago, there were people in Sumer drinking beer. If a man worked at one of the temples, he received a ration of two pints a day. Others, "senior dignitaries" at the temples, were provided with ten pints, enough to rid them of sobriety as well as thirst. Sometimes they drank for the simple pleasure of drinking; sometimes they drank to pay homage to the goddess Ninkasi, "the lady who fills the mouth," and who, in her role as celestial brewmeistress par excellence, presided over the country's production of malt beverage. It was, to say the least, extensive; the Sumerians made eight different kinds of beer from barley, another eight from wheat, and at least three from a mixture of grains. The more of the refreshment that Ninkasi's subjects drank, the more they honored her. The subjects were very fond of honoring.

Also at the time, there were people in Egypt drinking beer, which they called *hek*. For them, the beverage was a by-product—or, more appropriately, a bonus—of bread-baking. The Egyptians began by steeping barley in water, allowing the grain and the liquid to mingle in unhurried fashion. The result was a kind of paste, which was then stored in the open air in a vat of some sort, allowing warm Nile breezes to blow over it until it achieved the perfect consistency.

> Then [the Egyptians] kneaded [it] into a dough. Next, it was lightly baked to turn it into bread and then soaked in water; dates may have been added at this stage to sweeten the mixture. Then, it was put into a warm place to allow fermentation to occur and finally squeezed through a cloth or fine sieve so that the sweet liquid could be drained off into a pot.

After all this the pot was raised to the lips of the thirsty—perhaps too many sets of lips, perhaps too many times. "Banquets frequently ended with the guests, men and women, being sick," it has been noted, "and this did not in any way seem shocking." Further, alcohol-induced illness "was considered a suitable subject for art. A recovered fresco of the second millennium B.C. shows a woman banqueter turning from the table to vomit into a bowl held by a servant."

A lot of bowls were filled this way. So many, in fact, that after a while a backlash set in, and the Egyptians became one of the world's first populations to encourage abstinence, at least on a part-time basis. "Do not get drunk in the taverns in which they drink beer," cautions *Wisdom of Ani*, written about 1400 B.C.; if you do, your companions are likely to "repeat words which may have gone out of your mouth, without your being aware of having uttered them."

There were people in the northern lands drinking beer. Some of them were alive, some were not. The Scandinavians believed that "the spirits of their dead warriors were taken to an enormous banquet hall, Valhalla, where they feasted every day on copious amounts of ale." Thus they would remain valorous, or perhaps foolhardy, as ready to do battle in the afterlife as they had been on earth.

There were people along the banks of the Danube and the Rhine, between the North and Baltic Seas, early Germans and very much alive, also feasting copiously, "drinking rivers of beer," allowing the rivers to overflow within them and delighting in the sensations of flood.

There were people in Babylonia overflowing. Hammurabi, the most famous of their lawgivers, was troubled by their excesses but even more by the unscrupulous practices of the establishments in which his countrymen raised their mugs. His code condemned alehouses for selling beverages that were priced excessively and brewed weakly, finding the former fraudulent and the latter inimical to the whole point of drinking. He put some of these places out of business, while forcing others to change their ways. He was a consumer advocate long before the notion of consumers.

But he did not deny either the pleasures or the importance of beer, which "some authorities regard . . . as the critically important product, demand for which induced people to practice agriculture in the first place."

In India, wine seems to have been the preferred libation. Husbands downed it; their mistresses downed it; their wives did not. For reasons unknown to posterity, the wives were not allowed to quench their thirsts with alcohol; rather, they had to satisfy themselves olfactorily. The glasses would be filled and the wives would lower their noses, take a few deep breaths, then pass the glasses along and watch the others imbibe. It was a demeaning practice. It must also have been a pleasant consolation; the Indians concocted their wine from rice, grain, sugar, molasses, and honey, so that the potion was as fragrant to inhale as it was sassy to consume.

There were people in China drinking wine, and they sometimes sacrificed their fellow Chinese to the gods in the process, the earth on these occasions becoming moist with a combination of fermented grape juice and fresh blood. The Chinese also drank wine when they worshiped their ancestors, which is to say that they took their potion seriously, not socially. In fact, they tried to discourage merriment of any kind in the act of slaking thirst, the Han Dynasty going so far as to fine citizens for drinking in groups of more than three—unless, that is, one of the three was on his way to eternity.

There were people in Persia drinking wine, and a myth came to be told about how the beverage was discovered. One year, it seems, the grape harvest was so bountiful that the Persians, lovers of fine fruit though they were, could not make use of it all. Fearful of waste, old King Jamshid ordered the surplus to be stored in large jars in the cellar of his palace. Servants filled dozens of such jars, hundreds of them, sealing them tightly and then stacking them on the shelves that lined the walls of the underground corridors next to the dungeons. The jars were guarded as zealously as the prisoners with whom they shared the space.

Several months later, when the king ordered the fruit to be brought to him so that the men and women of his court might enjoy it out of season, he made a shocking discovery. The jars were still there but the grapes were not; they had been replaced with "a strange-tasting dark purple juice," of which the king took a single whiff and gasped. Mystified and disappointed, he ordered his servants to get rid of the stuff. They were to return the jars to the basement and, in large letters, write the word poison on each. If the grapes could not be reclaimed—which is to say, if this perverse process of alchemy could not somehow be reversed—at least the members of the royal household could be warned of the vile product that had so inexplicably been created.

Shortly afterward, one of the women in Jamshid's court, distraught at the betrayal of her lover, decided to commit suicide.

> She wandered down to the king's cellars, found the jars labeled poison, and helped herself to a few swallows from one of them. She immediately began to feel better. Then, after a few more swallows, she grew drowsy and fell asleep. When she awoke the next morning, she rushed to tell the king that his "poison" was not poison at all but was actually a pleasant and unusual drink.
>
> King Jamshid promptly sent for some of the "poison" and sampled it himself. He, too, began to feel relaxed and lighthearted. Jamshid thereupon rechristened the mysterious beverage *zeher-e-koosh*, or "the delightful poison," and decreed that henceforth a share of grapes from every harvest should be preserved in exactly the same manner.

There were people in Greece drinking wine, no less a figure than Socrates supposedly swearing that it "does of a truth 'moisten the soul' and lull our griefs to sleep." The Greeks found that their griefs slept even more soundly when they blended their wine with spices and flavorings, perfumes and unguents. Then they diluted it further, the usual formula being three parts water to two parts grape.

There were people in Rome drinking wine. They, too,
potion. But as time went on this seemed to them count
diluted wine, diluted pleasure. So the Romans began to a
making their wine stronger and stronger as the empire got we
weaker, the beverage perhaps not a cause of the empire's eventual fall
but almost surely an effect.

There were people in Etruria drinking wine, probably taking it
straight, and afterward, with as steady a hand as possible, recording
their euphoria by drawing "scenes of bibulous merriment" on the walls
of their caves. Then, inspired by their art, they created more bibulous
merriment in real life.

There was no one drinking liquor in the ancient world; the principles of distillation would not be discovered until much later—the first
century A.D. according to one account, but more likely the seventh.
The first distilled libation, brandy, was probably not blended until the
eleventh century by a Spanish physician, a gentleman who seems not
to have cared what his invention cured so much as what it momentarily
alleviated.

But half a millennium later, by the time the British had begun to colo-
nize North America, setting up outposts in Virginia and Massachusetts,
Rhode Island and Pennsylvania and the Carolinas, there would be a variety of distilled drinks available to men and women, not just brandy,
and there would be improved means of brewing grains for beer and
processing grapes for wine. The Americans would welcome them all.
The Americans would drink them all, rivers of mind-altering potables of
their own that produced scenes of bibulous merriment of their own, not
to mention inspiration and stimulation and comfort, as well as heartache
and illness and dissolution and, finally, early in the twentieth century,
the Eighteenth Amendment to the Constitution of the United States,
perhaps the worst idea ever proposed by a legislative body anywhere in
the world for the ostensible goal of a better society.

In fact, alcoholic beverages would come to be more than just a staple of diet for the New World colonists; they would serve as an almost indispensable accompaniment to liberty: sparking the urge to separate from the Motherland, igniting patriotism, stoking the passion for
growth and prosperity and a government that was the perfect reflection
of its citizens' desires.

It was, or so it seems in retrospect, as if freedom were an engine and
spirits the fuel of highest octane.

1

The First National Pastime

We read in our histories that the Revolutionary War was conceived in the watering holes of colonial America, but almost as an aside, and we never ask why.

Why did New York merchants gather at Burns's Tavern on Broadway to plan a boycott of British goods in response to the Stamp Act?

Why did Bostonians organize their tea party at the Green Dragon Tavern?

Why did Virginia's Committee of Correspondence, and later the Intercolonial Committees, conduct their insurrectionary business at the Sir Walter Raleigh Tavern in Williamsburg?

Why did Samuel Adams and John Hancock and their friends fan the flames of independence at the Black Horse Inn in Winchester, Massachusetts?

Why did Captain John Parker make Buckman's Tavern on Lexington Green the headquarters for the Minutemen?

Why did Ethan Allen and the Green Mountain Boys convene at the Catamount in Bennington, Vermont?

Why did John Adams meet George Washington for the first time at the City Tavern in Philadelphia? Why, in fact, was it considered "the great gathering place for members of Congress"?

Why did Thomas Jefferson begin writing the Declaration of Independence at the Indian Queen Tavern in the same city, a brimming glass of Madeira next to his bottle of ink?

Why did Jack Jouett, "a Southern counterpart to Paul Revere," mount his horse outside the Cuckoo Inn for a ride to Monticello, his goal to warn Jefferson of a British attack on Virginia?

, Why did "disgruntled artisans, storekeepers, and militiamen" congregate at Philadelphia's Four All's Tavern, or the Wilkes and Liberty, to rail about the concentration of wealth in the hands of a few?

Why did other colonists whose names have not survived the years assemble at other drinking houses to express their grievances and decide on their actions and form more tightly the bonds of their resolve? Why did they swarm into the Bunch of Grapes and the King's Head and the Blue Anchor and the Indian King, reading aloud the latest news of rebellion in the newspapers "and either applauding or howling with rage"? Why, in fact, would Henry David Thoreau one day write that "the gods who are most interested in the human race preside over the tavern"?

Why did none of these councils take place in the gods' more traditional home, the church, or in town halls or schoolhouses, places of business or private residences?

Some of them did, of course, but not many and not often, for no other meeting place of the time offered the same guarantee of high attendance and devout attention as a tavern, even when the topic was as important as relations with England. Which is to say that no other activity of the time, perhaps not even the conceiving and implementing of freedom itself, was as important to the colonists as the consumption of alcoholic beverages. Booze was food, medicine, and companionship in the early days of America: ichor, elixir, and *aqua vitae*. It was how the tongue got loose and the mind receptive, how the body unlimbered and the future grew bright. It was a boost for one's courage, a shield against loneliness, a light in the midnight hours when the stars were hidden and the moon otherwise occupied. Even the Pilgrims, thought to be so ascetic, so unwilling to yield to temptations of either the flesh or palate, packed a plentiful supply of "hot waters," probably gin and brandy, into the cargo hold of the *Mayflower*.

Most of it survived the voyage. Not so on future trips. "William Bradford, in 1630, was expecting a consignment of two hogsheads of mead for his colonists, but found no more than six gallons when the boat arrived, the remainder, which was about 100 gallons, 'being drunke up under ye name of leakage and so lost.' "

In fact, booze of one sort or another was attendant to so many activities of the time that it sometimes seemed as if the activities were but an excuse for the booze, a kind of cover story. Specifically, it was beer that made grain worthwhile and wine that gave sanction to grapes. Cider was "the main point of every apple tree north of the Carolinas" and rum the "only prayer for the present world."

The latter was certainly the most popular beverage in the present world, or at least that portion of the world bordered by the Atlantic on one side and the Appalachians on the other. South and west of it, on various islands in the Caribbean, molasses was being produced in large quantities from sugarcane. Much of it was exported to the colonies to be distilled into rum. "What wasn't consumed in New England," writes Edward Hamilton, "was shipped to Africa and traded for slaves to provide the labor to grow more cane in the Caribbean."

But these islands manufactured their own rum, too, and like Cuban cigars a few centuries later, it was both illegal for Americans to purchase and irresistible for them to consume. "As the first president of the United States, George Washington ordered a barrel of the best Barbados rum for the inauguration party."

What it all meant was that the tavern could not help but be the most venerated of early American institutions. The best people went to them. The best people owned them. In seventeenth-century Massachusetts, for example, only voters and church members, "the colony's elite," were allowed to purchase and operate taverns, and they often became a home away from home for those who inhabited them. To elected officials they were an after-hours seat of government, to shopkeepers a shop at which they could enjoy the indulgences of being a customer, to members of the clergy a place to contemplate the Almighty's designs without being plagued by thirst of demonic proportions.

This does not mean, however, that our forebears were a collection of tumble-down drunks and back-street hooligans. A few were, of course; that was inevitable. Even the best taverns suffered from the occasional outbreak of "Drunkenness, Swearing, Cursing, Perjury, Blasphemy, Cheating, Lying, and Fighting," and at taverns that were not the best, this kind of rowdiness was as common as a refill. In fact, early in the eighteenth century, the Massachusetts General Court and the Boston Town Council began suspending the licenses of owners who permitted inappropriate behavior on their premises, and the definition of "inappropriate" became more and more expansive as the years went by.

But there were also colonists who, for reasons of their own, did not partake at all, looking upon those who did with bemusement or disgust or a combination of both. And there were colonists who liked their liquor in moderation, putting away their bottles short of the point of full inebriation—social drinkers, we would call them today. William Bradford might have bemoaned the mead that did not arrive, but neither did he "want his people to be too drunk, complaining when, as he served as governor of Plymouth, his soldiers were 'so steeld with drinke as their peeces were too heavie for them.'"

And then there were colonists who became *so* "steeld" that they built up a kind of homeopathic resistance to glazed eyes, slurred speech, and an unsteady gait. They were "in a certain degree *seasoned*," as a contemporary observer put it, "and consequently it [was] by no means common to see an American *very* much intoxicated."

But a human being who seasoned himself undertook a difficult process, one that was expensive and imprecise and required vast quantities of alcohol for the proper results. How vast no one can say; in the years before independence, neither beer nor wine nor liquor was taxed, and thus the colonies had no reason to keep records of sale or consumption. The first educated guess is for the 1790s. There is, however, no reason to think that the figures were much different a decade or two, or even a century, earlier.

> An average American over fifteen years old drank just under six gallons of absolute alcohol each year. That represented some thirty-four gallons of beer and cider (about 3.4 gallons of absolute alcohol), slightly over five gallons of distilled liquors (2.3 gallons of absolute alcohol), and under a gallon of wine (possibly .10 gallons absolute).

It took a lot of dedication to put away so much hooch, not to mention a lot of time. Some of the colonists bent their elbows before the cock's first crow in the morning and did not straighten them again until the sun had grown weary and been several hours gone.

6:30 A.M. The instant they awoke, many Americans reached for bottles of rum or brandy and poured themselves a healthy serving. The object was to open the eyes wide and quickly, jarring the innards to abrupt alertness, hot waters instead of a cold shower. "The custom," it has been supposed, "owes something to the dram of whiskey on which the Highland Scot counted to set the system going after the stagnation of sleep." It might also owe something to the belief that so strong a jolt to the system so early in the day could not help but keep the system running at peak efficiency. And possibly, since rum was known in its native West Indies as "killdevil," the imbiber sought a spiritual, as well as spirituous, state for the sunrise hours.

Then again, it might simply have been that Americans loved their liquor so much they could not wait to get started. After all, the British from whom they were descended, whom in reality they still *were*, had long thought of alcoholic beverages as essentials; "the consumption of strong drink," in fact, "was connected with every phase of life from apprenticeship." For this reason, it is estimated that there were some 17,000 "gin-houses" in London alone in the mid-eighteenth century, and if some critics at the time thought the beverage they provided was a "liquid fire by which men drink their hell beforehand," others thought of it as a brief taste of heaven on earth, an antidote, crisp and bracing, for "the thickness and dampness of the atmosphere." And a modern historian, writing about England in the same era, has guessed that "drink, like gambling and violence, was a palliative at a time when life was so precarious."

7:00 A.M. Now that they had prepared their internal organs for the day, the colonists washed down their breakfasts with more alcohol, possibly a second portion of rum, which they either drank or sloshed over their bacon as it cooked. Or they might do their sloshing with beer, it being the habit of some women of the era to break their toast into small pieces and put them into a bowl and then liberally douse them with brew. If, for some reason, neither rum nor beer was available, our ancestors would find something else to pick them up, "anything from cherry brandy to wine mixed with sugar and water."

Perhaps there was an infant in the house. If so, he would be given the last few drops of alcohol. As he got older, he would graduate to larger amounts. "I have frequently seen fathers," wrote a colonist who was not disapproving, "wake their child of a year old from a sound sleep to make it drink Rum, or brandy." No less an authority than John Locke, the British philosopher who so inspired Thomas Jefferson and other architects of American independence, believed in the benefits of toddies for toddlers. Even better, though, was something known as "small beer," a weaker version of its namesake, although Locke cautioned that a child should drink it only "after he has eaten a piece of bread."

The first Americans were not trying to make sots of their offspring. They were providing them with spirits because spirits were the beverages of the household, not to mention the society. In fact, in the case of older children, the colonists were trying to prevent a sottish future by "seasoning" their hostages to fortune, accustoming them to alcohol in the hope that they would become so used to it in its various forms that it would not affect them much as young men and adults. It seemed like a good idea at the time. It seemed like an even better one when a cantankerous adolescent, rebelling at the demands of his dependent state, sipped a little early morning intoxicant and suddenly turned mellow, if not even beatific.

11:00 A.M. Gunsmiths and glassblowers, coopers and farmers, educators and preachers—almost all men who worked for a living, and more than a few women, put aside their labors for a few minutes to enjoy what they called the "eleven o'clock bitters," a cross between, and predecessor of, the modern coffee break and happy hour. Tension dissolved in the solvent of alcohol; energy, or at least the illusion of it, returned to the honest toiler, and the day's labors could continue. Did they continue a little less efficiently? Perhaps, but then no one can say how they would have continued *without* the respite for hooch.

1:00 or *2:00 P.M.* If the colonists were having dinner at the local tavern, as was often the case, they might begin with a rum flip, which seems to have been the most popular mixed drink of the time. The recipe called for two parts beer, one part rum, an egg or small amount of cream if desired, and sugar to taste. The ingredients were poured into a tankard, then stirred and brought to a near-boil by a poker that had been heating in the tavern's fireplace. The poker was called a loggerhead, and sometimes a customer would have a flip or two too many and begin to argue with another customer; the men would raise their voices, redden in the jowls, curse at each other in unforgiving tones. Soon one would reach for the poker to settle the issue. The other would try to wrest the instrument from him, or to secure one of his own to even the odds. Thus the expression "at loggerheads."

Other popular mixed drinks in colonial America—the word "cocktail" does not make its English language debut until early in the nineteenth century—sound as if they could just as easily be served today at one of our franchised singles bars, a paper umbrella in the glass and a plastic toothpick, spearing pieces of canned, syrupy fruit, on the side.

Rattle-skull: Brandy, wine, porter, nutmeg, and lime
Meridian: Brandy and tea
Calibogus: Rum and white spruce beer

Bombo: Rum, sugar, water, and nutmeg
Mimbo: Rum, sugar, water, and no nutmeg
Stonewall: Rum and cider
Cherry bounce: Rum and cherry juice
Sitchell: Rum, whiskey, water, vinegar, and molasses
Manathan: Rum, beer, and sugar
Whistlebelly: Sour beer, molasses, and bread crumbs
Sillabub: Warm cream, wine, and sugar
Sangaree: Madeira, water, sugar, and nutmeg (or some other
   spice)

4:00 P.M. This was the afternoon version of the "eleven o'clock bitters," a companion period of refreshment and relaxation. In Portland,
Maine, among other places, the two drinking times were so important
to the populace that they were fixed into the day by the bells in the town
hall tower. No other sounds were so eagerly awaited, unless they were
the opening of a bottle and the splashing of liquid into a glass.

6:00 P.M. The choice at supper might be small beer or a hard pear
juice called perry. Then again, it might be cider, wine, or a liquor made
from almost anything that could be distilled. As an amateur poet from
Massachusetts wrote to a friend in England:

> If barley be wanting to make into malt,
> We must be content and think it no fault,
> For we can make liquor to sweeten our lips,
> Of pumpkins, and parsnips, and walnut-tree chips.

8:00 P.M. At the tavern in the evening, a variety of alcoholic beverages served as raw materials of colonial dissent, juices to get the juices
flowing when the talk turned, as it almost always did, to policies of the
Crown and their effect on the New World. It might be export duties or
some other form of taxation; it might be the paltry sums of money that
England was willing to pay for fine Virginia tobacco and the Motherland's insistence that the crop not be sold to other countries at higher
rates; it might be the certainty of abuses yet to come.

Booze also had a tendency to make those expressing their discontent think of themselves as more eloquent than the normal run of patriot and more sagacious than the common brand of philosopher. In
fact, so closely were alcohol and rebellion linked in the minds of many
that a person who refrained from the former was sometimes thought

to be too weak-willed for the latter. "In Charleston," writes historian Norman Gelb of one such fellow, "George Walker refused to drink damnation to the king of England. It was enough reason for him to be tarred and feathered, paraded through the town and pelted by onlookers with whatever came to hand."

11:00 P.M. As a shield against nocturnal chills, the colonists might employ a hotchpotch, which was a manathan served warm. Or they might lift a mug of something else to inoculate themselves against heat, humidity, snow, rain, the blackness of night, the rigors of the forthcoming day—or perhaps just to toast themselves for having made it through another twenty-four hours in the punishing wilds of the New World. Americans enjoyed toasting one another and were diligent in seeking excuses, although no one is quite sure when the practice began. It probably goes back at least to the Middle Ages, "when people were baffled by drunkenness," and might have believed "that the Devil entered a person's body when he opened his mouth to drink. Clinking glasses supposedly frightened him away." If so, there was enough of a din in the New World colonies to keep Satan and his entire army of fallen angels cowering in a corner until the final judgment.

And, oh yes, a glass of mulled cider "was particularly good for infants at bedtime; it guaranteed parents a restful night."

Of course, not all Americans drank at all these times; schedules varied widely from place to place, even from day to day. Some people, though, drank at still other times, it having become customary in the future United States for alcoholic beverages to be lapped up by the occasion as well as by the clock.

Working. Not only were laborers rewarded for their efforts with two official booze breaks a day, they were encouraged to take a nip here and there in between, whenever thirst beset them; and to build a society from scratch—clearing a wilderness that did not want to be cleared, raising structures in the midst of the clearings, forming societies without appropriate models or reasons to believe they could ever endure—was to develop a thirst of the profoundest dimensions. In Northampton, Massachusetts, in 1737, sixty men set to work on a new meeting house, and were told by town officials that speed was of the essence. Could they finish in three weeks? How about two?

They finished in one. The secret to their success? They also finished, in the process of construction, sixty-nine gallons of rum and more barrels of beer and cider than anyone could count; they worked, in other words, in an almost constant state of inebriation, from the pounding of the first nail in the morning to the sawing of the last plank at night. As a result, it is not known how long the building remained upright, nor whether the corners were squared or the floors level or the roof strong enough to support the weight of even so insubstantial a creature as a sparrow. The men, one assumes, did *not* remain upright after finishing their tasks.

"Farmers," writes Alice Fleming in *Alcohol: The Delightful Poison*, "equally solicitous of their hired hands, placed jugs of rum behind the bushes and let the men help themselves as they toiled in the fields." And there were clerks who kept a jug in the desk and smithies who hid one near the forge; there were wagoners who slipped a bottle into a pocket and even the occasional seamstress who positioned a glass at the foot of her spinning wheel, and sometimes took so many sips that she began to spin herself.

Few people questioned these practices. Many endorsed them. Even so piously sober a figure as Increase Mather, the esteemed Congregationalist minister and one-time president of Harvard College, admitted that the trials of the working person were so great that he or she was entitled to the momentary salvation of liquor. It is "a good creature of God," Mather believed, and in small amounts would enable the builder or farmer or smithy to regain his strength and carry on with his tasks, thereby serving his Maker in a suitable manner.

But beer and wine and whiskey did not just revive the tiring toiler; in some cases they compensated him. Like tobacco, the subject of this author's next historical volume, alcoholic beverages were a form of currency in most of the colonies at one time or another, their status acknowledged by all and attempts to devalue it few, far between, and unsuccessful. One such attempt was made in Boston near the midpoint of the seventeenth century. The town fathers, believing that their employees labored with insufficient efficacy when they drank their pay, decided henceforth to remunerate in coin. Whereupon the employees came to a decision of their own. They would no longer work. It may have been the first American strike. It did not last long, however; the town fathers soon relented, and wages returned to liquid form.

Shopping. A storekeeper would often stand a keg of rum or whiskey near the front door of his establishment, a drinking cup attached to it by a chain. Customers and passersby alike were invited to help themselves. A large purchase almost always brought an invitation for seconds, and seconds often led to thirds, which, in turn, led to further, and sometimes totally unnecessary, purchases. The keg was, in many cases, as important to the success of a business as the products or services that it offered. It was a sign that the businessman valued his customer, and that the latter's preferences would be met.

Visiting. It was not considered hospitable in early America to allow a neighbor to drop in without offering him some refreshment. Sometimes, it has been noted, the neighbor would stop by for no other reason than the welcoming beverages. He would be offered a few sips by way of greeting and another few for farewell; in between the host might drink to his guest's health and the guest to his host's and the two of them might go back and forth like this so many times, each drinking to the other's health, that neither was feeling healthy anymore.

Soldiering. During the Revolutionary War, George Washington insisted on alcohol for his men, and once, when a shipment was delayed, he wrote an anguished letter to the president of the Continental Congress. "The benefits arising from the moderate use of strong Liquor," Washington stated, "have been experienced in all Armies and are not to be disputed."

Nor were they. Booze was dispensed daily to the colonial fighting forces, the usual amount being four ounces, although twice as much was handed out during the horrible winter of 1777–78 at Valley Forge, the men drinking for warmth or numbness or, if they were lucky, both. There and elsewhere, the rations were downed without delay, and it seems, according to journals of the time, that many soldiers talked about their beverages and the blessings they conferred as much as they talked about their foe. For instance, it was said of William Bacon, a captain during the French and Indian War, that he "showed more interest in recording the arrival of a new supply of rum than in what 'sacrifices' attended the troops once they were settled down in the wilderness."

By the time the war ended, there were 2,579 registered distilleries in the United States, with thirst enough in the newly created nation to support even more.

Marrying. A punch made from Jamaican spirits was commonly served at weddings, and after the bowl had been emptied, the men would sometimes throw their coats aside, roll up their shirtsleeves, and form themselves into a line, there to begin racing one another under the spell of alcohol-induced exuberance. The winner, he who sprinted the fastest while stumbling and weaving the least, was presented with a bottle of wine, which he might well decide to uncork immediately so that he could get a head start on the next spell.

Less commonly, and perhaps with the effects of Jamaican spirits intensified by beer, cider, and rum, the groom's friends might steal the bride, hiding her in the church basement or nearby woods and forcing the groom to find her before he could officially begin connubial life. Since the groom was as inebriated as the friends by this time, his attempts to locate the young woman were likely to turn into a kind of floor show; he would search in impossible places, utter rollicking oaths, trip over his own feet more often than he would manipulate them correctly. Those in attendance would hoot and whoop and laugh and cheer. Then they would fill up their glasses again, and almost surely do the same to his.

In truth, it might have been alcohol that contributed to the bride's appearance at the altar in the first place, for it has been said that the eighteenth century was a time in the American colonies "when kisses and drams set the virgins aflame."

Burying. Men and women from all stations of life were laid to rest with portions of rum in their caskets, a little something to ease the passage from one world to the next. Even paupers were so equipped, the thought being that a few postmortem belts would give them hope that the afterlife would be a more congenial experience for them than the one so recently terminated. But, understandably, most of the liquor at a funeral went to the mourners, who, still in the throes of mortality, found themselves chugging it in such quantity that there were times when they could no longer recall the cause of their bereavement or the extent to which it affected them. At the 1678 funeral of David Porter in Hartford, Connecticut, to mention but one case, the chugging went on for hours. The winding sheet and coffin, reported a man who stood at graveside, cost thirty shillings, but the hooch consumed by the rest of those at the service added up to more than twice as much. And when, in the same year in Boston, the wife of a noted Puritan minister passed away, more than fifty gallons of fine wine were imbibed by grieving attendees.

It was because of incidents like this that a noted Virginian, approaching the end of his life a few years later, gave his friends some instructions. "The debauched drinking used at burials, tending to the dishonor of God and religion, my will is that no strong drink be provided or spent at my burial."

Learning. In some colonial schools, the books were put aside for a few minutes each morning and afternoon so that the children, who might not have gotten enough liquor upon awakening, could be given a few more tastes to revive their flagging attention. The teachers joined in, just to be polite. The practice was considered as important a part of the classroom ritual as the rod and reader. When the students left for home, the teachers would often lock the door behind them and raise a glass in private.

Booze was no less important in the world of higher education, where students and faculty alike tended to satisfy their thirsts in greater quantity. Harvard, for a time, had its own brewery, eagerly patronized by all within the school's orbit, as a result of which lectures sometimes became unintelligible and commencement exercises so boisterous that rules had to be put into effect to limit "the Excesses, Immoralities and Disorders." There were no rules, however, to limit the brewery's production, and the occasional attempt by nondrinkers to do so was met with derision, even hostility. In fact, early in the college's history, some students complained to administrators that even without rules the production was insufficient; they were often deprived, sometimes "wanting beer betwixt brewings a week and a half together."

Something had to be done. Something was. Master Nathaniel Eaton and his wife, who supervised all food and beverage in college precincts for a time, were fired.

Adjudicating. A spectator at a trial would, if so moved, bring a bottle of cider to the courtroom with him. He would seat himself on a bench in back, take a sip, and pass the bottle up to the plaintiff. The plaintiff would empty a bit of the vessel himself, then forward it to his lawyer, who would, in turn, gulp down his own share of the pick-me-up and send the remainder along to the defendant. From the defendant, the cider was relayed to the defendant's counsel and from him perhaps even to the judge and jury, who were as likely to finish off the beverage and toss the bottle away as they were to return it to the spectator who had started it on its journey in the first place. "If the foreman of the jury became mellow in his cups," writes W. J. Rorabaugh, the foremost scholar of early American tippling, "the defendant stood an excellent chance for acquittal."

This being so, it seems that the distinguishing characteristic of colonial justice was probably not blindness as much as double vision.

Governing. According to some historians, town meetings would on occasion begin with a slug or two, the purpose being to focus the mind on the business at hand. If attendance was compulsory at these events, which seems to have been the case in at least a few places, a person who missed one without good reason was likely to be fined a certain amount of whiskey. The assessment would be added to the supply of spirits on hand at the next gathering, and the miscreant, assuming he showed up then, was welcome to join his fellow townsmen in a few nips before the session came to order. Or, if there were too many assessments, *dis*order.

Celebrating nationhood. In New York City, when the Constitution was ratified, "a brewer's wagon carrying a three-hundred-gallon cask of ale topped by a live Bacchus" rode through the streets. The banner on the side of it read: "Ale, proper drink for Americans."

Public gathering. In some communities, it was thought to be good luck to seal a full bottle of liquor into the cornerstone of a new church, school, or other communal building when a ceremony was held at the start of construction. There were, however, always a few who complained of the waste, insisting that an empty bottle, whose contents now resided in the stomachs of a few appreciative citizens, would do just as well. In Philadelphia, anyone who made a bid at an auction was rewarded with a drink. And at almost every other assembly of the time, from barn-raising to woodcutting bee to groundbreaking for a new road, from harvesting to husking to quilting, a vat of alcoholic beverages, prominently placed, served as the hearth, and bonhomie radiated outward from it in waves. No vat, no waves. This was a lesson that George Washington learned as a young man, and it enabled him, after a shaky start, to salvage what turned out to be a notable career in politics.

In his early twenties, he was an even more imposing figure than he came to be in later years, although the later years were when the painters and sculptors caught up to him, insisting that he pose for them and thereby make his immortality visible. He was "straight as an Indian," said his friend George Mercer, "measuring six feet two inches in his stockings and weighing 175 pounds. . . . In conversation he looks you full in the face, is deliberate, deferential, and engaging. His demeanor is at all times composed and dignified. His movements and features are graceful, his walk majestic, and he is a speeding horseman."

He was, in other words, a charismatic man in a critical time, an ideal candidate for public office.

Washington made his first attempt at such a position in 1755, at the age of twenty-three, seeking a seat in the Virginia Assembly. Although he would never express such a sentiment publicly, he believed that, despite his youth, he was the best man for the job in terms of both ability and attitude. The voters, however, did not; they rejected Washington overwhelmingly. There were several reasons for the defeat, but none more important than the fact that, a year or so earlier, the aspiring legislator had insulted the very people he hoped would elect him.

The French and Indian War was raging at the time, the two title groups allied against British territorial interests in the New World, hoping at the least to stop further expansion, at most to reclaim lands that the colonists had already usurped and settled. Washington distinguished himself quickly, forcing a French evacuation of Fort Duquesne, within the boundaries of today's city of Pittsburgh, and leading his men with a daring and grasp of strategy far beyond what could be expected from one with such limited military experience. Word of his triumph spread quickly; all who knew the young soldier assumed a bright future.

Shortly afterward, there was a lull in the fighting and Washington returned to his home colony of Virginia, hoping to rest, tend to his farm, and renew some friendships. It was not to be. Through one of those friends he learned that the nearby county of Frederick was about to be attacked by small, guerrilla-like bands of Native Americans. Some of them were already on the march, and were expected to join forces with others in a day or so, pooling their weapons and their wills. They would attack, Washington's friend told him, in less than a week.

The young soldier made his way to the county's largest town, Winchester, and not only warned the residents of the danger but urged them to resist it, to take up arms and hold their ground. He even offered to lead the local militia into battle himself, despite the fact that the jurisdiction was not his. He spoke to the men as inspirationally as he could, talking of duty and courage and responsibility to future generations.

Winchester wanted none of it. The militia colonel told Washington that his men had already heard rumors of the impending assault, and had decided on flight, not fight. Only if the natives cut off their routes of escape would they put up resistance, and most of them assumed it would not be enough, that the aggressors would overpower them and they would die with their families. It was not what they wanted, they said to their colonel, but if it was what fate had in store, so be it.

Washington was incensed. What kind of soldiers *were* these? He berated them for their pessimism, their cowardice, their unwillingness to act in their own behalf; it was a monologue of uncharacteristic severity and passion. Biographer James Thomas Flexner tells what happened next:

> Washington then went to a stable and tried to impress [the word, in this context, means to compel service for military purposes] a horse. The owner barred his way. He drew his sword and took the horse. Immediately, he was surrounded by a mob of inhabitants who, wishing to keep their animals for their own personal escapes, offered to "blow out my brains."

Washington managed to "stare them down," however, and rode out of Winchester as fast as he could, cursing the mob of inhabitants for their lack of fortitude.

But when the next election came along, the mob found itself with an unexpected chance to get even, for there on the ballot, next to the names of people that Winchesterites either admired or tolerated, was a single name they had lately come to revile: George Washington. For abusing them verbally, they avenged themselves electorally. Hugh West won the assembly seat that year with 271 votes. Thomas Swearingen came in second with 270. Washington finished a distant and discredited fourth with 40, which perhaps comprised the total number of Frederick Countians unfamiliar with the details of the Winchester incident. Washington was bitterly disappointed; he had not realized how deeply the feelings against him were running. He was also determined not to fail the next time.

Two years later, and two years wiser, Washington stood again for the Virginia Assembly, relying on the passage of time and the growth of his reputation to have eased hard feelings, and on rum, punch, cider, wine, and beer to have persuaded those who still *did* resent him to let bygones be bygones. Washington saw to it that 144 gallons of these beverages, in all their glorious potency, were delivered to as many polling places as possible, and he further made sure that supporters of his were stationed alongside the beverages to invite voters to indulge before making up their minds about the candidates.

Dip your mug, friend, one would say.

Colonel Washington does not want you to make so important a decision while suffering the pangs of thirst, another would chime in.

Yet another would urge that the mug be drained to the last drop, thirst being a malady known to return within seconds of what seemed a cure.

The voters drank. Still, the colonel was concerned, edgy. To the man who served as what we would today call his campaign manager, Washington had previously expressed the hope that he had not spent with "too sparing a hand."

He had not. The eventual father of his country got 68 more votes than runner-up Thomas Bryan Martin. West, seeking reelection, found himself 100 votes in arrears of the winner and Swearingen 350 behind. W. J. Rorabaugh analyzes the results of Washington's strategy as follows: "For his 144 gallons of refreshment, he received 307 votes, a return on his investment of better than two votes per gallon."

Washington did not originate the practice of trading booze for votes. It was a common one at the time, and was known to many, more colorfully than clearly, as "swilling the planters with bumbo." More often than not, the office-seeker joined the planters in swilling, the man and his constituents loading up their glasses and then tipping them back like friends of long standing, toasting the former's success at the latter's hands, and as soon as the glasses were empty refilling them and toasting again.

But it was not just the quantity of alcohol made available by a candidate that mattered at the time; no less important to the outcome of an election was his "manner and style of dispensing it." Rorabaugh writes of a contest a few years later than Washington's and many miles to the south. "The favored aspirant in one Mississippi election," he relates, "poured drinks for the voters with so much personal attention that it seemed like he would win. After his liquor was gone, his opponent, a Methodist minister, announced to the crowd that he also had whiskey to dispense, but that he would not be so stingy as to measure it out. 'Come forward, one and all,' he invited, 'and help yourselves.' The generous person won."

In addition to revealing generosity, a candidate supplied liquor to those at the polls, and drank a fair measure of the product himself in their presence, to demonstrate his "good nature and congeniality in his cups . . . thereby confirm[ing] his egalitarianism." In other words, he showed that he was a leader by providing the spirits and that he was one of the boys by quaffing them openly and sociably. In a fledgling republic, it was an unbeatable combination.

Not to mention a much-appreciated show of gratitude. There was a feeling at the time "that voters deserved recompense when so many traveled so far to exercise the suffrage." The higher the proof, the greater the recompense. And the larger the turnout; as historian Arthur M. Schlesinger has written, the presence of alcohol at the colonial polling place had "the beneficial effect" of drawing large crowds to democracy.

Still, not everyone approved. As early as 1705, a Virginia statute forbade this kind of electioneering. In 1753, an editorial in the *New York Independent Reflector* "expressed dismay that so many persons should barter their franchise for 'Beer and Brandy.' " And in 1791, a Frenchman named Ferdinard Bayard was journeying through Virginia, keeping a sharp eye on the customs of the new nation and reporting back to his friends at home, who were in the midst of a revolution of their own. He took in the doings at the polls with dismay. He saw "the candidates offer drunkenness openly to anyone who is willing to give them his vote." He saw the voters accept the offers, the buying and selling of democracy, and for so ignoble a medium of exchange. He did not know that the United States, so admirable by most contemporary accounts, had so unsavory a side.

Had M. Bayard gotten to North Carolina in his travels, he might have been even more appalled. It was reported that, on one election day in the colony, a man seeking office drove up to his local courthouse in a wagon "with a couple of tin cups, and a ten-gallon keg between his legs." He jumped to the ground, secured his horse, and began energetically emptying the keg into the cups, circulating the cups among the voters until the keg was empty and he had won their virtually unanimous support at the polls. That it was registered with foggy eyes and shaky hands, and that some of the registrants did not remember their support the next morning, probably did not trouble the new electee.

And a few decades later, a fellow named George D. Prentice was asked to report on the polls in another southern state for a publication called the *New England Weekly Review*. It was an assignment he never forgot. "An election in Kentucky lasts three days," Prentice wrote, never having been exposed to such a marathon before, "and during that period

whiskey and apple toddy flow through our cities and villages like the
Euphrates through ancient Babylon."

The most prominent foe of campaigning by whiskey and toddy in
early America was James Madison, who, running for reelection to the
Virginia Assembly in 1777, decided to take the high road: he would not
debase the electoral process by bribing the voters with alcohol, would
not create a carnival atmosphere at a serious venue. He explained that
"the corrupting influence of spirituous liquors, and other treats" was
"inconsistent with the purity of moral and republican virtues." It was an
admirable position, a principled stand; Madison's reward was a smashing defeat at the polls, his first and only. Like Washington, he found a
brilliant career in politics delayed by insufficient regard for constituent
thirst.

Others objected to booze at the polls because it deemphasized the
content of a candidate's character and granted him office for the content
of his casks. "I guess Mr. A. is the fittest man of the two," opined a
woman of the time in South Carolina, analyzing the results of a local
race, "but t' other whiskies the best." It was the latter for whom the
woman voted.

With the passage of time, the use of alcoholic beverages to purchase
elective office became less and less common. Existing laws against it
came to be enforced; new laws were passed and taken seriously by authorities; dignity and positions on issues began to count more than persuasion by potables. Yet the tradition persisted in a few races and in
a few places, not only through colonial times but into the nineteenth
century and even, in one comical instance, up to the dawn of the twentieth. In his book *The Big Spenders*, journalist and bon vivant Lucius
Beebe tells of a man who went pointlessly, and expensively, overboard.
It was "Montana's peerless Senator William Andrew Clark who, when
seeking election to the United States Senate at the turn of the [twen-
tieth] century, miscalculated by a comma the population of the city of
Butte, Montana, and provided the free distribution among 45,000 en-
franchised voters sufficient whisky for 450,000."

After his years as president, years when an estimated one out of every
four dollars that Americans spent on household expenses went toward
the purchase of alcohol, George Washington retired to Mount Vernon,
settling into a routine to which he had aspired ever since his hiatus during the French and Indian War. He rose with the sun, ate and drank

breakfast, and rode across some of his 8,000 acres to inspect both crops and men, diligent about it, Cincinnatus in his natural habitat. Either before or immediately after the ride, he spoke with his gardener, asking him how the shrubs were doing, what flowers should be planted next and when, whether patches of the lawn needed to be fertilized or sections of the fence mended. The gardener was a man whom Washington respected greatly, and whom he compensated not only in cash, but with "a generous allotment of rum," if not the expensive Barbados variety.

Later, perhaps after a nap, Washington took a walk, retracing some of his morning paths. Most days, he followed the walk with a cup of tea. Upon finishing, he might receive visitors; he did so almost daily, and when night fell, he wrote letters by candlelight, keeping up as best he could with the voluminous mail he received himself.

He also made his own liquor, not only for personal consumption but for sale, a decision he owed at least in part to his estate manager, James Anderson, "who persuaded Washington to turn over one of his unprofitable small farms to raising rye for whiskey. Soon Washington had a thriving operation that turned a profit of £83 in 1798, producing not only whiskey but apple, peach and persimmon brandy."

In addition, Washington built a brewery on the grounds to produce a molasses-based beer, which he savored both in the tasting and the sharing with guests. They would drink it at meals, and sometimes unaccompanied by food, as they sat in large chairs on the veranda, looking out on the Potomac and across to the federal city, still under construction but already bearing the name of Mount Vernon's master.

Thomas Jefferson installed a brewery at Monticello, but seems to have paid little attention to it, especially after his wife died, for it was she who looked after its operations and most often partook of the beverage. Jefferson was a devotee of the grape, becoming an expert on both viniculture and vintages and advising not only the two presidents who had preceded him, but the two who followed, on their own wine purchases.

His cellar was a particular source of pride, probably the best-stocked in Virginia, if not the entire nation, and Jefferson designed and built a dumbwaiter specifically to ferry bottles of libation from its shelves to the dining room; without it, his staff would have had to make too many trips. Jefferson usually drank three glasses a day, surely agreeing with Galileo, whom he had read and long admired, that wine was "light held together by moisture," and delighting in its magical properties as he and his companions sipped and sipped and sipped.

Samuel Adams worked at, and later managed, his father's brewery in Boston.

John Hancock, in his college days, availed himself of Harvard's beer-making capabilities, many times sitting in his room and washing down his studies until late at night. His preference, though, was to imbibe more publicly; he was a frequent presence in the taverns that surrounded the school, and in later years became a fixture at a variety of others. "John Hancock drank here" was a claim that could probably have been made more often than "George Washington slept here."

John Adams "emptied a large tankard of hard cider" on most mornings, usually as early as 4 a.m., before either sitting down to breakfast or starting in on his books. Cider was, in fact, a beverage he had begun to appreciate during his own days at Harvard. "I shall never forget, how refreshing and salubrious we found it, hard as it often was." In later years, Adams would also come to appreciate the beer that was made in Philadelphia, and, partaking of that city's supply of Madeira, "found no inconvenience in it." He also spoke, although a little less directly, on behalf of rum, saying, "I know not why we should blush to confess that molasses was an essential ingredient in American independence."

Still later, and to Adams's everlasting sorrow, his son Charles, depressed by his inability to earn a living as a lawyer, would die of a number of ailments that seem to have been caused, at least in part, by alcoholism. It is perhaps for this reason that old man Adams rewrote his personal history. He said, contrary to the record, that in his younger years he had been "fired with a zeal against ardent spirits, and the multiplication of taverns, retailers and rum shops . . . and grieved to the heart to see the number of idlers, thieves, sots and consumptive patients . . . in those infamous seminaries."

Adams's older, more distinguished son, John Quincy, did not quite achieve the alcoholic state. "All his life," though, writes Richard Brookhiser, "he would be a serious drinker—as an old man he would correctly identify eleven out of fourteen Madeiras in a blind tasting."

Patrick Henry tended bar in Virginia and happily yielded to requests from his customers to play the violin while they quenched their thirsts and altered their perceptions.

John Jay seldom went to a social gathering of any sort without taking up a position at the punch bowl, acting as unofficial greeter as he served cup after cup of liquid fire to himself and others.

James Otis "had a big eloquent mouth which looks, in his portrait, capable of taking in all the liquor credited to him." In truth, it took in so much liquor that he was eventually stricken with gout, the drinker's curse, which was the major torment of his life until he lost his mind for a number of other reasons with fifteen years still to live.

Before his legendary ride, Paul Revere is reported "to have stopped at the home of Isaac Hall in Medford [Massachusetts]. Hall, a captain in the minutemen and a rum distiller by trade, gave Revere two drafts of rum to fortify him for his journey." His memory was not affected. It was *one* if by land and *two* if by sea, and Revere easily kept the numbers straight.

Martin Van Buren was born in his father's tavern.

John Marshall was "a hearty, gregarious fellow who liked to drink with his friends in the local taverns." And when he ran for a seat in the U.S. Congress, the taverns were his favorite campaign stop.

William Penn, on the other hand, did not care for such establishments. They were too noisy for him, too rambunctious. But he knew how important alcohol was to his fellow citizens, and did not disapprove. In fact, he would occasionally enjoy, or at least tolerate for the sake of amiability, molasses beer or a punch of rum and water.

Ethan Allen, a man of "gaudy legend" and a prodigious drinker, even by the standards of the time, was once said to have gotten even more potted than usual, knocking down one Stonewall after another at Stephen Fay's tavern in Bennington, Vermont, although not seeming the worse for wear to those who chugged along with him. Immediately afterward, he and his cousin Remember Baker said farewell to Fay and set out on a long, perilous journey through the woods. Thereupon sprang up one of those gaudy legends, which one believes at his own risk.

When the drinks began to wear off, the two lay down beside a sun-warmed rock and fell into deep sleep. Some time later, Baker was awakened by an ominous, dry, hissing sound. Turning his head, he saw to his horror a huge rattlesnake coiled on Allen's chest, striking again and again at the arms, the shoulders, and the neck of the still sleeping giant. Springing to his feet and grabbing his gun, Baker moved cautiously to prod the snake away. Before he could do so, however, the snake slithered onto the grass, its lifted head weaving, its body fantastically writhing. Utterly astounded, Baker saw that the snake was looking at him cross-eyed! Then, incredibly, it emitted a mighty hiccup and hiccupped again as it disappeared into a blueberry thicket. Baker was still staring in frozen astonishment when Ethan Allen awoke and began to curse the "damnable blood-sucking mosquitoes" that had bitten him in his sleep.

James Madison might have disapproved of alcohol at the polls, but he welcomed it at other venues and on other occasions. Twelve years after losing his bid for a Virginia Assembly seat, Madison, now a member of the new nation's House of Representatives, introduced a bill to encourage American brewing by placing a heavy tax on imported beers. It passed easily. Madison was among those who toasted the measure's success, although perhaps too much; Gouverneur Morris thought the man "a fool and a drunkard."

At the Washington, D.C. boarding house where justices of the Supreme Court resided when court was in session, an edict passed by the jurists themselves permitted wine to be drunk only in wet weather and then only for the sake of health. After his term in Congress, now serving his nation as chief justice, John Marshall dissented. From time to time, he would tell his associate Joseph Story to look out the window and check the skies. More often than not, Story reported sun, an absence of clouds, fair weather as far as the eye could see. Marshall adapted nicely. "All the better," he told his younger benchmate, "for our jurisdiction extends over so large a territory that the doctrine of chances makes it certain that it must be raining somewhere."

"The chief was brought up on Federalism and Madeira," Judge Story later explained, "and he is not the man to outgrow his early prejudices." Story went on: "The best Madeira was labeled 'The Supreme Court,' as their Honors the Justices used to make a direct importation every year, and sip it as they consulted over the cases before them every day after dinner, when the cloth had been removed."

Benjamin Franklin was also fond of Madeira, and why not? It was a hearty beverage, holding up well to the rigors of importation from the West African island that gave the drink its name, and it was also able to withstand extremes of temperature better than other wines. Franklin's preference was widely known among his companions. One day, one of them asked for advice, wanting to know how he could "preserve my small-beer in the back-yard? My neighbours are often tapping it of nights." Franklin needed but a moment. "Put a barrel of old Madeira by the side of it," he said, "let them but get a taste of the Madeira, and I'll engage they will never trouble thy small-beer any more."

Franklin knew as much about oenology as he did electricity and penny-saving. But he believed that the blessings of wine, and indeed of all alcoholic beverages, could be realized only through moderation. Franklin warned repeatedly of immoderation's perils. "Nothing more like a Fool," he wrote as Poor Richard, "than a drunken Man." And "he that drinks fast, pays slow."

Chief among the blessings, he thought, was eloquence. " 'Tis true," he said, "drinking does not improve our faculties, but it enables us to use them; and therefore I conclude that much study and experience, and a little liquor, are of absolute necessity for some tempers, in order to make them accomplished orators."

Franklin was known to put aside his Madeira from time to time in favor of other thirst-quenchers, long enough on one occasion to devise the recipe for "a passable spruce beer." But it was wine that meant most to him, wine that captured his heart and tickled his fancy, wine that inspired him to write the lyrics for songs of praise. Among them may be found the following verses:

> 'Twas honest old Noah first planted the Vine,
> And mended his morals by drinking its Wine;
> And thenceforth justly the drinking of Water decry'd
> For he knew that all Mankind by drinking it dy'd.
> Derry down—
>
> From this piece of History plainly we find
> That Water's good neither for Body or Mind;
> That Virtue and Safety in Wine-bibbing's found
> While all that drink Water deserve to be drown'd.
> Derry down—

Wine bibbers, Franklin believed, should thank their gods for the way they had situated elbows in human arms; because of it, "we are enabled to drink at our ease, the glass going exactly to the mouth."

In the pages of his newspaper, *The Pennsylvania Gazette*, which, by the way, would occasionally urge women to soak their breakfast toast in milk rather than beer, Franklin published an alphabetized list of more than 200 synonyms for the intoxicated state, phrases ranging from "he is Addled" to "he's had a Thump over the Head with Sampson's jawbone" to "he got the Indian Vapours"; from "he's drunk as a Wheel-barrow" to "he makes Indentures with his Leggs" to "he has Sold his Senses"; from "his Head is full of Bees" to "he's Eaten a Toad & a half for Breakfast" to "he Knows not the way Home." As much as any other single piece of evidence, as much as the prevalence of taverns or the ubiquity of booze at polling places or the constant clanging of the bells that rang

for bitters, the extensiveness of Franklin's list testifies to the role of alcoholic beverages in colonial America, to their importance to people
like himself and Washington and Jefferson, to Adams and Marshall, to
Henry and Revere, to Jay and Hancock—in other words, to people who
made up, in the words of Arthur Schlesinger Sr., "the most remarkable
generation of public men in the history of the United States or perhaps
any other nation."

Eventually, Increase Mather's phrase came to be incorporated into law,
several statutes in early America referring to alcoholic beverages as "a
good creature of God" and insisting that they be treated with appropriate reverence. And some people seemed to credit them with the
Almighty's own powers. One such fellow, his name lost to history and
his use of language at times jabberwockian, wrote the following about
rum or whiskey or hard cider:

> It sloweth age; it strengtheneth youth; it helpeth digestion; it cutteth
> flegme; it abandoneth melancholie; it lighteneth the the mind; it quick-
> eneth the spirits; it strengtheneth the hydropsie; it healeth the strangurie;
> it pounceth the stone; it expelleth the gravel; it puffeth away ventosities; it
> keepeth and preserveth the head from whirling, the eyes from dazzling, the
> tong from lisping, the mouth from snaffling, the teeth from chattering, and
> the throat from rattling; it keepeth the weason from stifling, the stomach
> from wambling, and the heart from swelling; it keepeth the hands from
> shivering, the sinews from shrinking, the veins from crumbling, the bones
> from aching, and the marrow from soaking.

The belief that booze was medicinal—or, as in the preceding case,
that it comprised an entire pharmacopoeia—was not unique to the first
American settlers. It goes back at least as far as the ancient Greeks, who
would steep mandragora root in wine and provide it to patients before
surgery. They would also pour wine directly onto wounds, believing
it to be a healing agent, and would at other times blend alcohol with
opium as an analgesic. A similar faith in the curative powers of hooch
is recorded in the Bible, where, to cite but one of many examples, Paul
advises Timothy to drink wine for a recurring but unspecified illness.
And in medieval times, there were physicians who prescribed beer or
wine or brandy for longevity, among them the father and grandfather
of the rabidly austere monk, Savonarola.

Thomas Jefferson was no less a believer. When his daughter Maria
fell sick with an unrecorded malady, Jefferson saw to it that she ate
lightly and drank sweet wine; no other course of treatment, he felt cer-

tain, offered a better chance for recovery. Other Americans turned to beer, thinking it the only sure cure for scurvy and the likeliest remedy for headaches and sore muscles.

More commonly, though, our forebears relied on stronger stuff for what ailed them, and few things ailed a woman as much as the pains of bringing new life into the world. In England, "from the moment she realized she was pregnant she had dutifully taken the advice offered by the renowned London midwife Mrs. Jane Sharp in her childbirth manual and drunk a glass of sage ale every morning to strengthen the womb." When labor began, she sipped wine that had been warmed with sugar and spices, hoping "to keep up her spirits through the long ordeal." In the New World, it was rum that she most likely imbibed, usually mixed with milk.

Rum-soaked cherries were the prescription for a cold, hot brandy punch for cholera, rye for the shakes, and rye or almost any other kind of whiskey for colic, laryngitis, and aging, as well as for "the trembles, the slows, the puking fever, the tires," not to mention "snakebite, frosted toes, and broken legs." Spirits taken in the morning would ward off malaria, according to the eighteenth century's conventional wisdom; later in the day, a good stiff belt would energize the lethargic, cheer the depressed, and soothe the beleaguered—or at least distract them for a while. Taken in quantity, large quantity, "horse doses of brandy or rum," the good creature got even better, serving as an anesthetic, and it was enough to make many an early American get over his fear of surgery, if not actually long for the touch of blade to skin.

Nor was there a reason, thanks to alcoholic beverages, to fear excesses of temperature. Andrew Barr writes that "in the northern colonies, European settlers drank spirits in the belief that these would help to protect them against the extremes of the climate. In cold weather, they drank spirits because they gave them a feeling of warmth. In hot weather they thought that spirits warmed their bodies after sweating: They believed that sweat conducted heat from the inside to the outside of their bodies, leaving the inner parts in need of warmth and fortification."

In the majority of cases, Americans poured their beverages into their mouths and allowed them to flow profusely south. Sometimes, though, they applied them externally, dipping pieces of cloth into a bottle of rum or vat of hard cider and attaching them to the afflicted parts of the body, permitting the liquor to seep through the skin, to work its wonders by absorption.

In fact, one searches in vain for a disorder which, in the view of the men and women of long ago, would *not* yield to the restorative powers of liquor. It was aspirin and penicillin, cortisone and antibiotic, all rolled into one—the first wonder drug, the great American hope against nature's perversities, the focal point for belief in a healthier life.

(Well, one does not search *entirely* in vain. It is a digression, but an irresistible one, to point to something that never occurred to the colonists, but did come readily to the minds of earlier Americans, specifically, to a remote tribe of Mayans known as the Huaztecs. More than a thousand years before the first white man appeared on their shores, they were treating certain kinds of diseases with wine enemas. The patients would "lie down and, extending their legs, have the wine poured into their anus [sic] through a tube until the body is full." Other tribes in this part of the world would administer enemas of tobacco smoke, the medicine men separating the rectal aperture as far as they could and exhaling their pipes like smokestacks into the regions just beyond. These practitioners, as is apparent, were a wildly experimental lot in their quest for health and vitality. Give them an opening . . .)

The reasons for the American belief in alcohol as tonic are easily discerned, and the possible divinity of its origin is only part of it. Because beer and wine and liquor had such potent tastes—because they puckered the lips, burned a path down the gullet, and exploded in the stomach like tiny powder kegs—it was thought that they would toughen the body and thus better enable it to fight off disease. And the stronger the beverage, the stiffer the fight it would provide. Hard work was, after all, better for a person than idling, and the principle seemed similar; swallowing most kinds of liquor was a form of intense labor for the internal organs, and would toughen them correspondingly.

The converse, meanwhile, seemed equally true. Water, because it was nondescript in taste, sliding into the stomach with little more than its temperature to call attention to it, barely more noticeable than the air a person breathed, would reduce strength. Because it was clear, it lacked nutritional value; because it was free-running and insubstantial, it could not perform any salutary duties for the body. These views were so widely accepted in the colonies that, at one point, a life insurance company raised its rates 10 percent for the *non*drinker, believing him to be "thin and watery, and as mentally cranked, in that he repudiated the good creatures of God as found in alcoholic drinks."

But even if Americans had known the truth about spirits—that in certain quantities they are more of a palliative than a cure, and in larger quantities not even a palliative but a likely cause of all sorts of physical malfunctions—they would have downed them anyhow, perhaps no less eagerly, and not just because the taste and aftereffects excited them. In addition, other beverages of the time frightened them, or at least gave them pause, and in most cases with good reason.

Water. More than just nondescript, it could be dangerously dirty, an invitation to diphtheria, typhoid, or at the very least an upset stomach. There were few means of filtration in centuries past and they were not reliable; and there was no way to purify other than boiling. People who lived close to rivers would drop buckets into them, scoop out the water, and let it stand until the sediment sank to the bottom. Only then would they dare to taste it, and the process sometimes took several hours, with the dirt finally drifting down to occupy a quarter or more of the container. Even so, enough contaminants remained to pose a threat to well-being, and for that reason others eschewed the method altogether and simply waited for rain. They collected it in cisterns and drank their supplies until they gave out, stale and dusty though the beverage eventually became.

The purest water of the time came from springs, but these were usually found in lowland areas, whereas most settlers, wary of malaria and other diseases associated with such terrain, not to mention various and unsavory insect hordes that infested such places, preferred to build their cabins on high ground, a location that also afforded them greater visibility, and thus protection, when the French or Indians or British chose to attack. As a result, if spring water was their beverage of choice, they had to carry it uphill, and for most Americans the hardships of transit far outweighed the pleasures of consumption.

In New York there was a different problem, caused by "shallow brackish wells [which] made it certain that the drinker of water would not only quench his thirst but also be given a 'physic.'" In addition, he would have to endure a taste that was metallic, or possibly acidic, and one that lingered unpleasantly in the mouth long after the body had absorbed the fluid. No wonder one New Yorker of the era said that water served primarily as "an excuse to many persons for continuing the excessive use of strong drink."

Residents of other large cities also had to contend with the problem of water-as-laxative, and in Washington, D.C., sometime after the colonial era, the populace chose to keep its water in that condition rather than raise taxes to remove impurities. Why pay extra money to sanitize a beverage that no one wanted to drink in the first place? Why not just give up on the stuff and spend smaller amounts of money for safer, more stimulating drinks?

In thousands of smaller communities, the local stream did double duty as the local dump, and so contained almost as much garbage and human waste as it did water; the thought of drinking from such a reservoir did not even occur. Except, from time to time, as a punitive measure; forcing a few gulps of the stream down someone's throat was, on occasion, the legal response to civic offenses.

There were also those who objected to water because it appeared so commonly in nature. It was one of the few liquids human beings drank that did not require processing of some sort, and it was processing, many of them thought, which made a drink truly drinkable, adding flavor and color, aroma and punch. And as if all that were not enough, some of the New World settlers, among them men and women who would occasionally sneak a few sips of water in the privacy of their homes, refused to serve it to others, afraid that their guests would think them too poor to afford something from a bottle or mug or keg.

In short, water was dismissed by the majority of people in the colonial period as being "lowly and common; it was the drink of pigs, cows, and horses. Or, as Benjamin Franklin put it, if God had intended man to drink water, He would not have made him with an elbow capable of raising a wine glass."

Tea. In the words of a Pennsylvania pastor early in the eighteenth century, it was "a drink very generally used. No one is so high as to despise it, nor anyone so low as not to think himself worthy of it." Yet, for some people, tea was too expensive, especially when embargoes or warfare at sea reduced the flow of imports, and when taxes on the leaf, the result of a Parliament-sanctioned monopoly and the cause of the Boston Tea paty, were too high.

In addition, tea had even more of an image problem than water. For of all the drinks available in the New World, tea was the one most associated with foreigners, especially the ever more despised British. Colonists pictured them drinking their spiced-up water in expensive china cups, their fingers curled daintily, sipping tiny portions through tightly drawn lips as they lazed in their parlors or drawing rooms and dreamed up new taxes for their brethren in America—it could not have been a more unappealing vision to the rough-and-tumble forgers of a nation in the wilderness. And some of those forgers, in the years following the Revolutionary War, were so self-consciously proud of their independence that, regardless of what they thought about the taste of tea, they would no sooner drink it than they would smoke a pipe or take a pinch of snuff, which were also thought to be affectations of the haughty peoples across the ocean.

Yet even some of the British had begun to turn against tea. The author of *A New and Compleat Survey of London*, published in 1762, believed that too much of the liquid would be harmful to "the Stomachs of the Populace, as to render them incapable of performing the offices of Digestion; whereby the Appetite is so much deprav'd." And there were British and Americans alike who believed that "hot bread and too free indulgence in tea" would make a person's teeth fall out, which happened in those days with alarming frequency no matter what beverage he or she drank. The heat of the tea, people suspected, softened the gums and loosened the teeth. They also feared that it would wear away the enamel on the tooth, thus making a shambles of a mouth that had wanted nothing more than a few drams of refreshment.

Even among colonists who had once had a liking for tea, and it was said that in certain circles a gentleman or lady would find the time for two cups a day, the beverage eventually lost favor, especially after an American boycott of leaves from England. When it was over, some of the citizenry found themselves having so successfully adjusted to tea's absence that its presence no longer appealed.

Coffee. It is true that coffee had been gaining in popularity. It is true that the places in which it was consumed had begun to rival taverns in civic import. Scott Liell writes the following of the mid-1770s: "Many of the pressing issues that occupied the minds of Philadelphians found their fullest airing between the walls of the city's coffee houses, and its is no surprise that a frequent subject of discussion during that time was politics."

Yet coffee was even muddier than water, or so it seemed to many settlers of the New World, especially those unskilled at brewing it. It was even more expensive than tea in most of the colonies because it had to be imported from farther away. And since it was served just as hot as tea, people wondered whether it, too, in the long run, would diminish a person's dental capacities.

Milk. Too perishable. In the days before refrigeration, it was almost impossible to ship or store, and in the days before pasteurization, it was too often unhygienic. Americans were not a fastidious people in their early days, nor were they knowledgeable about, or in fact even remotely aware of, germs and bacteria and the microscopic worlds of menace that gave birth to them. But people drew the line at conditions that were obviously unwholesome, at beverages that smelled or changed color or seemed to harbor signs of pestiferous life. As J. C. Furnas writes, "Since neither the cows' rear ends nor the milker's hands got proper cleaning, the bacteriological content of all Colonial dairy products would probably have frightened a modern public-health laboratory into fits."

Not only that, milk was like the other nonalcoholic beverages of the period in that it provided a poor accompaniment to the monotonous regularity of the American diet. Hominy, hoe-cakes, porridge, bread, mush, grits, sometimes a seed cake or suet pudding—these were among the foods most commonly eaten by our colonial ancestors, and neither alone nor in combinations were they of much interest to the taste buds. Fresh fruits and vegetables were available, but only where, and when, grown; like milk, produce could not be safely transported or held for future use. Chicken and pork and beef could also be had, but not without inconvenience; salt was the only preservative widely used at the time and meat had to be slathered with it, virtually embalmed, if it were to keep for even a modest length of time. Other spices, which might have compromised the saltiness or enlivened the flavor of the meat, were hard to find and too expensive for the average budget.

Then there was the way the foods were prepared. The colonists did not have ovens; they either fried their meals over a fire or boiled them in huge pots, usually after dipping the individual courses into "extraordinary rivers of butter" or "oceans of grease." Afterward, they were tossed into the water and heated to the approximate temperature of perdition, so that the underlying food lost all semblance of taste and only the fat-laden coating, which by now could not decide whether to ooze like a wound or congeal like a rock, registered on the palate. Such a diet created a powerful thirst, and as far as the majority of Americans was concerned, only a special kind of beverage—distilled or brewed or fermented, not collected from rivers or rainstorms or the lower extremeties of cows—had the zip and fortitude to slake it.

Ironically, no one slaked in the early days of the new nation as the clergyman slaked, servants of the Almighty also proving to be servants to the grape or grain in liquid form. Sometimes it seemed as if sobriety troubled them more than Satan, as if they believed an empty bottle to be more of a threat to their earthly mission than an unrepentant sinner. Their souls might be bound for life everlasting, but their livers were not even going to make it out of *this* world in one piece.

Or *was* it ironic? Perhaps not. After all, with alcoholic beverages being perceived as their Boss's creature, men of the cloth might have believed it their duty to show a certain devotion to them, and in the process come to confuse intoxication with piety. Or they might have felt more acutely than most Americans the pangs of spiritual malaise in the forests and valleys of the New World, the Supreme Being sometimes seeming to be absent from an outpost as remote as theirs.

Whatever the reason, Reverend David Dudley Field of Stockbridge, Massachusetts, always served wine and brandy to his fellow clerics when they met to discuss the faith. There is no evidence that they imbibed to excess. But, said Leonard Woods, a cleric of the early nineteenth century as well as a professor of theology at Andover Seminary, "I could reckon among my acquaintances forty ministers . . . who were either drunkards, or so far addicted to drinking, that their reputation and usefulness were greatly impaired, if not utterly ruined." Some Americans, no less repelled by the situation than Woods, claimed that the reason church services were held but one day a week was that preachers were too nobbled the other six even to find the church, much less write a sermon and dispense salvation.

If they were not lushes before pledging their service to the Lord, they might well achieve the status a few moments later. Records show that at one minister's ordination in Woburn, Massachusetts, the supply of beverages included "six and one half barrels of cider, twenty-five gallons of wine, two gallons of brandy and four gallons of rum." There is no indication that any was left over, nor is there reason to suspect this occasion of being atypical. In colony after colony, ordinations had the same kind of reputation for being rambunctious, if not even perilous, as do high school graduation parties or fraternity initiations of the present, and in Virginia the ceremonies so often turned unruly that clergymen were fined half a year's salary for such behavior, not just to teach them a lesson but to cover damages to church property.

In part, the man of God was so susceptible to alcohol because of the way he passed his days. In Herbert Asbury's words, "even if he had wanted to do so, he could scarcely have remained temperate and still performed, satisfactorily, the duties of his office." During the week, those duties consisted mainly of calling on the families in his congregation to provide counsel, boost spirits, encourage belief, and remind people to worship with him on Sunday. But as was the custom in those days, and has been noted previously in this volume about people from all walks of colonial life, at each home he visited the preacher was offered a libation. "Add brandy to the amount of the capacity of the Bishop," says a recipe of the time for punch. If the bishop said no he was inhospitable; if he said yes he was soused. For most clergymen, the latter was not only the more politic choice, but the more pleasing. Those who did not want to admit this to themselves could rationalize their intoxication by believing it to be a means to an end: they were adopting the habits of the heathen to ingratiate themselves, and thereby increase the odds of converting them to the true faith. It was a stretch, to be sure, but some clergymen, especially the thirstier ones, were able to make it easily.

And besides, the cups were at least on a few occasions raised in the Almighty's behalf. How could a preacher refuse an opportunity to thank Him for blessings already bestowed or to ask for blessings in the future or to toast the prospects of dear ones recently departed? Just as the native tribes of America sent their prayers to heaven on trails of tobacco smoke, so did the first European colonists in the New World sometimes rely on streams of alcohol, the altered mental state thereby produced being so different from the normal condition of the psyche that it seemed to be evidence of divine visitations. Did such constant imbibing send "half the preachers round Albany to drunkards' graves," as was charged at the time? So be it. Nobody said the Lord's work was easy.

But neither was life an untroubled path for laypersons of the period. These were not just people who had left their homeland behind; these were people who had taken up arms against it, a far more drastic step. We might call the formal hostilities between America and England the Revolutionary War or the War of Independence, but it was in reality a civil war, with all of the angst and dislocation peculiar to that kind of conflict. One out of every four colonists alive during the struggle, or his or her parents, had been born in Britain, and for these people the pain was especially acute. Some of them welcomed the fighting, others were opposed, but almost all were, to one degree or another, horrified at the turn of events, amazed that war had actually broken out even though they had long seen it coming and could calmly and comprehensively list the reasons. They felt irrevocably cut off from family and friends across the Atlantic, and separated as well by wrenching differences in ideology and outlook that were being expressed more and more violently all the time. Alcohol did not just accompany these men and women when they plotted their freedom; it consoled them for the plotting's dreadful necessity.

It also stimulated the desire for freedom. In 1733, after many decades of disagreement over a variety of issues, virtually all of which involved money in one way or another, the British Parliament decided to tax one of the most important of all colonial foodstuffs. "Without molasses," writes John C. Miller in his book, *This New Man: The American*,

> New Englanders could not have enjoyed such delicacies as Boston baked beans, brown bread, and Indian pudding; Pennsylvanians would have been the poorer for want of shoofly pie and apple pandowdy; and Southerners would never have known the delights of molasses jack [and] corn pone. . . . Molasses was also used for medicinal purposes, curing meat, and pickling fish, and it was one of the basic ingredients of the soft drinks popular everywhere in the colonies.

But even more important, molasses was the basic ingredient of rum; in fact, almost half of the molasses brought to the New World from the West Indies went to the distilleries that produced the American national beverage. As a result, people were so upset about the tax that they did not even bother to protest or overtly rebel. Rather, they gave the Molasses Act the ultimate sign of disapproval; they ignored it, pretended it did not exist, neither seeing nor hearing nor speaking of the evil. They refused to pay the assessment and turned instead to product that they obtained illegally. "Far from being considered a crime," it has been written, "smuggling became an act of patriotism, and New England's sea captains became artists at sneaking their cargoes past British customs inspectors. In a single year, 1763, some fifteen thousand hogsheads of molasses were imported into Massachusetts, but taxes were paid on only a thousand."

The following year, the Molasses Act was repealed, although the tax was partially reinstated later in a different form, thereby keeping this particular set of hostilities alive.

But the British were not through. Seventeen-sixty-four was also the year in which Parliament passed the Sugar Act, one of the purposes of which was to impose so steep an excise duty on such sweet wines as

Madeira that Americans would stop drinking it and turn instead to port. It was the Portuguese who profited from Madeira; proceeds from the sale of port would go to England.

The colonists were irate. "Some of them boycotted both port and Madeira," Andrew Barr reports, "declaring that they would 'think themselves better entertained with a good glass of beer or cider.' Others drank smuggled Madeira instead." Let the British disregard the American thirst; the Americans would disregard the British mandate.

It was all to be expected. The citizens of the New World colonies needed their Madeira. They needed their rum. They needed their beer and cider, their syllabubs and manathans, needed them when ties with the Motherland were fraying even more than when they were strong. For they had started life anew in a part of the world in which every person was displaced, every institution untried, every parcel of land untamed and forbidding. Some goods could not be had; some services did not exist. England was a nation fully developed and efficient in its functionings; the colonies, in their youngest days, were more like an obstacle course. How were the settlers to cope? Where was the reassurance provided by familiar scenes and customs of long standing? Why had the Americans put an ocean between themselves and the only homes they had ever known?

There were insecurities of other kinds as well, more narrowly related to specific occupations, and these too led the colonists to beverages of serious intent. Farmhands drank because of the transitory nature of their employment and their unfamiliarity with the soil in this distant landmass. Laborers drank because their tasks seemed harder in a such a place, unlubricated by routine. Stagecoach drivers drank because of their rootlessness and their passengers because of the uncertainty of their destinations, the coach stopping "every five miles to water the horses and brandy the gentlemen."

Doctors drank because they cured so few patients. Patients drank because they were so seldom cured. City dwellers drank because rapidly growing populations left them in turmoil and countryfolk drank because of loneliness and students drank because, as is the case at present, they were living their rebellious years.

And then, as the nineteenth century turned, a new anxiety appeared at the horizon, a giant with an even more gigantic shadow, a presence without precedent in all the world's history. It was the Industrial Revolution, and some Americans, although not knowing what to call it—the term, in fact, does not seem to have been coined until 1848—or even precisely when it appeared, cowered at their initial intimations of it, reacting instinctively, sensing at some level that in time it would steal their jobs and their ways of life and never return them again. Its galloping technology seemed not only relentless but totally oblivious to consequences; new textile machinery was being invented, as was the cotton gin, the power shovel, the cast-iron plow, the cutting torch, the sliding rest lathe, the thresher, the steamboat, and the submarine—one of them right after the other, from the beginning of the century to the end. Factories were springing up to process cotton, refine sugar, roll brass, manufacture cold-cut nails, and mill flour, the latter in some cases equipped with a wondrous thing called an automatic production line. It was a brave new world, the first one ever, and living in it, even in its very first days, seemed to require as much courage as it had taken years before to fight the war for independence.

Each of these developments was a kind of death knell. Each of them weakened the value of a previously existing trade by enabling it to be performed faster and more cheaply, and usually with fewer people involved, than had been possible in the past. Human beings had never expected such a thing, this obsolescence of the individual rather than of the object. What were they to do? Was there any place to turn for consolation?

In fact, there was. There were a lot of places, and the colonists turned to them desperately: to bottles and barrels, to cups and glasses and mugs, to taverns and inns that were tried and true and comforting. And, as things worked themselves out, the very kinds of industrial processes that were distressing Americans and making them even thirstier than they used to be were at the same time improving the quality of drink to which they now felt so driven. "The Industrial Revolution touched the distilled spirits industry as well as other manufacturers," writes Oscar Getz. "New and better methods of distillation were invented. Distillers, whether on farms or in towns, expanded their facilities, using more and larger stills, more and larger mash tubs and running the finished product into larger barrels instead of into jugs and crocks."

Technology taketh away; technology giveth.

It has been said that, for all these reasons, Americans of the eighteenth and early nineteenth centuries were more in need of psychiatric assistance than any generation before or since. But, of course, there *were* no psychiatrists at the time—with the possible, unofficial exception of bartenders with generous ears—nor were our forebears the kind of people to have relied on psychiatrists even if they *had* existed. They were too self-reliant, too inner-directed. What they could not accomplish themselves, they assigned to their God; what their God could not accomplish, they would leave undone, assuming that that was what He had intended all along. They did not turn to booze because it provided answers, but because it made the questions easier to ignore.

In time, the importance of alcoholic beverages to Americans was reflected in the marketplace. At the end of the eighteenth century, a bushel of corn brought the farmer who grew it twenty-five cents. More often than not, this was barely enough to justify the time and effort. But if the farmer converted his grain to whiskey, he could sell it for four times as much money, and sometimes more than that. "Even if the farmer did not do his own distilling," we are told, "and had to give a commercial distiller half the output in payment for his service, he could increase the value of his corn by 150 percent." Since the eighteenth century was a bountiful time for American agriculture, most farmers had more than enough grain available after providing for their families and livestock to make the production of whiskey an irresistible prospect.

In addition, whereas dampness or mildew could destroy grain in storage, booze would not spoil no matter how long it was kept. Sometimes its taste would even improve with age. And when the potion was ready to be sold, it could be transported with relative ease. A horse that carried only four bushels of grain to market could carry the liquor made from twenty-four bushels.

Getting smashed was even being kind to animals!

In 1791, Secretary of the Treasury Alexander Hamilton, himself an infrequent drinker, got an idea. The new country was spending a lot of money to defend itself against attacks from the people who were its original inhabitants. Why not raise that money, at least in part, by placing a tax on whiskey? Why not, in other words, make revenue dependent on thirst? It seemed to Hamilton, and to others who shared his notion, that this would ensure all the men and materiel the United States ever needed to keep angry natives at bay.

Hamilton also thought that the tax would have other beneficial side effects. For one, it would even eliminate the advantage that whiskey had recently gained in the marketplace, as the previous year a tax had been imposed on molasses and rum. For another, it would force at least a few of his countrymen to cut back on their guzzling. "The consumption of ardent spirits," he once said, "is carried to an extreme which is truly to be regretted, as well in regard to the health and morals as to the economy of the community."

The proposal, though, was a controversial one. Some people opposed it on principle, as they had opposed similar taxes originating in the British Parliament over the years. Others opposed Hamilton's measure on the grounds that defense was already financed by existing levies; better to spend those monies more prudently than to seek new sums. Jefferson, who tended to dislike anything Hamilton supported, called the tax "an infernal one," and Albert Gallatin, who lambasted the bill in the Pennsylvania Assembly, claimed it would be an unfair burden on farmers, whose importance to the nation was such that the government ought to be easing their loads.

The opposition failed, however, and Congress initially set the levy at seven and a half cents for each gallon of whiskey that was distilled from domestic grain. Before long, it went to nine cents, and climbed to eleven cents per gallon if the liquor was produced from an imported product like molasses. An additional charge of sixty cents a year was added for each gallon of capacity in a farmer's still. Hamilton thought these numbers perfectly reasonable.

Farmers did not. As Gallatin had predicted, they were outraged. They had just fought a war to free themselves from a government that taxed them excessively without their consent; were they now to allow the same thing to be done by another government, one which had ostensibly been created to right the previous wrongs? Were they to accept injustice because their new oppressor had a familiar face and a nearby address? They were not, they decided, and several of the farmers wrote to Congress to explain their opposition, claiming that the new law

> appears unequal in its operation and immoral in its effects. Unequal in its operation, as a duty laid on the common drink of a nation, instead of taxing the citizens in proportion to their property, falls as heavy on the poorest class as on the rich; immoral in its effects, because the amount of duty resting on the oath of the payer, offers, at the expense of the honest part of the community, a premium to perjury fraud.

The farmers also complained that "the powers necessarily vested in the officers for the collection of so odious a revenue are not only unusual but incompatible with the free enjoyment of domestic peace and private property." Specifically what they objected to, in the words of historian Bernard A. Weisberger, was the tax's intrusiveness. "It allowed collectors to snoop in barns, closets, and cellars looking for hidden untaxed spirits," Weisberger writes. "And anyone wishing to challenge an assessment had to leave home and farm untended in order to take his case to the federal court in distant Philadelphia."

The opponents' case was a strong one, they believed, and they had expressed it eloquently and persuasively.

Congress paid no attention.

In southwestern Pennsylvania, where an estimated 25 percent of all American stills were located, and where the liquor trade was especially profitable and the Scotch-Irish citizenry more than usually obstreperous, the farmers vowed to fight the legislative indifference. They warned tax collectors that the law would be no protection for them; they should stay away, not try to enforce it. When they showed up anyhow, the farmers took after them with a vengeance. According to Alice Fleming, "a federal marshal in Allegheny County was attacked for trying to enforce the hated law, and an angry mob set fire to the home of the regional tax inspector and threatened to march on Pittsburgh." And there were other attacks, other fires, other threats, all too many of them acted upon; revenue agents became as despised in whiskey country as the British had been a few years before.

A more common tactic against them, though, was tarring and feathering, the farmers keeping themselves well stocked with both of the necessary ingredients and applying them at will. They were also quick to punish those among their neighbors who cooperated with the authorities. The rebels would plunder their crops and scatter or butcher their animals and damage their homes or barns and sometimes even tear the clothes right off their bodies. When a colonist named William Faulkner offered his house to the government as an office for the revenuers, his former friends set out with sharpened blades to give him the closest haircut of his life.

Hamilton was furious. He ordered the farmers to obey the law and to obey it promptly, citing the common weal, citing also the fact that the federal government, through its purchases for the military, was the biggest single customer of western Pennsylvania hooch; thus, he explained through gritted teeth, it was in the best interests of those who manufactured it not to treat the government's agents with such brutal disregard.

The farmers would not listen. They not only continued their resistance, but stepped it up. "They formed an army, several thousand strong, marched on Pittsburgh and took it. They approached the governments of Britain and Spain with plans for a separate republic." Neither nation was interested, but the western Pennsylvanians would not allow themselves to be discouraged. As soon as one plan failed, they came up with another, and they gave their all to each in its turn, forming themselves into small, roving bands of marauders and making life as miserable as they could for their foes.

Not until President Washington, at Hamilton's insistence, sent a force of 15,000 militiamen to confront the insurgents, more than the number which had fought in any single battle of the Revolutionary War, was order finally restored. Leading the force was General Henry "Lighthorse Harry" Lee, father of Robert E., and he was eager for the command, spoiling for a fight. As George Brown Tindall explains, he did not get one.

> To his disappointment the rebels vaporized like rye mash when the heat was applied, and the troops met with little more opposition than a few liberty poles. By dint of great effort and much marching they finally rounded up twenty prisoners whom they paraded down Market Street in Philadelphia and clapped into prison. Eventually two of these were found guilty of treason.

The Whiskey Rebellion, this episode in American history is called, and it is an even more appropriate name than it seems. There is some dispute over the derivation of the word "whiskey," but it more than likely hails from the Scottish *qubiske*, which means to move away rapidly, and refers, in the words of Oscar Getz, "to a light chaise apparently invented by the Scotch-Irish whiskey smugglers to escape tax collectors" a long time ago in their homeland.

But in this land, which in fact as well as name wanted the rest of the world to think of it as united, the rebellion was the most embarrassing of incidents. The end came in 1794. Washington pardoned the two traitors, and most of the other farmers in western Pennsylvania agreed to start paying the tax, although they were not happy about it, and in most cases, when they handed over the money, not even civil. They believed that the tax was a hostile act imposed by a thoughtless and arrogant and pusillanimous assembly of improperly elected officials who did not care in the least about the citizens they claimed to represent.

Which was yet *another* reason for them to drink.

2

The General and the Doctor

t was early in the colonial experiment, probably 1622, when the London Company, which held the charter for Virginia, told Governor Francis Wyatt that there was too much boozing going on in his jurisdiction. It was a stain on the reputation of both colony and company, an "infamy [that] hath spread itself to all that have heard the name of Virginia." The members of the company were embarrassed. Not only that, they were angry. They demanded "speedie redress."

This is the first known plea for a change in American drinking habits—the first, at least, from an official body as opposed to the occasional, aggrieved individual—and like most of those that followed, it might just as well have been whispered into the wind. Increase Mather made such a plea half a century later, and few people even knew of it, despite the importance of the topic and the eminence of the speaker. Here, *in full*, is what he said about the lineage of alcoholic beverages: "Drink is itself a good creature of God, and to be received with thankfulness, but the abuse of drink is from Satan, The wine is from God, but the Drunkard is from the Devil."

As we have seen, most of Mather's countrymen heeded the endorsement and ignored the caution. Occasionally a fine was assessed for public tipsiness; "in 1693, a fellow by the name of Joseph Biddle was 'found guilty of being drunck, by ye jury and was amerced forty shillings.'" Occasionally a sot was placed in the stocks or tied to a post and whipped in sight of his fellow villagers or forced the wear the scarlet letter

47

"D" for drunkard. In some communities, Boston the largest among them, the names of inebriates were posted in well-traveled venues for all to see, the goal being to shame them into a change of behavior. There were even a few cases of clergymen, perhaps playing pot to their parishioners' kettle, dismissing immoderate tipplers from the church, commanding them to mend their ways. One such excommunicant was a New England woman named Ruth Fuller, who in 1685 was seen "holding on to the gate before her house, drunk." Never again would she kneel before the Lord in her accustomed pew.

But these were the exceptions in early America, not the rules. More than a hundred years would pass from the London Company's warning until a significant attempt was made at redress, and the attempt would be a failure of such magnitude that its lessons should have been remembered by the legions of redressers who came along after yet another hundred years had passed.

One day, the estimable Dr. Samuel Johnson would be so impressed by General James Edward Oglethorpe that he would offer to write the man's biography. Not that Oglethorpe was much to look at: his face was too narrow, his nose too thin, and the color of his hair, somewhere between brown and blond and varying with the light, too hard to identify. His lips curled up effeminately; he could not do anything about it. But he "was aggressive, determined, and endowed with a powerful moral sense." He had "a fine honed conception of what constituted religion and morality." He "thought highly of his own abilities and never doubted for a moment that his training and experience would triumph over any problems he might face across the sea." The Englishman, then, was ideally cast for the role of America's first prohibitionist.

Yet it was not a role he had envisioned as a young man. The son of financially secure parents, Oglethorpe was born in London in 1696. He studied at Oxford and joined the military immediately after graduation. His first rank was that of ensign in His Majesty's Life Guards, but he did not stay there long, and in fact scaled the various levels of military hierarchy so quickly that, before reaching his twenty-fourth birthday, he had become a general and distinguished himself in England's war against Turkey. He was the George Washington of England before the George Washington of America had even been born.

A civilian again at twenty-six, Oglethorpe ran for a seat in Parliament and won, even though he did not appeal to the voters' thirsts. In fact, among the positions upon which he campaigned was the restricted use of alcoholic beverages; he "expressed his approval . . . by proposing a further duty on importations [of liquor] 'as well as to discourage the pernicious use of spirits, such as gin, etc., as to encourage the drinking of malt liquors.'" Such a duty would eventually be enacted; much of the credit would belong to young James Oglethorpe.

It was all going so well for him, so predictably, his life following a broad, well-worn, upper-middle-class path. Barring detour, there would soon be a wife from a family as prominent as his, a large flock of children, and eventually a title. He would manage his estate, and in the process see to the grapes in his vineyard. But he would never drink too much wine at a sitting, and would encourage similar restraint in others. He would grow old gracefully, continuing to serve his nation in one way or another, and would be rich in rewards as well as years. His ancestors would be proud, his descendants inspired. The story, it seemed, could have been written before the events.

But then something happened, something that James Oglethorpe could never have foreseen, something that would knock him off his path and send him down byways he did not even know existed, much less would have chosen to pursue. Given that powerful moral sense of his, though, he would never have cause for regret, or at least would never express such a feeling. He would do his new duty exactly as he saw it, the same way that he had been prepared to do the old.

It seems that a friend of his, a young architect named Robert Castell, about whom history knows little, had died of smallpox while in prison for his debts. Oglethorpe was shocked by the news, all the more so when he learned that the disease had not been treated, and perhaps had not even been diagnosed, by doctors who had looked in on the gentleman. Moved by his sorrow, Oglethorpe demanded information. How had doctors in the employ of the Crown been so remiss in their duties? How had such a fine fellow come to so inglorious an end? Was there anything anyone could have done? If so, why was it *not* done? Was there anything Oglethorpe could do now?

The answers to these questions provided yet another shock. Oglethorpe visited the prison in which Castell had died and found that it lacked even the most basic of medical facilities, facilities that could easily have saved his friend's life. Not only that, it was overcrowded, understaffed, rodent-infested, and so dark and filthy as to be unfit for habitation by any living creature, much less a decent human being who had simply failed for a time to make a sufficient wage. The food provided almost no sustenance and, for but a few pence, an inmate could fuddle his brains on varieties of gin known as "Kill-Grief," "Cock-my-Cap," and "Comfort." The air stank of things decomposing, the guards were sadistic on their more humane days, and the cells were achingly small, permitting an adult male almost no room to stretch his muscles and take a few steps. As a result, prisoners were pale, emaciated, enfeebled to the point of illness and despair.

Oglethorpe was horrified. Shortly afterward, he made a second trip to the prison, this time accompanied by several members of a specially appointed Parliamentary committee. They saw what he had seen and smelled what he had smelled and reacted as he had reacted. With their unanimous support, Oglethorpe then "presented to the House of Commons three reports in which he charged the respective jailers and their deputies with the sale of offices, breaches of trust, enormous extortions, oppression, intimidation, gross brutalities, and the highest crimes and misdemeanors." It was an incendiary document. It was also a practical one, leading to the elimination of the worst of British penal abuses and an improvement in some of the others.

But Oglethorpe was not satisfied. He wanted more. An idea had occurred to him, actually something closer to a mission, and he was determined to make it a reality. It meant more than the wife, more than the family, more than the estate that awaited him in a few years at the most. It was so new a notion, yet he felt so strongly that it might have been his goal, his consuming passion, all along.

Oglethorpe arranged an audience with King George II, and after an exchange of pleasantries, the young man asked the monarch to release a hundred or so inmates to his personal custody. Any hundred, from any prison in the realm. He told the king that he wanted to make a point. He would take the miscreants to the New World, he said; he would found a new colony, just below South Carolina, and thereby enable these poor men and women to start their lives over again, giving them a chance to achieve the kind of fulfillment that circumstances had so cruelly denied them in the land of their birth. "If given an opportunity," he believed, "an individual who might have failed in his first chance could possibly succeed in his second." The colony would also,

Oglethorpe said, in so many words, serve as a military buffer against the Spanish in Florida.

George II was dubious.

Oglethorpe told him that human beings under God had a responsibility to their fellow human beings.

George II was still dubious.

Oglethorpe said he had a good name for the colony.

The king wanted to know it.

Georgia, Oglethorpe said. What do you think?

The king wished the reformer fair winds and calm seas.

General James Oglethorpe and 116 former inmates of London prisons set sail from England on November 17, 1732. The seas were not calm and the winds were sometimes violent, but the settlers arrived in Charles Town, South Carolina, two months later, staying long enough to be welcomed by those subjects of the Crown who had preceded them, then heading south as planned. On February 12, 1733, "on a tract ceded by the Indians and lying on the banks of the Savannah River, ten miles from its mouth, they began to erect the town of that name."

But before they cleared the forests, scattered the natives, and built their homes, Oglethorpe assembled his charges and handed out supplies. Having brought "10 tons of Alderman Parson's best beer" from the Motherland, he decided that an allotment of forty-four gallons would be a fair amount for each family's needs. But he dispensed them with a warning. He said the colonists should treat the beer respectfully, even warily, and they should never, under any circumstances, drink anything stronger. Most of all, they should avoid rum, which was to Oglethorpe poisonous, "a fatal Liquor."

Then he made a mistake. He also apportioned sixty-five gallons of molasses to each family, assuming that they would use it to sweeten their foods and feed their livestock and perhaps even brew some more beer when the original quantities were gone. Which they did. But, for the most part, they used the molasses for rum, and their output was so great that the colony became, on a per capita basis, the New World's leading producer of the beverage, its citizens developing an almost continuous thirst that led to an almost continuous buzz that led, in turn, to almost continuous distilling. The Georgians could not help it, or so some of them said at the time; the perils of dwelling in so primitive a place were so great and unceasing that only with rum's assistance could they "keep up their Courage."

Oglethorpe could not believe it. Such an unholy misuse of molasses, such a pathetic ignorance of what truly constituted courage. As biographer Phinizy Spalding tells us, the general

> honestly believed that the presence of rum in Savannah had caused more than twenty persons to die in less than a month. . . . The various "burning Feavers," "bloody Fluxes," convulsions, and other horrors were conquered only with the greatest difficulty. The ministrations of a doctor were essential, but Oglethorpe was convinced that his own hawklike antirum crusade played the major role in the decline of Savannah's summer sickness.

He was also convinced that rum subverted the utopian goals of his community in other ways. Take the case of the lighthouse in Savannah's harbor, a building that seemed ever under construction, never fated to open. Oglethorpe did not understand. He asked some associates to look into the matter, to tell him why it was taking a more-than-adequate number of able-bodied men so long to complete so simple a structure. Their reply, however, did not satisfy him; he would have to conduct his own investigation, just as he had done at the English prison.

And, as had happened back home, Oglethorpe made upsetting discoveries, although in this case he could not claim they were unexpected. What he found was that the laborers were creating the lighthouse in the opposite manner from the Almighty's creating the world. He had worked for six days and rested one; they worked one, rested six. The reason? What else: rum, damnable rum. It sold for so little in Georgia that the men could buy a week's worth of stupefaction on but a single day's pay. And that was not only what they did, but all they wanted to do. Unlike the men who would later erect the meeting house in Northampton, Massachusetts, and speed up their labors because of spirituous refreshment, the southerners slowed to a crawl. The lighthouse would get built eventually; ships would just have to be a little more careful in the fog for the time being. Bottoms up!

But just as Oglethorpe was not surprised by such behavior, neither were the colony's trustees in England; all the while, the general had been writing to them of his problems. They supported him as best they could from afar, sometimes sending messages to let know how much they appreciated his efforts, encouraging him to keep on. But after seeing what was happening at the lighthouse, Oglethorpe decided he wanted something more from the Motherland: specifically, a pronouncement from the king on the subject of alcoholic beverages in the

New World. Fearing that his name would forever be associated with the debauched state of his eponymous colony, George II was quick to reply.

> Whereas it is found by Experience that the use of Liquors called Rum and Brandy in the Province of Georgia are more particularly hurtful and pernicious to Man's Body and have been attended with dangerous Maladies and fatal Distempers . . . No Rum or Brandy nor any other kind of Spirits or Strong Waters by whatsoever name they are or may be distinguished shall be imported or brought to shore.

Thomas Penn, the proprietor of Pennsylvania and the late William's son, disapproved of the ban, telling Oglethorpe "that rum added to water, especially during the American summertime, was absolutely indispensable." To the king Penn seems to have said nothing, but others joined him in believing the proclamation a mistake, that it had been issued "without sufficient appreciation of the nature of the country and the disposition of the people."

It had also been issued without appreciation of the economic needs of those people, who, as a result of the edict, could no longer export their timber to the West Indies because all that the Indies could offer in return was the molasses that was turned into Oglethorpe's "fatal Liquor." The result was the end of trade, and financial hardship for all, imbiber and abstainer alike.

Nonetheless, the prohibition in Georgia was not a total disaster. For South Carolina, in fact, it was an absolute boon. Rum-sellers from the older colony had no sooner heard of liquor's demise next door than they loaded their wagons with liquid fire and thundered across the border. They also loaded their boats and sailed down the coast. Then they dropped off their cargo and loaded their moneybags, their thirst-crazed customers greeting the South Carolinians as if they were a liberating army and thereupon getting loaded themselves.

Oglethorpe, infuriated, tried to repel the purveyors, and even pleaded with officials in South Carolina to close down one particular tavern after fourteen of his colonists drowned while sailing back home after patronizing it. The tavern remained open. So did the mouths of Georgia's thirsty ex-cons.

Yet Oglethorpe was undeterred. He next step was to see to it that a law was passed in his domain to forbid the purchase or consumption of South Carolina spirits. He was certain of the wisdom of such an edict, confident it would work. He was wrong. In most cases, members of the constabulary would not even arrest a fellow colonist for so inoffensive an offense as whistle-wetting. If they did arrest him, juries would not convict. If juries convicted, judges would not sentence. After all, the law enforcers and the judges and juries were buying liquor of their own from South Carolina; they might have been sots, but they would not be hypocrites.

The first American experiment with prohibition lasted from 1735 to 1742. As a way of life, however, it never really got started. In fact, one of Oglethorpe's denizens thought it might have been counterproductive, "as it is the nature of mankind in general, and of the common sort in particular, more eagerly to desire and more immoderately to use those things which are most restrained from them."

In the decades to come, there would be reformers who learned from the Georgia example, who would lament man's thirst for alcohol and try everything within their power as individuals to reason or frighten him out of it; they would not, however, seek a remedy through legislation, would not believe such a thing was possible.

But the reformers who came after them, particularly late in the nineteenth century and early in the twentieth, would be inspired by what General James Oglethorpe had attempted to do, so noble had been his motives and so unwavering his dedication. Their own motives would also be noble, but their methods, they vowed, would be more efficient than his, even ruthless if necessary, and they would not stop until they had gone so far as to rewrite the Constitution of the United States.

A physician by trade, although much more than that by inclination and ability, Benjamin Rush ministered to many of early America's leading families, the Adamses and Hancocks among them, and one of his pupils in medical college was the future president William Henry Harrison. Rush served the Continental Army as surgeon general and, no less concerned with the effect of injury upon the mind than the body, came to be known as the father of American psychiatry. He was a member of the American Philosophical Society and a co-founder of both the Philadelphia Bible Society and Dickinson College; he was a congressman, a delegate to the First Continental Congress, and a signer of the Declaration of Independence. Later in life he financed a school for children of African descent and helped establish the first formal group of abolitionists in the United States. He studied agriculture and astronomy, patterns of human immigration and animal migration, whatever caught his attention, whenever it happened to catch.

But it was medicine that occupied most of Rush's time. Only 10 percent of the doctors in colonial America had medical degrees and Rush was among them, having earned his at the University of Edinburgh in Scotland and then returned to the New World to become the leading figure in his field. "The "Hippocrates of Pennsylvania," he was called, even though some of his ideas, like those of his most distinguished contemporaries, later proved erroneous, and a few were so misguided as to be harmful. Rush believed, for example, that certain diseases, such as yellow fever, were best treated by bleeding the patient—and not just bleeding him, practically emptying him out. He insisted that human beings could lose 80 percent of their blood without risk, a calculation even more destructive than it sounds given the fact that Rush grossly overestimated the amount of blood that a human being contains. "The ultimate proof of his theory," writes a sadly amused Daniel Boorstin, "was that any patient who was bled long enough would eventually relax!"

Rush sought to improve the health of the community as well as that of the individual, and here he was on firmer ground. He urged his fellow Philadelphians to clean their streets, keep their water supplies as pure as possible, and dispose properly of sewage and other refuse, which is to say, refrain from throwing it in the nearest street or waterway. He believed that people should exercise regularly, eat and drink in moderation, and avoid distilled spirits altogether. The latter was especially important to him; as surgeon general, he tried to eliminate the daily rum ration for the army, insisting that it was not, as its advocates claimed, salubrious; rather, it led to fatigue and promoted "fluxes and fevers." As far as American fighting men were concerned, Rush was fluxed and fevered himself; they paid no attention to his views.

Nonetheless, in 1772, he "embarked on a lifelong campaign against ardent spirits from a medical standpoint in a pamphlet entitled *Sermons to Gentlemen Upon Temperance and Exercise*." Then, in 1785, he published a far more extensive document, perhaps the first American temperance treatise to stimulate serious debate. It was called *An Inquiry into the Effects of Spiritous Liquors on the Human Body*, and, among other things, it tells of the terrible fate that awaits the person who lubricates himself too freely with demon rum: "In folly, it causes him to resemble a calf,—in stupidity, an ass,—in roaring, a mad bull,—in quarrelling and fighting, a dog,—in cruelty, a tyger,—in fetor, a skunk,—in filthiness, a hog,—and in obscenity, a he-goat."

Stating the same general message in different terms, and in a different form, Rush included a chart in his *Inquiry*. It provides specifics on the disintegration of the imbiber, based on the quantity of alcohol imbibed, according to a scale that Rush devised himself that ranges from 0 to 80, although 0 to 80 *what* he does not say.

		VICES	DISEASES	PUNISHMENTS
10	Punch	Idleness	Sickness	Debt
20	Toddy, egg rum	Gaming, peevishness	Tremors of the hands	Jail
30	Grog, brandy and water	Fighting, horse-racing	Inflamed eyes, red nose and face	Black eyes and rags
40	Flip and shrub	Lying & swearing	Sore and swelled legs	Hospital or poorhouse
50	Bitters, infused in spirits & cordials	Stealing & swindling	Jaundice, pains in hands & feet	Bridewell [a local prison]
60	Gin, brandy & rum in mornings	Perjury	Dropsy, epilepsy	State prison
70	The same in mornings & evenings	Burglary	Melancholy, palsy, apoplexy	Ditto for life
80	The same during day & night	Murder	Madness, despair	Gallows

Rush was hopeful that mankind could avoid the fates so precisely detailed above. He predicted that, by early in the twentieth century, alcoholic beverages would be "as uncommon as a drink made of a solution of arsenic or a decoction of hemlock." To bring his goal into being, he proposed that Americans disassociate themselves from spirits gradually, perhaps quenching their thirst for alcohol with beer or light wine. If the taste of liquor was absolutely essential, he thought a weak rum punch might do, and recommended that once a person got used to one level of weakness, he dilute the beverage even further, watering it a little more each day until he weaned himself off rum entirely. "For the transition period between drunkenness and temperance," writes Herbert Asbury, "[Rush] recommended the use of laudanum or opium mixed with wine." Even better, Rush told people to satisfy their longings with a concoction called a switchel, whose ingredients were sugar, vinegar, and water. As the recipe suggests, the drink never caught on.

Benjamin Rush believed that, consumed to excess, "strong" alcoholic beverages were a curse not just to the person who drank them but to the society of which he was a part. They were "anti-federal," he stated, because they encouraged "all those vices . . . calculated to dishonor and enslave our country." Thus if a person availed himself of them temperately, or, better yet, not at all, the new republican government would operate more efficiently, and the vices enumerated in the preceding chart, like perjury, burglary, and murder, would be almost nonexistent. It sounds terribly naïve today; to Rush and some of his fellow citizens of the Enlightenment, an age that was so hopeful about the potential of mankind, so confident of its prospects, our dubiousness would have sounded cynical.

But Rush did not think that all distilleries should be shut down, all stores of liquor destroyed or made illegal. He conceded that spirits had their uses—two of them, in fact, both strictly medicinal. He prescribed them as a safeguard against fainting, and as a means of helping people protect themselves against fever or chills after exposure to inclement weather. In the former case, he recommended a spoonful or two, in the latter he referred to "a moderate quantity of spirits," which, he said, "is not only safe, but highly proper."

So far, so good. But the doctor went on to explain that the spirits "will more certainly have those salutary effects, if the feet are at the same time bathed with them, or half a pint of them poured into the shoes or boots." To pour them into the stomach, Rush taught, was to invite disease, not bring about a cure. It was obvious, he declared; all one had to do was note the altered condition of the lush as he indulged his thirst: the flush to the skin, the slurred speech, the headache and queasy stomach, the changes in personality—each was a harbinger of illnesses to come, and, according to other alcohol opponents of the time, even more of them awaited the boozehound than appear on Rush's chart. In addition, there were biliousness, Bright's disease, diabetes, fetid breath, "frequent and disgusting belchings," goiter, idiocy, immorality, indigestion, itching, liver disorders, loss of common sense, poor appetite, scurvy, stomach rumblings, uncleanliness, and vomiting. And then there was that most dreaded of all physical indispositions, that "mild foretaste of what awaited the drunkard in hell," spontaneous combustion.

Yes, spontaneous combustion.

One of the first of these reports came from the French town of Rheims in 1725. Supposedly a woman named Nicole Millet, who had not "gone to bed sober these past twenty years," as her husband recalled, suddenly burned to death while sitting in a chair which was itself "hardly burned" at all. A doctor who examined the charred remains of Madame Millet recognized the signs and pronounced her fate. "She died," said M. Claude-Nicholas leCat with appropriate solemnity, "*by the visitation of God.*"

Benjamin Rush added to the lore in the United States by claiming that he once saw a hard-drinking man belch near the flames of a candle and become "suddenly destroyed." Charles Dickens gave further respectability to spontaneous combustion, or at least further publicity, by offering it as the explanation for the mysterious disappearance of Mr. Krook in his novel *Bleak House.* And, back to the real world, or what some swore was the real world, one George McCandlish, a member in good standing of the Reform Club of Jackson, Michigan, provided his own testimony on the subject a few years later.

> In the fall of 1867, during my drinking days, I was going home one night badly set up, and when I came to the High Bridge, between Oil City and West Oil City, I looked down and saw a man lying at the bottom of the ravine apparently dead. I was a good deal frightened, and went and called the chief of police; and along with two policemen and Drs. Seys and Harding, we picked up the man, and found that he had fallen over, in a fit of intoxication, and broken his neck. I was summoned as a witness before the coroner's jury, and saw the *post mortem* examination performed by these two physicians. After removing the top of the skull, for the purpose of examining the condition of the brain, they tested it for alcohol, by holding a lighted match near it; and immediately the brain took fire, and burned with a blue flame, like an alcohol lamp.

Even so renowned a figure as the philosopher and psychologist William James was being taught about spontaneous combustion at Union College in New York in the 1860s. The school's president, Dr. Eliphalet Nott, happened to be very much a believer, and he liked to preach the virtues of sobriety by telling his students of the young man who had been found "roasted from the crown of his head to the soles of his feet . . . standing erect in the midst of a widely extended silver-colored flame, bearing . . . exactly the appearance of the wick of a burning candle. . . . It was purely a case of spontaneous combustion."

These tales were the UFO sightings of their time. They were told with relish and heard with awe and repeated in whispers both excited and furtive. But there is no proof of their authenticity, and for all of the horrible fascination of the accounts, they did not accomplish their goal. Americans would not be frightened into doing something so unnatural as turning their backs on alcoholic beverages. If abstinence was ever to appeal to them, if the teacup was one day to replace the beer mug, the dairy farm the vineyard, and the stream the distillery, those who advocated the reforms would have to come up with a different approach altogether.

The Father of Prohibition
and Other Kinfolk

t is a tale that the popular historians believe and the academic historians suspect, and the latter, claiming there is little evidence and nothing that can be proven beyond doubt, are probably right. But this author has decided to tell it anyhow, for two reasons. First, the characters, at least, are real. Second, there are fictions that make up for the inaccuracy of their details by the truth of their general impressions, they are like novels whose inventiveness renders an era as effectively, in its own way, as do the diaries and data and journalism of the period. The story of Billy James Clark and Lebbeus Armstrong might be one of those fictions. Then again . . . ,

The time was March 1808, and the place Moreau, New York, in Saratoga County, about fifty miles north of Albany as the crow flies. It could not be called the middle of nowhere; it was worse than that, the fringes. The gray skies and bare trees of winter were symbols of the entire year in this part of the country, which could be cold and damp and uninviting regardless of the season. Yet if Moreau lacked charm, it did not lack bustle, a sense of purpose. It was "the heart of a rich timberland, and the millowners, raftsmen and loggers who populate[d] it spen[t] a major part of their leisure hours getting rampaging drunk."

Billy J. Clark, twenty-three years old and uncommonly thoughtful for such a young man, did not spend *his* hours like this. He was a doctor who had recently read Benjamin Rush's *Inquiry* and had considered Rush's points long and hard. As we join him, he is sitting before the fire in his home, perhaps, as is his custom, stirring it idly with a branch. Because of his occupation, he has been "afforded exceptional advantages for observing and studying the effects upon the people of the prevailing intemperance," and this is what he ponders tonight.

Actually, both of Clark's occupations have given him these advantages. Before entering medical school, he was a bartender in Vermont, and at least at the beginning, he found it an enjoyable line of work. He was not averse to joining his customers for a round or two, was more than willing to sneak a few sips for himself when serving others. He kept the good times going, did bartender Billy, and he defined the good times the same way as everyone else in the establishment.

That was then. Now a man of a different stripe, Billy J. Clark keeps tending to his fire, looking into it and listening, lost in some kind of reverie. Suddenly, he is struck with an idea, one that seems so obvious he cannot imagine why it has not occurred to him before, and so beneficial to the whole of mankind that he believes there is not a moment to lose. He throws the branch into the fire, springs out of his chair, rushes outside. He leaps onto his horse and at full gallop makes "a three-miles journey under a black, wet sky, splattering himself from hat to boots with clayey mud."

The journey ends at the home of a man he has known and admired for many years, ever since he stopped tending bar: the Reverend Lebbeus Armstrong. Clark knocks at the preacher's door, bursts inside, and utters these words: *"Mr. Armstrong, I have come to see you on important business. We shall all become a community of drunkards in this town unless something is done to arrest the progress of intemperance!"*

The quote, complete with italics and exclamation point, is from Reverend Armstrong's book, *The Temperance Reformation*, which is meant to be a historical record but might instead be the very kind of fiction referred to a few paragraphs back. It goes on to state that, on the same night, the two men put their heads together and came up with the Union Temperance Society of Moreau and Northumberland, the first organization of its kind in the United States. They shook hands on it, then dropped to their knees to pray for the assistance from above that they knew they would need.

Within a few weeks, more than forty men with hard-drinking pasts became charter members of the group. Most of them were farmers, one a fellow who had a habit of coming in from his fields and swigging a mug of rum so fast that, in addition to suffering from an occasional bout of the West Indian Dry Gripes, he nearly died a time or two. He was ready to turn over a new leaf. All of them were. Reverend Armstrong and Billy J. Clark had seized the moment perfectly.

According to one version of what happened next, the aspiring abstainers were summoned to the village's only meeting place, Peter Mawney's tavern, to agree on a constitution. Mawney was a friend of the men and had long been their servant in thirst suppression; one assumes he had not been told the purpose of the get-together. Among the salient points of the document said to have been written that night are the following:

> ARTICLE IV. No member shall drink rum, gin, whiskey, wine or any distilled spirits or compositions of the same, or any of them, except by advice of a physician, or in case of actual disease; also, excepting wine at public dinners, under a penalty of twenty-five cents, provided that this article shall not infringe on any religious ordinance.
>
> Section 2. No member shall be intoxicated, under penalty of fifty cents.
>
> Section 3. No member shall offer any of said liquors to any other members, or urge other persons to drink thereof, under a penalty of twenty-five cents for each offense.
>
> ARTICLE XI. It shall be the duty of each member to accuse any other member of a breach of any regulation to Article IV, and the mode of accusative process and trial shall be regulated by a By-Law.

The constitution was adopted without dissent.

Billy James Clark was voted secretary of the society.

Reverend Lebbeus Armstrong declined an office.

Peter Mawney told his ex-friends to get the hell out of his tavern and never come back.

The Union Temperance Society of Moreau and Northumberland, which reportedly met thereafter at the schoolhouse across the road from Mawney's Tavern, soon became a prototype. Or, just as likely, it did not. Just as likely, Reverend Armstrong exaggerated the extent of his contributions to temperance, and the first such organizations were founded a few years later, perhaps in Andover, Massachusetts, perhaps by ministers belonging to the Connecticut Church conference, perhaps by others living elsewhere. Regardless, it seems that by 1820, similar groups had been formed in other states as well, notably Pennsylvania, Rhode Island, New Hampshire, Vermont, and Maine.

Among the sources of inspiration for such bonding was delirium tremens, the d.t.'s, the waking nightmare of the man who has been too long and devotedly at the bottle. The disorder usually begins with a nail-biting bout of anxiety, often accompanied by the shakes and then moving quickly to periods of paranoid hallucination.

> One man, for example, envisioned a rattlesnake chasing him as people tried to shoot it; another was convinced that those present in the room were attempting to shoot him; a third imagined at various times during his hallucination that his fellow steamboat travelers were plotting to kill him, that a tavern landlord had the same intent, and that his wife wanted to poison him. Yet another was afraid that "mice had come to eat his library."

"Finally," it has been written, "the victim falls into a deep sleep and enters an acute alcoholic depression. Either death or complete recovery follows."

The term "delirium tremens," if not the actual condition, seems to have made its American debut at about the same time that the first temperance groups were warning people about the horrible consequences of alcohol. Thus the malady was the ideal accompaniment to a hard-sell membership drive; the casual drinker was urged to sign on before the d.t.'s could pay him a visit, and the serious drinker to enlist before the d.t.'s took up permanent residence in his gray cells. Suddenly, temperance seemed not just the path to better health, but to continued, sentient existence.

Most of the initial groups were loosely organized, meeting irregularly and following no particular agenda. They were tentative, not sure of either the wisdom of their mission or the odds of success. They were small, some of them numbering fewer than a dozen members. In many cases, they seemed little more than social clubs, although without the booze they could often be a little short on conviviality.

But before the nineteenth century was a third over, more than 5,000 antidrink societies had come to life in the United States, 700 in New York State alone. The combined enrollment was thought to be a million and a half, perhaps more, and the groups were gaining in sense of commitment and perseverance no less than in membership. There was a kind of youthful energy to them, an optimism, a belief that they could bring the words of their temperance constitutions to life just as their nation had made a reality of its political constitution.

Alexis de Tocqueville understood. He knew that the success of the movement had more to it than just disgust at the consequences of demon rum. "Americans of all ages," he would write after visiting the United States and returning to his native France, "all stations to life and all types of dispositions are forever forming associations." And Ralph Waldo Emerson understood. He knew that Americans liked to dedicate those associations to noble ends. "What is a man born for," he asked rhetorically, "but to be a Reformer, a Remaker of what man has made?"

Yet these early advocates of temperance were not zealots, not single-minded, rock-jawed, fire-breathing tub-thumpers. Not by any means, not yet. Alice Fleming writes that most of them "took a fairly lenient approach to alcohol. Like Benjamin Rush, who was a patron saint for many, they were against 'ardent spirits'—rum whiskey, and brandy—but they had no objections to weaker drinks like cider, wine, and beer. Moreover, although they condemned drunkenness, they argued for moderation in drinking, rather than total abstinence." And they appealed to each of their fellow citizens to limit his own consumption voluntarily; they did not seek laws to force him or divine intervention to make him feel guilty for lapses.

All of that changed, however, with the first of the reform groups to spread beyond the borders of a single community or state. It was the American Society for the Promotion of Temperance, founded in Boston in 1826 and soon to shorten its name to the American Temperance Society. According to its first official statement, the group

> has, after devout and deliberate attention to the subject, resolved in the strength of the Lord, and with a view to the account which they must render to Him for the influence they exert in the world, to make a vigorous, united and persevering effort, to produce a change of public sentiment and practice, with regard to the use of intoxicating liquors.

At the start, the men who adopted the preceding position allowed themselves to drink, as the name says, temperately. A few of them, at least, enjoyed a beer or a little wine with a meal, or even a shot of whiskey on a special occasion, believing that there was little harm in a little drink. They were proud men, used to making decisions for themselves and sticking with them; by demonstrating that they could yield to temptation, but only to a point of their own choosing, they proved that they were in fact temptation's masters.

Before long, though, problems arose. Some of the members of the American Temperance Society began to suspect others of abusing the principle of self-determination. As the society increased in size, the suspicions increased as well. To an extent, it might have been a matter of envy, with those who forced themselves to drink only an ounce or two of alcoholic beverage a week looking longingly at those who downed three or four ounces, or a pint. Then the former began to lash out at the latter, to accuse them of a self-indulgence that made a mockery of the society's purpose. And both former and latter united in looking even more longingly—and resentfully—at those who consumed a quart or more per seven days. There was too much freedom here, too much individual initiative; one man's temperance was another's license, and this kind of thing could only lead to anarchy. The founders of the American Temperance Society decided to rethink their initial tolerance.

What they concluded, after a minimal amount of debate, was that distinctions of quantity were henceforth irrelevant; no longer could there be such a thing as a little harm, no longer could an individual make his own choices. The society, meaning those who served as its officers, would do the deciding for the membership as a whole, and the decision would be final.

Those who disagreed, although few, were vocal; they continued to insist that moderate drinking had no real effect on either a person's health or his chances for eternal glory. But the extremists carried the day. Henceforth, a member of the American Temperance Society would have to give up alcoholic beverages altogether. According to several historians, when the member agreed to this, the letter "t," for total abstainer, was placed next to his name on the society's rolls. The individual thus became a teetotaler.

To many, the new absolutism was simply a means of eliminating weakness and hypocrisy from the temperance ideal. But to others, it was hypocrisy of a profound nature, not to mention a rigidity so much at odds with human nature that it could not possibly succeed. George Brown Tindall, in his two-volume narrative of the American past, called the triumph of the despots "a pyrrhic victory that caused moderates to abstain from the movement instead."

One of those moderates was Abraham Lincoln. As a child, Lincoln had observed the effects of beer and wine and liquor on the small towns in which he lived, and generally found them troublesome. He had seen drunken husbands mistreat their wives, drunken wives ignore their children, drunken children forget their studies and commit acts of pointless violence, sometimes even against themselves. He was dismayed by all of it. Alcoholic beverages, he said, were "like the Egyptian angel of death, commissioned to slay, if not the first, then the fairest born in every family."

But as a young adult, Lincoln could not resist the occasional experiment. He had a few drinks one night, a few more another, trying to find either a taste or an aftereffect that pleased him. He found neither. Instead, he complained that when he imbibed too much—and he came to find that even a minimal amount was too much for him—he felt "flabby and undone"; as a result, he was even more mystified than he had previously been about the appeal of alcohol to others. Someone had to do something about it, he thought, and perhaps he could make a contribution himself. He became an enthusiastic supporter, although it seems not actually a member, of the Washingtonians, one of the most prestigious temperance societies of the time. "According to the near-mythic account of its origins, Washingtonianism began with six Baltimore artisans who adjourned from a tavern to attend (and ridicule) a temperance meeting. Instead they found themselves converted to the doctrine of self-reform . . . and set out to reclaim other working-class drinkers."

By 1842, Lincoln was a legislator in Illinois, and sufficiently respected by the Washingtonians to have been invited to address the group's annual convention in Springfield. They expected, and surely hoped for, a diatribe, a Manichaean rant on the role of spirituous refreshment in society. They did not get it. "When all such of us as have now reached the years of maturity first opened our eyes upon the stage of existence," Lincoln told his audience, "we found intoxicating liquor recognized by everybody, used by everybody, repudiated by nobody. It commonly entered into the first draught of the infant and the last of the dying man." But then, choosing his words carefully, keeping his tone measured, he sounded the same note that Increase Mather had sounded long before. "It is true that even then it was known and acknowledged that many were greatly injured by it; but none seemed to think the injury arose from the use of a bad thing, but from the abuse of a very good thing."

In other words, Lincoln was advising the Washingtonians to reject the radical position that they had already taken, and he went on to make his views even clearer. Use rather than abuse, he emphasized. Do not confuse a good thing for a bad. Bend your elbow, but not so much that it gets fixed into position. No one, it seems, listened.

Two years later, Lincoln spoke out again. He was disgusted by the hard-line policies of virtually all American temperance groups. He was also eager for the votes of the beer-drinking population of his home state. He wanted nothing to do, he said, with an abstinence that was imposed on people. "Prohibition will work great injury to the cause of temperance," he announced presciently. "It is a species of intemperance within itself, for it goes beyond the bounds of reason in that it attempts to control a man's appetite by legislation and makes a crime out of things that are not crimes. A prohibition law strikes at the very principle upon which our Government was founded."

Still no one paid attention, no one in the movement, at least. A student of history and an avid reader since childhood, Lincoln probably knew that, in 1777, the Second Continental Congress had called on states to "pass laws the most effectual for putting an immediate stop to the pernicious practice of distilling grain." But the states would not do it. The federal government gave up the idea and turned its attentions elsewhere.

Now, Lincoln watched with sorrow as the idea was revived. Almost overnight, laws became a holy grail to the antiliquor forces, laws not to tax or regulate or modify, but to put that immediate stop to both the manufacture and consumption of beer and wine and whiskey. Was such a desire a direct contradiction to the temperance movement's adjective? No matter; the groups would hold onto the word proudly, perversely, shrewdly. "Abstinence," some of them feared, had too final a sound to it; potential members, as Tindall pointed out a few paragraphs ago, might be frightened off, coaxed to act against their own best interests. But "temperance," ah . . . temperance was a soothing assembly of syllables, in both sound and meaning. It suggested a course that any person could follow, one that was worthy of approbation by all men and women of reasonable nature. The leaders of the alcohol reform organizations, in other words, words that belong to the present rather than the mid-nineteenth century, had decided to spin the American public.

By doing so, they might have been false to others but were unshakably true to themselves. Almost to a man, they loathed the individual whose thirsts were under control. "The moderate drinker," as has been pointed out, "made Temperance propaganda look bad. The spewing

drunk in the gutter was a fine Exhibit A, but not the well-tailored gentleman having a cool sherry cobbler at the bar on a warm afternoon and
going his urbane way certainly none the worse for it, probably rather
better."

And so temperance became a thing more and more *in*temperate, although Lucius Manlius Sargent, "the cultivated Boston classicist," who
had once tried to persuade both secondary schools and universities to
eliminate all references to wine in ancient Greek and Latin texts, was
fanatical even among the fanatics. Sargent despised moderate drinkers.
They made his hair itch, his teeth grate. They were playing with fire;
he wished them burns. After contenting himself for a time with simply
denouncing such renegades, he came up with a plan. He suggested that
men and women who enjoyed raising a glass or two at a social event be
segregated from decent society and placed on a diet of hard liquor, the
highest alcoholic content available. No food, no other forms of beverage, just rotgut—morning, noon, and night. This, Sargent explained,
would end their miserable lives more quickly, "and take the burden of
their support off the hands of family or society."

Despite such occasional outbreaks of lunacy, the temperance movement in the United States thrived in the first half of the nineteenth
century, a growth industry in a growing nation. By 1840, it is believed,
one out of every ten adult Americans had either joined an antibooze fellowship or signed a pledge to abide by the goals of one. Furthermore,
there were now temperance novels being written, temperance newspapers being published, temperance poems being recited, temperance
songs being sung, and temperance dramas, like *The Drunkard* and *Ten
Nights in a Barroom*, being performed in theaters that had once been
vilified by a different breed of reformers for the licentiousness of their
productions. There were temperance hotels, temperance restaurants,
temperance steamboats—you could not get a drink on any of them, not
so much as a thimbleful, not a small beer or a weak punch or a single glass of diluted wine. There was even some talk about temperance
towns, entire dry communities, although these would not appear until
later in the century, when the best known would be Harvey, Illinois.

And perhaps most surprising, at least to some observers, was the appearance of temperance societies in our nation's capital—of all places.
Members of Congress formed them. Other members of Congress joined
them, and "badly needed" they were, said people who should know, "for
the heavy perfume wafting up from the legislative chambers was a good

third Old Monongahela rye, the other two ingredients being chewing tobacco and unbathed statesmen."

The result of all these temperance organizations and locales, according to Mark Edward Lender and James Kirby Martin, was unprecedented. "From a high of just over seven gallons of absolute alcohol per capita annually in 1830," they tell us, "consumption estimates fell to slightly more than three gallons by 1840—the largest ten-year drop in American history."

The estimates might be exaggerated, the numbers perhaps not as accurate as Lender and Martin would wish. Nonetheless, a drop there was, surely the first ever in America for so long a period as a decade, and if on the one hand this seems a remarkable occurrence for a country with such a pickled past, on the other it appears inevitable, perhaps analogous to the later growth of the American labor movement in response to dehumanizing conditions in factories and sweatshops. Temperance boomed, in other words, because of legitimate abuses that demanded attention, because of suffering and irresponsibility and inaction, because of injustices that affected not just tipplers but the entire society.

Temperance boomed—there is no better way to say it—because it had to.

Had George Washington seen it coming? Perhaps. It is true that he won elective office with the aid of alcoholic beverages, and that he manufactured and sold them for profit later in life. But he did not drink to excess himself, and as president tried to inspire similar restraint among his fellow Americans. Specifically, Washington set out to discourage them from drinking liquor by promoting trade with France for wine. This, he explained, "would at least be more innocent to the health and morals of the people than the thousands of Hogsheads of poisonous Rum which are annually consumed in the United States."

Thomas Jefferson also might have seen it coming. He, too, tried to turn Americans to wine, although he took no official actions on its behalf. Rather, he set an example at his own table, and offered his opinion on alcohol whenever he was asked, and often when he was not. "No nation is drunken where wine is cheap," he told people, "and none sober where dearness of wine substitutes ardent spirits as its common beverage."

To those Americans who could not abide the grape, or who had difficulty finding it, Jefferson urged beer as a preferred libation. In fact, while president, he invited a contingent of Bohemian brewers to visit the United States and give public demonstrations of their craft, hoping to inspire his countrymen to take it up themselves. "I wish to see this beverage become common," Jefferson wrote to a friend, although it never did at Monticello, "instead of the whiskey which now kills one third of our citizens and ruins their families."

But neither man was successful in his efforts. Early in the nineteenth century, before temperance's heyday, the average American male ingested almost half a pint of hard liquor a day, more than ever before or since. To such a pass had things come that the army "dared not bar the recruitment or reenlistment of habitual drunkards. If such a policy were adopted, warned the surgeon general [one of Benjamin Rush's successors], the army might have to be disbanded." The same could be said about the navy, and about almost all lines of civilian work. Rare was the tavern with an empty chair when the sun went down, the forge went cold, the shop doors were locked for the night.

In some cases, tippling to extremes was fatal. "Instance the murder of John Scott in Catskill," said the Reverend Lebbeus Armstrong, admittedly not the most impartial observer, "which was solely the effects of spirituous liquors. After spending the evening in filling and emptying the jovial glass, a quarrel at length arose, about a pipe and tobacco, which terminated in bloodshed and death."

In New York at about the same time, a pair of ruffians named James Wall and Aaron B. Stookey were convicted of murder. The judge, in sentencing them to death, stated as a matter of fact that booze had been the undoing of the two men. They did not disagree, and it was to a far, far drier place that the two of them soon went.

And in 1852, New York Governor Washington Hunt commented on the "extraordinary number of capital offenses" that his state had recorded the previous year. Giving the matter due consideration, he concluded, "This melancholy fact must be attributed, in a large degree, to the prevalence of intemperance in our cities and larger towns."

But even if he did not take another person's life, and most drunks, of course, were not killers, an individual who had drifted too many sheets to the wind wreaked other kinds of havoc on his community, breaking the social contract in almost all of its provisions. He ruined property, alienated friends and inflicted wounds, both physical and emotional, on members of his own family, wounds that were in many cases so severe they could never be healed. Then as now, the latter was the most insidious effect of inebriation: beaten wives, terrified children, family environments so toxic that out of them could come nothing but more malefactions, more violations of the social contract. There are no statistics to confirm the extent of this kind of hardship in the early nineteenth century, but several case histories survive, and they are as painful and personally affecting to read as an account from this very day's newspaper.

> As I was riding in my sleigh I came up with a lad about 16 years old, very raggedly clothed—although an utter stranger to me, I was prompted to give him an invitation to get into my sleigh, which invitation he gladly accepted. No sooner had he taken a seat, than he commenced telling a tale which touched the very fibres of my soul. Said he, "I am an abused child"— the tears gushed from both his eyes—What is the matter? said I. "My father," he replied, "is a drunkard—he spends all he can get for rum—he returns home from the stores, fights with mother, who is as bad as my father— he has licked me (to use his own words) till gashes have been cut by the lashes of a green hide, till the blood has run all down over me. I have got no learning. I can't write any, and read but a very little—my father won't let me go to school, but keeps me all the time to work, and then beats me for doing no more."

Children of drunkards became drunkards themselves. It was not inevitable, as we often think today, but it happened with some frequency and more often than not at a young age, with boys and girls sometimes developing a taste for alcohol from all the trips they made to the local tavern to bring home beer or liquor for dad. They would take a pitcher or bucket along with them and have the bartender fill it to the top. Then, walking home, they would stop for a sip or two, in part to lighten their burden, in part to satisfy their curiosity, to be like the old man, like a grownup. If the initial taste was appealing, they would dip in again right away; if not, they would try the beverage a week or a month or a year later, hoping to understand the attraction, and would in many cases not give up until they understood it fully, overcoming their resistance and making the booze first a treat and then a habit. After all, it was both for so many people who were older than they, more experienced in the ways of the world, and those in that category were also supposed to be wiser. "Give me whiskey, a little drop of whiskey," said an emaciated little girl named Lucie Zucheriechi to a visitor in New York's Presbyterian Hospital in the middle of the nineteenth century, "and I will give you a kiss." The visitor turned away. The little girl coughed. Not long afterward, she died of cirrhosis of the liver.

Some bartenders would warn youngsters not to start down this path. They would sell them the alcohol, but tell them that sampling it was not good for them; they should leave the stuff for the parent, which would cause problems enough. Most retailers, though, did not care what the kids did, as long as they paid for the beverage up front. In the majority of states, not even the legislature seemed to care; either there were no statutes referring to youthful intoxication or the lawmakers, ablaze with civic irresponsibility, did not allow American citizens to start slurping down spirits until the ripe old age of ten.

But for no group of people was alcohol abuse as much a problem as it was for Native Americans. In fact, it seems to have been during this period, the first half of the nineteenth century, as the temperance movement was gaining momentum and the d.t.'s began to make an impression on recalcitrants, that the Native American as mean and frequent drunk became a national stereotype.

Like most stereotypes, this one is true to a degree. There are researchers today who believe that men and women of Mongolian descent are susceptible to alcoholic beverages in a way that other races are not, that they have a gene which "permits little alcohol in the body without severe symptoms from flushing to palpitations to dizziness—that is, becoming sick drunk." Other researchers disagree, finding all human beings essentially the same under the skin, although it is not clear whether this position is founded in science or so-called political correctness.

Some of those who reject a genetic explanation for Native American drunkenness believe that it is instead a kind of infection. They say that alcoholism is "another European-derived ailment from which American Indians had no immunity." They say that alcoholism is a plague, with explorers from the Old World playing the role of rats. They say that the original settlers of the New World, living first in a pre-Columbian paradise and then in a post-Columbian nightmare, never had a chance.

They are wrong. The natives were fond of alcoholic potions long before the white man invaded their shores, with different tribes drinking different kinds of beverages to different extents. They were doing it as far back as history can detect and for all the reasons that the Brit and Frenchman and Spaniard were doing it later, as well as for another reason that was probably more important than the rest of them combined. Many tribes, it seems, found intoxication a state much like the trances that their mystical religions encouraged, so that the more trancelike the level of consciousness—which is to say, the more closely it resembled *un*consciousness—the closer they felt to their gods. It was easier for them to pray in such a state, easier for them to believe their prayers were being answered.

They drank, in other words, not to raise hell but to avoid it. They assumed their gods would approve, and did not care about the reactions of mortals of different skin colors and faiths.

"Alcohol also offered a tempting release of aggressions," says historian Alan Taylor in his volume *American Colonies*. These aggressions were "ordinarily repressed with great effect, because Indian communities demanded the consistent appearance of harmony."

But the white man was not an innocent, not in the least. He was more an accomplice, a tempter. He contributed to the stereotype of indigenous peoples as victims of alcohol in ways that were indefensible regardless of the natives' genetic makeup or religious beliefs, and he did so by converting the original settlers from the alcoholic beverages they made themselves to products of European origin, which were in almost all cases stronger and less pure. The natives were not used to this stuff, could not handle this stuff. They consumed the booze that the white man provided and the booze consumed them, sinking them into deeper levels of stupefaction than they had ever known before. Or, as they often thought of it, ascending to higher realms of spiritual ecstasy.

And so, initially at least, they were appreciative of the white man's libations. The Spanish introduced them to Mexico and South America early in the sixteenth century, and it seems to have been Henry Hudson who brought them to North America in 1609. He and his fellow explorers aboard the *Half Moon* were sailing into New York Bay, keeping their eyes open for a water route to the Indies and their ears open to tales of the natives and their fondness for hooch. They heard about prodigious thirsts, outrageous behavior, hallucinatory visions. At least one historian believes that they also heard some etymology, Hudson and his men learning that the name Manhattan derived from the term *manahactanienk*, which means "the island of general intoxication."

Hudson got the natives generally intoxicated. Finding a party of Delawares fishing in the bay, he offered some spirits. The chief looked at his men; the men looked back at their chief. For a few moments, no one spoke. It was not the gift that gave the Delawares pause; it was the giver. Whether they had seen Europeans before or not, they had surely heard of these people from faraway lands, these men whose appearance was so strange, whose customs were even stranger, whose presence in the New World could not be satisfactorily explained. The natives did not know whether to trust them. Were they providing the liquor in friendship, a simple gesture of amity? Or did Hudson have some kind of ulterior motive; were the spirits a means to a nefarious end? They did not know. Neither does history.

Eventually, the chief took a cup from Hudson and slowly, warily, transferred the contents to his mouth and throat At first nothing happened; white man and red man continued to eye each other with suspicion as the fire water worked its way into the chief's internal passages. Once it did, he became another human being altogether. "After a burst of wild hilarity," John Kobler relates, "[the chief] fell into a stupor so profound that his comrades believed him dead. But when he finally recovered, he described his sensations with such enthusiasm that they all clamored for some of the same." Hudson provided it, and he and his men carefully noted the results.

Some time later, in what is now Hudson Bay, with the Europeans still no closer to that water route to the East, they encountered a different band of natives who sent "a hail of arrows" upon them, killing one of their contingent and terrifying the rest. They next day, finding himself not only surrounded by the natives but low on provisions, Hudson had to swallow his pride and mask his fears and venture out to meet with them. He proposed that they barter: they would give him food; he would give them booze. The motives here are a little clearer.

> This was not done in a spirit of friendliness: mindful of Sebastian Cabot's famous advice that "if [a native] may be made drunk with your beer or wine you shall know the secret of his heart," Hudson now plied his Indian guests with "so much wine and aqua vitae that they were all merrie.' Unfortunately, they soon became so "merrie" that they were unable to tell him anything about the supposed passage that led to the Indies.

The story was the same in other parts of the New World, with different tribes of natives encountering different parties of white men. John Le Blanc, an Ottawa chieftain of the seventeenth century, acquired "a lifelong passion" for spirits with his first taste of the European variety. When asked what he thought the beverage contained, he answered without hesitation. "Hearts and tongues; for when I have drunken plentifully of it, my heart is a thousand strong, and I can talk, too, with astonishing freedom and rapidity."

But Europeans had no desire to make the original Americans stronger and more verbose. The more they saw of the natives' territory, the more they wanted it for their own; the more they saw of the natives' vulnerability, the more certain they were of the way to proceed. Their goal became, quite simply, to "fuddle [the natives] with rum." George Thomas, an eighteenth-century governor of Pennsylvania, admitted as much when he said that white traders "take advantage of [the natives'] inordinate appetite for [liquor] to cheat them out of their skins and their wampum, which is their money, and often to debauch their wives in the bargain." In other words, the white man's booze, which might have been a gift at the start, had become a weapon, no less deadly than a firearm or bow and arrow, and it was wielded with the same kind of malevolent precision.

Which the natives knew all too well. "Rum will kill us," the Shawnees and Onondagas admitted, with other tribes knowing it as well, "and leave the land clear for the Europeans without strife or purchase."

Rum killed them, all right, and when it did not actually take lives, it ruined them, for as Edward Behr points out, "liquor addiction went hand in hand with mortal disease. The Columbia River Indians died en masse, and some, such as the Chinooks, were virtually wiped out." The members of other tribes recorded their angst in "extraordinarily lyric poems, passed down from generation to generation by survivors." Behr reprints one of them, its lyricism lost to a degree in translation, but its sorrow no less apparent.

> I am afraid to drink but still I like to drink.
> I don't like to drink, but I have to drink whiskey.
> Here am I singing a love song, drinking.
> I didn't know that whiskey was so good.
> And I am still drinking it.
> I found out that whiskey is no good.
> Come, come closer to me, my slaves,
> And I'll give you a drink of whiskey.
> Here we are drinking now.
> Have some more, have some more of my whiskey.
> Have a good time with it.
> Come closer to me, come closer to me, my slaves,
> We are drinking now, we feel pretty good.
> Now you feel just like me.

Of course, not all white men dealt with the native Americans in so vile a manner, and some even tried to stop their countrymen from behaving with such callousness. They passed laws, set up government agencies, sometimes even came to blows with their fellow Europeans. They argued about the place of the red man in society as they would later argue about the place of the black. At the very least, they refrained from selling or giving alcoholic beverages to people of such susceptibility.

But the good guys were either a minority or a majority without sufficient will. The "holocaust," as more than one modern observer has called the conquest of the American tribes by alcohol, continued. "Is it to be wondered at, then," Governor Thomas said, speaking of the native not only in Pennsylvania but elsewhere, "if when they recover from the drunken fit, they should take severe revenges?"

Severe indeed, so much so that New Amsterdam and Providence Plantation, among other early American colonies, "forbade sale of drink to Indians within the settlements, not from regard for the red man's welfare, but because he was a menace when under the influence." And the menace took many forms. Driven to a fury by the very alcohol that had made them such easy prey to deception, the natives would attack white settlements and leave not so much as a single man, woman, or child alive unless by oversight, and not so much as a single residence uncharred unless the wind died down and refused to fan the fires they had so promiscuously set. Some of the most painful memories of frontier Americans, as set down in their diaries, are of making their way westward, across the vast New World prairies and coming upon the remains of Indian massacres. On occasion, they would find the bodies of victims either rotting or still writhing, personal effects scattered across the landscape as if flung by an angry god, creatures of prey watching from above, preparing to swoop down from the sky or mountain ledge and feed as soon as the tourists went on their way. Many were the pioneers who turned back or made lengthy detours around these scenes; no one who saw them could proceed with confidence.

On other occasions, it was the white man who, under the influence, struck the first blow. He led his fellows in raids whose purpose was to establish territorial supremacy, gain revenge or simply work off the corrosive effects of their own liquor. One account tells of whites firing guns into a native village until they ran out of bullets, and then hurling rocks and tree limbs until these too were exhausted, and finally flinging their empty bottles of booze until they exhausted themselves. The Europeans were no less vicious than their adversaries in cases like these, and no more likely in the aftermath either to question or repent of their deeds.

And at still other times, it was the natives fighting with one another, the alcohol blinding them in their rage, making their violence indiscriminate, a mindless monster with no point other than to express itself. Comanche did battle with Comanche; Cheyenne lay in wait for Cheyenne; Arapaho laid waste to Arapaho. William Henry Harrison, as governor of the Indiana territory in 1801, reported on the tribes near Vincennes, observing that "in all their frolicks they generally suffer most severely themselves . . . kill each other without mercy. . . . A Wea chief of note well known to me was not long since murdered by his own son. . . . Little Fox, another chief who was always a friend of the white people, was murdered at mid day in the streets of town by one of his own nation."

It was for these reasons, the accumulation of such horrible and scarcely human incidents, that men and women of sober disposition and properly functioning conscience, appalled by what was going on around them, by what *had* been going on around them since before their nation was even a nation, the actions of European and native alike, began to decry the great and deadly American thirst. They searched their hearts and raised their voices, and the loudest voices of all, to the surprise of many, now seemed to be coming from the pulpit.

Gradually, and almost without being noticed, the clergy had been coming around. No longer were its ordinations bacchanalian revels; no more did men of God accept drink after drink from the families in their congregations; no more did the "good creature" seem so good or even as certainly descended from the Almighty. The pastorate had seen the light, and a great many of its members were casting aside their old ways and believing that their new call was to lead the country to redemption through abstinence. Or at least to give it a try.

It was the Quakers who spoke out first. Even while the Revolutionary War was being fought, their leaders began "to labour for a Reformation in Respect to the Distiling and Use of Spirituous Liquors amongst Friends and the Polluting Practice of keeping Taverns, Beerhouses, etc." Few people took the labor seriously; Quakers were not much more popular in colonial America than abstinence.

But as the years went by, the Quakers' position seemed the right one to more and more men of the cloth. "Who hath woe?" asked the Reverend Lyman Beecher in the following century, and one can hear him crying in joyful supplication, ratcheting up the enthusiasm with each succeeding question. "Who hath sorrow? Who hath contentions? who hath babbling? who hath wounds without cause? who hath redness of eyes?" And then the most famous man of God of his day pauses just the right amount of time to work up just the right amount of fervor among his congregants before bellowing out the totally expected answer that will nonetheless bring forth a rollicking chorus of amens, if not even a sound more joyful than that, something flat-out cathartic, to serve as punctuation. "They that tarry long at the wine!"

Another cleric of note, the Reverend Justin Edwards, was no less passionate, declaiming that whiskey "has been among the more constant and fruitful sources of all our woes. Yet such has been its power to deceive men that while evil after evil has rolled in upon them, like waves of the sea, they have continued till within a few years knowingly and voluntarily to increase the cause. . . . Ministers preached against drunkenness and drank the drunkard's poison."

Not anymore they didn't, at least not in the same horrifying quantities as before. To the Reverend Lebbeus Armstrong of Moreau, New York, a nonpartaker of long standing and sincere motives regardless of the veracity of his book, "temperance seemed to have been sent by Providence for the salvation of men. It had been foretold by the prophets of old and was part of God's plan for blessing the world." The majority of his brethren now seemed to agree.

And some of them acted more than they spoke. Felix Francisco Varela y Morales, a Cuban born educator and pastor, organized temperance groups in New York City in the 1830s. A decade later, Father Theobald Mathew, who had "come hot from Ireland to the New World to promote total abstinence," became an idol in his new land.

> The president of the United States gave a banquet for him, and the United States Senate voted him the privileges of the floor, an honor given only once before, to the Marquis de Lafayette on his triumphal tour of 1824–5. The reasons for this hero's welcome were that the Washingtonians had so resoundingly dramatized the efficacy of teetotalism in reforming drunkards; and that Father Mathew, practically single-handed, had imposed the teetotal pledge on the majority of the drunkenest nation in Christendom.

The last sentence exaggerates. The transformation of the clergy, however, cannot be exaggerated; the old sots had seen the light and become new men. But there were people who wondered why, people who, knowing their Bible, knew that Paul had told Timothy to have a few sips of the grape for his recurring illness. And they knew about other references in the Good Book that encouraged the use of alcoholic beverages, either directly or by implication, such as Jesus' turning water into wine. What were God's earthly representatives in nineteenth-century America going to make of tales like these, appearing as they did in the Lord's own manual? How were they going to explain them by way of justifying their new outlook?

They were not. Instead, they simply disregarded such references. The Bible, after all, is a wondrously all-encompassing volume, and as the masters of the altar began to change their attitude toward booze, they found their new point of view emblazoned in scripture as clearly as the old. They found Eli's telling Hannah to get rid of her wine, an angel's assuring Zechariah that his son would drink no liquor and thus be filled with the Holy Spirit, and even Paul's doubling back on himself to declare that it was good neither to eat flesh nor to drink wine, and more forcefully, that drunkards should be included with murderers and sodomites as candidates for the fiery throes of eternal damnation.

It was from passages like these that the American Temperance Society took its cue. Henceforth, it "resolved in the strength of the Lord . . . to produce a change of public sentiment and practice, with regard to the use of intoxicating liquors." Other societies also invoked the Lord, and upon this rock they began to build their movement, a movement which, as John Allen Krout points out, came at a time of great religious awakening in the United States, an explosion of interest in matters divine and otherworldly. This meant that temperance now

> took on the attributes of a great revival. . . . Temperance workers were evangelists preaching a new gospel, and they stated its dogmas in the pulpit phraseology of the day. Persons who responded to the powerful appeal and signed the pledge were known as "converts." For the programs of the societies into which the "converts" were gathered the evangelical prayer meeting served as a model. Appropriate verses, set to familiar gospel tunes, were sung with all the fervor of religious exaltation. The emotional appeals of the speakers and the "testimony" of the pledge-signers strongly suggested the revivals of the evangelical sects.

It must be admitted that not all clerics supported the alliance between temperance and faith. Bishop John Henry Hopkins of the Episcopal Church of Vermont said that he was opposed to it because it "gave prominence to one particular vice, contrary to doctrines of the Bible." Further, he explained, "The outward reformation of a single vice is nothing, when the heart remains unsanctified and the curse of God still hangs upon the soul." But Bishop Hopkins's voice was not the voice of the choir; most pastors of the time seemed pleased enough to be making inroads on a single vice, seeing it as a starting point, a foothold on the path that would lead to the eventual salvation of their flocks.

But as all of this was going on, another front was opening in the war against alcoholic beverages, one that proved equally energetic, equally purposeful, and at least at the outset, equally effective. Temperance groups of secular orientation, harkening back to Benjamin Rush's charge that hard drinking was "anti-federal," began to wrap their pleas for sobriety in the flag. What sense does it make, they asked, for us to have left the Old World for a better life in the New when we are destroying that life by drinking ourselves into oblivion? What sense does it make for us to have won our independence from King George III when we have become subservient instead to the bottled blandishments of the devil? For what possible reason should we invite one unfeeling demagogue to substitute for the other?

In the zeal of this new patriotism, there were temperance groups going so far as to rewrite the Declaration of Independence, substituting for the ruler of England the name of a different monarch: "The history of *Prince Alcohol* is a history of repeated injuries and usurpations, all having in direct object the establishment of an absolute tyranny of these States."

And "We, therefore, the Representatives of the united States of America . . . solemnly publish and declare, That these United Colonies are, and of Right ought to be, Free and Independent States; that they are absolved from all allegiance to *Prince Alcohol.*"

God and country. The combination was irresistible, especially to politicians, who now began to support the temperance movement whether they believed in its goals or not, just to bask in the glow of its righteousness. And what better way to demonstrate that support than through legislation? Legislation, after all, is what a legislator does, and a yes vote on an antidrinking bill revealed such a person to be compassionate and virtuous, a responsible member of a republican society, a worthwhile candidate for even higher office, if not even perpetual salvation. A no vote seemed to say he was opposed not only to the welfare of his constituents, but to the stated goals of the nation in which they dwelled.

As a result of these perceptions, state lawmakers began to turn out bills and acts and statutes the way plantations were turning out cotton and factories were mass-producing cloth for apparel. By 1852, Oregon, Massachusetts, Maine, Minnesota, Rhode Island, and Vermont had declared alcoholic beverages to be illegal substances. In 1853, Michigan did the same; in 1854, Connecticut; in 1855, Delaware, Indiana, Iowa, Nebraska, New Hampshire, New York, and Pennsylvania. These were the first such laws in America on the statewide level since General James Oglethorpe had so wisely given up on prohibition more than a century earlier in Georgia, and they were modeled, every one of them, in almost every particular, after "An Act for the Suppression of Drinking Houses and Tippling Shops," which came thundering into existence with all good intentions and dire consequences in the state of Maine in 1851.

The act was Neal Dow's idea, and he could not have believed in it more avidly or sold it to the populace with greater passion. A blockade of a man, a tiny but altogether secure fortress, Dow stood five-foot-two in height but seven-foot-three in enthusiasm, disposition, and manner. His hair was dark and curly, and he parted it on the right and swept it down over his ears on both sides to the base of his neck; he appeared, from certain angles, to be wearing a helmet. His eyes were steely, making him seem both farsighted and unyielding. He dressed well at all times; there were no such things as informal occasions to Neal Dow, as there were no such things as matters of casual interest.

A self-made man, of which the nineteenth century had many, Dow rose from modest circumstances to become successful not just in one line of work, but in three: tanning, timber, and banking. What mattered most to him, though, was not the way he made his money, but the beverages on which other people spent the money that *they* made. For Neal Dow was regarded by many people of his time as the first real hero—or villain, depending on your point of view and preferred means of thirst-quenching—of American temperance, and a later generation would refer to him as the father of Prohibition. On a weekend afternoon, he would have his horses hitched to his carriage and would ride through the seedier sections of Portland, pointing out ill-clad people and ramshackle housing, and say to those who accompanied him, "Rum did that." It was a simple view of life. Unambiguous. It came naturally to a fellow whose maternal grandfather, a similarly uncomplicated soul, bore the name—not a nickname, but the actual, honest-to-goodness appellation, as recorded in black and white on his birth certificate—of Hate-Evil Hall.

After leaving the business world with enough money to last him the rest of his life, Dow felt that he should give something back to the community. Having already, through various lobbying efforts, "succeeded in preventing the drunken excesses so long associated with Fourth of July celebrations in Portland," he volunteered to do a turn as fire chief. The pay was poor, the opportunity to serve great; it was just what Dow had been looking for.

One day, a liquor store went up in flames and the new chief had a choice to make: open the hoses and keep the place in business, or let it burn and make a point. Reportedly, he did the latter, ordering his men to watch the blaze rather than fight it, and by no means to attempt to liberate the inventory. Although Dow denied the story at the time, and repeated the denial in his autobiography, he did leave room for doubt, admitting that the burning store made "a most brilliant and beautiful spectacle."

We also learn from his autobiography that Dow reversed long years of precedent in Portland by eliminating booze from the city's firehouses. If one of his men sampled some spirits elsewhere and showed up for work under the influence, or went out for a meal and came back with brew or wine or whiskey on his breath, he was sent home and ordered to stay there until he was not only sober but stone-cold sorry. "This was no easy task," Dow conceded, but when his deputies finally rebelled, deciding to force the issue, their adversary was more than ready.

> "Mr. Chief [said a firefighter of stentorian voice, who stood a good foot taller than Dow], I ask you to respond to this toast: 'Brandy and water—water for the fire, brandy for the firemen.'" Naturally there were loud shouts, and amid the vociferous cheering, largely ironical, a small minority, I dare say, sympathizing with my view, I rose to respond. I tried to keep the company in good-nature that it might listen, as it did with respect, while I improved the opportunity to enable me naturally to close with another toast as follows: "Brandy and water—water extinguishes fire, and brandy extinguishes firemen."

Horace Mann, the famous educator, was perhaps Dow's biggest fan, finding him one of the nation's outstanding mortals, an inspiration to young and old, male and female alike. Mann called Dow "the moral Columbus," and said that the prohibitory law he struggled so hard to pass was as important to the human race as "the invention of printing, or any other great strides in the progress of civilization." Not so. There were differences galore. Among them: Gutenberg's press worked; Dow's law did not.

His zeal, though, was understandable. Portland was the city in which the bells had rung out the hours for bitters in colonial times, 11:00 in the morning and 4:00 in the afternoon, and they continued to chime a century later. Dow recalled that there were seven distilleries in Portland when he was a boy, and more grog shops than any other kind of commercial enterprise; in fact, at one point there was a licensed liquor dealer for every fifty residents, a ratio probably unmatched by any other American city of its size. A journalist visiting the outskirts of the community, what we would today call a suburb, told of entering a store that sold a variety of products and looking at the account book. "Eighty-four per cent of the entries were for rum," he found. "Boots and shoes, dress goods, sheeting and shirting, hats and caps and groceries appeared at rare intervals, but rum was splotched over every page."

As its name indicates, Portland was a port city and it attracted sailors who were as averse to sobriety on shore as they were to large waves on the sea. Mingling with overworked landlubbers and women whose husbands were still at sea themselves, these men were the final ingredient in a dangerously volatile populace. Dow either witnessed, or was told tales about, dozens of incidents of violence, lust, and bad manners. He believed them all, took them personally. He loved the place of his birth, and vowed that when he grew up he would make it better. In fact, he would make the whole state better.

Toward this end, Dow in time gave up the firehouse as he had given up the business world and began to work full-time to persuade the Maine legislature to take action. At his own expense, he traveled from one end of the state to the other, month after month, year after year, trying to gain support for a measure that would dry out the inhabitants and keep them dry. He urged citizens, urged politicians, urged citizens to urge politicians and politicians to urge citizens; he cornered people on the street or in their offices and stores, planting that squat, uncompromising body of his in front of them, not letting them go until he had explained the reign of terror that was being conducted by alcoholic beverages. It is said that in 1846 alone, Dow trekked 4,000 miles and collected more than 40,000 signatures on a petition that referred to traffic in alcoholic beverages as "an infamous crime" and sought to outlaw it.

The first time the legislature brought the matter to a vote, it failed. But Dow tried again, and in 1851 the state of Maine gave its approval to "the law of Heaven Americanized," as one of its advocates referred to it, and began the legally mandated suppression of drinking houses and tippling shops.

The measure was all-encompassing. Simply put, it "prohibited the sale, the keeping for sale, and the manufacture of all intoxicating liquors. Heavy fines were imposed for the first two violations, and imprisonment for the third." When the authorities, in their pursuit of enforcement, happened upon a supply of spirits, they were empowered to confiscate it and destroy it on the spot. They were also empowered to close down the establishment that sold it.

Dow believed that the law would be a boon to his fellow man. It was certainly a boon to him. So famous did he become as the result of his efforts, and so admired by those who shared his views, that he ran for mayor of Portland and won easily. Now, rather than depending on others, he could lead raids on drinking establishments himself. It was the best part of the job. He was like a man with a sweet tooth who had suddenly fallen into a tank of caramel.

On one raid, Dow was reported personally to have poured $2,000 worth of rum and whiskey into the gutters outside City Hall, laughing as he did, inviting others to join in. On another, he saw to it not only that the liquor was rendered undrinkable, but that all the kegs and bottles were shattered and that a number of glasses and mugs were broken into even smaller pieces. Dedicated imbibers watched Dow's forays with long tongues and heavy hearts. Some called him "the sublime fanatic"; to others he was "the prince of fanatics." To all he was a scourge such as they had never known before.

In his autobiography, Dow evaluated the legislation that had brought him such renown.

> After the enactment of the Maine law, a considerable portion of the state, including Portland and most of the larger towns, was practically free from the liquor-traffic. The change for the better, substantially throughout Maine, was marvelous, apparent not only in a decrease of drunkenness and of the long and varied list of disturbances which radiate from a rumshop, as miasma rises from a swamp, but in evidences of industry, thrift and material prosperity rewarding well-directed labor. This was a revelation to many, who, having given little thought to the subject, had regarded the prophecies of the advocates of Prohibition as fanciful, if not fanatical, dreams.

It was a pretty picture, and Dow painted it again and again, not only on paper but in lecture halls and street corners, before audiences large and small, whenever someone asked him about the fruits of his labors and the commitment that had brought them into being.

It was not, however, an accurate picture; the dreams *were* fanciful. Maine's drinkers proved as clever in their defiance of the law as Dow was adamant in its enforcement. Some of the former, especially those who owned taverns or worked as bartenders, reasoned as follows. Okay, it's illegal to *sell* booze. But nobody said anything about giving it away for free, right? So what if we sell, say, soda crackers—yeah, nice, crisp soda crackers; nice, crisp, *salty* soda crackers—for maybe five cents apiece, which is what a shot or a beer would cost in the days when it was legal. Then we provide the hooch for free. How about that? Or, if people don't want crackers, we could sell them, let's see, salted nuts, salted pretzels, spiced ham, summer sausage, olives, hard-boiled eggs, sauerkraut, pickled herring, pickled pigs' feet, sardines . . .

It was all quite ingenious, and all good for business; Maine's drinking population was delighted that Dow's law could so easily be skirted. In time it became a subject of jokes and disrespect, as did the legislators who had voted for it and those in their precincts who believed in it. But the humorist George Ade sounded a cautionary note, one whose wisdom would not be apparent until many decades had passed. "The trouble with the drink places," he wrote, "was that they tried to think up cute ways of making a fool of the law instead of wisely endeavoring to keep up a semblance of decency and placate the non-customers." In other words, the barrooms would win the battle in a manner that damaged their reputation and thereby increased their chances of losing the war.

Another loophole in the Maine law, which was also an allowance made in Article IV of the charter of the Union Temperance Society of Moreau and Northumberland, as well as a provision of almost every prohibitory law to follow, was that alcoholic beverages could be sold for medicinal purposes. Never was a term riper for loose interpretation. If you had a friend who was a doctor, or if you knew a doctor who, for a small honorarium, was willing to give you a prescription—and most men of medicine were happy to take your money for a service so easily performed as scribbling a few lines on a piece of paper—you could treat yourself with a mug of rum or crackling rye or hard cider for even so minor an ailment as thirst.

As was the case in Maine, most of the states that passed laws between 1851 and 1855 worked their way up to prohibition gradually, starting with looser restrictions or local ordinances that were a kind of—no pun intended—dry run. In 1838, for example, Massachusetts wrote into its statute books the widely and justly ridiculed "Fifteen-Gallon Law," a comic masterpiece of the legislator's craft that made it illegal for a person to purchase *less* than fifteen gallons of beverage on any single trip to the dramshop. The theory was that some people would not have enough money to buy that much booze, while others would not have the means to transport such a quantity to their abodes.

The theory was absurd. Buying fifteen gallons at once meant, among other advantages, cutting down on the number of trips a customer had to make for his refreshment. It also ensured even the heartiest imbiber that he would not be likely to run out for a while. Were there people who could not afford so large an amount? Of course, but they could work around their lack of capital by pooling their money with friends. Were there people who could not convey so large an amount? Of course, but in addition to pooling cash, they would pool bodies and horses and wagons, loading up fifteen or thirty or even forty-five gallons of liquor and getting back home so tired and thirsty from their exertions that they spent the rest of the night dipping into their cargo for relief. Then they divided up the remainder and happily went their separate ways.

But were there also people who, as the law envisioned, could not deal with the huge prescribed amount, or who could not find others with whom to split the cost or share the physical burdens? Yes, but the fifteen-gallon minimum was not a hindrance in these cases, either. What the customers did, with their favorite bartender's complicity, was play a little game with words. They told the bartender that they wanted fifteen gallons and a gill (a quarter of a pint) of their favorite libation. They paid for it all, drank the gill on the premises, then sold back the fifteen gallons for the same amount of money that it had cost. The cash might change hands, it might not; the fifteen gallons never budged. The men and women who addressed their thirsts like this were often so pleased with themselves that they had a second gill to celebrate.

And so it went. Laws that had as their goal the promotion of temperance instead promoted more imaginative ways to quaff, encouraging them precisely as a mother's admonition to stay clean leads a child to don his Sunday best and head for the nearest mudhole. This was true not just in Maine and Massachusetts, but in all states that had voted controls on alcohol. The historian John Kobler did some computing, using figures from the Department of Commerce and the Bureau of Internal Revenue, and determined that between 1850 and 1860, the golden age of God-and-country temperance, as well as the period of greatest alcohol-related legislative activity to date, per capita consumption of beer, wine, and whiskey in the United States increased by 63 percent over the previous decade. Even if Kobler has miscalculated somewhat, and even taking into account the rampant boozing in states and territories without legal barriers, it is obvious that the laws did not do what they were supposed to do.

But so many people had joined temperance societies earlier in the century, and so many continued to join. So many had signed the pledges and gone to the meetings and rededicated their lives, swearing not only that they would remain dry themselves, but would insist that others of their acquaintance do so as well. What happened to them? Had they defected? Had they only been kidding in the first place?

Neither. For the most part, they stayed and they were serious. But a certain percentage of them had sworn allegiance to the cause for reasons other than a desire to abstain. Some wanted to placate their families, to get wives and mothers off their backs, and as a result would slip out to the barroom when they were supposed to have been at temperance meetings. Others enrolled in the movement *because* of the meetings, enjoying the ambience, the fellowship, much as their grandchildren would sign up for the Rotary or Kiwanis or some other society of gregarious male intercourse—Americans, as de Tocqueville said, are "forever forming associations."

Still others, while believing that they themselves could hold their liquor, and while continuing to do so at clandestine moments, enrolled in temperance societies to set an example for the boisterous drunks of their acquaintance, or the community as a whole; this was the "do as I say, not as I do" crowd. And then there were those who wanted the boost in self-esteem that came with belonging to a body of such noble aims as the American Temperance Society or the Washingtonians. Rectitude by affiliation.

But there were also drinkers who joined temperance organizations in all sincerity. They *wanted* to give up the habit, *believed* that teetotalism was an achievable goal, only to learn the hard way that it was in fact beyond their grasp. For these people, returning to the bottle was a terrible disappointment; they had thought better of themselves, better of human nature on the whole. They were comforted, however, by the knowledge that, whatever punishment awaited them for their lapses, dismissal would not be one of them. They could quit the society if they so desired, but they would never be evicted. Temperance organizations were so eager for the social cachet and political clout that came with high membership that they would rather keep a boozer on the rolls than drop his name for noncompliance. In fact, there seem to have been cases of members who were deceased holding on to their positions, even members who had not existed in the first place, whose names were merely fictions of the recording secretary or some other officer of the group. There were phantoms of temperance in addition to true believers.

Such were the politics of the antialcohol movement as the nineteenth century proceeded past the midway point, and the movement, like the rest of the fabric of American life, ripped apart at the seams.

The civil war that was actually called the Civil War was the great national heartbreak. Never before had so many citizens been visited by so much tragedy; never before had so much been at stake or had so much uncertainty attached to the outcome. Friends turned against friends and siblings against siblings; the small civic groups that were the souls of their communities did not meet anymore; the shops became places of unease and the churches places of despair; and able-bodied men walked out on their farms and other businesses to take up weapons— this fabric that was no longer whole had been made up of so many small patches.

The fighting began in 1861, when the South Carolina militia, under General Pierre G. T. Beauregard, opened fire on federal troops at Fort Sumter in Charleston, South Carolina. When peace finally returned to the country four years later, more than 600,000 Americans, both Union and Confederate, were dead, although more from disease than bullets. Part of the reason, as historian Simon Winchester points out, is that the military man of the time was the victim of an "inescapable irony."

> [The war] was fought with the mortar and the musket and the miníe ball,
> but not yet quite with anesthesia or with sulphonamides and penicillin.
> The common soldier was thus in a poorer position than at any time before:
> He could be monstrously ill treated by all the new weaponry, and yet only
> moderately well treated with all the old medicine.

There is no way to know precisely how many men were killed in the fighting, although some estimates place the total at almost 3 percent of the male population. There is no way to know precisely how many were injured, no way to measure the psychological costs for winner or loser or bystander. As for the financial costs, including pensions for soldiers and their survivors and interest on the loans that financed the carnage, these are also hard to reckon, but according to John Steele Gordon, "the American national debt rose from $65 million to $2.8 billion" during the years of hostility.

Since most of the battles were fought in the South, most of the damage was also situated there, as the bodies of the deceased bloodied the soil and entire communities fell to the musket and the torch. Farmlands were trampled under the crashing hooves of horses; factories were destroyed and manufacturing came to a halt. Officially, the South surrendered; more accurately, it was vanquished.

The temperance movement was also a victim of the Civil War and the tensions that led up to it, losing many of its supporters and almost all of its momentum. As a result, not a single state passed a prohibitory law between 1856 and 1879. Even more harmful to the movement was the fact that several of the states which had passed measures between 1852 and 1855 gave up on them, either repealing them, modifying them into weaker versions, or simply not troubling to enforce them any longer.

But the problem was not just that temperance advocates lost their lives. Thousands fell to illness and ammunition, it is true, yet an even greater number of dry disciples seem to have given up on the cause before the first shot was even fired. These were people who, faced with a wrenching choice, one they had never wanted to confront in the first place, had come to believe that slavery was a more malicious kind of bondage than drinking, and, this being the case, their first priority should be to eliminate the former. They stopped preaching temperance, stopped demanding the cooperation of legislators; they would get back to the struggle against liquid fire, they promised themselves and one another, but only after slavery had been forever abolished and the Union stitched back into a single entity again. It might take a while.

Temperance's only accomplishment during the Civil War was to eliminate, once and for all, the daily ration of rum for the Union navy. But neither the Union army nor any of the Confederate forces was moved to similar action, and thanks to friends and neighbors and "patriotic businessmen," sailors from the North managed to get their hands and lips on their favorite libations anyhow. There is no evidence that any group of Americans, military or civilian, North or South, cut back on consumption of alcoholic beverages, either voluntarily or otherwise, while the battles raged.

Actually, most people seem to have drunk more, and those temperance organizations that remained intact from 1861 to 1865 were sorely frustrated. Some of them suffered in silence, knowing the time was not right for them to speak. Others spoke, decreasing neither the volume nor the output of their rhetoric. In fact, they publicized their rage at inebriated soldiers to such an extent that the army was moved to cooperate with them from time to time, the Union occasionally punishing its jug-bitten warriors by making them stand on a box for two or three days with a log on each shoulder; if one of the logs fell, the penalty was extended. But this kind of thing did not happen often, and it did not change anything.

Reformers applauded such action, urged that it become standard procedure, wanted even heavier pieces of timber. They feared that booze would lead to military disaster. Soldiers, on the other hand, prayed that it would lead to a few hours of blessed distraction.

The most famous of the temperance protests, because it was rebuffed so wittily and at such a high level, has been recounted by many. It concerns a meeting between dry leaders and President Lincoln, a meeting that the drys demanded because of complaints about Ulysses S. Grant, the Union general who was thought to lapse into sobriety less than almost any other American of the time. How much Grant really drank is a matter of some dispute, but it must have been a significant amount, as a major general named John Rawlins was at one point assigned to Grant's staff primarily to keep his leader's thirst under control. If Grant could mount a horse, remain upright on it for a reasonable period of time, and bark out commands that others could follow, Rawlins had done his job. That, at least, was what many thought. Hence the gathering at the White House, and an impassioned plea from the temperance contingent for Grant's dismissal.

Lincoln listened respectfully to the charges. Then he fixed his eyes on the man who had done most of the talking. "Doctor," he said, "can you tell me where General Grant gets his liquor? . . . for if you could tell me, I would direct the Chief Quartermaster of the army to lay in a large stock of the same kind of liquor, and would also direct him to furnish a supply to some of my other generals who have never yet won a victory."

This incident and others made Grant a symbol of booze's perceived blessings during times of stress and hardship, and a refutation of those who would, by fiat, deny those blessings. A few years later, when the old soldier occupied the White House, the industry figured out a way to thank him while at the same time flooding its own coffers with money that never should have been there. An association of distillers known to history as the Whiskey Ring cheated the federal government out of almost $3 million in excise taxes over a six-year period, with some of the funds being kicked back to Grant's associates to finance his second presidential campaign. Officials of the Treasury Department were involved. So was Grant's private secretary, Orville E. Babcock, who forged his boss's signature on messages to the ring and received gifts from its members, "including a thousand dollars, a diamond stud, and even the services of a 'sylph.'"

There was never any proof that Grant knew about the conniving; in fact, he was regarded as a "tediously truthful" man by those who served with him in the army and as "scrupulously truthful" by Hamilton Fish, a member of his cabinet and himself "an example of absolute probity." The scandal, though, was further evidence to many that Grant was much too close to the bottle and the bottlers, and that any kind of association with whiskey or the people who produced it could only lead a human being—and, in this case, the nation he led—to misfortune.

Neal Dow was appalled. Grant's opposite as a soldier just as he had been as a civilian, Dow held the rank of brigadier general in charge of the Thirteenth Maine Regiment, and took no chance of being misunderstood. Within minutes of meeting his men and telling them to stand easy, he announced a complete ban on alcoholic beverages of all sorts at all times. The men thought he was kidding. Even those who knew his views assumed that he would adapt them to the horrible circumstances of war and the needs it created.

But he would not, and the fighting men of his command saw no choice but to fight their commander. They tried to order spirits for medicinal purposes; with conventional medicines being hard to procure and largely ineffective, this was a common practice. Andrew Barr, in fact, writes of a "sixteen-year-old soldier in a St. Louis hospital [who] was apparently 'kept alive' by 36 ounces of brandy a day. In a Virginia hospital one patient was given 48 ounces of eggnog (as well as two or three bottles of porter) every day for several weeks; another got a half-pint of egg and brandy every two hours; a third was to have as much of this mixture as he could take."

But Dow abhorred the practice. He turned down every request his soldiers made for medicinal alcohol, even though he found it a "great inconvenience" to have to spend so much time on the subject. The men, understandably, were furious. They thought Dow was trying to undermine not merely their pleasure but their health. They did everything they could think of to make life even more inconvenient for the "Napoleon of temperance," who wrote:

> One of them, while serving as a staff-officer, filled out an order whereby
> I was sent on horseback, twenty-four miles, on a mission that might have
> been performed as well by an orderly. He got the order signed by the com-
> manding general, who, afterwards, assured me that he had no idea that it
> was addressed to me.

But the temperance movement would have lost ground during the Civil War even if there had been a whole battalion of Neal Dows trying to impose their will on the troops, even if supplies of conventional medicine had overflowed and worked with modern efficacy, even if temperance advocates had stormed the White House daily to rail against the Ulysses S. Grants of the world. For one thing, the Union decided to tax alcoholic beverages to help pay for the fighting. Liquor retailers were charged a $20 license fee, and manufacturers had to hand over a dollar for each barrel of malt liquor they produced and 20 cents for each barrel of distilled.

Of course, it was not the first time that such a measure had been enacted. Early in the eighteenth century, there were colonies that "welcomed the alcoholic traffic as a source of revenue, devoting the proceeds to defense needs or other worthy objects. In this fashion the Connecticut legislature in 1727 appropriated the yield of that year's rum levy to Yale College." The Whiskey Rebellion, late in the century, was the result of a tax on thirst, and the government took a cut not only from whiskey but from other kinds of booze during the War of 1812. None of these assessments, though, was as steep as the present one, and all were in time reduced even further and then, to choruses of public cheering, repealed.

When temperance advocates heard about the Civil War fees, it was they who cheered. They thought of them as a penalty for those who produced and sold whiskey, a moral judgment being rendered in financial terms, and nothing, they believed, could be more appropriate.

In reality, the armies of abstention should have been the leading foes of the new monies, fuming and fussing rather than voicing their support, because what the taxes did, for the first time, was make the liquor industry an important part of the American economy, and as has since been pointed out, this "furnished the wets forever after with one of their most cogent arguments against prohibition—the immense loss of government revenue." The distillers were now full investors in democracy.

But more than anything else, the temperance movement suffered between 1861 and 1865 because the war was so cruel. For these few painfully long years, the alcoholic stupor that had been a curse in peacetime became a pleasure, if not even a necessity. Booze helped to drown out, in Joseph P. Cullen's words about the First Battle of Bull Run, "the soul-searing moans of the wounded and dying which echoed through the still night air." It helped to dim the vision of the "motionless forms [that] covered the ground in grotesque shapes, as if someone had carelessly heaved them from a wagon." And most important, it helped to dull the realization of what the horrible sounds and ghastly sights meant: that the ways of life Americans had previously known were being forever altered.

And of all places, the commonwealth of Massachusetts, home of the "Fifteen-Gallon Law" and then statewide prohibition, was one of the leaders in acknowledging the new reality. A specially appointed legislative committee released a wartime report on alcoholic beverages, the conclusions of which were summarized as follows:

1 . It is not sinful or hurtful in every case to use every kind of alcoholic liquors as beverages. It is not, therefore, wrong in every case to sell every kind of alcoholic liquors to be used as beverages.
2 . It is the right of every citizen to determine for himself what he will eat or drink. A law prohibiting him from drinking every kind of alcoholic liquors, universally used in all countries and ages as a beverage, is an arbitrary and unreasonable interference with his rights, and is not justified by the consideration that some men may abuse their rights, and may, therefore, need the counsel and example of good men to lead them to reform.

Many soldiers were so desperate for relief from the terror and ennui of their days that not only did they pour spirituous beverages into themselves when medicine wasn't available, they turned to medicine when the spirits ran out. In particular, they turned to patent medicines, consuming entire bottles of these supposed cure-alls at a single sitting. Some of the stuff had an alcohol content of 44 percent, 88 proof; it could addle their brains even more than their favorite whiskey. It could cross their eyes, roil their gullets, send them spinning into nightmares less real, and therefore more manageable, than the ones in which they lived every day of their wartime lives.

This was not social drinking. There was no society anymore. The booze was to obliterate.

4

The Crusaders
and Their Crusades

obert E. Lee surrendered to an apparently sober Ulysses S. Grant at Appomattox Court House, Virginia, on April 9, 1865. The following year, a group of reformers called the Sons of Temperance changed their membership requirements and admitted daughters. The year after that, the women outnumbered the men.

Before long, the same was true in other societies, and then new societies came into being, one right after the other, made up entirely of women. They were old and young, rich and poor, educated and unlettered—in the aftermath of the Civil War, females poured into the temperance movement as if a dam had broken and released a force too long and too unnaturally confined. They took control of it, remade it according to their own beliefs, and added to it their own distinctive methods. Is their sudden enlistment surprising? Perhaps. But more surprising is that it took them so long to get around to it.

Actually, there were a few women's temperance groups before the war, the first of them possibly going as far back as 1805. Later, the Washingtonians admitted the Martha Washingtonians, the women subservient to the men but not seeming to mind. "Who can be independent," they said, "when thousands of weeping mothers and sisters have followed their nearest and dearest relatives, broken-hearted, to a drunkard's grave?"

But the first females to swear enmity against alcohol did not accomplish much; they did not attract many others or inspire a durable passion. And women who tried to align themselves with men's groups were not in all cases welcome. In 1852, writes Catherine Gilbert Murdock, a couple of ladies decided that they should address the Sons of Temperance at their annual convention in Albany, New York. They were told to forget it.

> Outraged, the two women, Susan B. Anthony and Mary C. Vaughn, formed the Woman's New York State Temperance Society, appointing Elizabeth Cady Stanton president. Thus the temperance movement, albeit rather backhandedly, inspired three of the nineteenth century's most important women leaders to form separate women's groups.

But stories like this were the exception. The majority of temperance organizations were eager for the support of women and actively encouraged it, even if they were not willing to offer full and equal participation. Reverend Armstrong, one of the early advocates of female activism, explained. "Instances of female influence," he said, "which have been successful in averting predominant evils . . . have been numerous in every age, and have been so recorded in the book of divine inspiration."

Of course, Armstrong believed that the *most* predominant evil was intemperance, and in pleading with women to join him in combating it, he assumed he was speaking to a receptive audience. After all, females had long been the primary victims of alcoholic excess—slapped, punched, pushed, pinched, spanked, ignored, or otherwise mistreated by drunken husbands, and sometimes even by their children. "You might say it's a disgrace," spoke a woman in the slums of Chicago late in the nineteenth century, "to have your son beat you up for the sake of a bit of money you've earned scrubbing, but I haven't the heart to blame the boy for doing what he's seen his father do all his life; his father forever went wild when the drink was in him and struck me to the very day of his death."

Elizabeth Cady Stanton thought this kind of thing all too common and was disgusted by it. "Let women's motto be 'no more union with drunkards,' " she cried, and said it again and again, that all should hear. Reverend Armstrong believed that those who did hear would listen, make her words a rallying cry which would sound from one end of the nation to the other.

They did not. Rather, women allowed their history of second-class citizenship and fear of male reprisal to override their self-interest, powerful though the latter was. They had gotten too used to bearing their hardships with stiff—and sometimes swollen—upper lips, found it too familiar a course.

But it was not just mistreatment by men that prompted them to act. Women were also mistreating themselves, a number of them turning to alcohol for reasons of their own, which might include forgetting the abuse that their drunken mates had inflicted on them. Then there were those who, like some Civil War soldiers, got hooked on various medicinal compounds containing alcohol, as well as those who, in preparing their families' meals, used alcohol in recipes and over the course of time began to sip more than cook. In that case, it was but a short step for a woman to make liquors of her own in the kitchen, and, when she did not want to be bothered, to take a few more steps to the local tavern, sneaking in through a special entrance in the rear and buy beverages that she would take home and consume behind drawn curtains.

The history books seldom report such incidents; not surprising, certainly, because they were little publicized at the time. Everyone, it seems, had a stake in the cover-up. Husbands were embarrassed to admit that their wives drank; wives were embarrassed to have fallen victim to so coarse a form of behavior; and women in the temperance movement were embarrassed to admit that their own sisters were part of the problem. Although, to be sure, not the largest part; even as the twentieth century approached, it was reckoned that no more than one out of every five people admitted to a hospital for treatment of alcohol abuse was a woman.

But it was, perhaps, because women were sometimes doubly cursed by alcohol—through the husbands who treated them violently, and, less often, through their own abuse of themselves—that they were finally motivated to act in large numbers. The Civil War was over, and wives and mothers and daughters were all out of patience for suffering of any kind. They were determined to make the peace a safe and sober one; they would take up arms of their own symbolically.

It was a man, however, who led them: Diocletian Lewis, "beautiful, bran-eating Dio," whose "large, rotund body and well-formed head make him at once a striking and conspicuous figure. He stands nearly six feet high and weighs over 200 pounds. His complexion is fair, eyes blue, hair formerly auburn, now white. His skin is fresh, with a peachy hue. His nature is peculiarly sympathetic."

Lewis was, in other words, the very picture of hardiness and vitality. But he did not just look fit; he *was* fit, so much so that he made of fitness a vocation, writing a book called *New Gymnastics*, inventing the beanbag and the wooden dumbbell, and decrying halitosis and sexual promiscuity and anything else that seemed a threat to the blissfully salubrious state. It was he who coined the expression, "A clean tooth never decays," and the teeth in which he seemed most interested belonged to ladies. He gave them all sorts of advice: brush thoroughly, brush often, wear short skirts and light clothing, avoid corsets at all costs, and spend at least a few minutes every day strolling about with twenty-pound sandbags on your head to improve posture.

In addition to being an admirer of the opposite sex, Lewis was a man of deep religious conviction. The latter made him believe in the efficacy of prayer, the former in the ability of women to cast spells over men, to persuade by enchantment. Combining these two articles of faith, Lewis found himself speculating one day that women might be able to put drinking establishments out of business simply by assembling in front of them in what he called "Visitation Bands," and, while male customers watched and listened, communicating their displeasure to the heavens. Just the sight of them, and the incantatory effect of their monologues, Lewis thought, might be enough to affect masculine behavior. It had happened before, after all. In 1834, a group called the Female Moral Reform Society began to picket prayerfully outside of New York brothels, and the tactic was successful enough to spread for a time to other cities. It is not known, though, whether Lewis had ever heard the story.

His friends, apparently, had not. They told him his notion sounded nonsensical, preposterous even; not only would it not work, it would turn the female participants into laughingstocks. But Lewis disagreed, and in a way his determination foreshadowed that of Mohandas Gandhi, whose strategy for reform in India in the following century would be based on a similar principle; which is to say that there is something in even the most aggressive of people that makes them susceptible to certain kinds of passivity, a mechanism whereby the weak or underprivileged are somehow able to exert their will over the strong—provided that the weak are unyielding and the strong, at bottom, humane. Gandhi called the notion *satyagraha*, which refers to the force of truth being employed in a good cause.

But. Would it work? Would theory translate into practice? Lewis needed a sounding board, someone with whom to share his belief, a person he could trust above all others to give him a fair hearing and advise him wisely and honestly. He went to his mother. She, not his friends, would be the judge. If the idea seemed reasonable to her, Lewis would somehow put it to work.

As the long-suffering wife of a chronic and unredeemable dipsomaniac, a man who enjoyed the distiller's handiwork far more than the company of his family, Delecta Lewis proved a rapt audience for her son. More than that, she became a kind of research assistant, reacting so enthusiastically to Diocletian's concept of female power that she told him she would test it herself, and promptly.

Lewis wondered what she meant. He opened his mouth to ask, but was too late; his mother had already excused herself from the room and gone upstairs to change. When she came down again a few minutes later, attired in one of her most dignified outfits, she thanked her son for the inspiration, told him she would see him later, and assured him no harm would befall her. He asked her where she was going. She closed the door behind her without answering.

Delecta Lewis had turned on her engine. She gathered up steam and tooted some kind of silent whistle and chugged down tracks that only she could see until she arrived at the tavern where her husband did most of his guzzling. She parked herself in front of it and—how else to say it?—simply prayed the damn thing shut. That is, she closed her eyes, gritted her teeth, and invoked the higher powers of the Lord in full-voiced fashion until the patrons, sensing the strength of her resolve, the irresistible rays of it, and perhaps even the stronger emanations of Him whom she beseeched, either straggled out of the barroom or stopped straggling in. They were not sure why. Neither was she. There does not seem to be a direct connection here between cause and effect, between a woman's prayers and a man's decision to ingest a little less alcohol than usual. Somehow, though, Delecta had found one. Encouraged, even a little amazed at her success, she reported back to her son. Encouraged and amazed himself, he determined to try the approach on a larger scale.

What followed is known to history as the Women's Crusade. It began on December 24, 1873, in the small, southeastern Ohio town of Hillsboro. Despite a population of fewer than 5,000 souls, and a reputation as a good, God-fearing community with an industrious corps of residents, Hillsboro was home to thirteen saloons—the word, just coming into widespread use at the time in the United States, derived from the French *salon*, although in America it connoted drinking venues of far seedier ambience—and another eight businesses, such as hotels and drug stores, that sold spirits on the side.

For the wives and mothers of Hillsboro, many of whom were leading lives similar to Delecta Lewis's, this was twenty-one gin mills too many. The women decided to act, and on the eve of the birth of the Lord, eight and a half years after the end of the Civil War, the time finally seemed right. "Carrying their knitting and zephyr work, or embroidery," writes Gilbert Seldes in *The Stammering Century*, "they . . . advanced in a long procession to the saloons. Some of them did not even know what saloons looked like. They believed 'that those second-rate looking places were barber shops.'" They were about to learn otherwise.

At the head of their ranks was not Lewis, but one of his disciples, a short woman, slight of build, almost sixty years old. Mrs. Elizabeth Jane Trimble Thompson considered herself an easygoing sort, law-abiding; she had never made a wave in her life and refused to associate with the kind of people who did. But she was "the mother of a promising son who drank himself out of jobs as a minister and a teacher, was confined for a time to an inebriate asylum, and died at the age of thirty." She was, in other words, ready to supply herself with a missal and take on a den of iniquity, even though, when Lewis had lectured in Hillsboro two nights earlier, pleading with the women to act, Thompson had not even attended; "family cares," as she put it, had kept her at home.

Nonetheless, she agreed to join a Visitation Band. What she did not agree to do was serve as its leader, and when she was chosen for the role by those who *had* listened to Lewis, she said she did not know whether she was up to it; she would have to ask the Almighty for guidance. Her friends understood, and Thompson removed herself to a private place. She had no sooner begun to pray than her daughter approached "with tearful eyes" and brought her a Bible opened to Psalm 146, an admonition that she had read many times before, but one that struck her now with an entirely new meaning. "This is the way," the Good Book stated, "walk ye in it." She decided she would.

Her husband was not pleased. In fact, he "was properly alarmed at what he called a lot of tomfoolery. His wife reminded him that the men had been in the tomfoolery business for a long time, and remarked that 'it might be God's will that the women should now take a part.'"

Perhaps, but Mr. Thompson, a former governor of Ohio who counted himself a temperance supporter of unquestioned loyalty, would have preferred that the cause be left to men, or if not, at least to women other than the one he had married. He told her precisely that.

Elizabeth Jane Trimble Thompson was used to listening to her mate; like most women of her time, she had made a virtual career of spousal obedience. But in this case, she would not be cowed. She was nervous as she faced her disapproving husband, and would later be even more nervous as she and her sisters assembled at the First Presbyterian Church of Hillsboro, whence they set out for the front lines, putting their bodies where their beliefs were. But she knew she was doing something important, something that mattered more than anything she had ever done before.

She assembled her troops, issued the marching orders. "We will sing that good old hymn, 'Give to the Winds Thy Fears,'" she said, "and as we are singing let us form in line, two by two, the small women in front, leaving the tall ones to bring up the rear, then let us at once proceed to our sacred mission, trusting along in the God of Jacob."

Less than two weeks later it was over, and the results were scarcely to be believed. A clergyman from Boston who happened to be present at "the miracle of Hillsboro," and who had not even known it was in the planning stages, explained how it worked.

> I came unexpectedly upon some fifty women kneeling on the pavement and stone steps before a store. . . . There were gathered here representatives from every household of the town. The day was bitterly cold; a cutting north wind swept the streets, piercing us all to the bones. The plaintive, tender, earnest tones of that wife and mother who was pleading in prayer, arose on the blast, and were carried to every heart within reach. Passers by uncovered their heads, for the place whereon they trod was "holy ground." The eyes of hardened men filled with tears, and many turned away, saying that they could not bear to look upon such a sight. Then the voice of prayer was hushed; the women began to sing, softly, a sweet hymn with some old familiar words and tune, such as our mothers sang to us in childhood days. We thought, Can mortal man resist such efforts?

The answer, apparently, at least in the short run, was no. Every single one of the offending twenty-one establishments in Hillsboro, Ohio, either closed its doors or stopped selling alcoholic beverages. A few went up for immediate sale; others became emporia of a different kind, offering products to which no one could object. Charley Beck, a rough-hewn German who owned a beer garden that catered to an especially boorish clientele, was one of the last holdouts. He vowed that the women would never break him, swore that his tenacity was superior to theirs and he would outlast them, come what may. But he heard *so* many prayers, *so* many hymns; there were all those clasped hands and shrill voices and fervent expressions—he did not think it would ever end, and even if it did, he did not think the words would ever stop echoing through his brain. What was a man to do? "Ach," he is supposed to have said, "vimmins, shut up vimmins, I quits," and he covered his ears and ran down the street in search of refuge.

Even Joe Lance, the tougher-than-nails proprietor of a dive called the Lava Bed, was no match for the delicate but persistent crusaders. According to one account, Lance withstood the praying about as long as Charley Beck did, then admitted even more thoroughly to defeat. He sold every bottle of liquor that the Lava Bed owned, then sold the place itself and bought a cart and began a new life peddling seafood in the streets. No more whiskey and water for Beck; from now on it would be whitefish and walleye.

Prayer, it seemed, if uttered by the right mouths and directed toward the right ends, was a tool for civic justice no less than an indispensable element of faith. But in his book *The Americans: A Social History of the United States, 1587–1914,* J. C. Furnas suggests that something quite secular was going on in Hillsboro as well, that self-interest on the part of the victims of the crusade might have had as much to do with its accomplishments as the chorus of heavenly importunings. "The saloonkeeper," Furnas writes, "recognizing among the crowd of bonnet-and-shawled self-righteous in his barroom the wife of the banker who held his mortgage, the wife of the lumber and coal dealer to whom he owed $653, the mother of the county attorney and the daughter of his family doctor was unlikely too roughly to resist their holy bullying."

Whatever the reason, the Women's Crusade was off to a promising start. But that is all it was, a start. From Hillsboro, it moved to Washington Court House, Ohio, where a gentleman named Smith stood in front of the saloon he owned with his arms folded across his chest and his jaw carved so deeply into a scowl that it seemed as if it could never be displaced. He explained to the Lewis-inspired abstainers before him that there were no such things as prohibitory laws in either the town or the state. Thus, he explained, being as patient and polite as he could, the ladies were interfering with his legal right to make a living, to provide for himself and his family, and to be a productive member of society. They were, in other words, behaving criminally. He told them to leave. Otherwise, he said, he would summon the authorities.

The crusaders' spokesperson was Mrs. George Carpenter. She listened to Smith with patience and politeness of her own, but refused to budge, either literally or figuratively. When he finished, she replied that, right or not, she and her troops had "vowed to Heaven that we would not cease until the selling of liquor was stopped in this town." The barkeep might have had the law on his side, but the temperance troops were operating under a higher authority.

"Do you mean to come here and pray every day until I stop?" Smith asked.

Mrs. Carpenter answered in the righteous affirmative.

Smith stroked that jaw of his, the scowl remaining in place, then told the ladies to stay right where they were as he slipped back into the saloon and found a quiet corner. What he thought about in there, what mysterious transformation came over him and why it came at all, not to mention as quickly as it did, no one knows. Perhaps Smith had been told of Hillsboro, and thought his cause hopeless. Perhaps something Mrs. Carpenter had said made him see an error in his ways. Regardless, when he emerged a few minutes later, he was pushing a barrel of beer in front of him and groaning at the effort. The crusaders looked at him questioningly. He smiled back. Then he invited them to destroy the barrel, to break it into bits, and this they did—with stones and sticks and bricks and glee. Smith even got caught up in the spirit of things himself, and went back inside for another vat, a second round of ruination.

Before the day was over, every container of alcohol that Smith owned, large and small, wood and glass, had been toted outside his place of commerce and demolished. The contents gushed into the main street of Washington Court House, turning the loose-laying dirt into a mud of some 30 to 40 proof. Animals lapped at it but soon gave up, confused and happy. Smith's customers shook their heads at the waste. As for the crusaders and their supporters, they stepped around the spirituous torrents at their feet and pumped their fists at so dramatic a show of good sense.

The crusade spread in other directions: east to Wheeling, West Virginia; northwest to Ripon, Wisconsin; southwest to Carthage, Missouri; and north to Minnesota, where some women wrote their own hymn.

> And where are the hands red with slaughter?
> Behold them each day as you pass
> The places where death and destruction
> Are retailed at ten cents a glass.

To their repertoire of song and prayer, the ladies sometimes added stenography, jotting down the names and addresses of the men who entered the saloons, shaking their heads and tsk-tsking as they did. It was a pointless exercise; the lists went nowhere, were seen by no one, and would not have mattered even if they had been. But they had the appearance of official disapprobation, and seem to have inspired many a devotee of bottled refreshment to skip his favorite rum shop for an evening. And at one such location, some women managed to rig up a set of locomotive headlights, turning them on at nightfall and shining them through the front window of the saloon, exposing the bibulous revelry within to all who passed by, making it seem all the worse for being so starkly visible.

But not everywhere did the Women's Crusade meet with acquiescence. There was the occasional barman who reacted to interference with his trade by throwing fruits, vegetables, and eggs at the reformers, or perhaps flinging handfuls of sawdust from the saloon floors into their faces. He cursed at them, threatened them, in a few cases even loosed dogs on them. "In Cincinnati," we learn from Herbert Asbury, "the proprietor of a beer garden mounted an old cannon at the entrance to his place and threatened to blow the ladies to kingdom come. One of the women promptly clambered upon the gun and led the others in prayers."

Sometimes bartenders "baptized" the women with buckets of warm, sudsy beer, dumping the liquid over their heads so that they would return home from their labors smelling not of triumph but of conversion to the other side. On one occasion, and a bitterly cold one at that, a saloonkeeper turned a powerful spray of water on the crusaders, causing Asbury to remark that the "line of praying crusaders resembled a row of icicles." And in yet another town, a gang of thugs who had been deputized by the mayor to enforce a spur-of-the-moment decree against public praying threw a seventy-year-old woman down a flight of stairs and, after she landed, struck her on the arms a number of times with wooden clubs.

Once in a while, instead of remaining in the street, the ladies would march inside the saloons to pray within easier earshot of their audience. But this also put them closer to retribution, and there were newspaper reports of bartenders who "blocked up their chimneys to send the women gasping and coughing into the street, sprinkled pepper over burning coals to make them sneeze, opened their doors and windows to freeze them and sloshed filthy water across the floor to discourage kneeling." Some owners even locked the women inside their joints for the night, so that they now had to pray for escape as well as an end to inebriation.

It was, of course, reprehensible behavior, as reprehensible as that of the drunken, violent husbands which had in so many cases brought the ladies to the saloons in the first place. But it is important to understand what the crusaders had in mind, the larger point of their exercises. They were not just trying to persuade individual barflies to change their ways and go home to loved ones; no less were they trying to publicize their larger goal of an end to alcohol by achieving a kind of martyrdom, and the more unjustly they were treated, the more likely they were to succeed.

This is not to say that they were masochists, nor that they tried to bring out the worst in their tormentors, goad them to extremes. But they were more than willing to endure the mistreatment that so often befell them, well aware of the public relations value of being pummeled or pelted or doused in view of a sympathetic crowd, or a crowd that would *become* sympathetic in the process of watching such deeds. They knew that it would reveal their position to be a worthy one; why else would otherwise sane and peaceable human beings subject themselves to such abuse? And they knew that through their pain and humiliation they would win followers, the tender-hearted being attracted to temperance, regardless of their previous feelings on the matter, simply because they felt such compassion for the movement's foot soldiers.

As for the saloonkeepers who attacked them, behaving so abominably as to make bullies blush, they were inadvertently promoting the cause of temperance themselves, and perhaps, in the final analysis, doing an even better job of it than the women.

The Women's Crusade gave birth to a Children's Crusade. Boys and girls who had long been instructed by their parents to take the longest detour possible around the local saloon were now being told to station themselves right in front of the nefarious place, and in some cases, especially if their numbers were large enough to ensure safety, even to walk through the door. More often than not, a child would recite a pledge, perhaps one that had been popular among the children of temperance for several decades.

> This little band do with our hand
> The pledge now sign to drink no wine,
> Nor brandy red, to turn our head,
> Nor whiskey hot that makes the sot,
> Nor fiery rum to turn our home
> Into a hell where none could dwell—
> Whence peace would fly, where hope would die,
> And love expire 'mid such a fire;
> So here we pledge perpetual hate
> To all that can intoxicate.

Or a child might sing a song of supplication.

> Father, dear father, come home with me now;
> The clock in the steeple strikes one.
> You said you were coming right home from the shop
> As soon as your day's work was done.
> Our fire has gone out, our house is all dark,
> And mother's been watching since tea,
> With poor brother Benny so sick in her arms,
> And no one to help her but me.

Or a child might simply walk up to the man pouring the drinks, and in a voice throbbing with innocence ask him, and the men sitting across the bar from him, where he could find his daddy. Even the most rabid of boozers, those who would not think twice about throwing a spoiled tomato or a bucket of beer at a fully grown female, would gulp at the sight of children in their midst, would understand the terrible apprehension they felt, and would at least for the moment regret their choice of libation.

The Women's and Children's Crusades were short-term accomplishments. Diocletian Lewis claimed that, as a result of them, more than 17,000 drinking establishments were abandoned in Ohio alone in a period of two months. National figures compiled by the Internal Revenue Bureau, as it was called at the time, show that a significant number of breweries went out of business during the peak years of the crusades, and that the production of malt liquors dropped more than it ever had before. And an article in the *New York Observer*, with Tiffin, Ohio, as its dateline, said that "the assessors and gaugers of the ninth district of Ohio tell us that, as a result of the temperance movement, not one of the eight distilleries in the district is now in operation. The sale of all kinds of liquors, beers, and ale has fallen off more than 60 percent."

But it did not fall off for long, either in Ohio or anywhere else that women and children crusaded, no matter how sincerely or energetically. Most saloons that closed as a result of prayer vigils opened again a few days later; sometimes, in the case of Washington Court House, there would be more saloons up and running after the reformers had descended than before. Sometimes they would come back and pray the places shut again, but then they went away and the saloons had another reopening—and whereas the dry brigades eventually grew tired of returning to the same place every few weeks to invoke their Higher Being, the customers never tired of appearing anew to lift a glass of spirituous beverage. And, the Lava Bed's Joe Lance excepted, most saloonkeepers had no desire to change jobs.

Perhaps inspired by the crusades, the publicity they received if not the longevity of their results, a man from Dwight, Illinois, named Leslie E. Keeley announced a method of his own for eliminating the alcoholic thirst. It was not intimidation, legislation, or public humiliation. Nor did he rely on prayer or reason or financial penalty. For Leslie E. Keeley was a doctor—a graduate, in fact, of the Chicago medical college named after Benjamin Rush—and in his view, the craving for hooch was to be regarded no differently from the onset of mumps or measles or cholera. "Drunkenness is a disease," he told a newspaper interviewer in 1879, "and I can cure it."

Among the scoffers, and there were many at first, was Joseph Medill, the editor of the *Chicago Tribune*, who thought Keeley a charlatan and said as much in print.

> Dr. Keeley responded by asking the editor to send him "half a dozen of the worst drunks you can find in your city." Medill did so. When they had completed Keeley's four-week treatment, they returned to Chicago. Medill was amazed. He scarcely could recognize them. "They went away sots," he wrote in his paper, "and returned gentlemen." The future of what became known as the Keeley Cure was assured.

But the ingredients of the Keeley Cure remained a mystery. The doctor advertised it as "double chloride of gold," but never seems to have explained beyond that. In 1890, he opened a sanitarium in Dwight and found himself immediately besieged with reform-minded tipplers. They were given three injections a day with a needle, it has been said, that was "one of the large nineteenth-century bore—like having a garden hose shoved into a bicep."

Painful it might have been; expensive it was not. Stewart H. Holbrook tells us that patients were charged $25 a week for four weeks. They "roomed in the sanitarium but were obliged to board out; Dr. Keeley provided that they should 'have free access to the best brands of liquor.' After the first two days, however, they had lost all appetite for it. They 'could not bear the smell of the stuff.' "

Holbrook goes on to wonder "if there is a single village in the United States, incorporated before about 1900, which cannot recall at least one fellow citizen who was a graduate of the Keeley Cure." There were so many such citizens, in fact, that they were eventually organized into a Keeley League, which, in 1895, claimed some 30,000 members in 359 chapters all across America, every single one of them a satisfied customer, none of them a victim of demon rum at any future time.

Or so Dr. Keeley would have had people believe. Other physicians, however, claimed that his methods were dangerous and relapses "so frequent as to cast grave doubt as to the value of the medication." They had a point. When Keeley died in 1900, his sanitarium died with him, albeit more gradually, and the cure he so boldly touted became even more controversial, less popular, and finally obsolete. Today it is known by few people, and most histories of temperance do not even bother to mention it.

Nor do they mention Sylvester Graham, although he attached his last name to the cracker that is still with us. A nutritionist, by inclination if not training, Graham thought a thirst for spirits might be the result of poor dietary habits. He recommended that Americans give up meats and fried foods, and eat more slowly and cheerfully. He also recommended his cracker—and, in fact, since it was made of unbleached flour, it was a more healthful product than most commercially manufactured bakery goods. But few were the people who found it a satisfactory substitute for demon rum.

It was not that Keeley and Graham the crusaders could not win. It was that, human nature being what it is, the victories could not endure.

5

The Importance of Being Frank

The Women's Crusade was a series of brush fires, frightening in intensity but quickly extinguished. The Woman's Christian Temperance Union, on the other hand, was a carefully orchestrated conflagration—and it was the American public schools that took most of the heat.

Woman's, as the group liked to point out in its early literature, "because they felt that if men had an equal place in its councils their greater knowledge of Parliamentary usage, and their more aggressive nature would soon place women in the background, and deprive them of the power of learning by experience."

Christian, despite the occasional reservation that "we would shut out the Jews."

Temperance, which meant "the moderate use of all things good and total abstinence from all things questionable or harmful."

Union, to acknowledge the fact that "women extended their hands to grasp any that were held out to them in loyalty to the Gospel of peace and good-will."

The WCTU succeeded the crusaders and shifted their emphasis. No more would females kneel in front of saloons in all their passion and vulnerability and send their prayers winging up to the empyrean. Oh, perhaps a few of them would, in a few isolated places and a few exceptional cases, keeping up the old ways where they seemed to be effective; but for the most part the WCTU decided to ignore the strategies of Diocletian Lewis and concentrate on the classroom, on

111

younger and more impressionable minds than those of barroom habit-ués. The group would teach children to regard alcoholic beverages as Satan's own potables; it would leave the salvation of their elders largely to other groups, mainly because it doubted whether salvation was even possible once a man or woman passed a certain age.

Unlike the Women's Crusade, which no sooner got underway than it leaped into the headlines, the WCTU started slowly, spending several years on the back pages of newspapers—if, that is, it caught the editors' attention at all. It was founded in 1874, the year after the miracle of Hillsboro, and the woman who worked hardest in the group's formative days was Frances Elizabeth Caroline Willard, whose severity in appearance was matched by her severity of manner, at least to those who did not know her well. She parted her hair in the middle, tugged it down tightly behind her ears, and peered at the world through plain, wire-rimmed spectacles. Sometimes her lips hinted at a smile, but seldom did they deliver; she did not see much through those lenses of hers that lightened her heart.

To her friends she was Frank. Less humbly, she would in time be compared to Joan of Arc, and regarded by at least one historian as "the most formidable woman in America." The WCTU would call her "The Uncrowned Queen of American Womanhood." One of the group's members, a more than usually devout follower, admitted that in times of crisis she would drop to her knees, cast her gaze hopefully upward, and call out in a voice that no one nearby could ignore, "Help me, God, or Frances E. Willard."

But no one would have guessed that she would one day be referred to in such adulatory terms, least of all herself. She was born in Churchville, New York, in 1839, into "a rarely endowed home." So said Anna Gordon, a later acolyte of Willard, who then defined the phrase in a gust of barely comprehensible prose. Willard's was "a home sheltered from adverse chance to soul or to body by the father's strength of heart and arm and will; with the mother-climate warm within, winning out and fostering all wholesome developments—a richly nurtured child-garden, where the sturdy small plants struck deep root and spread wide leafage to the air, catching every drop of pure knowledge and every beam of home-love falling within its rays. Here the 'rosy-white flower of the child's consciousness unfolded its five-starred cup to the bending blue above.'"

The reader must, at this point, take a breath.

Frances Willard's Churchville home might have been a richly nurtured child garden, and perhaps the same could be said about her later childhood homes in Oberlin, Ohio, and Janesville, Wisconsin. But young Frank did not grow confidently from their soil. She was timid, self-doubting; she found herself unattractive, even repellent, and in her autobiography did not shrink from relating the similar conclusions of others. An acquaintance asked how she felt about being so homely. Other acquaintances whispered behind her back. Her music teacher thought her appearance "a great pity."

Yet she did not lack for ambition. Willard would later say that she wanted to grow up to be a saint. Failing that, she would settle for politician. In a manner of speaking, she ended up combining the two.

But she began life a tomboy, her red hair cut as short as a boy's, her chest as flat, her limbs as lean and sinewy. She often wore trousers, and as she got older would sometimes accompany them with jackets and ties, looking for all the world like an undersized but terribly industrious young man. And, like a young man, Willard had an eye for the ladies. Her adolescent years were marked by a series of crushes, one after another, deep swoon leading to deep swoon. In later life, she wrote about one such object of her affection, recalling that "the flame of the ideal burned in my breast for a sweet girl of sixteen, Maria Hill by name. . . . That was my first 'heart affair,' and I have had fifty since as surely as I had that one.' "

Another whose name stayed with her, even several decades after the fact, was Maggie. Frank could not sleep because of Maggie, could not eat, could not control the wild beating of her heart when her inamorata was nearby or even prominently situated in her thoughts. Finally, she confessed her feelings to her mother. She said she had written Maggie a letter, telling her that "I love you more than life, better than God, more than I dread damnation." Then she sighed and swallowed hard, fearing her mother's reaction, prepared for the worst and ready to believe she deserved it.

"Oh, Frank!" Mrs. Willard said after a few moments, and it was not what the daughter had expected, not in the least. "Pray Heaven you may never love a man." So much for the notion that the "mother-climate" was impressed with her husband's "strength of heart and arm and will."

But Frank Willard *would* love a man, or would try to, pretend to—one of those. In her early twenties, she was engaged to Charles Henry

Fowler, a respected educator who would one day be a bishop in the Methodist Episcopal Church. Even Willard had to admit that he was a "man of brilliant gifts." But the relationship was stormy while it lasted and did not last long, and when she looked back on it in her autobiography, it was with a disappointment she could not disguise. "In 1861–62," she wrote," for three quarters of a year I wore a ring and acknowledged an allegiance based on the supposition that an intellectual comradeship was sure to deepen into unity of heart. How grieved I was over the discovery of my mistakes the journals of that epoch would reveal."

Perhaps if she had met Neal Dow. Perhaps if their paths had somehow managed to cross and they could have sat together in private and talked about their shared beliefs and the depth with which they held them, perhaps then she would have found an intellectual comradeship ripening into unity of the heart. For Willard had studied Dow's life and his law and admired him greatly, but only from afar; much as she wanted to, she would never enjoy his company. She would, though, tell people that he was an idol of hers, the only male ever to earn a place in her pantheon. She would even vote for him for the nation's highest office; the Prohibition Party, founded in 1869 by dissident Republicans and dedicated to women's suffrage as well as to the elimination of drink, nominated Dow for president in 1880. But it was Republican James Garfield who took the White House that year with 4,454,416 votes. Democrat Winfield Scott Hancock finished a close second, tallying 4,444,952. Dow came in fourth, well behind the Greenback labor candidate, his vote total slightly more than 10,000.

To Willard, though, it was the electorate that had failed, not Dow. One of the last goals of her life—and she might even have whispered it on her deathbed—was that Dow's birthday, February 20, be observed by the United States as National Prohibition Day. It never happened.

The best she could say of other men, and this of only a few, was that they were "good and gracious." Willard even seemed to prefer dogs to the human male; when she got one of her own, she named it Prohibition, and was thought to have lavished more care and attention on it than most women supply to their mates.

This, then, was Frances Elizabeth Caroline Willard: intelligent, well-spoken, unwavering in her resolve, stoic in some ways and sensitive in others, a good friend and a bad enemy. This was the woman who, more than any other, was responsible for the Woman's Christian Temperance Union, which she took pride in organizing and managing and describing as "the sober second thought of the Crusade."

Yet in its first decade, for all the results it got, the WCTU might as well have been a sewing circle, a place for like-minded ladies of untroubled circumstance to stitch their hearts away and talk over tea about their favorite recipes and methods of canning. It was that genteel, that irrelevant to the outside world.

But it was building momentum—slowly, laboriously, sometimes so far under the surface of its daily activities that the members themselves were not even aware of it. The WCTU was attracting a little notice here and changing a few minds there and persevering, just plain-old persevering, until suddenly, in 1885, there was a turnabout, the seeds so patiently planted finally bearing fruit—erupting into fruit, in fact—surprising those who had planted them as much as anyone else. The group's annual report for that year says the following: "Ten States have, during the last twelve months, followed the example of the great Empire State [New York], in making, by legislative act, the study of physiological temperance a part of the required course of instruction in their public schools." The report goes on to list the states, and to credit the Lord for the actions of their legislators.

This, however, is the conventional believers' rhetoric. It was the WCTU under Frances Willard, not a supernatural entity, that brought the states around, and would bring even more around in years to come. The group "harried state and territorial legislatures so relentlessly that within twenty years every one of them except Arizona had enacted laws making such education compulsory in its public schools. Congress imposed the same law upon all schools under federal control." And the WCTU's efforts turned out to be all the more effective because they coincided with laws that, for the first time, made attendance compulsory in American public schools. What the DARE drug education program is to today's classrooms, the WCTU was to yesterday's.

But the actions of the states were not enough for Willard. She wanted more than a dry curriculum in the schools; her own organization, she insisted, must provide the texts. She wanted to teach that alcohol is "a colorless liquid poison," and that it "sometimes causes the coats of the blood vessels to grow thin. They are then liable at anytime to cause death by bursting." She wanted to teach that the children of drunkards are weak-minded and tend toward insanity as adults. She wanted to teach that even a tiny amount of alcohol would kill a dog or cat, and therefore do immeasurable harm to a child. How could Willard be sure that such lessons would be a part of the American curriculum unless the Woman's Christian Temperance Union wrote the books, distributed them, and carefully monitored the results?

Lawmakers, for the most part, gave Willard free rein, afraid that opposition would make them seem unconcerned about the physical and moral health of youngsters. They were also afraid of alienating the drinkers in their constituencies, and reasoned that those folks would find WCTU schoolbooks less of a threat to their thirsts than either Diocletian Lewis's crusading womenfolk or prohibitory laws. And they were afraid of incurring the reformers' wrath; like DARE, the WCTU was thought of as an acronym, its enemies swearing that the letters stood for "We'll See to You."

Thus was born the group's Department of Scientific Temperance Instruction. That its aims were noble and the problems it meant to address were in some cases serious threats to society was, or should have been, acknowledged by all people of good will and common sense. That many of its publications were no more scientific than Benjamin Rush's booze-in-the-shoes cure for a cold seems, at least by those who fought against alcoholic abandon, to have gone unnoticed. That the department appeared more intent on intimidating than enlightening, on simplifying rather than cogently explaining, was similarly unmentioned in all but the most rabidly wet of circles.

Kindergarten students, for example, studied from books that showed radiant teetotalers, crippled tipplers, and no kinds of human beings in between. They were taught to shout in unison, voices impassioned and enunciating with utmost clarity, "Tremble, King Alcohol, we shall grow up!" And they were asked, and in most cases required, to affix their names to pledges; to their classmates who were reluctant to do so, they sometimes chanted.

> Young man, why will you not sign the pledge,
>   And stand with the true and the brave?
> How dare you lean over the dangerous ledge
>   Above the inebriate's grave?

In elementary school, children learned that apples are God's bottles and grapes are God's bottles, but some men "take the juice of the apples and grapes and make drinks that will harm our bodies. They put the drinks in glass bottles, but we will not drink from such bottles. We will DRINK FROM GOD'S BOTTLES."

Or they would drink without any bottles at all. A WCTU pamphlet featured a drawing of a hand with the fingers numbered and a lesson inscribed on each:

One, two, three, four, five fingers on every little hand;
Listen while they speak to us; be sure we understand.

1.—THERE IS A DRINK THAT NEVER HARMS
It will make us strong.

2.—THERE IS A DRINK THAT NEVER ALARMS
Some drinks make people wicked.

3.—A DRINK THAT KEEPS OUR SENSES RIGHT
There are drinks that take away our senses.

4.—A DRINK THAT MAKES OUR FACES BRIGHT
We should never touch the drinks that will put evil into our hearts and spoil our faces.

5.—GOD GIVES US THE ONLY DRINK—'TIS PURE, COLD WATER

There were also stories to be read aloud, and discussed with the class afterward.

Daddy was disgusted with Neighbor Jones. "Swigs beer like a sponge! Drank ten glasses, one after another,—made a fool of himself,—and had to be carried home dead drunk!"
    Billy asked, "Daddy, how much did you drink?"
    "Only one glass," said Daddy, virtuously.
    Billy had been studying fractions. "One glass is ten per cent of ten glasses," he calculated. "Mr. Jones was a fool to drink ten glasses. Were you ten per cent of a fool, Daddy?"

For teenagers, the WCTU published a book called *Hygienic Physiology*, by Joel Steele. Among other things, the author recommends several demonstrations for teachers to perform in class. One begins with the placing of an egg white in a cup. Then, writes Steele, the teacher is to tell her students that another name for an egg white is albumen. The students repeat the word: Albumen. Next, the teacher pours pure alcohol or strong brandy over the egg white, the potion's very appearance in a classroom sometimes causing gasps. She waits a few moments as the egg white becomes "hard and solid," and calls this change to the boys' and girls' attention. Then she says, "Remember, children, your brain is largely an albumenous substance." She points to the ossifying egg white. "We would never want anything like this to happen to it, would we?"

If the teacher desires, says Steele, she may use a calf's brain instead of the egg white.

And it was not just the Department of Scientific Temperance Instruction that produced texts and tracts, songs and poems, demonstrations and drawings. As the years went by, the WCTU, adopting as its motto "Do Everything," broke up into so many subdivisions that outsiders often thought it a virtual corporation with a huge staff and limitless resources. In truth, it was a small band of volunteers who more often than not operated on a shoestring, but with a remarkable degree of efficiency, each of its parts functioning precisely as the master plan of Frances Willard envisioned. There were, during the group's years of peak influence, departments of, or for . . .

Suppression of Social Evil, which opposed doing virtually anything, even getting a haircut, on Sunday.

Christian Citizenship, which opposed gambling.

Work Among Mormon Women, which opposed bigamy.

Work Among Foreigners, which included "Germans, Indians, Chinese, Scandinavians and Colored People."

Unfermented Wine at the Lord's Table, which tried to persuade various churches to substitute grape juice for wine at their services.

Social Purity, which tried to outlaw prostitution and lead its practitioners onto a more virtuous path.

Mercy, which sought to prevent cruelty to animals and criticized the use of bird feathers by hat makers.

Purity in Art and Literature, which is self-explanatory.

Inducing Corporations to Require Total Abstinence in Their Employees, which is also self-explanatory.

Overthrow of the Tobacco Habit, which after a few years became the Department of Narcotics and broadened its aims.

The WCTU "even joined the late-century campaign for bland foods, in response to the fear that a spicy diet would foster desire for stimulating drink."

And it was Willard, more than anyone else, who made such a breadth of ambition possible. She was an organizer of superb skills, a CEO long before the term was invented, and an exceptional one at that. Had *For-*

tune and *Business Week* and other such publications been around back then, they would surely have profiled her, and CNBC would have called for interviews, asked her to provide advice for the aspiring captains of industry in the audience. Certainly print and broadcast media alike would have covered the opening of the Woman's Christian Temperance Union Temple, which, in 1890, was one of the "newest, tallest Chicago skyscrapers."

Willard saw to it that those who worked in the building made use of new machines called type-writers and even newer machines called Dictaphones, the latter of which were gifts from a supporter named Thomas Alva Edison, who disapproved of both tobacco and alcohol. The type-writers constantly wrote; the Dictaphones constantly took notes; the lessons from the Woman's Christian Temperance Union just kept on coming, one line of goods after another from one more American factory, albeit one more socially conscious than most.

Willard was also an educator of more depth and sophistication than her foes were willing to admit. She read and approved all that her organization published, contributing a great deal herself and editing meticulously. As a result, she put modesty aside on one occasion to pronounce the materials "great without arrogance, wise without *hauteur*, familiar without degradation." Perhaps she did not believe every word of them, but so devoted was she to the WCTU's goals that she was probably willing to take some license, permitting some small lies or exaggerations for the sake of the larger good. Most people believe that the Bible, after all, is not literally true in every single detail.

Actually, Willard had once been an educator in the more formal sense, serving as president of the Evanston (Illinois) College for Ladies and then, when the school merged with Northwestern University in 1873, becoming that institution's first dean of women. She was a reformer here, too, instituting an honor system for female students and referring to it proudly as a form of self-government. She was well liked on campus, a favorite of students and faculty alike, and might have stayed on, not departing to help found the WCTU and thereby influence the entire course of the American temperance movement, if it had not been for the fact that, after Willard had been employed at Northwestern for but a short time, the school appointed a new president, a man with whom the dean of women was not comfortable. She thought him competent, knew him to be a good choice for the job according to most standards, but believed there was no way she could work for him,

regardless of how much or little direct contact they had. She was almost
certainly correct. She left the school soon after he took office, and never
regretted her decision. He did not regret it, either.

The man's name was Charles Henry Fowler.

Millions of boys and girls learned about alcoholic beverages from the
Woman's Christian Temperance Union, both directly from the group's
publications and indirectly as a result of the influence that the ladies
exerted on other educational sources. Even *McGuffey's Reader*, the most
commonly used schoolbook of its time, warned children about the perils
of beer and wine and whiskey. In one edition, it denounced the system
by which most communities granted permission for saloons to operate.
According to *McGuffey's*, these places were thus

> Licensed—to do thy neighbor harm,
> Licensed—to kindle hate and strife,
> Licensed—to nerve the robber's arm,
> Licensed—to whet the murder's knife.
> Licensed—like spider for a fly,
> To spread thy nets for man, thy prey;
> To mock his struggles, crush his soul,
> Then cast his worthless form away.

The parents of America's students, however, did not learn the lessons.
In the decade preceding the WCTU's founding, adult men and women
drank 62 million gallons of liquor. In the group's first ten years of existence, the total jumped to 76 million. The comparative figures for wine
over the same period are 21 million gallons and 27.5 million gallons,
and for beer 647 million gallons and a billion gallons. And between
1879 and 1898, which was the term of Frances Willard's presidency of
the WCTU and the height of its power, the amount of all alcoholic beverages gulped down in the United States more than doubled. In each of
these cases, the increase in consumption was greater than the increase in
the country's population through both birth and immigration, although
a great many immigrants brought drinking habits with them.

This does not mean, however, that the Woman's Christian Temperance Union failed in its mission. In fact, given the strength of the
customs it opposed, it is probably more accurate to say that the WCTU
succeeded, but on a much smaller scale than it had hoped.

For one thing, the WCTU, with some 200,000 members in every
state and territory and 10,000 local units, was the first company of re-

formers to make an impression on brewers and vintners and distillers. In previous years, these people had read of temperance activities with a grin or a yawn or a roll of the eyes, then tried to figure out how best to increase production to keep up with demand. They did not know the names of temperance advocates, did not bother with the specifics of their approaches; they certainly did not believe that the anti-imbibing cause was serious enough to merit real opposition.

But the WCTU frightened the booze barons; "organized mother love," as Willard referred to her group's guiding principle, was a more powerful threat to them than the occasional, disorganized shows of rebellion that had preceded it, and the barons reacted first by gathering information, then by organizing and spending money. Distillers, for instance, formed something called the National Protective Association, which "subsidized newspapers, subverted politicians and engineered fraudulent elections wherever a prohibitory amendment confronted the voters." The United States Brewers' Association also tried to manipulate public opinion, and by the first decade of the twentieth century would be charging its members 3 cents for each barrel of beer they produced, a total of almost three-quarters of a million dollars a year, the sum going to a war chest to fight the scourge called temperance.

The WCTU also succeeded, at least according to its own lights, by promoting the first real attempt at national prohibition, and working for a constitutional amendment to bring it about. It did not happen, not then at any rate, but the group's diligence was an inspiration to those who came after it, leading both women and men to believe that what had once seemed impossible was now merely difficult. The ladies also labored tirelessly on the state level. But fruitfully: by late in the nineteenth century, in large part because of WCTU efforts, three-fourths of all American states and territories had voted legislation to outlaw, or at least place limits on, the manufacture and sale of alcoholic beverages— this despite the best efforts of the brewing and distilling lobbies.

But just as important, if less quantifiable, the WCTU's agenda was so diverse—which is to say, so appealing to so many women in so many ways—that it helped to make activists out of females from all walks of life, something which no association of any kind had managed to do before, not in significant numbers. And Frances Willard and her compatriots did not just encourage women to enter the public arena; they made them believe that they were welcome, and that through their zeal and diligence they could influence the course of events. And Willard and her colleagues did not just teach catch phrases and exhortations; they shaped attitudes. They formed themselves into a tough-minded, smoothly running organization that was paid the ultimate compliment of being considered a threat by those who opposed its aims.

Temperance, in other words, as crucial as it was to the members of the Woman's Christian Temperance Union, was, seen retrospectively, just a starting point. "In the early days," as Gilbert Seldes wisely points out,

> nearly every item in the program of women's rights was approached on that side which bore a relation to drink. Women wanted to hold property so that the drunken father might not ruin their children. They wanted divorce made easier so that the virtuous wife might elude the drunken husband. They wanted to speak in public, to be lawyers and doctors and bankers, so that the drunkard in delirium tremens, or in his grave, might not leave the wife and mother penniless. They were interested in phrenology, and diet, and dress reform, and participated in most of the other movements of the time, but above everything was the dominating desire to destroy the demon Rum.

Eventually, most women came to decide that the best way to destroy it was to vote it out of existence, and from here they proceeded quickly and logically to the decision that the voting booth was the place to bring about the other reforms: property rights, divorce rights, employment opportunities. If there had been no temperance movement in the United States, the campaign for suffrage would still have begun and still have succeeded, but it almost surely would have been delayed, perhaps by a matter of decades, and it might not have been accepted so equally. Suffrage's foundation was temperance, and no structure remains standing for long unless the foundation is solid.

So solid, in fact, that the liquor interests intruded here as well. As Miriam Gurko reports, "They put pressure on Congressmen and state legislators, threatening to work at election time against those who supported woman suffrage. They warned all the businessmen and farmers who depended on the liquor industry—the coopers who made the barrels, the farmers who grew the grain, the railroad men who transported the liquor, the local dealers and saloon keepers who sold it—to work against suffrage and to keep their wives and daughters from joining suffrage organizations."

Further proof of how seriously the WCTU was taken comes from the number of influential members it attracted, women who contributed to the movement by making it at once more visible and respectable. Most of them operated on the local level, in their towns or counties or states, where they were the leaders of the community, the wives of the influential. One woman, though, transcended all boundaries but the oceans. She was Lucy Ware Webb Hayes, wife of President Rutherford B. Hayes, temperance's first female celebrity and the proud recipient of the nickname "Lemonade Lucy," which she earned by her refusal to serve alcoholic beverages at the White House, no matter what the occasion, no matter who was attending. Her husband, also an abstainer, gave his blessing.

But it was a controversial decision. Reporters muttered under their breaths; politicians complained more audibly. Both were used to copious amounts of high-proof refreshment at executive office functions; listening to their reactions to Mrs. Hayes's edict, one might have thought that what they drank was more important to them than what they reported and debated. Said one observer of the time, a frequent guest of the Hayeses and not a happy one, "At the White House, water flows like champagne."

Lemonade Lucy let them talk. She turned her back to her detractors and carried on with grace. "I have young sons who have never tasted liquor," she explained, as she was often asked to do and did without hesitation. "They shall not receive from my hand, or with the sanction that its use in the family would give, the first taste of what might prove their ruin. What I wish for my own sons I must do for the sons of other mothers."

Members of the White House staff, however, sensing the mood of discontent at social events within their walls, began to work around the First Lady. According to one story, a steward managed to concoct something called Roman punch, a blend of egg whites, sugar, lemon juice, and rum, the latter of which was slipped into the bowl without Mrs. Hayes's knowledge. The steward offered the beverage to the guests in glasses or, according to another story, froze it and concealed cubes of the libation in oranges, which were provided in plentitude for dessert. Either way, White House regulars were said to be desperately thankful for the punch and referred to the table at which it was served, with sincerity more than wit, as the "Life Saving Station."

It is not certain that Frances Willard abstained from alcoholic beverages all her life. Most accounts, especially those of her friends and associates, say she did. But historian Thomas R. Pegram thinks differently. "In the early 1870s," he writes, "Frances Willard, soon to become the chief symbol of female temperance, drank wine while traveling in Europe and took a daily medicinal glass of beer with dinner during a rocky tenure as a college dean."

Nor is it certain that she was a lesbian, at least not as we understand the term today. It seems just as likely that she was asexual, and derived her private satisfactions from the feeling of an idealized sisterhood. She might have lived with women in a kind of union that was referred to as a "Boston marriage," a pairing of females meant to satisfy the emotional needs of the participants rather than the physical. As the author Phyllis Rose points out, "such relationships were seen as healthy and useful" in the nineteenth century, and were not uncommon, especially in the wake of the Civil War, which had prematurely ended the lives of so many potential husbands and coarsened the outlooks of many other American males, making them undesirable companions for a lady of refinement.

Regardless, it cannot be denied that Willard's attachments to women were strong, and that she received as powerfully as she gave. Witness the following example, an excerpt from the introduction to Willard's book, *The Autobiography of An American Woman: Glimpses of Fifty Years.* The sentiments are those of Hannah Whitall Smith, a distinguished and respected lady, the mother-in-law of both Bertrand Russell and Bernard Berenson.

> There is a creature in the sea called the Octopus, with a very small body but with immense arms covered with suckers, radiating from every side, that stretch themselves out to indefinite length to draw in all sorts of prey. Miss Willard seems to have the same characteristic of being able to reach out mental or spiritual arms to indefinite lengths, whereby to draw in everything and everybody that seem likely to help on the cause she has at heart. Hence I, who have felt the grip of those arms of hers, have come to call her in our private moments, "My beloved Octopus," and myself her contented victim.

The problem with men, Willard told a reporter in the fullness of her years, was their habits. They smoked and drank, and it was this, more than anything else, she insisted, that kept the sexes apart, made truly meaningful communication impossible.

Don't women smoke and drink, too? the reporter asked.

They used to, Willard replied, but women had now evolved to a higher plane of existence; men, she predicted, would one day join them, although she could not say when, or whether she would welcome their eventual ascension.

It was, of course, an unrealized prophecy. Not only would men fail to rise; women would drop a few notches as the decades passed: smoking more, drinking more, and sampling a variety of other vices previously unknown to most and doing so in recklessly uninhibited fashion. Frances Willard never knew this, though, or else never admitted it to herself; there are truths that even reformers, *especially* reformers, cannot bear to acknowledge.

The end for her came in 1898. She was fifty-nine years old, and had spent so much of that time swimming upstream against society's tides that she had few resources left. She lay in bed one day, after several weeks of lessening vigor, unable to rise, unable even to focus on the latest edition of *The Union Signal*, the WCTU newspaper. "There came an intent upward gaze of the heavenly blues eyes," writes Anna Gordon, known to Willard as "Little Heart's Ease," one of a small battalion of women keeping an anxious vigil around her. Then, Gordon says, "there were a few tired sighs, and at the 'noon hour' of the night, Frances Willard was

> Born into beauty
> And born into bloom,
> Victor immortal
> O'er death and the tomb.

The WCTU lived on, but it was not the organization it used to be, and never would be again. Willard had not only been its leader, but was its very essence, the origin of its commitment; she was unique in both her devotion and her skill, and what is unique cannot be replaced. The group continued to swear by education, producing thousands of pages of do's and don't's for classrooms all over the United States, but it did not lobby as much as it once had for national prohibition. The rough-and-tumble world of politics, which had never appealed much to Willard, appealed even less to the post-Willard WCTU: all those sweaty men in their smoke-filled rooms, all that crude behavior and unseemly language, such malodorous bravado. In fact, Willard's successors came to believe more than ever that, if people were addressed calmly and guided properly—that is to say, if they learned their lessons, the *proper* lessons, well enough, at a young enough age—they would behave in a righteous manner without the threat of sanctions.

Long before Willard's death, however, there were other individuals and other groups taking a harder line, and it was they, not the Woman's Christian Temperance Union, who would lead the movement to its final reward.

6

Hatchetation

t is not easy to tell the truth about a legend. It is not easy to *know* the truth. Some of what has been written is falsehood and some is hyperbole and some is verifiable fact, and it can be difficult to distinguish among them. A legend serves the same purpose to those who chronicle it as a manikin does to a clothing designer; it provides a frame upon which the individual drapes his own materials for his own purposes, satisfying both himself and the marketplace. The goal is not accuracy so much as an eye-catching appearance.

This is especially true of the woman who stars in the present chapter, clomping across its pages in such brusque, melodramatic fashion. She was everything that a worldly man disdains, everything that a cultured lady ignores, everything for which a nonacademic historian longs, that he may provide his readers with a few moments of diversion from the rest of his tale, all the earnest strivings and carefully catalogued names and dates and places. Did the woman deserve to be disdained? Often. Did she deserve to be ignored? Never. Does she deserve to be explained? For a great number of reasons, perhaps most of all because she was uniquely, almost unpardonably, American.

She began life as Carry Amelia Moore, her first name spelled like the verb instead of the female because her father did not know any better. He was "a thoughtful but restless Irishman," it has been said, a cattle trader and tobacco farmer who had never spent much time in school. Some years later, tired of questions and wisecracks and puzzled expressions,

127

Nation changed the spelling herself to the more conventional Carrie. But by the turn of the twentieth century, having taken as her second husband a vagabond of a minister named David Nation and become convinced that alcoholic beverages were the express route to perdition, she returned to the original spelling, telling people that, as things turned out, her father had been prescient, not unlettered; her name was a sign that she had been put on this earth specifically to "carry a nation" for temperance.

Her first encounters with alcohol came as a young girl in her birthplace of Garrard County, Kentucky. She would sit at the breakfast table and watch her grandfather filling his tank for the day. As Nation later described the scene, the old man "put in a glass some sugar, butter and brandy, then poured hot water over it, and, while the family were sitting around the room, waiting for breakfast, he would go to each member, and give to those who wished a spoonful of this toddy, saying, 'Will you have a taste, my daughter, or my son?' "

But he was not as generous as he sounds. No one got more than a single spoonful from Grandpa, and he poured the rest of the cocktail—and a substantial quantity it was—down his own throat. Then he "went for a rather aimless ride on his horse, after being wrestled to the saddle by his colored servant, Patrick." Young Carry would look after him quizzically, asking herself why he seemed like one man before he drank and like another, far less pleasant sort by the time he mounted up. What was it about the toddy and why did he need it so badly?

Her mother, though, was the true character in the family, a woman so severely unbalanced that her delusions could have stocked an entire opium den without any help from the opium. Mrs. Moore suffered through, or perhaps enjoyed, several breaks with reality in the course of her lifetime, but the most pronounced came shortly after her daughter was born. For no reason that anyone can ascertain, she suddenly decided that she was royalty—and not just royalty in general, but a specific, flesh-and-blood monarch who was currently sitting on a throne across the sea and apparently doing so as an impostor. That high-minded, straight-laced, dour-faced woman in Buckingham Palace notwithstanding, *she*, Mrs. Mary Moore, Garrard County's own, was Her Royal Majesty, Queen Victoria of England!

Carry's mother felt the truth of this new identity in her bones, and wasted no time in revealing it. She spared neither expense nor effort, giving up her gingham dresses and donning purple robes, putting aside her cotton bonnets and fitting herself with a crystal and cut-glass tiara. And sometimes, all done up in her regal finery, Mrs. Moore would venture out into backwoods Kentucky to inspect her domain in a carriage drawn by silver-caparisoned horses. On one of these tours, says Nation's biographer Robert Lewis Taylor, she was preceded by her husband's "choicest slave, a giant called Big Bill," who wore "a scarlet hunting coat" and carried "a brass hunting horn" to announce his royal mistress.

> [She] set off to call on the King of Belgium, but failed—could not, in fact, locate the palace—and on another she bawled out the Duke of Buckingham, who was hoeing a patch of onions. She knighted three or four farmers, one of whom struck back, and stripped an itinerant tinker of all his lands in Sussex. The man's first reaction was good-humored, not to say bawdy, but he later threatened to take her into court and get the property back.

The queen's paraphernalia, the crown and robes and horses, were provided by her husband, who had been selling more cattle and tobacco than usual of late, turning a nice profit, and who, although quite baffled by his mate's masquerades, spent his money so cheerfully on them that today's psychobabblers would dismiss him out of hand as an enabler. To Carry, not burdened with such insights, he was the best father imaginable. "I have met many men who had lovable characters," she later wrote, "but none equaled him in my estimation. He was not a saint, but a man—one of the noblest works of God."

His wife thought highly of him, too; she named him Prince Consort.

In time, Carry became weary of palace life and began to keep to herself. She left home for a while to serve as a nurse in the Civil War and finally decided on a permanent escape at age nineteen by marrying a veteran named Charles Gloyd, a doctor who "was as much scholar as physician, and spoke and read several languages." Gloyd had decided to give up medicine to become a schoolteacher, and met his intended when he arranged for room and board at the Moore residence shortly before taking up his first position in the classroom.

In addition, he met the queen, who was troubled by Gloyd from the outset, and not just because of his status as commoner. She sensed in him both an undercurrent of violence and a disregard for the teachings of the church. She warned her daughter that a union with such a man could not possibly come to any good. In fact, "she issued a royal ban against his speaking to Carry; also, the two were prohibited from being alone together in a room. The decree set up an awkward situation; the house was of limited size, and the young pair often had to skirmish, with quick dashes and sorties, to avoid finding themselves *tete-a-tete* in an unoccupied chamber."

But the monarch's daughter, headstrong even then, did not listen. She and her intended set a date and went through with the ceremony as planned, young Carry Moore becoming a Gloyd and eagerly anticipating a new life in different, more romantic places.

Her mother, though, was right. It seemed that the groom had long been a heavy drinker, addicted to the bottle before the war broke out and driven deeper into liquid dependency by his experiences under fire. He even showed up in an inebriated state for his nuptials, so much so that his breath reeked and his skin was flushed and he could barely remain upright, teetering as the preacher asked for his responses and uttering them thickly. Later in the day, after continuing to imbibe and almost passing out two or three times, Gloyd regained enough control of himself to impregnate his new wife. Then he collapsed in a heap and was out for the rest of the night.

His bride, on the other hand, barely slept at all, and we may imagine her terror: a young woman lying in a marriage bed for the first time next to a vile stranger who smelled of decay and indifference and had handled her roughly, the darkness in the room seeming to shut her off from all that she had ever known and perhaps all she had ever dreamed. She was no longer a child, nor merely a daughter; she could not go home again. But she did not feel like a wife, and was all of a sudden aghast at the prospect of a new home with the unconscious hulk beside her, this Charles Gloyd fellow. She must have cried, shuddered; what should have been a glorious beginning had turned out to be a defilement, and it was unlikely that the dawn would bring any relief.

In the weeks following, Gloyd drank even harder. For one thing, it was what he did, the way he spent his time. For another, he seems to have been traumatized by his hasty marriage, giving every sign of regretting it as much as his wife did. It was he who came up with a solution, though, by pickling his innards so much that he collapsed again, this time into a fatal heap, dropping dead a mere six months after the couple had taken their vows. Three months later, a daughter was born to his widow. Carry called her Charlien, and loved her all the more for the vile shortcomings of her father.

It was not easy. Charlien was a trial, a child who needed constant care, a nurse as much as a mother, and even then she could not have been saved. She grew up to be a psychotic, "a wretched girl [who] was in and out of . . . institutions, took to drink, became cured, developed 'chronic mania,' suffered a relapse and made what her mother declared was an authentic recovery in 1910."

But in the beginning, her body tormented her even more than her mind. As a toddler, Charlien developed a sore on the inside of her cheek which eventually ate its way through the skin and left her face a hideous sight, her teeth exposed like those of a skeleton. Several painful operations, spread over much of her adolescence, managed to close the hole, but in the process, for reasons not entirely clear to doctors, her jaws locked shut. They stayed that way for almost eight years. During that time, Charlien took her nourishment through a metal tube, which could be inserted only by knocking out several of her front teeth.

Her mother kept on loving her, though: praying for her, paying her medical bills as best she could, and complaining only in private moments and then almost immediately afterward feeling guilty. But a rage was building in Carry Nation, something powerful and formative; the worse Charlien got, the more Carry blamed her departed spouse. A sober man's seed, she believed, would never have produced so troubled an offspring. First her grandfather at the breakfast table, then Gloyd on his wedding day—what was it, she asked herself, about men and their demonic thirsts?

When Charlien was eleven and at last approaching physical normality, her mother married again, this time hooking up with David Nation, an itinerant preacher who was nineteen years older than his bride and as unpromising in his own ways as Gloyd was in his. A photograph of the time "reveals what on first glance appears to be a shifty Old-Testament prophet dressed in a high-crowned black hat and a funereal, ill-fitting mail order black suit. He wears a long white beard that straggles down offensively over his cravat, his eyes have the self-righteous grimness of a man about to set up a lynching and his mouth is a downturned crescent of autocracy, bitterness and disappointment." So pronounced Carry's biographer, Taylor, almost a century later.

But the bride saw none of it, and without the powers of hindsight there might in fact have been nothing to see. Carry's second husband was not the irresponsible specter of a man that the first had been, and a shifty Old Testament prophet was a major improvement on a shifty Civil War vet with the devil's own taste in beverages. Had David Nation been married before? What of it? So had his wife. Perhaps it meant that both were less likely to repeat their previous mistakes.

With Charlien in tow, the newly constructed family hit the road, living an almost nomadic existence, village-hopping through the Bible Belt for several years—renting a tiny house in one town, a room or two over a dry-goods merchant in the next—until finally alighting in the small community of Medicine Lodge, Kansas, in 1898. There, David Nation told Carry that he had had enough; it was time to settle down, establish roots, become a part of something permanent. He would preach or teach or something else of a sedentary nature; she was to stay home and engage herself in the tasks that the Lord had intended for the daily routine of a man's wife: cooking the meals, washing the clothes, cleaning the house. The Nation family, said its patriarch, would finally get conventional.

The matriarch shook her head. She told him he could not have come up with a worse idea if he had been husband number one working on his fatal drunk. She, too, had come to a decision about the course that life should take, and housewifery was not part of it. Henceforth, this woman who had known so much misfortune of her own would try to protect others from a similar fate; this woman who had seen firsthand what strong beverage could do would try to shield the vision of others. She would immerse herself in the good works and noble purposes of the Woman's Christian Temperance Union, and single-handedly raise the group to a new prominence. She might be a different sort from Frances Willard, who would in fact pass away that very year, but she defined evil in the same way, and shared Willard's belief that it was the male of the species, so consumed by lechery and the wantonness of thirst, who more often than not brought it about. Carry Nation was a few months shy of her fifty-third birthday and ready for action.

Theoretically, the Barber County chapter of the WCTU should not have existed. It should not have been needed. Kansas was legally dry at the time and had been since 1880, when it became the first state to prohibit alcoholic beverages after the Civil War. The vote was over-whelming; it was God-and-country temperance all over again, and this time, its supporters vowed, it would not be waylaid by either events or indifference.

But the law was flouted at least as often as it was obeyed, and Nation took the offenses personally. She not only helped to found the Medicine

Lodge chapter of the WCTU; she became its president, and immediately decided that her minions had to change their method of operation, to forget about all those lessons in the schoolroom and start making some lessons available in the street. This is a reform group, she told her followers; time to get out there and start reforming.

She began by following the lead of the Women's Crusade, praying at the doors of the Medicine Lodge saloons. Sometimes Nation went alone; more often a few of the WCTU's bolder members accompanied her, although they usually stood in the background—and in almost no time she became the town's leading curiosity. People stopped, looked, listened; they did not quite know what to make of this newcomer to their town, so aggressive was she at a time when women were supposed to be submissive. After a while, Nation started bringing her hand organ with her, and stationing herself as close to the saloon as she could without actually crossing the threshold, she would break into song, accompanying herself to "Nearer, My God, to Thee" or "The Prodigal Son" or another number, the title unknown, whose verse went,

> Touch not, taste not, handle not,
> Drink will make the dark, dark blot.

The hour of day did not matter, nor did the day of the week nor season of the year. Weather, alignment of planets, larger issues in the world around her such as war and peace, poverty and plenty—all irrelevant. If the drinking establishments were open, the president of the Medicine Lodge chapter of the Woman's Christian Temperance Union was planted in front of them, each in its turn, her visage set in a harrumph, making that pointedly purposeful music of hers, speaking her prayers loudly enough to be heard inside almost every business in town, not just the barrooms.

And neglecting—oh, so sorely neglecting—the care of her husband's wardrobe and domicile.

Her commitment made Nation an instant hero to the forces of abstention all through Barber County. They had never seen anyone like her before, and could not believe how fortunate they were to have so primal a force of nature so resolutely in their camp. More and more of them joined her on saloon duty, and those who did not—and there were many who lacked the courage, or perhaps the theatrical flair—stopped her on the streets to congratulate her or wrote her notes of support.

One Sunday, strolling into church just moments before the service began, she found herself on the receiving end of a standing ovation.

But she was restless, unsatisfied. It was not that she longed for more acclaim; she does not seem to have been the victim of a conventional ego, although the unmistakable signs of it would appear later in her career. What she wanted now was a world in which fewer human beings drank alcoholic beverages and, as a result, caused hardship and deprivation for others, especially women and children. To accomplish this, she decided, she would have to confront the law-breaking booze-swillers of Medicine Lodge head-on, not by way of overheard words to the Almighty. She would have to show them the depth of her zeal, the breadth of her anger and disregard. She could not do this with a script; the prayers she spoke were neither fiery nor specific enough. It was time to start ad-libbing from the heart.

"Rum-soaked rummy!" she began to holler at the patrons who dared to enter saloons while she stood watch.

"Ally of Satan!" she would scream at others.

"Makers of widows!" she bellowed at still more.

The lady was indomitable. Pug-faced, almost six feet tall and more often than not dressed in the cold black of an avenging angel, Carry Nation backed down to no living person, male or female. In fact, in a few years more she would even storm into the training camp of John L. Sullivan and try to knock the heavyweight boxing champion of the world to the canvas, or at least to reason with him, because he drank so much beer during workouts. So, at any rate, it was reported. But, according to biographer Taylor, when Nation appeared at the entrance to the camp,

> Sullivan retreated to the rear. In the presence of reporters, the crusader permitted herself a string of essentially masculine epithets and dared the giant to come out. Puzzled bystanders agreed that the implication was that, in any bare-knuckle fight, she could beat him to a pulp. Sullivan, a gentleman behind the façade of beer fumes, declined to be drawn from his lair, upon which Mrs. Nation made the open declaration that he was yellow.

It was understandable, then, that lightweights and middleweights and other lesser forms of male would cower before Nation, and decide, when she showed up at their favorite gin mills, that their thirsts could best be alleviated in some other way or in some other establishment or at some other time. Even men who defied her and stayed to throw down their shots and inhale their drafts anyhow found that her presence outside the saloon doors cast a pall on the atmosphere; they could not addle their brains with the peace of mind they usually enjoyed, knowing that so unforgiving a presence waited to harangue them when they finally departed. Carry Nation was, often literally, a sobering influence.

Yet she was still not content, and it was as simple as this: Kansans continued to drink; she must be doing something wrong. But what? It was a mystery to her, and more than that, a curse. She did not lack energy, did not lack resolve, did not lack courage; she did not, in other words, lack any of the ingredients that normally led to the realization of any goal a person might set for herself. She said her prayers, respected her elders, looked after her child.

But perhaps, she came to decide, there *was* something missing: a proper stage, the kind of platform that would enable her to attract a larger audience and the influence that would undoubtedly come with it. She might be doing everything right after all; she just might be doing it in the wrong place.

So it was that on a mild spring day in 1900, the sky milky above her and the sun indecisive, Carry Nation arose early, careful not to disturb her husband, and sneaked out of town in the family wagon. Her destination: "the harmless, half-asleep town of Kiowa, twenty-five miles distant," on the border that Kansas shared with the Oklahoma territory. It seemed that a few weeks earlier, Nation had heard a voice in the middle of the night. She took it to be God, and the instructions He gave her were clear. "Go to Kiowa!" He said, as Nation later told the tale. "Take something in your hands, throw it at those places and smash them."

So she did. Using the stones, bricks, bottles, and pieces of wood and scrap metal that she had loaded into the wagon before departing, Nation reduced almost every grogshop in Kiowa to the kind of rubble normally associated with far more sophisticated weapons. She flung, heaved, hacked, whipped, grated, chopped, sliced, diced, minced, and practically pureed. Drinkers ran for cover; saloonkeepers roared in fury and bewilderment, but do not seem to have fought back. Kiowa's teetotalers stood on the sidelines, bewildered themselves but undeniably pleased; they rooted for Nation until their voices squeaked and rasped and finally gave out. A force of nature indeed, and without doubt on the side of the just.

At one watering hole, Nation knocked the bottles off the shelves behind the bar by firing one rock after another at them, like a fellow at a shooting gallery at the county fair, trying to win a kewpie doll for his best gal. Pieces of glass flew in all directions; streams of booze ran freely, making a waterfall as they gushed from the shelves and across the bartop and stools to the floor.

At another saloon, this one owned by a man named Lewis, Nation

> ran out of armament when the place was little more than two-thirds down in ruins, and the logistical failure appeared to drive her berserk. It was a minute or two before she spotted, and seized up, the billiard balls from Lewis's recreation area, and as she did so, a boy of about fifteen tried to scuttle from a foxhole near the bar to a position of improved camouflage. Mrs. Nation fired a bowling ball at his head, missing only by inches. . . . Then she overturned several tables—swiped them aside with one arm— kicked the rungs from a dozen chairs, pulled all fixtures from their moorings, booted a cuspidor over a black iron stove, and, as before, smashed the expensive front windows.

Back in Medicine Lodge on this day, David Nation woke up alone. He got out of bed, looked around for his wife, could not find her. He walked through the house with a puzzled expression on his face. He prepared his own breakfast, not happily, and wondered where his Carry had gone.

After visiting a few more joints in Kiowa and achieving similar results, Nation found herself confronted by the mayor of the fair town along with the marshal and several members of the council. They were not happy. In fact, they threatened the intruder with jail, explaining that the destruction of property was also prohibited by law. Nation explained right back. Alcoholic beverages were also prohibited by law; surely they were aware of that. "Men of Kiowa," she continued, "I have destroyed three of your places of business! If I have broken a statute of Kiowa, put me in jail. If I am not a lawbreaker, your Mayor and Councilmen are. You must arrest one of us."

She had a point, and after she made it she wiped her hands on her dress as if to be rid of Kiowa once and for all. Then she gave the town fathers one last icy look and walked away. No one stopped her, nor did anyone go to jail, not on this occasion, although Nation would later reckon that she had been incarcerated some thirty-three times in her life for a total of 170 days, and was once treated so shabbily that she "was not allowed a pillow; I begged for one, for I had La Grippe, and my head was as sore as a boil."

The mayor, though, fumed. He shook his fist at Nation's back as she made her exit and warned her never to set foot in his town again. She did not even turn around to acknowledge him. She had done what she set out to do and that was that; she climbed up into her wagon for the trip home with conscience clear and head unbowed. "Peace on earth," she shouted, urging her horse forward, her wheels spinning out dust, "goodwill to men!"

Many years later, she would reflect on the siege of Kiowa, and what it meant not only to her but to others. "The first smashing was like the opening of a battle," she wrote, obviously believing that she had won. It "resounded o'er the land a talisman of destruction to the liquor traffic."

Back in Medicine Lodge a few days later, Nation dropped into a hardware store. She might have been looking for something in particular; she might have been just idly browsing—but after a few minutes she turned the corner of an aisle and, seeing a display of hatchets before her, stopped and took it in. She picked up one of the instruments and held it in her hands, getting the heft of it; perhaps she tapped the side of the blade on a shelf to affirm its solidity. She might even have swung it a time or two, adjusting her grip, trying to determine the proper angle of attack. As for the proper *object* of attack, she seems already to have decided.

No one knows precisely what she felt at the moment, but it must have been very similar to what Tony Gwynn felt the first time he picked up a baseball bat—a perfect mating of person and object, of objective and means. Did Nation hear another celestial voice? Did she feel a renewed sense of mission? Had she at last found that missing piece of the puzzle? We are told only that she bought the hatchet, and within a matter of days headed out of Medicine Lodge again, sights firmly set on the big time.

At the turn of the century, Wichita was the second largest but most rip-roaring city in all of Kansas, the best irrigated oasis in the entire, nominally dry state. "Forty-odd joints ran openly with no concealment other than curtained windows and doors," it has been written. "Each displayed a modest sign, 'Sample Room,' the current cryptogram for saloon, especially in dry territory. A few more were operated in conjunction with eating places. Another reason Wichita attracted Mrs. Nation was that a majority of Kansas wholesale liquor dealers had their warehouses there."

Attracting—or, more appropriately, repelling—Nation all the more was the city's homonymously named Hotel Carey, one of the finest drinking establishments anywhere in the Midwest, a place both elegant and boisterous, where the swells brushed elbows with the hoi-polloi and the old-timers with the newcomers, and everybody seemed to find everybody else an indispensable part of the atmosphere.

The place was a landmark, a magnet for visitors whether they stayed there or not, and the special attraction was the bar. Even nondrinkers would stand in the doorway on occasion and peek in, admiring the materials and workmanship, if not the purpose. It "was more than fifty feet long, gracefully curved, made of gleaming cherry wood rubbed, always, to a high polish by proud attendants who felt that there was no place like a home-away-from-home. The brass rail, the cut-glass decanters, the enormous museum-piece mirror, the cherry tables—all were spotless."

Until Nation got there. "Smash! Smash! For Jesus' sake, smash!" she roared, and having looped her pursestrap through her belt to keep her hands free, she descended upon the Hotel Carey and took her new blade to it like a swatter to a horde of suddenly sluggish flies. With the very first swing she could tell that the hatchet was a better medium for her message than her previous armaments. It was faster and sharper; it broke things into smaller, less repairable pieces, and it seemed, by its exceedingly menacing appearance, to reduce the odds of violent reprisal to almost zero. Another advantage, as Gilbert Seldes has pointed out, was that the hatchet could be wielded again and again, never leaving Nation's hands, whereas a stone or brick or bottle or billiard ball, "however effective, could only be used once; when she ran out of ammunition, she had to retreat." In other words, the hatchet was an automatic weapon, at least as employed by the Medicine Lodge marauder.

And she could not have been more pleased. "God gave Samson the jawbone!" she explained at a later date. "He gave David the sling, and he has given Carry Nation the hatchet!"

After wrapping things up at Wichita's premier hotel and drinking den, which was now no longer so premier, Nation tiptoed out of the wreckage and moved on to venues of more modest appointment, delivering one unbidden encore after another. She scattered customers, battered tables, slivered bars, shredded glasses, decapitated stools, pulverized windows, bashed in gaslights, launched ash trays into suborbital flight, and in one place, absolutely enraged, ripped down a sign that said: "All Nations Welcome But Carry."

But it was not just alcoholic beverages that enraged her, nor the men who so selfishly and self-destructively lapped them up. In some cases it was the view, the images that assailed her as she thundered through the doors of iniquity. She describes one such image as follows:

> The first thing that struck me was the life-size picture of a naked woman, opposite the mirror. . . . I called to the bartender; told him he was insulting his own mother by having her form stripped naked and hung up in a place where it was not even decent for a woman to be when she had her clothes on. . . . It is very significant that the pictures of naked women are in saloons. Women are stripped of everything by them. Her husband is torn from her, she is robbed of her sons, her home, her food and her virtue, and then they strip her clothes off and hang her up bare in these dens of robbery and murder. Truly does a saloon make a woman bare of all things.

It was an eloquent plea, and Nation followed it in some saloons by yanking such pictures off the walls. In others, she ripped them from their frames and tore them to bits, or applied her hatchet to them and hacked them into unrecognizable strips, like pieces of fabric that had been shredded by an animal's teeth. She had an abiding sense of dignity, did this large and fearsome woman; when it was offended, she reacted in a most undignified manner.

With daughter Charlien as an ever-present reminder of the wages of copulation, Nation had no patience for anything that even suggested so debasing a deed. Sometimes on her saloon-hopping forays she would run into couples embracing in public. Her pulse would thump, her blood pressure soar. She would whack the offending lovers with her hatchet handle or an umbrella or some other object easily at hand, and consign them to the raging furnaces of eternal damnation. She thought of it as a public service. She did not tell them why she felt so strongly.

From Wichita, Nation advanced to several other locations in Kansas, small towns and large, the latter including the second best-irrigated oasis, Topeka, where, in the dead of winter, she was joined by two other hatchet-wielding females.

> The three raiders plodded through the deepening snow across Kansas Avenue, to note there were no guards on duty at the elegant entrance to the Senate Bar, Topeka's finest drinking establishment. Whereupon Mrs. Nation, Mrs. White, and Miss Southard pushed open the door and entered without disturbing Benner Tucker, the popular and efficient bartender, who was busy polishing glasses. He became aware of his visitors when he heard pounding and the tinkle of breaking glass.

Bartenders in other gin mills heard the same sounds, and they and their patrons ran for cover. Newspaper reporters, meanwhile, were running in Nation's direction. They were the staff aces, the front page stars, the kings and queens of coverage, and they raced to the scenes of carnage with pencils pointed like stilettos and they wrote and wrote until their fingers were sore and the lead was blunt. Never before had the press paid so much attention to temperance; never before had one of its advocates been such good copy. Carry Nation was like an athlete who not only performs physical feats of remarkable aplomb, but can talk about them afterward with exuberance and wit.

In fact, her reputation was by now such that a man named Ed Blair wrote a poem about her. He called it "She's Coming on the Freight, or, The Joint Keeper's Dilemma." It is reprinted here in full, which is precisely what Nation did with it in her autobiography.

> Say, Billy, git ten two-by-four
>   'Nd twenty six-by-eight
> 'Nd order from the hardware store
>   Ten sheets of boiler plate,
> 'Nd phone the carpenter to come
>   Most might quick—don't wait,
> For there's a story on the streets
>   She's comin' on the freight.
>
> O, many years I've carried on
>   My business in this town;
> I've helped elect its officers
>   From Mayor Dram clear down;
> I've let policemen, fer a wink
>   Get jags here every day;
> Say, Billy, get a move on, fer
>   She's headed right this way.
>
>
> I don't mind temp'rance meetin's
>   When they simply resolute,
> Fer all their efforts bring
>   But mighty little fruit;
> But when crowbars and hatchets
>   'Nd axes fill the air—
> Say, Billy, git the boiler iron
>   Across the window there!
>
> It beats the nation—no, I think
>   The Nation's beatin' me,

When I can pay a license here
  'Nd still not sell it free;
Fer I must keep my customers
  Outside 'nd make 'em wait,
Because the story's got around
  She's comin' on the freight.

There, Billy, now we've got her—
  Six-eights across the door,
'Nd solid half-inch boiler iron
  Where plate glass showed before;
But, Bill, before that freight arrives
  Ye'd better take a pick
'Nd pry that cellar window loose,
  So we can get out quick.

By this time, Nation had attracted an informal cadre of followers, groupies, not large in number but every bit as fevered as their leader. Some of them adopted her techniques, practiced them in their own communities, going off on rampages of their own in the belief that it was all to the greater good of society. And now those techniques had a name—hatchetation, which is what Nation called her unique style of temperance promotion. Leaving Kansas to her subordinates, she proceeded to hatchetate in such faraway places as Des Moines, St. Louis, Chicago, Detroit, and eventually Philadelphia, Atlantic City, and even New York, where the recently retired heavyweight champ, John L. Sullivan, was running a saloon. "If she comes to my place," he is supposed to have said to a newspaperman, hearing of his bete noire's proximity, "I'll throw her down the sewer."

Learning of the statement, the temperance bandita smiled. As far as she was concerned, Sullivan was not threatening her so much as issuing an invitation. She accepted it. She made straight for the ex-champ's lair, threw open the door, and stormed in, telling the bartender to summon her boss. She put her hands on her hips, tapped her foot on the floor.

The bartender went upstairs to Sullivan's office.

Nation waited.

The men on the barstools and in the booths grew suddenly quiet, sipping their brews and whiskeys nervously, looking at one another out of the corners of their eyes, and wondering what would happen.

Nation waited some more.

There was a clock on the back wall of the place, near the cash register, and the hands slogged their way around it.

Finally the bartender returned with a message. "Tell her I'm sick in bed," Sullivan had told him to say, and he did not come downstairs; in fact, he did not appear again in his own place of business until Nation had departed, furious at the old boxer's cowardice yet as pleased as could be with her own performance.

But that was the problem. It *was* a performance. Almost everything she did these days was a performance, the spontaneity having long since gone out of her saloon-wrecking, mainly because so many stories had been written about her over the years and so many people had read them and formed expectations about her and forced her to feel the pressure of living up to them. Nation had read the stories too, and could not help but become self-conscious about the woman they portrayed. The result was that she had inadvertently begun to parody herself, to *do* Carry Nation rather than to *be* Carry Nation. She knew what was happening, but the awareness only puzzled and disappointed her; it did not lead to a solution.

Moreover, Nation did not fare as well in the cities of the East as she had in the smaller towns and villages of the heartland. In New York and Philadelphia and Atlantic City, there were few if any laws to restrict alcoholic beverages; this meant that, instead of swinging her blade, which would have put her behind bars, Nation had to resort to verbal havoc, which in turn meant that she was far more likely to be ridiculed than feared. She huffed and puffed, ranted and raved, but could accomplish nothing except her own particular brand of burlesque. Soon the newspapers began to cover her with their humorists instead of their top newshounds, thereby guaranteeing the ridicule and slowly but surely breaking Nation's heart. There is no more effective way to neutralize a zealot; she does not mind infuriating people, even sets out to do it, but she cannot survive the laughter bred of disdain.

Also in the East, Nation became troubled by what she perceived as a lack of support from headquarters. The Woman's Christian Temperance Union had long been of divided opinion about its most famous member: skittish as to her means, admiring of her results. On a more personal level, she was just not the kind of woman with whom Frances Willard and her genteel circle would have socialized, not even the kind they were comfortable acknowledging. An editorial in *The Union Signal* came as close to endorsement as Nation ever got, saying that she has a method all her own, and one which is not found in the plan of work of the W.C.T.U. . . . whose weapons . . . are not carnal but spiritual. While we cannot advise the use of force . . . we are awake to the fact that Mrs. Nation's hatchet has done more to frighten the liquor sellers and awaken the sleeping consciences of Kansas voters than the entire official force of the state has heretofore done.

But the editorial concluded, regretfully, that "more harm than good must always result from lawless methods."

It certainly appeared that way, for consciences soon dozed again, perhaps falling into a deeper slumber than ever. It was the same thing that had happened to the Women's Crusade; within a few days of Nation's cyclonic passage through either city or hamlet, rebuilding would begin. Saloons with which she had had her way were repaired, or if the damage had been too great, replaced by new ones; and those that had closed out of fear or prudence before she arrived—a substantial number—opened again confidently.

At most of these places, business was just as good after Nation's blitzkrieg as it had been previously, and sometimes even better, for the hatchetater's visit made the establishment a tourist attraction at the same time that it elicited a healthy outpouring of sympathy for the owner, who thus became, at least for a time, a local luminary. As for the reassembling of the clientele, it was not just a joyful occasion; it was like a reunion of war buddies. The men returned to the joints and shook hands and hugged one another and shared impressions of the terror that was Carry Nation, swapping tales of the hardships to which she had subjected them. Then they laughed, sighed, and clinked glasses, drinking up as if tomorrow might never come. They were brothers in adversity, soulmates in survival, former inmates of the foxhole.

And so Nation discovered what so many other people of radical persuasion had learned before her: a reformer leaves few monuments that the ways of mortal man and woman do not quickly erode. Her father's spelling was a mistake after all. Her best efforts to the contrary, she could *not* carry a nation for temperance.

Still, as the twentieth century slid through its first decade, she entered her declining years in good cheer, continuing to take pleasure in describing herself as a "bulldog, running along at the feet of Jesus, barking at what He doesn't like." What with frequent lectures, newspapers she published called *The Smasher's Mail* and *The Hatchet*, and a ragingingly pro-self autobiography called *The Use and Need of the Life of Carry A. Nation*, the lady was making more money than ever before, and was no less fervent than she had been back in Medicine Lodge. She was, however, almost entirely the performer now.

And she added to her earnings, if detracting from her credibility, by selling autographed pictures of herself. Some were conventional head-and-shoulders shots; others were staged action poses, Nation pretending to lower her trusty blade on a saloon door, her face a mirror of pious vituperation. These moved so well that she soon expanded the line to include tiny souvenir hatchets. The price for the latter was a dime at first, then a quarter, and finally, when the traffic would bear it, fifty cents. She told her customers that, in addition to being poignant reminders of a holy cause, they made wonderful lapel pins.

She reminds one, at this stage of her life, of the has-been comedians and over-the-hill actors of today who peddle merchandise to which they have attached their names on the Home Shopping Network, or some other outpost of low-end cable television. They make money, although most of them have a lot of it already; they surrender self-respect, although they seldom realize it, assuming that visibility, regardless of the surroundings, confers a certain status in the eyes of those who watch. But Nation's fate was sadder than theirs. The comedians and actors were in show biz to begin with; Nation was a woman who believed that her calling was divinely inspired.

But if the reformer forfeited her pride, she did not give up her humanity. She had always been a compassionate woman beneath the bluster—the bluster, in fact, was her means of enforcing compassion—and she took advantage of her late-blooming prosperity to buy a home in Kansas City, Kansas, for the wives and widows of drunkards. "In the first years, when the idea seemed novel (and the quarters regally comfortable), wives flocked in by the score," writes Robert Lewis Taylor, and Nation provided them with shelter, counseling, and hope, each an indispensable item for women in their position. It was one of the first places of its kind in the United States, and although Nation could afford to keep it open for only a few years, she was responsible for either saving or enriching the life of virtually every woman who stepped through its door.

Eventually, though, her name began to fade. The public memory is a short one, and when too much time has elapsed between a celebrity's glory days and the present, newcomers step in to usurp the spotlight.

Nation's last appearances were in carnivals, where she shared the attention spans of passersby with the strong man and the rubber man and the tattooed lady. In settings as absurd as these, her fulminations against demon rum played more comically than ever, as a kind of vocal slapstick. She was one more booth in the sideshow, one more stop along the midway. She was trying to be true to herself, yet there were so few ways remaining.

Her last public pronouncement, or at least the last one to be recorded and entered in the histories, came in the wake of President William McKinley's assassination in 1901. She applauded it. McKinley, she believed, although apparently without evidence, had been a closet tosspot, and those people always got what they deserved. Had she still mattered to people, her words would have caused an uproar. As it was, few people paid attention, and even fewer bothered to comment.

Her marriage was long over by this time. David Nation did not get around to divorcing his wife until 1902, but he had stopped living with her many years before and given up on the relationship well before that. He was bitter about the circumstances. "My life has been made miserable by this woman," he told the *Topeka Journal*, "who means no good in this world. She has robbed me of all my happiness, and dragged my name, along with hers, down to the mire of notoriety. . . . She smashed all those saloons against my advice and she alone is to blame for the punishment she has received. I want nothing more to do with her. I am done with her."

David Nation wanted obscurity. He got it. Once he removed himself from his wife, he faded almost entirely from history's view.

As for Charlien, she endured a wildly alternating cycle of good years and bad, and had eventually come to reside at the State Lunatic Asylum in Austin, Texas. Nation was livid about it. She did everything she could to win her daughter's release, in the process angering not only asylum officials, but Charlien's husband, one Alexander McNabb, whom the bride had met and lured to the altar during one of her good years. He loved her, he claimed, and wanted to remain her man no matter what, but even he had come to believe that an asylum was the best place for this poor, tortured soul. He pleaded with her mother to leave her there and simply visit from time to time, as he was planning to do.

Nation refused. She wanted Charlien out in the world, and eventually her efforts succeeded. The young woman was released into her mother's custody in 1910, never again to reside within padded walls, although, as might be expected, never to function as a completely normal human being, either. It is not known what happened to McNabb at this point.

It was also in 1910 that Nation entered a gin mill with mayhem on her mind for the final time. The city: Butte, Montana. The joint: May Maloy's Dance Hall & Café. Nation strode through the door "with the avowed intention to destroy a painting, and was met at the entrance by the proprietor herself, a young and powerful woman, who went hammer-and-tongs at the astonished crusader. The encounter was brief, terrible, and one-sided. The old champ went down, and went away to Arkansas."

In the first week of June in the following year, five months after having suffered a stroke and sixty-four years after her birth, Carry Nation died of "nervous trouble" at the Evergreen Hospital in Leavenworth, Kansas. She was asleep at the time and there was no flock of fluttering gentle-ladies at her bedside with hankies in hand and poetry books open across their laps. Nor was there a friend of long standing to remark on the trajectory of a life, to try to understand the connection between beginning and end and make sense of the steps between. And there was no one to say that, considering all she had been through as a child and a young bride, Carry Nation probably deserved more credit for her kindness and lucidity than she did blame for her outrageousness.

She was buried, according to her own instructions, next to her mother, the former queen of England, in the small town of Belton, Missouri. But so controversial had Nation become that not until the following decade would the people of Belton see fit to mark her grave, and even then it was done grudgingly, after much debate. The granite shaft finally erected bore a sentiment that did not run to excess.

CARRY A. NATION
Faithful to the Cause of Prohibition
"She Hath Done What She Could"

Nation remained controversial among members of the Woman's Christian Union as well. At the end of the twentieth century, when President Sarah F. Ward published a history of the group's first 125 years, Nation's name did not appear even once.

1

The Wheeler-Dealer
and His Men

Gradually, almost imperceptibly, women were losing control. They were falling back to the periphery of the temperance movement, becoming second-class citizens for a second time. They had had their day, had tried their methods, had fallen short of their goals. The public schools were still teaching WCTU lessons, but not enough people seemed to be heeding them; national prohibition was no closer to reality than it had ever been, and state and local legislators seemed to be repealing antibooze bills as often as they were passing them, finding that it was too much trouble to make them work.

More important, Americans were not only continuing to raise their glasses and empty their bottles, but were picking up the pace. In 1878, per capita consumption of alcohol was eight gallons; twenty years later it stood at seventeen. There were more saloons than ever before, more rowdy patrons, more violent behavior and arrests for drunkenness, and more suffering families.

And so the men took over the movement once more, and never again would they relinquish control. But they had paid attention to their predecessors and had learned from them; they would know what to do in the future and what to avoid. They would be more subtle in their tactics than Carry Nation; more single-minded in their approach, and less reliant on education, than the Woman's Christian Temperance

Union; and, unlike the Prohibition Party, they would work within the framework of the existing two-party system. They would seek guidance and support from the Almighty, as the women had done for so many years, but no less would they align themselves with the power brokers of the earth.

Yet they would not fail to give the women credit for what they had accomplished, and would come to believe that their most important contribution might simply have been their persistence. True, many people of both genders laughed at Carry Nation and Frances Willard and Mrs. George Carpenter and Elizabeth Jane Trimble Thompson and the rest of them, but at the same time they could not help but admire their dedication, not to mention the courage they displayed on an almost daily basis. At a time when most females humbly accepted the roles assigned to them by a male-dominated society, the women of the temperance movement took another path, not only expressing their beliefs but fighting for them, and not only fighting for them but returning to the fray time and again, often in the wake of humiliating defeats.

As a result, the Women's Crusade and the WCTU had resurrected the issue of alcohol abuse after what seemed to be the death knell of the Civil War, and they kept the issue firmly in the national consciousness in the decades following. Legitimacy through endurance—this was the status report on temperance as the nineteenth century entered its final decade or two. In the national *sub*consciousness, if there was such a thing, a complete, coast-to-coast ban on alcoholic beverages had now begun to hover, a ghost in the distance to be sure, but one that was visible at least in outline. That by itself, for a nation which had once drunk from one end of the day to the other, which had drunk in the stores and on the job and at its weddings and funerals, in its courtrooms and polling places and military encampments, and which still considered booze a good creature, one of the best of all creatures, and imbibed it in some cases to sloppy and destructive excess, despite laws forbidding it and family members condemning it—that by itself was a notable achievement for the soon-to-be-displaced women of American temperance.

A Congregational minister named Howard Hyde Russell had to walk past a brewery on his way to church every day, and it was not a pleasant experience. He held his nose, kept his eyes straight ahead, and quickened his stride, trying to put the building behind him as quickly as he could. And most of all he would distract himself by speaking to the Lord, asking Him "to stay the tide of sin and shame flowing therefrom . . . and whenever I passed a saloon I sent up a prayer, 'O God, stop this!' . . . [Finally] God plainly said to me, 'You know how to do it; go and help answer your own prayers.'"

So he did. On May 24, 1893, Russell founded the Anti-Saloon League of Ohio, and he did it "exactly where one would expect it to be founded—in the town where Frances Willard spent her early childhood, the middle western center of reform, Oberlin, Ohio." The organization, Russell liked to say, was of divine origin; he was merely the human intermediary.

The time could not have been more right. The temperance movement was in fact not moving at all in these days, but simply holding its ground, and even that had been proving a struggle. What was needed were not only new ideas, but new people to devise them and new organizational structures to implement them. Russell quickly stepped to the forefront. Within a matter of months, nine other states had formed groups similar to his, and more than 160 local societies became affiliated with them. In 1895, these groups merged, turning themselves virtually overnight into the most efficient temperance group yet to appear on the planet. It was called the Anti-Saloon League of America, and because of it, in the words of Arthur S. Link and William B. Catton, "the division between church and state almost ceased to exist in many southern and Midwestern states. The Leagues—with their general superintendents, organizers, and hosts of speakers—became the most powerful factors in politics in many states."

Russell chose the name himself, and he did so ingeniously, if not ingenuously, for even among imbibers there was at least partial agreement that, as a place of human concourse, the saloon had become a blight on the community. True, there were exceptions. Some saloons were opulent, designed to "conjure up an image of elegance and taste, and many such urban establishments in the late nineteenth and early twentieth centuries more than filled the bill." These were places that encouraged men to behave responsibly, to watch their language and keep their tempers and depart without protest when the bartender thought they had reached their limits. They sometimes admitted women, but only if escorted, and the women were expected to conduct themselves at least as decorously as the men.

Other saloons, although not so elegant, were even more important assets to their neighborhoods, refuges of a sort, clubhouses and meeting places "where men come together to exchange ideas, to laugh and boast and dare, to relax." And, as a clergyman of the era pointed out, they served more practical purposes as well.

> It was in the saloon that the working men in those days held their christening parties, their weddings, their dances, their rehearsals for singing societies, and all other social functions. . . . Undoubtedly the chief element of attraction was the saloon-keeper himself. . . . He was a social force in the community. His greeting was cordial, his appearance neat, and his acquaintance large. He had access to sources of information which were decidedly beneficial to the men who patronized his saloon. Often he secured work for both the working man and his children.

Or he shared the premises with others who did the securing. In 1898, sixty-three out of the sixty-nine labor unions in Buffalo, New York, held their regular meetings in saloons. The story was similar in other towns, as unions and various other groups affiliated with places of employment, political parties, and religious and charitable organizations set up shop in the barroom, where they provided valuable services to their constituents—handouts in addition to jobs, counseling and consolation, and meetings with the proper authorities. And then, afterward, they provided a round of drinks to celebrate.

If nothing else, this kind of establishment served as "the common lavatory for the entire city."

Which meant that, at its best, the saloon was an indispensable institution to the workingman, "the church of the poor," as one writer has called it, and on some occasions, harkening back to colonial times, even the site of the voting booth on election day.

But seldom did it achieve its best. More often, the saloon was the most unsavory spot around, or, in the words of an anonymous abstainer of the period, "the acme of evil, the climax of iniquity, the mother of abominations, and the sum of villainies." It attracted criminals and other undesirables, and encouraged them in antisocial activity. It also attracted children, boys and girls whom it hired to deliver buckets of beer called "growlers" to its take-out customers. In many saloons the paint was peeling, the wood chipping, the furniture in various stages of disrepair, the mirrors filthily opaque, the beer mugs and shot glasses nearly so. Floors were neither swept nor mopped; conversations were as foul as the ambience. Females of negotiable virtue and questionable hygiene sat at the bar and, crossing their legs at the knee, swung them in invitation.

In the back room, reeking even more of cigar smoke and stale beer than the front, there was probably a low-stakes poker game among men who could not afford even that. There are reports from the time of dogs wandering into saloons by mistake, taking a few whiffs, and then fleeing back to the street. Women of conventional virtue, even those who drank themselves, or at least had no objection to the drinking of others, were appalled by dumps like these, pleading with their husbands and brothers and sons not to go.

And they were everywhere, all over the place, all over all kinds of places. It is said that, late in the nineteenth century, there was one saloon for every 300 dwellers in American cities. In San Francisco, it was one for every ninety-six. They were large buildings in prime locations, centers of commerce and attention, and those who did not frequent them railed at their inappropriateness as focal points of trade. Most urban areas, not to mention a disproportionate number of small towns, had more saloons along their front streets and byways than churches, and more American boys of the time grew up to be barkeeps than preachers of the gospel.

Thus the wisdom of the name Anti-Saloon League; thus the widespread acceptance of its motto, "The Saloon Must Go!"

But in reality, the league wanted everything to go, not just rum shops of tawdry atmosphere, but *all* rum shops, in addition to *all* breweries, *all* distilleries, *all* vineyards, and, as a consequence, *all* customers and their horrible, unceasing thirsts. It was the most ambitious goal ever set by a consortium of teetotalers, but by claiming that it opposed only the saloon, the league was able to seem more moderate than it really was, a benefactor rather than a ruffian, and this in turn made it acceptable to men and women of less than radical bent.

In both its prowess and its duplicity, the Anti-Saloon League was like one of our modern political action committees. It would not credit a man for the virtue or good sense of his positions on other issues if he opposed the group in its single area of concern. It would, in fact, do everything it could to end the fellow's career; it would write letters, issue brochures, devise slogans, plan strategies, canvass neighborhoods, poll voters, staff headquarters, stuff envelopes, and provide speakers, the league plodding through these chores with the tenacity of bulldogs and "the patience of driver ants."

The results were impressive. By 1903, fully a third of all American citizens were living under some kind of mandatory abstention, and the total rose to about half the population, 46 million people, in 1913. The totals would have been even higher were it not for the fact that, in many states and localities, the laws were successfully challenged, repealed almost as soon as they were passed. And in other places, people did not respect the laws enough even to bother with a challenge; they simply carried on with their old habits and trusted to half-hearted and lackadaisial enforcement.

It was also in 1913 that a measure affecting the entire nation, or most of it, at least, was finally enacted. "The League took its blackjack to Washington," said one account, and saw to it that Congress approved the Webb-Kenyon Act, which banned shipments of liquor across the boundaries of dry states.

In part, the Anti-Saloon League accomplished all this through the printed word. Between 1909 and 1923, it published more than 100 million copies of its various pamphlets and leaflets. "Propaganda," declares Andrew Sinclair, "fell thicker than hailstones on the heads of the people." Among its pithier messages, which in today's culture would have ridden the bumpers of many a car and truck and SUV, were the following:

> You can't drink liquor and have strong babies.
> Sow alcohol and you reap disease, disgrace, defeat, death.
> Can you imagine a cocktail party in heaven?

But it may be that what the Anti-Saloon League did best, again reminiscent of the political action committee, was raise money, more money than temperance had ever raised before, enough to make the cause, for the first time in its history, as much a big business as a social movement. The WCTU chipped in. So did thousands of unaffiliated Americans, who contributed in their churches or else filled out subscription cards and sent the cash directly to ASL headquarters.

Some of it went to the campaigns of dry politicians; some was used to publicize, or just as likely to invent, the shortcomings of wet candidates. And to qualify as a dry, as far as the league's largesse was concerned, an office-seeker did not have to do anything so drastic as refrain from drinking alcoholic beverages himself. As J. C. Furnas writes with both wit and perception, "Many a frock-coated, string-tied legislator voting Dry and getting reelected by the grace and favor of the League was just as rugged a drinker as his colleague at the next desk who voted Wet partly because he believed in booze but partly also because most of his campaign funds came from the distilleries in his district." In other words, a dry did not have to abstain; he simply had to vote to force the condition on others.

In one mayoral race in Cincinnati, for example, the league found itself supporting a man who also happened to own two of the city's most popular bistros, well-known venues of late-night debauchery, of brawls and arrests and streetcorner-rattling dins. The places were hotbeds of vice, featuring the frequent misdemeanor and the occasional, but hardly uncommon, felony. Not surprisingly, a newspaperman decided to point out this seeming hypocrisy to an Anti-Saloon League spokesman. "Neat-mustached, starchily dressed," the spokesman "looked like the cashier of a middle-sized bank."

But he did not react like a cashier. He listened to the reporter's statement about the candidate and his gin mills with eyes growing ever narrower and cheeks ever redder, and when he finished, the spokesman practically erupted, blasting the reporter for intolerable naivete, inexcusable insolence. He told him that a man's job "doesn't have anything to do with his official actions." Surely, he implied, even a person with the intelligence of a journalist was smart enough to figure *that* out.

But before the reporter could answer, the spokesman, perhaps even redder and more glowering now than before, turned on his heels and stomped away. He would neither speak another word nor listen to one, and he would savage the names of both the reporter and the newspaper in his private conversations for weeks.

The spokesman's name was Wayne Bidwell Wheeler.

Like Carry Nation, and perhaps a majority of America's other proselytizing teetotalers, Wayne Wheeler had been scarred by alcoholic excess as a child. In his case, the mark was literal. Growing up on a farm outside Brookfield, Ohio, Wheeler used to spend his spare time watching the operations of a nearby farm, which was larger and more profitable than his father's spread. He would lean against a wall or sit on a fence as the men plowed and seeded the fields and tended to the large herds of livestock, and perhaps hope that someday he could work in such a place himself. Possibly even own one, raise a family there, give his life to the soil. He was not yet a dreamer of big dreams.

One day, a laborer on the farm had a few belts of whiskey, then began feeding a bale of hay to some horses. Wheeler stood close to him, too close, and the man accidentally stabbed him in the leg with his pitchfork. Wheeler fell backward, crying out, then quickly clutched at the wound to stop the bleeding, which seems to have been profuse. Other farmhands rushed to help, carrying the boy into the house and getting the leg bandaged. If his later account of the mishap is accurate—and one cannot help but suspect a bit of tailoring for dramatic effect—what Wheeler said at the moment was, "I hope that some day there won't be any more liquor to make men drunk." He also claimed that, even after many years had passed, he could still remember the terrible alcoholic reek of the man with the pitchfork, and the shimmery flush of his skin.

But even before that he had developed an antipathy toward spirits, if in much less painful a manner. Wheeler used to hear stories about an uncle who would get so thoroughly tiddled on his weekly trips to town that, coming home, he would more often than not fall off his wagon and not be seen again until the following morning, after family and friends had spent hours combing the roadside for him. They would find him in a ditch or under a tree and he would still be asleep; he would not remember what had happened, would be so hung over that he was afraid to open his eyes, much less acknowledge his rescuers.

What Wheeler said at *this* moment, although similar to what he said after being stabbed, was subtly and tellingly different. "I could never understand," he confessed, "why the saloons were allowed to make him drunk."

Consider a statement that Neal Dow had made about fifty years earlier—the subject different, the theme the same:

> My father once owned an old-fashioned silver watch, too large to be conveniently carried, which he often hung on a hook on the wall. One day, when a little fellow, I climbed into a chair to get at the watch, tipped the chair over, pulled the watch down, which, falling with me to the floor, was broken. When reproved for meddling with the timepiece, I urged upon my father that the fault was altogether with those who had left the watch within my reach. Years afterward, in relating the incident, my father would laughingly say that he had heard me make my argument for Prohibition, so far as it bore upon the removal of temptation, before I was six years old.

It is a confusion typical of reformers. It reveals an inability to distinguish between cause and effect, between disease and symptom. It demonstrates the kind of ignorance that inevitably leads to doomed attempts at remedy.

Wayne Bidwell Wheeler first met Howard Hyde Russell at Oberlin College. Wheeler was a student in his third year, a bright and inexhaustible young man known to his classmates as a "locomotive in trousers." He seems to have been ambitious to an almost indiscriminate degree, and thus was to some of his instructors a pet, to others a nuisance. "We wouldn't mind having you in the Glee Club, Wheeler," said his music teacher, to whom the boy fell into the latter category, "if you didn't try to sing all the parts yourself."

As for Russell, he was an alumnus who had returned to campus to preach against the wages of alcohol. By this time, Wheeler had outgrown his interest in agriculture and now planned a career in business; perhaps he would end up being that bank teller which, in some ways, he already resembled. But so moved was he by Russell's sermon, his fiery excoriations of demon rum and allied beverages, that he began to question himself. Perhaps there was something else he should do with his life; perhaps the Almighty, in that wondrous way of His, intended a different kind of business for young Wayne.

After the speech, the man met the boy and was immediately impressed. Russell found Wheeler well-groomed, well-spoken, well-mannered. Perhaps more important, he learned that Wheeler was powerfully motivated. His parents were not sending him to college; Wheeler had earned the money himself by spending two years as a teacher after graduating from high school, and kept the funds coming at Oberlin with part-time employment as a janitor. Education mattered to Wayne Wheeler; he would not be denied because of the penury of his father's farm.

Russell spoke to him about the temperance movement. Wheeler listened carefully, finding much of what he heard not only sensible but inspiring. Perhaps if there had been an Anti-Saloon League a decade and more ago, both his uncle and the man on the nearby farm would have turned out differently. Perhaps if the Anti-Saloon League were a powerful force in America in the next decade, many others would turn out differently.

Before they parted, Russell asked his companion to join the league; Wheeler, caught by surprise, suggested that the two of them pray together, and they dropped to their knees on the spot and bowed their heads in supplication. Thinking about the moment later, Wheeler said, "The simplicity and practical nature of the new organization captured me," in the main because the group "ignored all sectarian, political, racial, sectional or other subdivisions."

But it did not capture him immediately, at least not enough for him to make a commitment. Wheeler could not decide what to do about Russell's offer, and spent most of his senior year thinking it over, asking God for counsel on a number of occasions but not receiving any that he could detect. Finally he told Russell he would give the league a try, but only for a year; beyond that, he would make no promises. Russell found the terms acceptable and, as proud as a father showing off his firstborn to members of the family, he took Wheeler to an Anti-Saloon League gathering and introduced him as "The new David . . . who will hurl his missile at the giant wrong." He would keep hurling, as things turned out, not just for twelve months but for the rest of his life.

Wheeler's first assignment for the Anti-Saloon League was to get to know the politicians who controlled the small towns in the north of Ohio along Lake Erie, and to tell them that there was help available for them in their campaigns, financial and otherwise, if they wanted it. All they had to do in return was exactly, precisely, and undeviatingly what the Anti-Saloon League told them to do. They were not to think, not to question. If the politicians balked at the terms, well, perhaps the league could find other candidates who wanted to run for the same offices and would accept the dry alliance.

It was not an easy task, but Wayne Wheeler made the transition from college student to player of hardball politics quickly, and with an effectiveness far belying his years. When a candidate for the state senate named John Locke refused the Anti-Saloon League's help, calling prohibitory laws a form of fanaticism, Wheeler took after him with a vengeance. "He persuaded the ASL to buy him a bicycle, to give him the required mobility," writes Edward Behr. "He then tirelessly lobbied clergymen and leading citizens in the three counties casting their votes in the election. His next step was to persuade a prominent dry Methodist businessman, W. N. Jones, to stand against Locke, becoming, in effect, his campaign manager."

John Locke was the favorite in the state senate race, W. N. Jones a kind of afterthought who did not seem to have a chance. What he *did* have was the backing of the Anti-Saloon League, and "Wheeler on his wheel." It was more than enough. Jones won election to the Ohio senate by a comfortable margin. Most observers saw the result as an omen, some with a shudder, others with a sigh of contentment.

As for Wheeler, he was elated, both surprised by and impressed with his power, and in the years ahead he would become an absolute master at the issuance of righteous threats. He would even go so far as to issue a few to presidents of the United States. One was Warren G. Harding, who "was dissuaded from appointing Senator Shields of Kentucky to the Supreme Court by Wheeler. . . . Wheeler even opposed the appointment of Andrew Mellon, the industrial magnate, as secretary of the treasury, because Mellon had liquor interests."

In fact, says biographer Justin Steuart, at his peak, Wayne Wheeler, who was then running the Anti-Saloon League from an office across the street from the U.S. Capitol,

> controlled six Congresses, dictated to two Presidents of the United States, directed legislation for the most important elective state and federal offices, held the balance of power in both Republican and Democratic parties, distributed more patronage than any dozen other men, supervised a federal bureau from the outside without official authority, and was recognized by friend and foe alike as the most masterful and powerful single individual in the United States.

Steuart overstates the case. But not by much. And it is not an overstatement to say, as Steuart did, that a surprisingly high number of elected officials at the federal, state, and local levels "served under" Wheeler at various times. Nor is it an overstatement to report that many of those officials were openly obsequious to him. In 1921, Wheeler happened to be sitting in the gallery of the United States House of Representatives one day when a congressman below spoke critically of him. Not scathingly, not viciously; he simply said a few words in opposition to Wheeler's policies and methods.

Some of the man's fellow legislators, recipients of league donations and proud of every penny, responded by booing. Others joined in. The volume rose. So deep and rumbling were the hoots of displeasure after a matter of seconds that the poor speaker was forced from the podium by his colleagues, who then looked up at Wheeler like congregants turning toward a deity—or perhaps just employees looking hopefully at their boss—and gave a long, loud round of applause. Wheeler bowed slightly, accepting his due. It was not a typical occurrence in the hallowed halls of American government.

One is forced to ask why. How did it come to be that an individual who had never held office, who had never even run for office, and who did not represent a traditional power base, had acquired so much influence? What was his secret? How did he operate? When the journalist Lincoln Steffens put the question to Wheeler personally, he got a characteristically candid answer, one that could easily have come from a politician of more recent vintage bragging to a talk show host.

> I do it the way the bosses do it, with minorities. There are some anti-saloon votes in every community. I and other speakers increase the number and passion of them. I list and bind them to vote as I bid. I say, "We'll all vote against the men in office who won't support our bills. We'll vote for candidates who will promise to. They'll break their promise. Sure. Next time we'll break them." And we can. We did. Our swinging, solid minorities, no matter how small, counted.

Yet Wayne Wheeler's stature was not merely a reflection of the minorities he represented. There was, in addition, something in the man himself that bespoke an almost irresistible force. It was not his physique; Wheeler stood no more than five feet, six inches tall and was as thin as a soda straw. He wore wire-rimmed glasses, had a thatch of gray, thinning hair, and intimidated no one at first glance. Nor was it his voice, so thin and wheezy, as if it were being strained through some kind of abrasive object. More than anything, it might have been his smile, which was as chilling as the frowns of less subtle men. Wayne Wheeler's smile seems never to have gone as far back into his cheeks as a smile should, and his eyes forever peered over the shoulders of those he addressed, as if he could see something that no one else could see, or was at least determined to look. His eyes were bystanders when he smiled. It was the expression of a man who would not be disregarded.

And only once during the entire glorious run of the Anti-Saloon League did it happen, when President Woodrow Wilson refused another of those righteous threats that Wheeler issued to a chief executive, this one demanding that a worldwide prohibition of alcoholic beverages be written into the Treaty of Versailles. Wilson did not agree. He did not respond. He did not even mention the matter to his advisers. He figured he had enough problems with the postwar world as it was.

Wayne Wheeler thought him a coward.

But there was more to Wheeler's job than just threatening legislators and building cores of constituents. As he had done well at raising money for himself, paying his own bills at Oberlin, so did he begin to raise money for the Anti-Saloon League, and neither his associates in the state legislatures nor his "swinging, solid minorities," which included the WCTU and some old-line crusaders and their families, were of much use to him here. For money, big money, Wheeler needed other contacts, and he made them with the most solid and influential minority of all.

Henry Ford, Andrew Carnegie, Elbert Gary, Gustavus Swift, Henry Frick, Cyrus McCormick, Samuel Insull, Pierre Du Pont, John Wanamaker, Samuel Kresge, John D. Rockefeller Sr. and Jr.—these were the men who owned and operated the United States of America early in the twentieth century, the men who held its shares of stock, who sat on its boards, who reaped in considerable disproportion its rewards. And these were the men to whom Wheeler turned for the Anti-Saloon League's bankroll. For the most part, they were willing to provide it. Between 1900 and 1926, the two Rockefellers alone donated more than a third of a million dollars, and according to some reports, the younger Rockefeller actually purchased, and then razed, several breweries and distilleries, the rubble a much-appreciated present for Wayne Wheeler.

The irony was that, until recently, most of the barons of American industry had opposed the temperance movement on the grounds that the realization of its goals would lead to insurrection in the workplace. They knew—or should have known, whether they were willing to admit it to themselves or not—that they were in many cases abusing the men who worked for them, paying them too little and working them too long and hard in factories that were all too often grimy and dangerous and as wrenching to the soul as they were to the arms and legs and back. They knew, or should have known, that their employees felt no pride of craftsmanship because whatever craftsmanship existed was the machine's, not the man's. They knew, or should have known, that capitalism does not have to become so unjust that many of those who live under it come to disdain it. Accurate figures do not exist, but newspaper accounts, among other sources from the late nineteenth and early twentieth centuries, show that the number of Americans killed or maimed on the job was high enough to constitute a public health crisis, and that dissatisfaction with the conditions of employment had become an epidemic.

As for the jobs themselves—that is, the motions required to perform them, apart from the circumstances in which they were performed— they had become more specialized, more repetitive, less fulfilling. A printed account from England all the way back in the 1760s, when the Industrial Revolution was something of a novelty, warns that monotonous labor might, in the long run, produce insanity. In the years since, labor had only turned more monotonous, and although insanity might have been rare, discontent and depression were common. The workingman's lot was hard in the best of cases, tragic in the worst.

Yet there were few strikes against the system and even fewer outbreaks of violence. Production quotas were met and often exceeded; absenteeism was not a problem, nor was insubordination. The American factory, in other words, ran smoothly and efficiently most of the time, and one of the reasons, some people thought, was the availability of a pacifying beverage at the end of the day. Saloon owners often set up shop within walking distance of the factory gates, and saw to it that they were always well-staffed when the shift changed. They were happy to cash a paycheck, happy to take the proceeds right back in trade. As Tom Lewis, the president of the United Mine Workers' Union, said, "There is no easier way possible to make the unfortunate or oppressed worker content with his misfortune than a couple glasses of beer."

Upton Sinclair put it more eloquently. In *The Jungle*, his classic novel of the laboring man as beast of burden, he wrote that

> from all the unending horror of [the meat packing house] there was a
> respite, a deliverance—he could drink! He could forget the pain, he could
> slip off the burden, he could see clearly again, he would be master of his
> brain, of his thoughts, of his will. His dead self would stir in him and he
> would find himself laughing and cracking jokes with his companions—he
> would be a man again, and master of himself.

The salaries of American industry were just high enough to allow this expense—this, and very little else. And, in fact, a study conducted early in the 1900s "found that the workers who had the most menial and lowest-paid jobs spent the greatest amount of time in saloons, washing the workday away with beer."

But as factories and working procedures became more and more complicated, and machinery more demanding to run and efficiency ever more critical to the bottom line, the rulers of corporate America began to see a connection between sobriety and productivity. Actually, they had seen one previously. Two hundred years earlier, taverns in Massachusetts and Connecticut were forbidden to serve "apprentices and servants, lest the time belonging to the master should be spent in idleness." Attitudes, if not laws, were similar in other colonies at the time. No one wanted a dipsomaniac seeding a field or shaping a horseshoe or cutting a bolt of fabric to specifications. But neither did anyone want to monitor a fellow's drinking habits, or to be forced to abstain himself when thirst overtook him on the job. The means seemed too demanding for the end.

But now, factory owners began to think that a dry workforce was a goal worth pursuing. They realized that employees who drank might be less likely to complain about conditions than those who refrained, but the latter were less likely to slow up the assembly line through clumsiness or ineptitude. Or, in the words of Henry Ford, seeming quite public-spirited, "The speed at which we run our motor cars, operate our intricate machinery and generally live would be impossible with liquor." Privately, Ford also favored abstention for another reason. The Jews, he thought, were trying to conquer the world through "the use of liquor to befuddle the brains of Christian leaders," and the automaker, his own brain often seeming befuddled on virtually every subject other than the assembly line, would not let it happen.

In time, Ford became one of the Anti-Saloon League's strongest supporters, even proposing that the breweries in his state of Michigan be converted to distilleries—not for the manufacture of beverages, but for the production of denatured alcohol to power the next generation of internal combustion engines. Fortunately for the league, Ford contributed large sums of money as well as suggestions. He also set what he thought was an excellent example for his fellow industrial chieftans; whenever he learned that one of his employees was partial to spirits, even if the man consumed them moderately, privately, and after working hours, Ford fired him. And he employed a well-paid staff of company spies, known as the Service Department, to provide him with just such information. Henry Frick, in what one historian calls "a well-meant burst of paternalism," also forbade his men to drink either on or off the job, although he was not so quick to terminate. Among other companies that demanded twenty-four hours a day of abstention a century ago were the American Sheet and Tin Plate Company and a majority of the nation's railroads.

Some corporate leaders demoted the imbibing laborer; some harassed him or just allowed him to languish without promotion. But this kind of thing was a struggle for the ruling class, so much time did the pashas and their assistants have to devote to sniffing breaths and checking on dexterity and asking questions and peeking around corners. More and more, they began to long for the assistance of the law. Said the owner of a cotton mill in North Carolina, testifying before a committee of that state's legislature, "Gentlemen, there is a liquor shop, a dispensary, two miles from Selma, and you must shut up that place or I must shut up my cotton mill. It is for you to say which you will encourage in North Carolina, liquor mills or cotton mills —the two cannot go together."

Perhaps it was Andrew Carnegie who best summed up corporate America's new attitude toward alcoholic beverages. He told his employees that they should "never enter a bar-room, nor let the contents of a bar-room enter you," and the message became all the more important to him and his fellow titans between 1911 and 1920, when forty-one states passed workmen's compensation laws. Because teetotalers were less likely than sots to slip their fingers into the punch press, they were less likely to need their employers' money, and time, to recover.

Those who supposedly benefited from these edicts and maxims raged at the presumptuousness of them, at the interference in their lives. And when the leaders of their own unions, men who supposedly had their best interests at heart, began to align themselves with the heads of industry, as was happening more and more all the time, the working man felt more betrayed than ever. In fact, the *Literary Digest*, one of the most prestigious magazines of the time, conducted a poll of 500 labor leaders and found that two-thirds of them thought teetotalism was good for their members, whether the members thought so or not. Eugene Debs, who founded the American Railway Union and would later be the Socialist Party's candidate for president, suggested that his men devote their leisure hours to the contents of books rather than the contents of bottles. The Anti-Saloon League recommended moving picture shows. Other reform groups put forth other diversions: board games, card games, building models, collecting stamps.

The wage slave would have none of this, not to the exclusion of his alcohol, at any rate. Nothing else did for him at the end of the day like a shot of whiskey or a glass of beer, the latter being more common because the lower taxes on it resulted in a lower price. Sometimes, though, perhaps on a special occasion, a fellow would down a little whiskey and then quickly follow it with some suds—a boilermaker, it was called; and after what he had been through during his hours on the job, he figured he was entitled. However, he had neither the law nor his union on his side; the abstainers seemed to have all the clout, both in the boardroom and in the corridors of government.

So what was he to do, this fellow who toiled so long, so hard, for so little in the way of reward? Wayne Wheeler had some advice, and it is reminiscent of the equally cold-hearted sentiments offered by Lucius Manlius Sargent at an earlier time. "Start a saloon in your own home," he said to those who insisted on alcoholic beverages despite the increasing opposition. "Be the only customer. . . . Go to your wife and give her two dollars to buy a gallon of whiskey. . . . Buy your drinks from no one but your wife. . . . Should you live ten years and continue to buy booze from her, and then die with snakes in your boots, she will have enough money to bury you decently, educate your children, buy a house and lot, marry a decent man and quit thinking about you entirely."

The journalist William Allen White was not so facetious. In fact, he seems almost utopian in his insistence that the worker would be a better person in the end for the absence of alcohol.

> When the laboring man works eight hours and spends none of his time at the saloon, he will save up more money and better his economic status. This will lift more and more men from the laboring class to the economic middle class. And the more they attain they more they will want, which is just the condition that ought to prevail. That's why prohibition is a good thing. It's really part of the inevitable and approaching movement to get for the worker a greater share of what he produces.

In other words, the members of the working class could make more money if they gave up booze, and the members of the ruling class could make more money if the toiling class gave up booze. So it was not, as the occasional malcontent charged, a labor-management struggle at all. It was a goose-and-gander accord.

Wayne Wheeler must have smiled.

Soon he had more to smile about. It was called World War I, "the momentous event without which the League's crowning victory might have eluded it for many more years." Not that Wheeler was pleased about a conflict of that magnitude, nor that he welcomed American participation in slaughter on such a scale; although he does not seem publicly to have expressed himself on the war, there is no reason to assume he was any the less appalled by it than anyone else.

But he was a practical man, a big picture kind of guy, always had been; he believed that as long as slaughter on such a scale was taking place anyhow, it might as well serve the cause of a drier America. And it did. The Civil War had been a great disruption to the temperance movement, almost its final gasp, but the Great War only gave it further impetus.

President Wilson declared the United States a participant in the fighting on April 6, 1917. Shortly afterward, Congress passed the Food Control Bill, which rationed the domestic use of certain comestibles so that more of them would be available for military consumption. Among them were sugar and a variety of grains, principal ingredients in liquors and beer. It was especially necessary to slow the pace at which Americans used wheat and rye, barley and corn; the harvest of 1916 had been a poor one, virtually throughout the nation, and the next year's crop would not make up the difference, no matter how bountiful it turned out to be. Herbert Hoover, whom Wilson had appointed food administrator, asked grocers and their patrons to accept voluntary rationing of foods in short supply, and urged the latter to make at least one day a week meatless and another wheatless. Most Americans went along.

But the Anti-Saloon League wanted more. The Food Control Bill gave the president discretionary power to prohibit the manufacture of alcoholic beverages, and the league urged him to use it. A spokesman said that the many needed food more than the few needed potables, and he went on to cite the precedent of Rhode Island and Massachusetts, which had outlawed whiskey during the Revolutionary War so that corn and rye could be conserved. Were President Wilson to take a similar course, the league insisted, the whole nation would profit. "Brewery products fill refrigerator cars," said the group's 1918 yearbook, inaccurately, "while potatoes rot for lack of transportation, bankrupting farmers and starving cities. The coal that they consume would keep the railroads open and the factories running."

Initially, the president ignored the league. He did not care for either its tactics or its leaders. He wanted the breweries and distilleries up and running, not because their products were providing sustenance for the fighting man, but because they were providing sustenance for the Treasury. Money as well as food was needed to ensure proper mobilization, and since the Civil War, the federal government had become increasingly dependent on a thriving liquor industry; in fact, as the war began in Europe, the government was taking in $262 million by taxing alcoholic beverages, fully one-third of its total annual revenues. If those who made the stuff went out of business, or were ordered to reduce their output significantly, the United States would lose a lot of money precisely when it needed to be spending more than ever before on men and materiel.

But Wheeler reminded Wilson that in 1913 the Sixteenth Amendment to the Constitution had provided the first peacetime American income tax. Although it was not raising much money yet, the amount had been climbing each year, and projections said that it would continue to climb. By early in the 1920s, Wheeler assured the president, tax monies would easily make up for whatever the government lost on booze. He had done the math, he said, or had had it done for him; the president could take his word for it.

Wilson decided not to.

Wheeler persisted. Even if the numbers were off a little, everyone knew that a wartime economy is more prosperous than a peacetime economy: more workers are hired, extra shifts are added, output increases dramatically—the entire tax base, in other words, expands. And once the war ends, the economy stays in its higher gear, providing a boost for the nation's return to civilian life. One way or another, Wayne Wheeler told his commander-in-chief, the government would get its money without having to take the morally repugnant course of depending on alcoholic beverages.

Wilson was not swayed. He would go no further than the rationing of grains and sugar. But this led a number of distilleries to close because they could no longer obtain enough raw materials for their whiskey. And that, in turn, met with hearty approval in a number of places. In 1914, three years before the United States entered the war, alcoholic beverages were illegal substances in fourteen states, in no small part due to efforts begun many years before by the WCTU. But by the time the U.S. sent its troops to Europe, twenty-six states had passed prohibitory legislation, and during the war years, another nine leaped on the bandwagon—and for this increase the Anti-Saloon League was to a significant degree responsible. As it was for a variety of other measures approved by the federal government early in 1917. A partial list is provided by Mark Sullivan in the fifth of his six historical volumes, *Our Times.*

> *January 9.* The Senate passed the Sheppard bill prohibiting the manufacture, importation or sale of liquor in the District of Columbia. . . .
>
> *January 11.* The Senate passed a bill prohibiting the sending of liquor advertisements by mail into "dry" territory. . . .
>
> *February 21.* The House adopted a measure originating in the Senate forbidding shipments of intoxicating liquors into States which prohibited their manufacture and sale. At midnight June 30, when the law went into effect, twenty-two States automatically became "bone dry."

In September of 1918, believing that grains were still not being sufficiently conserved, Congress voted to shut down the breweries in addition to the distilleries. Wilson did not object. Nor did he object when, having gone this far, the nation's legislators decided to take the lone remaining step and declare a national wartime prohibition, which they did the same month. It was, however, a much less drastic action than it seems, a baby step, for as Charles Merz writes in *The Dry Decade*, "the bill carrying this provision did not become a law until fourteen days after the war was over and did not take effect until the seventh month of peace."

The Anti-Saloon League supported it all. The league also succeeded in outlawing the sale of alcoholic beverages at army camps and naval bases. This did not result, however, in a more sober military force; rather, it resulted in soldiers who had to go to greater, more surreptitious lengths than usual to tie one on. They had to deal with dubious characters, pay excessive sums, and arrange for meetings in places where they were not supposed to be. The ban was a large inconvenience, not an effective piece of legislation.

But Major General Leonard Wood, for one, chose not to acknowledge those violations. He told people that the new law was a godsend, and would lead to a much-improved caliber of young man in the nation's armed services. He cited Kansas, Carry Nation's old stomping ground, which had now been legally, if not actually, dry for more than three and a half decades, as an example. Kansas produced, in Wood's view, "the finest, the cleanest, the healthiest and most vigorous soldiers . . . that we have ever known. . . . Kansas boys were brought up in a clean atmosphere. They started right." Wood dared to hope that, before long, the whole United States of America would turn into Kansas.

But as pleasing as the prospect was to the major general, and as pleasing as the ban was to other foes of alcohol both in and out of uniform, the temperance movement got even more of a boost from the fact that most brewers in the United States at the time were of German ancestry, and in these fervid days of preparation and warfare, nothing German was socially acceptable anymore, especially not to the Anti-Saloon League. "Kaiser kultur was raised on beer," the league declared. "Prohibition is the infallible submarine chaser we must launch by the thousands. The water-wagon is the tank that can level every Prussian trench. Total abstinence is the impassable curtain barrage which we must lay before every trench. Sobriety is the bomb that will blow kaiserism to kingdom come. We must all become munition-makers."

It was not just the league that overreacted; so, too, did a majority of other Americans of the period, regardless of their opinions about alcohol. They treated their countrymen of German descent almost as shabbily as they would treat their countrymen of Japanese descent a generation later. They fought a war, of a sort, in their homeland, preposterous and one-sided though it was.

Jon Bradshaw writes about one of the fronts. "German language instruction was abolished in the public schools," he says, "and many German newspapers ceased publication." In addition, many German individuals ceased being employable, among them the violin virtuoso Fritz Kreisler, who was no longer welcome on the American stages upon which he had so proudly demonstrated his artistry for so many years. Beethoven's music was banned in Boston and Wagner's operas were booted out of the repertoire of New York's Metropolitan Opera.

It got sillier. Families of German background were ostracized to such a degree that they tried to disguise themselves with new names. "Strauss was changed to Stratford, Schmitt to Smith, Fritz to Fox and Rosenstein to Rose"; and one member of the Ochs family that owned the *New York Times* came to the conclusion that Oakes had a safer ring to it. Also receiving new identities were sauerkraut, which became "liberty cabbage," and hamburger, which turned into "liberty steak." German measles were now "liberty measles"; German shepherds were Alsatians; and dachshunds were "liberty pups," although in the latter case it did not make a difference, as some Americans, those of a perversely patriotic and bullying bent, cursed the animals and kicked them whenever they saw them in public, regardless of their new names.

German toast was rechristened French toast and frankfurters became hot dogs and both of the aliases stuck. Berlin Street in New Orleans would henceforth be known as General Pershing Street; German Street in Baltimore changed to Redwood Street; and that city's most famous and eloquent beer drinker, the columnist and social critic Henry Louis Mencken, yielded his position with the *Sun* newspapers for a time, fearing that his views, or even just his name, would stir up the rabid.

And Wayne Wheeler, still a locomotive in trousers, rubbing his hands together in gleeful satisfaction, presided over these bonfires of irrationality with a bellows. He wrote to A. Mitchell Palmer, the government's custodian of alien property and soon to be attorney general, and said he had been "informed that there are a number of breweries in this country which are owned in part by alien enemies. It is reported to me that the Anheuser-Busch Company and some of the Milwaukee companies are largely controlled by alien Germans. . . . Have you made an investigation?"

The charge was never proven, and the answer to the question seems to have been no; Palmer did not investigate. Nonetheless, Wheeler might have been onto something, although less than he thought. It was later learned that several breweries in the United States had been financing a group called the German-American Alliance, and that the alliance had been "engaging in pro-German activities since 1914."

It was no time for a fellow to be manufacturing a beverage called, say, Schlitz. Or Pabst. And the beer called Miller was a product of a man who had started out in life as Mueller.

But the sudsmakers also suffered from problems that had nothing to do with ancestry. So did the distillers. They were not, as some people charged, their own worst enemies—the Anti-Saloon League rightly and proudly claimed that distinction—but they had inadvertently become a close second. The reason, historian John Kobler believes, was greed, "gross greed. The League could wrap itself in the robes of morality and piety. The liquor industry could hardly delude anybody that its profits did not come first. The League used the churches as a staging ground for political action. The brewers and distillers used the saloons. In the end they defeated themselves."

And defeated themselves soundly, behaving with stupidity as well as greed, and making of the combination a guiding principle. For example, in Sioux City, Iowa, in the 1880s, saloons continued to do business despite statewide prohibition. The law was worse than ignored; it was laughed at between rounds. So the pastor of the local Methodist Episcopal Church, a nondrinker with a powerful sense of mission, began collecting evidence. He staked out the watering holes in Sioux City and took down the names of people entering, the dates, and the amount of time they spent therein. But unlike the Women's Crusaders, the pastor's list had a point; it would be evidence in a court of law. For more evidence, he gathered witnesses and persuaded them to testify and secretly confiscated samples of booze that never should have been served and stashed them away in a safe place, carefully labeled.

But he waited too long, accumulated too much; before the clergyman could present his case to the authorities, he was shot to death by the owner of a local beer garden. Although there was no doubt of the man's guilt—several people saw the crime and came forward to identify the assailant—he was acquitted by a jury of his intemperate peers.

At the next convention of the United States Brewers' Association, the incident was referred to in a statement that read, in part: "With pride and gratification, we record the fact that the fanaticism of the Iowa prohibitionists was frustrated in at least one instance, namely, the attempt to fasten the crime of murder upon a member of our trade."

For the member of their trade to have gotten away with the killing was horrid enough. But for the Brewers' Association to have implied that the bartender was himself almost the victim of injustice was egregious. Among the men and women of Sioux City who knew the truth of the crime there was outcry and indignation, and newspapers published by various temperance organizations saw to it that as many people as possible outside of Sioux City were also informed. The shooting became a rallying cry for opponents of alcohol, a specific instance upon which to focus their general, and growing, disgust. For people who were not opponents of alcohol, the shooting was, at least in a few cases, the beginning of doubt.

And then the following year, in Jackson, Mississippi, virtually the same thing happened. Again a citizen was murdered for attempting to prove illegal activity; again the gunman, a brewer, was acquitted; again his colleagues complained about the irrationality of the other side.

A more common tactic of the alcohol trade than murder, however, was bribery. In 1900, an official of the Pabst Brewing Company sent a memo to his fellow producers of malt beverage. "Dubois will surely be the next senator from Idaho," it read. "I think it would be for the interest of brewers to have his cooperation—he is aggressive and able—send me $1,000 to $5,000. I think it will be the best investment you ever made."

And at almost the same time in Pennsylvania, a grand jury was learning about the financial machinations of seventy-two different brewers and distillers, dealings that led to a hundred indictments on charges of illegal political activity, which was a euphemism for paying legislators to vote against dry laws. A New York grand jury found that a distillery had raised money for the express purpose of corrupting the state legislature. It also heard evidence that brewers paid enormous sums to newspapers, both for partial ownership shares and complete editorial control over subjects relating to alcohol. And in Texas, seven brewers pleaded guilty to bribery and were fined $281,000 plus court costs.

Of course, the Anti-Saloon League was also influencing politicians. It was threatening to offer or withhold contributions, to campaign for or against, to publish materials that informed or deceived, to make speeches that clarified or muddled or slandered—whatever it took. The league was just as ruthless as the liquor interests, but infinitely smarter. It often acted unfairly and almost as often unethically; seldom, though, did it do anything that was blatantly against the law. And with its cause seeming a more reputable one to a great number of people, its means could not help but be justified, at least to some extent, by the ends.

Not that William E. "Pussyfoot" Johnson cared about things like that. Image was irrelevant to him and the law a collection of niceties, like those little books of etiquette to which old maids and others of that ilk paid too much pointless attention. He, on the other hand, was a doer, a man among men, a taker of bulls by horns. Johnson had already lost an eye for the temperance movement when an antiabstainer hit him in the face with a stone. He was ready to risk more. Pussyfoot wanted to live in a dry America, and, if need be, he was willing to dry it out himself.

He got his name, it is said, by sneaking into bars and brothels under cover of darkness, treading oh, so softly, and then berating, and sometimes arresting, miscreants. He swung his fists at both men and bottles, and cursed at all who dared question him. He was the Anti-Saloon League's "most zealous spy and *agent provocateur*," the male Carry Nation, although without the comic overtones. In the middle of Prohibition, he would look back proudly on his efforts to bring it about. "I have told enough lies 'for the cause' to make Ananias ashamed of himself," Johnson said, referring to the notorious biblical teller of falsehoods. "Did I ever drink to promote prohibition? . . . In seeking hidden information, in perfecting criminal cases, I have drunk plenty of the stuff."

Means and ends, means and ends.

When the Nebraska legislature met to consider a prohibitory law early in the twentieth century, Johnson rushed to the scene to offer assistance. He was afraid, he said, that the elected representatives of the people would get bought off, and his concern was well-founded; he did not have enough money to buy them off himself. Something had to be done instead, he muttered to his allies, and what he decided on was a ruse. He ordered some stationery imprinted with the letterhead

John's Pale Ale, and, pretending to be the head of the firm that produced the imaginary brew, wrote to the state's leading distiller. Johnson told him they were brothers in purpose, fellow victims of the lunatic drys. He wanted to get those people off his back once and for all. Could the distiller give him some advice?

The distiller could. His reply to Johnson was both sympathetic and practical, including a list of detailed instructions for buying off politicians and subverting legal authorities without alerting the press or raising alarms in other quarters. Johnson, of course, alerted the press immediately, handing over the letter for publication and then raising alarms in every quarter possible. Like the case of the Sioux City preacher, the Nebraska distiller became a *cause celebre* for temperance.

Ultimately, though, it did no good. The law was defeated; Nebraskans voted to give alcoholic beverages renewed life. Johnson, however, had the satisfaction not only of making the vote closer than it would otherwise have been, but of further blackening the eye of the liquor industry.

So much did the industry come to loathe Pussyfoot that, at one point, a gang of renegade suppliers offered a $3,000 reward to anyone who would kill him. The target was livid. He thought he was worth more; he would rather have had people shoot at him than undervalue him.

The owners of a saloon in Haskel, Oklahoma, as it turns out, were glad to oblige. They let it be known that if he ever set foot in their place, they would drop him to the ground and fill him full of holes. Undaunted, Johnson slipped into a disguise of some sort, then strode into the Haskel saloon, slapped his money on the bar, and demanded some "real hell-fire." When the bartender provided a glassful of his best, "Johnson whipped out two pistols, pressed a muzzle against each of the owner's ears and marched him off to justice."

"Ethics be hanged," he later said in defense of his methods. "I more than accomplished what I was driving at."

An Ohio brewer, a man who had not been egged on by Johnson, also contributed, however unwittingly, to the case against his cause. "We must create the appetite for liquor in growing boys," he announced, with the Anti-Saloon League paying close attention, ready to spread the word on his behalf. "Men who drink . . . will die, and if there is no new appetite created, our coffers will be empty. . . . Nickels expended in treats to boys now will return in dollars to your tills after the appetite has been formed."

But perhaps the single most embarrassing incident of all for the wet forces involved the distillery in Kentucky that went out of business in 1913 after a long and profitable run. Hoping to make a few final bucks, a company official wrote to the president of the Keeley sanitarium in Chicago, the very place where, years earlier, the namesake physician had dispensed his "double chloride of gold." The distiller offered to help the sanitarium recruit future patients. "We can put on your desk a mailing list of over 50,000 individual consumers of liquor," the letter read. "The list of names is new, live and active." The distillery would provide the list, the official continued, "in quantities at the prices listed below." There was no reason, the letter writer implied, for the sanitarium ever to suffer from unoccupied beds.

A copy of the letter found its way to Wayne Wheeler, and he made sure that its contents were reported not only in the temperance press, which was expanding all the time, growing in influence as well as subscriptions, but in regular newspapers as well. The reaction came quickly and vituperatively. The liquor industry was blasted in newspaper editorials and magazine articles, in dinnertime conversations and casual chats among friends on the street or in the office or factory. Among the general populace, drys were gaining ground; wets were getting drier. The liquor industry seemed to be putting one foot in its mouth and shooting itself in the other, just taking turns, back and forth like that. Perhaps, on occasion, it *was* its own worst enemy.

Wayne Wheeler kept on smiling. The reason, some historians have suggested, although without any real corroboration, is that the letter from the Kentucky distiller was a fake and Wheeler was the faker and his scam simply thrilled him to pieces. "The Anti-Saloon League couldn't buy such publicity for a million dollars!" the league's honcho said, but that was as close as he came to a confession.

Of course, it does not necessarily follow that a product should be banned because some of the people who manufacture it are unscrupulous; otherwise, Americans over the years would have turned their backs on automobiles and appliances and processed foods and items of apparel and performances by any number of entertainers. But for many people at the time this was too fine a point; they took a less nuanced view of booze makers and their raging malfeasance. As George Ade would later write, deciding against any mincing of words, the United States eventually "went dry because the distillers, the brewers and the retail dealers in wines, liquors and cigars were a lot of overbearing dumbbells."

Everything was gong the Anti-Saloon League's way. The robber barons were making big donations to the group and a few of their employees, appalled at the heartlessness of the wets, were making smaller ones, a few cents out of each paycheck to the dry forces instead of the bartenders. The war was creating a spirit of self-sacrifice, not to mention xenophobia, which played into the league's hands, and brewers and distillers were doing their damnedest to lose the uncommitteds.

Moreover, in 1917 the American Medical Association announced for the first time an official opinion on beer and wine and whiskey, passing a resolution that said, in part, "whereas we believe that the use of alcohol as a beverage is detrimental to the human economy and whereas its use in therapeutics, as a tonic or a stimulant or as a food, has no scientific basis, therefore be it resolved that the American Medical Association opposes the use of alcohol as a beverage, and be it further resolved that the use of alcohol as a therapeutic agent should be discouraged."

The Anti-Saloon League, which had been pestering the AMA to speak out for years, was delighted that it finally had, and chose to dwell on its words rather than its deeds, as a significant number of doctors continued not only to imbibe themselves, but to prescribe alcohol for their patients: a little something to get the heart started, to calm the nerves, to aid digestion. The group also recommended liquor of one kind or another "in cases of fainting, shock, heart failure, exposure and exhaustion," and it was an accepted "method of feeding carbohydrates to sufferers from diabetes." Furthermore, it was, at least on occasion, an accepted method of dealing with ailments for which there was no accepted method of dealing.

But baseball star Ty Cobb came out against alcoholic beverages. Baseball manager Connie Mack "attributed the success of his teams to total abstinence." And the heavyweight champion of the world, Jess Willard, a very different sort of man from John L. Sullivan, said that if he had his way, "there would not be a drop of liquor made or sold in America."

So the athletes, in what seems to have been the first round of celebrity endorsements on either side of the issue, thumbed their noses at alcohol, although one cannot help but suspect that at least a few of them kept their mouths open and the liquid fire flowing.

Who was giving hooch the high sign? Presidential assassins, that's who. Temperance propagandists did a little research, and then joyfully pointed out that John Wilkes Booth took "his last shot of whiskey at a saloon near Ford's Theatre on the night he shot Lincoln. Charles J. Guiteau, another drunk, shot James A. Garfield. Leon Csolgasz, a saloonkeeper's son, was living in a saloon when he assassinated William McKinley. John Shrank, the failed assassin who shot Theodore Roosevelt, had been a saloon keeper and bartender for years." It seemed, to some, an irrefutable indictment.

And the league had something else in its favor, something that did not relate directly to the consumption of alcohol, but which, in the final analysis, might have been its most important advantage of all, the bedrock upon which its strength so firmly rested. The league had geography on its side, or, more specifically, geographical prejudice: the tendency of the person who lives in the country to resent one who lives in the city, and of the person who lives in the city to look with disdain at the country dweller. These are "ancient" feelings, says historian Will Durant, and inevitable, because the country dwellers "want high returns for agriculture and low prices for manufactured goods," while those of the city "want low prices for food and high wages or profits in industry."

It was the same in America in colonial times. Those who lived in the country, notes Eliot Asinof, looked down on the city because "the money people were there, the snobs of old European 'aristocratic' class lines. The United States Constitution reflected the hegemony of the arm, favoring rural conceptions over urban. Not accidentally, state capitols were set distant from the big cities: Albany, Harrisburg, Trenton. Agrarianism was the first dominant force in America, farmers its leading citizens."

So the roots of the prejudice are economic. But in nineteenth-century America, the prejudice became a more complex and sinister thing, and the reason was booming immigration. Between 1841 and 1860, more than 4 million Irish and Germans and British and French poured into the United States, which meant that, just before the outbreak of the Civil War, thirteen out of every hundred people in the United States were recent arrivals. Some tried to blend in, others merely to survive; regardless, the new Americans were a distinct presence, and could not help but make their new homeland a different place.

In the years that followed, even more people came, huge numbers of Poles and Czechs and Croatians and Italians, with immigration reaching its peak in the two decades leading up to Prohibition. Fourteen million men and women gave up the Old World for the New during those twenty years, almost 2,000 every day of the week, and a majority of the white Americans alive today are descended from them. No other nation in the history of the world had ever seemed so desirable to so many people from elsewhere, and none so readily extended a welcome.

More than anything else, it was the possibility of wealth and freedom that brought Europeans to American shores. Just as their ancestors had wanted to settle in El Dorado, or at least to locate and plunder it, so did the newer generation want to take up residence in the United States—and like the former, the latter had begun to take on the qualities of myth, seeming to promise, by the very fact of its existence, everything that life in their homelands denied. No one, it seemed, could consider the American prospect without exaggeration. In Vienna, writes Frederic Morton, "Brochures showed the Statue of Liberty glittering in solid gold and skyscrapers edged with diamonds."

But this was not just the vision of the Viennese; it was what refugees from almost every European nation thought they would find here. And even those realistic enough to know that precious metals were not commonly used as building materials, in this country or anywhere else, were nonetheless certain that riches of one form or another could be theirs if they only worked hard enough and believed hard enough. America was, after all, the land of the possible—this was *not* a myth. The immigrants were inspired by Carnegie; he was a foreigner. They were inspired by Rockefeller; he was the son of a peddler. They were inspired by Ford; he had had little formal education.

But exceptions always attract more attention than rules, and for that reason make much more dangerous models. The typical immigrant, writes Max Lerner, no sooner arrived in the United States than he

> found himself, dazed and bewildered, in a world with which his traditional peasant qualities could not cope. He had to get work immediately—work of any kind, at any pay, and with whatever hours and conditions—he became thus a ready prey for exploiting employers, swindling fellow countrymen, greedy moneylenders.

And ruthless landlords. The only living spaces that most of the newcomers could afford were almost unlivably small; Jacob Riis, who wrote the classic study of immigrant poverty in New York, *How the Other Half Lives*, described an apartment so tiny that he could barely take a photograph of it even by placing his camera in the hall and shooting through the door. And often these apartments were occupied by so many people that they had to take turns using the various pieces of furniture, of which there were few; and no matter where they situated themselves, they literally breathed down one another's necks. The apartments were carved out of buildings that had a larger population of rodents than of human beings, and through which waves of smallpox and other diseases wafted like breezes on a foul summer day. Toilets were at the end of the hall, or somewhere outside; they smelled like the last days of a dying species. These rooms, intended and rented as homes for human beings, were in truth "unfit for horses or swine."

It did not take long, under conditions like these, for the newcomers to lose what they had had most of when they landed: hope. It began to seem a waste of the little energy they had left at the end of the day, and of the little time that remained when the day's labors were finally over. In some years, in fact, statistics show that as many as 40 percent of them gave up on the United States and went home again. Yet reinforcements continued to come, unending masses of men and women and children, storming onto American shores, more Irish and Germans and British and French and Poles and Czechs and Croatians and Italians. If success was harder to achieve in the U.S. than they had originally thought—and people in the later waves of immigration were being warned by their predecessors that this was so—it still seemed more of a likelihood than it did in their native lands, and between the two the choice was obvious.

In 1907 alone, a record number of people—1,285,349, most of them from southern and eastern Europe—landed in America, enough to make a city the size of today's San Diego. There were now almost three times as many foreign-born men and women in the United States as there had been on the eve of the Civil War, and each boatload stretched the dream a little thinner. Each put a further strain on living quarters, a further strain on wages, a further strain on relationships. For many immigrants, there was only one thing to do with the tensions so great and expectations so fleeting—and a person who drank for reasons like these could be the meanest of drunks.

Meanwhile, a world away, on the farms that stretched across the vast plains of the Midwest and the softly rolling acreage of the South, life was remarkably similar to what it had been in the earliest days of the Republic. True, there were now trains to take the crops to market instead of wagons, and engines to run the plows instead of horses. But the same kinds of people lived in the same kinds of places and did the same daily tasks to the same, unalterable rhythm of the seasons. This meant that now, more than ever, the country was all the things the city was not.

It was, for one thing, "American." In New York, on the other hand, there were more Jews than in any other city in the world, more Italians than in any city but Rome, more Poles than in any city but Warsaw, and about the same number of Irish as in Dublin.

The rural areas were also Protestant, in some places still cleanly descended from the original settlers. Most of the middle Europeans and Mediterranean immigrants in the city, though, were Roman Catholics, and the animosity between the two sometimes seemed as bitter as it had been in sixteenth-century Europe, when the Protestant faiths were created out of dissatisfaction with the Roman. Bishop James Cannon Jr., next to Wayne Wheeler the most powerful man in the Anti-Saloon League, was said to have hated Catholicism second only to booze. "The mother of ignorance, superstition, intolerance and sin," was how he described the church under Benedict XV, the pope from 1914 to 1922, and that being the case, it was only natural, thought he and many of his fellow members of the league, that the Catholic would also be inordinately fond of spirits.

Thus, to the man of the country, the composite city dweller: a foreigner who was also a papist and a boozer, with the first two invariably leading to the third. And to the man of the city, the composite heartlander: a small-minded, straight-laced, intolerable rube who spent too little time broadening his outlook and too much fretting about the pleasures of others. "It was among country Methodists," believed Baltimore's H. L. Mencken, after alcohol had been legally banished from one end of the continent to the other, "practitioners of a theology degraded almost to the level of voodooism, that Prohibition was invented, and it was by country Methodists, nine-tenths of them actual followers of the plow, that it was fastened upon the rest of us, to the damage of our bank accounts, our dignity and our ease."

And the country was agrarian, the city industrial; the country quiet, the city raucous; the country spacious, the city confined; the country sparse, the city teeming; the country fresh, the city noisome; the country bound for salvation, the city going to hell, if not already its earthly embodiment. And in 1910, the country was half of American population, the city the other half.

It was in part because of perceptions like these that the men and women of the soil voted so overwhelmingly against alcoholic beverages when their states considered Prohibition. They also voted against them because of their feelings for yet another group of foreigners, the most ominous of all as far as some were concerned: the dark-skinned, dark-souled Africans, so different in appearance and custom. It is probably fair to say, as did historian John Kobler, that "among the hardest drinking, dry-voting legislators were some of the Deep Southerners whose chief concern was to keep liquor away from the black lest it impair his capacity for cheaply paid work."

Even more, these legislators, and the people they represented, wanted to make sure that black men stayed as far away from white women as was possible given their mutual occupancy of the same continent. Southerners seemed to fear miscegenation more than they feared crop failures or dust storms or locust infestations, and it was an article of faith among them that liquor turned otherwise peaceable blacks into "sexual hyenas," animals in whose presence no white woman below the Mason-Dixon line was safe. In fact, when a play called *The Nigger* opened in New York in these days, it portrayed booze as the fuel for black lasciviousness, and referred to a ban on it as "the only way in which we can attack the niggah problem." The Ku Klux Klan, concerned not only with that particular problem but with others of its own abhorrent invention, was an active and welcome supporter of the Anti-Saloon League.

Were those who lived in the American Midwest and South any less fond of alcoholic libations than other Americans? Certainly not. In fact, they were probably more fond of corn liquor and other forms of homemade moonshine, many of them having drunk such beverages for years and having handed down recipes from one generation to the next. But the times were different now, and opposing alcohol had become a statement they had to make, a political position they had to support, a means of being true to themselves by revealing the antagonism they had developed for the other America, an antagonism by which, in many cases, they now came to define themselves.

They were not unkind people, not inherently, and certainly not the fools that Mencken made them out to be. They were simply people who did not know what to make of the unfamiliar. How could they? They had had so little experience with it, living as they did, where they did, so far from seaports and the ships that landed there and almost daily brought forth new Americans who were so very different from, and thus so very threatening to, themselves. They did not hate the black man and the Serb, the Italian and the Pole, the Czech and the Croatian. They feared them, and it is not animosity that makes a person afraid; it is ignorance, a lack of knowledge, a narrow kind of living.

And so of course the Women's Crusade and the Woman's Christian Temperance Union and the Anti-Saloon League of America were born in the Midwest. Of course Carry Nation bombed in New York. It might have been a single country, but these were totally different audiences.

A constitutional amendment to make alcoholic beverages illegal from the Atlantic to the Pacific, from Canada to Mexico, from dusk to dawn and from cradle to grave, was first introduced in Congress in 1876, after having been a plank in the Prohibition Party's platform earlier in the year. Actually, the measure would have applied only to distilled products, not beer or wine, and would not have taken effect until 1900. Still, it was referred to committee and never heard from again.

The next attempt came in 1914. The bill was sponsored by Representative Richmond Pearson Hobson, Democrat from Alabama and naval hero in the Spanish-American War, who believed that alcohol attacked the reproductive systems of both male and female, destroying tissue, enfeebling capacity. He also claimed that booze "was the main cause of feeblemindedness and sexual perversion in women." Further, he stated, reflecting the biases of so many of his constituents, "Liquor will actually make a brute out of the Negro, causing him to commit unnatural crimes. The effect is the same in the white man, though the white man being further evolved it takes a longer time to reduce him to the same level."

The House gallery was packed with drys for the introduction of Hobson's bill, and they were one of the more ludicrous sights ever to appear in that location, having draped themselves with a petition which they said contained the names of 6 million fellow teetotalers, all of whom shared the same desire to have abstinence written into the Constitution. And there they sat, taking up space in the dignified chambers of federal government with this endless document wound around their torsos and shoulders and arms and legs like the world's longest daisy chain of dreams, rooting on their cause.

But it was not to be. One hundred ninety-seven legislators supported the booze ban, 190 opposed it. That was sixty-one votes shy of the two-thirds majority needed for passage. Andrew Sinclair's geographic breakdown of the result is instructive.

> Of the 197 members of the House who voted for the Hobson resolution, 129 were from cities of less than 10,000 people, while 64 of them were from country villages of less than 2500 people. Only 13 were from cities

containing a population of more than 100,000. Of the 190 opponents to the
resolution, 109 were from cities of more than 25,000 people, and only 25
from villages with less than 2500 inhabitants.

With the amendment failing a second time, its supporters unwrapped
themselves from their petition, this unwieldy paper boa of theirs, and
folded it into a huge, awkward mound and went home disconsolately.

The third time, however, was the charm. In the 1916 congressional
elections, with U.S entry into the Great War only five months away
and dry momentum on the rise, the Anti-Saloon League, as Wayne
Wheeler boasted to a journalist, "laid down such a barrage as candidates for Congress had never seen before, and such as they will, in all
likelihood, not see again for years to come." The result was that Americans voted into office more antidrink legislators than ever before, men
whose debt to the league was no less binding to them than their oath of
office. So in 1917, when the amendment came up again, there was little
doubt about the outcome.

Representative Hobson reintroduced his bill, this time under the co-
sponsorship of a fellow Southerner, Senator Morris Sheppard, Democrat from Texas, a gentleman whose name will appear later in this narrative, and who appeared earlier as eponym of the measure prohibiting the
manufacture, importation, or sale of spirits in the District of Columbia.
But although these two men had their names attached to the legislation,
the sentiments, and in some places even the language, were pure Wayne
Wheeler.

Whereas, exact scientific research has demonstrated that alcohol is a nar-
cotic poison, destructive and degenerating to the human organism, and
that its distribution as a beverage or contained in foods, lays a staggering
economic burden upon the shoulders of the people, lowers to an appalling
degree the average standard of the character of our citizenship, thereby
undermining the public morals and the foundation of free institutions,
produces wide-spread crime, pauperism and insanity, inflicts disease and
untimely death upon hundreds of thousands of citizens, and blights with
degeneracy their children unborn, threatening the future integrity and very
life of the nation.

Therefore be it resolved: By the Senate and the House of Representatives
of the United States of America in congress assembled (two-thirds of each
House concurring therein), that the following amendment is proposed to
the States, to become valid as part of the Constitution when ratified by the
legislatures of the several States as provided by the Constitution.

Section 1. After one year from the ratification of this article the manufacture, sale or transportation of intoxicating liquors within, the importa-

tion thereof into, or the exportation thereof from the United States and all territory subject to the jurisdiction thereof for beverage purposes is hereby prohibited.

Section 2. The Congress and the several States shall have concurrent power to enforce this article by appropriate legislation.

Four months after the United States officially entered World War I, the Senate approved Hobson-Sheppard by a count of sixty-five to twenty. Four months later, the House also assented, 282–128. The bill did not prohibit the drinking of alcohol, only the buying and selling of it. Or as Sean Dennis Cashman points out in his book, *Prohibition: The Lie of the Land,* "It was the trade and not the article itself that was beyond the pale."

One of the reasons Hobson-Sheppard passed so easily was that, in those days, the country was different from the city in yet another way; it had a great and unfair advantage in terms of legislative apportionment. Cashman gives a single example where dozens are possible. "In New York State," he writes, "one voter in Putnam County had as much representation as four voters in Rochester, five in Syracuse, and seven in some districts of New York City."

The large margins in House and Senate were also ensured by a last-minute blitz from the Anti-Saloon League, which seems to have been spearheaded by Howard Hyde Russell, a final hurrah for the old man who had started it all, then taken a willing back seat to his protégé, Wayne Wheeler. Russell had remained in that position throughout the campaign against alcohol, but now thought the time right to take a step of his own. So he

> entered into a holy conspiracy with Sebastian S. Kresge, the dime store tycoon, to force the measure through. Together they sent out thirty-five different high-powered letters of financial solicitation to 135,000 select businessmen and manufacturers. Thirteen thousand responded with contributions. A few days before the submission vote, the two apostles met in Kresge's Detroit office and out of the 13,000 contributors selected the 2,400 who seemed most promising. By telegram, they urged them to flood Congress with cries demanding submission of the amendment to the states.

As Russell later bragged, "We blocked the telegraph wires in Washington for three days."

The *Washington Times* might not have known about the telegraph wires, but it was well aware of the league's behind-the-scenes prominence. It believed that "if the ballot . . . were a secret ballot, making it impossible for the Anti-Saloon League bosses to punish disobedience, the amendment would not pass."

It may be true. And it may be true, as Mencken said, that in a great many cases "a congressman is a man who prepares for a speech on prohibition by taking three stiff drinks." But it is also true that, just as a certain number of citizens joined the early temperance societies knowing they would continue to drink moderately themselves, but wanting to set an example for others, so too did some members of the House and Senate vote for that purpose. Wet was their natural condition, but they were sincere in their belief that dry was best for the society as a whole. "Hypocrisy," says the French essayist La Rochefoucauld, "is the homage that vice pays to virtue," and it might well have been the explanation for many a legislator's vote on national prohibition, and then his retreat to his office for a private nip or two.

With the vote having turned out as it did, it was now time, as Hobson-Sheppard itself said, for "the legislatures of the several States" to approve. Three-fourths of them, or thirty-six, would have to ratify the ban on booze within seven years for it to become the Eighteenth Amendment to the Constitution of the United States.

Strange as it seems, this part of the process was pleasing to both sides. Drys thought seven years more than enough time to get the job done. After all, even before wartime prohibition, more than half of the states had enacted prohibitions of their own; surely they would approve the same ban for peacetime, and on the national level, and this being the case, only a few more states would have to join them.

Wets, on the other hand, chuckled smugly to one another, although some of it might have been false bravado, an expression of hope more than confidence. They believed—or claimed to believe—that there was no way in the world for thirty-six bureaucracy-laden governmental entities, regardless of their views on alcoholic beverages, to do something so drastic, so untraditional, so disruptive to their own economies and tax bases and personal habits, as vote for a permanent prohibition of alcohol under *any* set of circumstances, much less with such rapidity. After all, this was still the land that the Founding Fathers had created, and there was not so much as a single teetotaler among them.

But drys, more perceptive as usual, knew that the change had already come. It had been a slow and painstaking process, perhaps starting as long ago as the day when the Benjamin Rush first put pen to paper in the cause of a more sober nation: one person persuaded at a time, one convert preaching to a friend, one vote purchased here and the next vote there, one local law passed and then another and another, one corporate head changing his mind and then another and another, one set of prejudices played upon, one set of sympathies evoked. What remained, then, was not for minds to be changed, but for the changing of the minds to be formalized, and then acknowledged by one and all in an official forum.

Mississippi was the first state to ratify the Eighteenth Amendment, on January 18, 1918, and fourteen other states followed suit before the year was out. Here again the country's voice was louder than the city's. "In Michigan," Cashman discovered, "electors in Antrim, Alpena, Livingston and Midland counties had as much representation even in the state house as two-and-a-half electors in Detroit."

In the first two weeks of 1919, twenty more states fell into line before the steamrollering zeitgeist. In most cases, the votes were not close, the outcome long expected. Then, on January 16, with bitterly cold winds whipping across the slumbering farmlands of Nebraska, perhaps the heartland's very heart, legislators in the capitol of Lincoln met in august and sober assembly and also said yes. They were the thirty-sixth affirmative vote—and it had not taken seven years for them to be recorded, but a few days less than one! Drys were giddy, overjoyed—more than that, *vindicated.*

Wets could not believe it. They had had no idea how thoroughly they were being outmaneuvered and how long the outmaneuvering had been going on, and once they found out it was too late for anything but stupefaction. Eventually, forty-six states would approve the Eighteenth Amendment, many of them simply continuing the prohibitions that already existed within their borders. Connecticut and Rhode Island were the only two states that—one should forgive the word—abstained.

All together, some 5,090 elected officials, an average of more than a hundred in each ratifying state, voted for the end of demon rum and its fellow intoxicating potions. There is no way of knowing how many of them were puppets of the Anti-Saloon League, nor how many first learned about the effects of alcoholic beverages from the Department of Scientific Temperance Instruction of the Woman's Christian Temperance Union.

Nine months later, Congress passed the National Prohibition Act, meant to be the muscle behind the Eighteenth Amendment. It, too, was largely the work of Wayne Wheeler, but it became popularly known by the name of Minnesota Congressman Andrew Volstead, who, despite being less than enthusiastic about a dry America, had acceded to Wheeler's wishes and sponsored the measure in the House of Representatives.

President Wilson did not like it. He vetoed the Volstead Act, only to have Congress override him by a tally of 176 to 55. In truth, he did not care for the rejiggering of the Constitution that had brought the act into being in the first place. "I am in favor of local option," he explained. "I am a thorough believer in local self-government."

The Volstead Act allowed people to keep possession of all the alcoholic beverages they had purchased prior to July 1, 1919; in so doing, it proved the greatest incentive to hoarding ever known to men and women of spirituous thirst. The act also required that the beverages be consumed at home, something that men and women of the Republic were more than willing to do. In addition, it permitted them to manufacture their own wine and hard cider, up to 200 gallons a year, provided that these were imbibed by members of the family, also at home. They could also make something called "near beer," a brew that contained one-half of one percent alcohol, compared to 3.5 to 5 percent in conventional beer, and was so pitiably weak, said Will Rogers, that "you have to take a glass of water as a stimulant immediately afterward." Factories could continue to turn out industrial alcohol, alcohol used for medicinal purposes, and sacramental wines. And, as a sop to farmers, they were allowed to produce sweet cider which would in time turn to hard.

What the Volstead Act did not allow was the sale or commercial manufacture of any other alcoholic beverages under any other conditions. People who brewed or distilled were subject to a fine of $1,000 or a jail term of six months. For second offenders, it was $10,000 and five years. The act also provided for the padlocking of any place that sold booze. Personal property used in the transportation of alcohol, such as cars, boats, and planes, was to be seized by the government and auctioned to help pay the costs of enforcement.

The agency in charge of enforcement was the Bureau of Internal Revenue, which did not become the Internal Revenue Service until the 1950s. Its main man in New York, Colonel Daniel Porter, spoke confidently about what the Volstead Act would mean. "The penalties for violation are so drastic," he said, "that the people of New York will not attempt to violate it. There will be no violations to speak of."

In Washington, D.C., Daniel C. Roper, Commissioner of Internal Revenue, disagreed. Sort of. "The Prohibition Law will be violated—extensively at first, slightly later on, but it will, broadly speaking, be enforced and will result in a nation that knows not alcohol."

Unfortunately, Mark Twain was dead, and unable to be queried. Had he been alive, he might have remembered his trip to New Zealand in 1895, where a prohibitory law was also under consideration. Twain told an audience in Christchurch

> that if prohibition came to town, they could expect difficulties. He told them that in America, a few years before, a stranger came to a dry town and discovered that the only place he could get a drink was at the pharmacy. When he asked the pharmacist for a drink, he found he needed a doctor's prescription, except for snakebite. "The man said, 'Where's the snake?' So the apothecary gave him the snake's address, and he went off. Soon after, however, he came back and said, 'For goodness' sake, give me a drink. That snake is engaged for months ahead.'"

The stage, then, was now set for what many would regard, despite daily dollops of evidence to the contrary, as "The Noble Experiment."

8

The Blues and How They Played

Pussyfoot Johnson was looking forward to the new law. "This is a big moment for me," he said, after exaggerating his own role in bringing it about, "because from this day the flag of my country will no longer float over any brewery or distillery."

The Reverend Billy Sunday, one-time major league baseball player turned evangelist, was looking forward to the new law. "The reign of tears is over," he told the faithful, his voice soaring even more than it usually did when moved by the Spirit. "The slums will soon be a memory. We will turn our prisons into factories and our jails into storehouses and corncribs. Men will walk upright now, women will smile and the children will laugh. Hell will be forever for rent."

Dr. Henry Lee Smith, the president of Washington & Lee University in Virginia, was looking forward to the new law. He thought that Americans were about to take "the longest and most effective step forward in the uplift of the human race ever taken by any civilized nation."

William Jennings Bryan was looking forward to the new law. Three times a candidate for the presidency of the United States, he had afterward served as Wilson's secretary of state, and in that capacity had refused to provide liquor and wine at State Department functions, thereby bringing back memories of Lemonade Lucy and earning the enmity of most of the Washington diplomatic community and all of the press corps. He did not care. Let them drink grape juice and water, he thundered, and served both. "You shall not bury the Democratic Party in a drunkard's grave," he bellowed, and made sure he served the grape juice before it fermented.

Josephus Daniels, secretary of the navy, was looking forward to the new law. The Eighteenth Amendment, he told friends, "will last as long as the preamble [to the Constitution]." He did not stop there. "The saloon is as dead as slavery," he declared. He was sure of it.

Miss Christine Tilling of the San Francisco chapter of the Woman's Christian Temperance Union was looking forward to the new law. She thought of it as "God's present to the nation," and was confident that others would see it that way, too.

Michigan pastor and Prohibition Party member Edward B. Sutton was looking forward to the new law. When someone told him that public sentiment was not ready for it, he pounded his fists in fury. "Public sentiment was not ready for the Ten Commandments when they were first given!" he said.

So spoke some notable drys as the days grew short for beverages containing alcohol. They were confident and belligerent, relieved and prayerful. They toasted themselves with fruit juice and soft drinks and and coffee and tea and their glasses clicked resoundingly. They had climbed a mountain so tall that they could not even see the summit when they started, and in the euphoria of the moment, planting their flags at the peak, they had no misgivings, or at least none that they would admit to one another.

Wets, on the other hand, feared the end of an era, the disappearance not only of certain kinds of libations, but of a way of life, a style of conviviality that was at once comfortable and stimulating, not to mention deeply and eternally American. "Goodbye forever to my old friend booze," wrote Ring Lardner, and you could almost hear a saxophone in the background, wailing in languid sympathy. "Doggone, I've got the prohibition blues."

He was not alone. On the last night that alcoholic beverages were legal in the United States of America, a night that was the tippler's equivalent to the Black Thursday that would begin to deflate the stock market a decade hence, there were expressions of woe from all quarters, especially the nation's largest metropolis.

In New York City, where heavy snow was falling and the thermometer read 18°, mock obsequies marked the approach of midnight. . . . Tom

Healey, the owner of the Golden Glades Restaurant, a resort renowned for its ice-skating extravaganzas, had a coffin paraded around the dance floor for everybody to throw his last bottle and glass into. Louis Fischer, who ran Reisenweber's café, had sent black-bordered cards to his regular clientele, bidding them to a funeral ball. The ladies who accepted received vanity cases in the shape of coffins. At midnight, six waiter-pallbearers carried a real coffin across the room to the elaborate strains of Chopin's "Funeral March." . . . The most elaborate mummery was staged by a visiting Philadelphia publisher, George Sheldon, who took over an entire dining room at the Hotel Park Avenue. His guests, 200 of them, wearing black clothes as instructed, were seated at tables covered, like the wall and candlebra, with black cloth. The tableware had black handles. Napkins and glasses were black. The waiters, all in black, served black caviar. An enormous black coffin full of black bottles occupied the center of the room, and a black-clad band played funeral dirges. Following a midnight toast, the lights went out and spotlights framed a mournful *tableau vivant*. At a rear table two couples poured the last drops from a black bottle into their black glasses, sobbing and dabbing at their eyes.

Not all American drinkers behaved so theatrically. Many were in their homes when midnight struck on the appointed night, either asleep or in the company of a small number of family and friends. Among the latter were those who listened to the tolling of bells from a nearby church or town hall, so different from the bells that had sounded the eleven o'clock bitters in colonial times; then they bent their elbows back once or twice, said "Bottoms up" to one another, and went to bed quietly, puzzled by how puzzled they were. Some slept well; others tossed and turned. Just because they had seen it coming for weeks and months and years did not mean they were ready for it.

A British spiritualist named Sir Oliver Joseph Lodge tried to offer consolation. He was making a tour of the United States as Prohibition descended and told of a conversation he had recently had with his son. The son was dead, Lodge pointed out, but he claimed to have as good a postmortem relationship with the lad as he did premortem, and said he could summon him up at will for a chat.

When last he did, the elder Lodge went on, he gave his son the details of the Eighteenth Amendment. The son listened raptly to the whole, convoluted, improbable tale, trying to make sense of so authoritarian a step having been taken by so democratic a country. Then he told his father not to worry. Furthermore, he told his father to tell the whole of America not to worry. There is "strong drink in the great beyond," said Lodge, Junior; the thirsty needed only to be patient.

They were not. It was the here and now that concerned them, not the future, and the here and now seemed as bleak a prospect as the American wassailer had ever known. How would he cope? How would *she* cope? What would become of them? Was there any chance they would wake up tomorrow and find it had all been a dream?

The Eighteenth Amendment to the Constitution of the United States became the law of the land on January 16, 1920, at 12:01 A.M.

Some Americans began to adjust at 12:02. Others had been adjusting for months or years, ever since their various states passed prohibitory laws and they were forced to choose between resourcefulness and thirst. Among those who opted for the latter were people who decided to make their own beer in their own kitchens or basements or bathrooms. They were steelworkers in McKeesport, Pennsylvania; autoworkers in Dearborn, Michigan; dockworkers in Bayside, New York; textile workers in Lowell, Massachusetts; miners in Parkersburg, West Virginia; oil men in southern California; farm equipment salesmen in Dubuque, Iowa; small businessmen in Paterson, New Jersey; store clerks in Bridgeport, Connecticut; seamstresses in Dayton, Ohio; secretaries in Gary, Indiana—they were, in other words, the men and women of the lower-middle-class neighborhoods, and by slaking their thirsts as they did, they brought back the pre–Industrial Revolution days of cottage industry. In the process, they found a project that the whole family could enjoy, a means of sharing quality time long before the phrase became popular.

> Mother's in the kitchen
> Washing out the jugs;
> Sister's in the pantry
> Bottling the suds;
> Father's in the cellar
> Mixing up the hops;
> Johnny's on the front porch
> Watching for the cops.

During Prohibition, Americans produced as much as 700 million gallons of beer in their homes each year, defying the Volstead Act and enraging the Anti-Saloon League. The air became thick with new kinds of industrial fumes; it was on some occasions possible for a person to walk an entire town or city block, if not more, without ever losing the scent of brew from the residences he passed. And after a man of unknown identity had paddled a canoe the entire length of the Mississippi River, he told the friends who greeted him in New Orleans that the telltale odors of home brew had been with him since Minnesota.

It could hardly have been otherwise. People were malting, mashing, boiling, hopping, fermenting, siphoning, settling—all the things that a professional brewer might do, but amateurishly. They had neither the touch nor the training of a pro, only a sudden and desperate incentive, and so their beverage usually did not taste as much like the pre-Prohibition substance as they had hoped; it was too weak or too flat, too sweet or too bitter. Nor did it have the same effect. "After I've had a couple glasses I'm terribly sleepy," reported one partaker of home brew. "Sometimes my eyes don't seem to focus and my head aches. I'm not intoxicated, understand, merely feel as if I've been drawn through a keyhole."

H. L. Mencken did not feel attenuated after swigging down his own new-style suds, but neither did he feel safe. "Last Sunday I manufactured five gallons of Methodistbrau," he related, "but I bottled it too soon, and the result has been a series of fearful explosions. Last night I had three quart bottles in my side yard, cooling in a bucket. Two went off at once, bringing my neighbor out of his house with yells. He thought the Soviets had seized the town."

Another man, however, had a recipe for home brew that he claimed was not only harmless, but as tasty as the commercially manufactured beverage had been in the oh-so-recent good old days. He was Fiorello LaGuardia, congressman from New York and later the city's mayor, and no respecter of the Eighteenth Amendment or any of its promoters. In fact, the law frustrated him so much that he decided to demonstrate his feelings publicly and dare the authorities to stop him. He invited the press. He invited his fellow lawmakers. He invited the constabulary. Then he attired himself in bartender's garb and angled those mischievous lips of his into a big smile as he stood before newsreel cameras in Room 150 of the House Office Building in Washington, D.C.

He made sure the cameras were rolling. He gave the men behind them time to compose and focus their shots. Then, proceeding slowly so that they did not miss anything, and speaking as clearly as possible, for posterity as well as for the microphones, LaGuardia went to work. He blended two parts malt tonic, "heretofore of interest only to anemics and easy to obtain at almost any drugstore," to one part "near beer." He stirred the ingredients and allowed a few seconds to pass to heighten the suspense. Then he drank up and licked his lips. The cameras zoomed in. "A brewmaster was standing by to sample the mixture," historian Geoffrey Perrett records. "He pronounced it delicious."

The assembled crowd applauded eagerly, all except the cops. They turned away in frustration and began to talk among themselves. Should they arrest the guy? They decided not to, figuring it would probably not be wise to slap handcuffs on a member of the U.S. House of Representatives, especially not as he stood in the midst of a group which had just given him so warm an ovation.

Still, the New York State Prohibition Bureau was not amused. It warned that anyone in the Empire State who tried to follow the La-Guardia formula, especially in large proportions, would not only be arrested but, through the severity of his punishment, made into an example. Yet many did; the congressman became a Julia Child for Prohibition-wracked imbibers from Buffalo to Staten Island, from Plattsburgh to Elmira. LaGuardia's recipe was also a hit outside New York. "Newspapers all over America carried stories of his exploit," writes Edward Behr, "and one city editor wired him: 'Your beer a sensation. Whole staff trying experiment. Remarkable results.'"

Before long, grocery stores were openly abetting the household brewing industry, not only by stocking malt tonic, which had never been part of their inventory before, but by displaying the cans as prominently as issues of the *National Enquirer* or *TV Guide* are displayed in today's supermarkets. Signs advertised specials; people were urged to buy in quantity and save money.

As for the equipment necessary to make beer and other alcoholic beverages at home, it became remarkably easy to acquire. Almost overnight, small stores sprang up in many neighborhoods to service the booming new industry. They sold "hops, yeast, malt, corn meal, grains, copper tubing, crocks, kettles, charred kegs, bottle tops and other supplies." They provided booklets of information and precise measuring devices; they were staffed by knowledgeable people, eager to help. The police were not happy about this and sometimes harassed both owners and customers. But that was all they did or could do; since the shops neither sold proscribed products nor directly encouraged people to use the products to perform Volstead-defying activities, they were not against the law. They were, rather, the equivalent of the "head shops" that sprang up for a later generation—abetting illegality, winking at illegality, but not, strictly speaking, engaging in illegal acts.

Sinclair Lewis's *The Man Who Knew Coolidge*, normally a law-abiding sort, saw nothing wrong with the stores or the equipment or the recipes. He saw nothing wrong with emptying a glass or two in a nation that had lost its mind and decided to frown upon the practice. He didn't *really* know Coolidge, as it turned out, but he knew his times, and could speak for them as authoritatively as anyone else. "If a fellow feels like making some good home-brewed beer," he said, "there ain't any reason on God's green earth that *I* can see why you shouldn't take advantage of it, always providing you aren't setting somebody a bad example or making it look like you sympathized with law breaking.

"No sir!"

A person who wanted to produce liquor at home could also do so. As was the case with beer, he had to put up with a great deal of inconvenience and results that more often than not disappointed, but many was the adventurer willing to try. The first thing he did was buy a so-called alky cooker for $12; if that was too expensive, he made use of a kettle or even a big pot that he already owned. Then he bought some corn sugar mash, the purpose of which was almost solely to make whiskey and the sales of which increased sixfold between 1919 and 1929. He heated the mash slowly in the kettle until it reached a temperature of 180 degrees Fahrenheit. At that point, vapors of alcoholic steam began to rise like smoke from a smoldering cigarette. The crucial moment had now arrived.

As quickly as he could, the fledgling distiller, forced so unjustly into this new and demanding avocation, trapped the steam by placing a cloth over the top of the kettle and then wringing it into a bowl. The yield was pure alcohol, 100 percent, 200 proof. Although too deadly to drink in this form, the liquid was then used as a base to create facsimiles of almost every kind of booze known to pre–Eighteenth Amendment man. Adding water, glycerine, and juniper oil, for example, resulted in bathtub gin, one of the most popular of the era's ersatz beverages, so named because of the container in which it was often prepared or stored to accommodate large and constantly renewing thirsts.

But mind-altering potions of some sort could be made from almost anything, if one were inventive, patient, and sufficiently thirsty. Fruits, vegetables, flowers, grasses, various medicinal compounds, cleaning agents, cosmetics—all could be pressed into service one way or another. "In southern Florida," Perrett writes, "all that anyone had to do was take a coconut, bore a hole into it, leave the milk inside, add a tablespoon of brown sugar, and seal. Three weeks later they had a pungent, potent, treacly concoction called cocowhiskey."

And for those who could not figure out how to concoct a satisfying libation on their own, or who had no one to advise them, the federal government was pleased to offer assistance. Well, perhaps not pleased, but at least willing, however inadvertently. Before the Eighteenth Amendment took effect, the Department of Agriculture had published a number of brochures telling people how to create alcohol from "apples, oats, bananas, pumpkins, and parsnips, and in true bureaucratic fashion, the department continued to distribute them after Prohibition." Which is to say that the same folks who had passed the law forbidding liquor were now providing detailed instructions on how to break it. It should surprise no one to learn that the pamphlets were even more popular after January 16, 1920, than they had been before, nor that commercial publishing houses began to turn out their own texts, suddenly discovering a whole new line of how-to literature with an avidly receptive audience. At libraries, books on brewing and distilling were checked out in unprecedented numbers as the 1920s got underway; many libraries had to order additional copies, and in some cases to insist that they not circulate.

But there was more to homemade booze than just the buzz. For some households, the manufacture of alcoholic beverages was also a source of much-needed income. Call it, almost literally, a form of trickle-down economics. According to a survey conducted in 1925 by the Federal Council of Churches in Christ in America, "The illicit liquor traffic has become a means of comparative opulence to many families that formerly were on the records of relief agencies. In one New England industrial town a row of somber tenements has been adorned with Stutz and Packard cars purchased with the profits of a new-found illicit livelihood." In other towns, less ostentatious cars appeared in front of houses, or perhaps an extra piece of furniture showed up in the living room, more food was placed on the dining room table, more clothes were hung in the children's closets, or more evenings were spent at the motion picture theater or the concert hall. Cottage industry, after all, makes for a more prosperous cottage, as an anonymous poet in the *New York World* was quick to realize.

> Mother makes brandy from cherries;
> Pop distills whiskey and gin;

Sister sells wine from the grapes on our vine—
Good grief, how the money rolls in.

And yes, as the poet acknowledged, it was possible to make a kind of wine at home, even without a personal vineyard. The simplest method was the one so coyly explained by salesgirls at various New York department stores. And what salesgirls they were—short-skirted and bobbed-haired, lusciously dimpled and bright-eyed, full-chested and very carefully programmed. What they did was offer their customers blocks of grape concentrate that were sometimes the size of a pound of butter, sometimes a little smaller. Bacchus bricks, at least one company called them, and the come-hither members of the sales force might pitch the bricks by saying something like this to the men and women, although mostly men, who gathered around them so curiously:

"There's nothing to it, ladies and gentlemen," the young woman would begin, flashing a smile all the way back to her molars, "nothing at all. To get started, what you do is dissolve our brick here in a bowl of water." (She places the brick into the bowl.) "Then you wait a little while." (She waits, sloshing the brick in the water, keeping the molars visible.) "When you're done waiting, voilà, you have a wonderful, thirst-quenching grape beverage. See?" (The water has turned purple.) "It's the perfect thing for a hot, summer day. Or any other day, for that matter. Isn't it great?"

Murmurs of assent from the audience.

"But there's something I have to caution you about," she would continue. "After the brick is completely dissolved, you've got to be sure not to pour the beverage into this jug." (She holds up a jug.) "And then you've got to be even more sure not to put the jug into the cupboard, away from the light, for exactly twenty-one days. Got that, three weeks? No more, no less. Because if you *do* pour the liquid into this jug and hide it away from the light for exactly twenty-one days, three weeks, you won't have sweet-tasting, harmless grape juice anymore." (She shakes her head.) "Oh, no. What will happen, see, is the juice will turn into wine—that's right, *wine*—into sherry or port or burgundy, and, depending on what you do with it, you might be breaking the law!

"And, just as important, be sure you don't stop up the jug with this cork." (She holds up a cork.) "You see, if you *do* stop it up with this cork, you will only be helping the juice to ferment. Have all you folks got that?"

Every single word.

"Okay, one more thing. The jugs and the corks—and you see the cork has our patented red rubber siphon hose, the best you can find anywhere, at any price—are for sale this week only when you buy three bricks for the price of two. Just don't use them for the wrong reason.

"May I take your orders?"

Some ethnic groups, Italians and Greeks prominent among them, did not need Bacchus bricks. They had long been making wine at home, finding the manufacture something of an art form and the consumption an integral part of their cultures; some of them had, as a result, become as skilled at turning out fine vintages as the professionals. Rather than forcing them to stop, the Eighteenth Amendment provided all the incentive they needed to increase production by teaching the skill to their friends, relatives, and other countrymen. They saw to their family's needs and perhaps supplied what they could to others, selling their beverages to strangers, giving it away to their *paisans* and *sigenis*. It was not what the law had in mind. "The spectacle of immigrants making and drinking their wine," writes Andrew Sinclair, "drove the drys to paroxysms of fury, so that they recommended the deportation of alien violators of the Volstead Act." Even if, by turning out less than 200 gallons a year, they were *not* violating the act.

Both immigrants and longer-established citizens alike made so much wine, beer, and whiskey during Prohibition that glassmakers struck it rich. "Manufacturers capitalized on the new enthusiasm for home drinking," writes Catherine Gilbert Murdock. "John T. Flynn, in a 1928 *Collier's* article, listed the thirty-five different cocktail glasses he found at one New York department store, in addition to shakers, hip flasks, and a variety of wine glasses. As early as 1923, department store ads mentioned wine and cocktail glasses by name. The respectable hostess required a knowledge of glassware akin to that of her Victorian grandmother."

And why was such knowledge required of the respectable hostess? Because it was with Prohibition that the cocktail party, for the first time, became an American institution. Prior to 1920, most people did most of their drinking in taverns and saloons and restaurants; these were, after all, where the booze was sold and the seats were comfortable and the companions familiar and welcoming. But now the families that produced their alcohol at home were bound by Volstead to serve it at home; they were hardly going to dip a few jars into their gin-brimming bathtubs and head for the ball game or town park or church social. Rather, they invited their friends to visit, and they kept the glasses as full as they could for as long as they could. Hitting the sauce had once been a public activity; the Eighteenth Amendment now converted it to a more personal occasion within the old four walls.

The Anti-Saloon League had not expected anything like this. Neither had the politicians who nestled so dependently in their pockets. They had not singled out the home production of alcoholic beverages for special penalties in Volstead because they believed that people who were used to quality beer and wine and whiskey would not stoop to merchandise that was both inferior in taste and difficult to manufacture. Early on, when a reporter asked A. B. Adams, chief chemist of the government bureau that tested beverages for alcoholic content, whether he thought people would become do-it-yourselfers, he said there was little chance. "It's too much trouble for uncertain results," he opined. "They may try it once or twice, but not more."

One of the many ironies of Prohibition was that, having long accused the wets of suffering delusions because of their drinking habits, the drys now began to develop delusions of their own.

People who did not make their own, and who preferred to do their drinking outside the home, took themselves to places called speakeasies, the most plentiful of Prohibition businesses. They were like gas stations in the 1950s, fast-food joints in the 1960s, or realtors' offices in tony commuting suburbs in the 1990s. In Manhattan, it is said, the humorist Robert Benchley "once walked the north and south lengths of Fifty-Second Street between Fifth and Sixth Avenues counting speakeasies. He put the total at thirty-eight." Federal officials believed it to be the wettest block in America, populated by so many clandestine watering holes that a woman who lived in one of the block's few private residences had to put a sign on her door, pleading with people not to ring the bell. Sometimes they rang anyhow. They thought she was kidding when she swore she had no intoxicants for them, or else that she was lying to throw off the cops.

In the entire city, according to an estimate by Police Commissioner Grover Whalen in 1929, there were 32,000 speakeasies, which was more than twice as many as the number of legal drinking establishments before Prohibition.

It was the same in Chicago and Los Angeles, in Denver and Detroit, in Mobile and Fargo, with speakeasies springing up so often and changing locations so suddenly in their attempts to avoid detection that the drinking man and woman could barely keep up with them—although he and she were always willing to try. Some of the places, logically enough, had been saloons until the new law; even so, transforming them meant work for many a skilled craftsman. "Door fitters were in especial demand," writes Henry Lee in a light-hearted volume called *How Dry We Were: Prohibition Revisited*, "for the high-minded new décor insisted on elimination of the swinging doors that had graced the old, open saloons. In addition to decorum, the proprietors felt, thick oak defenses would slow down any raiders while the evidence was being poured down the drains. Too, when the Feds hit on the nasty device of actually padlocking raided premises, a need developed for several doors. No sooner was one locked with all the majesty of federal law than a second door was opened practically alongside, and the clientele suffered no inconvenience."

With people of lesser means brewing their own beer and distilling their own liquor and dissolving their own Bacchus bricks, the speakeasies tended to cater to a wealthier clientele, people who could afford quality and the effort of others to provide it; hence the high-minded décor of which Lee writes. There were exceptions, of course; some well-heeled people made their own beverages and some down-and-outers went to speaks on occasion and a few of the speaks they patronized were as lowdown as the worst of the saloons that had preceded them. But many of them were several steps up the social ladder, and these places, especially in New York, attracted not only the well-to-do but the celebrity crowd: athletes, artists, the stars of Broadway and vaudeville and the silver screen. They stepped out of their fancy cars, waved to gawkers on the sidewalk, and disappeared within for a few glasses of their favorite. Even politicians who should have eschewed such places were often in attendance, working the crowds, flouting the Eighteenth Amendment as a means not only of satisfying their thirsts and proclaiming their status, but of informally campaigning among wets.

Take New York's mayor, for example, an ethically dubious and rampantly self-promoting man about town named Jimmy "Beau James" Walker. Known to frequent a variety of drinking parlors, and to arrive and depart either with his mistress on one arm or belles of less intimate acquaintance on both, Walker was a perfect symbol for the era: too sophisticated to obey the law and too brash to hide his disobedience. His favorite drink at this time when he should not have had such a thing was a Black Velvet, consisting of top-shelf champagne and Guinness stout. He would down a few himself and buy a few for others, especially the newspaper reporters of his acquaintance, with whom he was as likely to talk cocktail recipes as he was the intricacies of urban management.

"One afternoon," writes Jules Abels, "there was a rumor that he had been shot. The reporters flocked to his office. 'Gentlemen,' he said, 'at this time of day I am not even half-shot.' "

Walker did his drinking at places where the elegance was more often than not overstated, plush and furtive establishments that offered their customers the chance to break an unpopular law in the kind of setting never before associated with crime. A gentleman might be required to wear a tuxedo, a lady an evening gown. Appointments varied, of course, but might include a solid oak bar with brass fittings, thick carpets, gilt-edged mirrors, and overhead, tinkling chandeliers and frescoed ceilings. Fine paintings or quality reproductions might hang on the walls, and small pieces of sculpture, perhaps busts of famous statesmen or warriors, men who would have had the fortitude to keep the Wayne Wheelers of the world at bay, might sit on marble pedestals in the corners, sometimes under specially installed spotlights that set them off dramatically.

A few speaks boasted kitchens that were supervised by famous chefs, and stylishly dressed waiters placed the food on tables draped with fine linen and set with silver and crystal. Small porcelain vases held freshly cut flowers. Some of these joints were so high-class as to offer live entertainment, singers and dancers and musicians who were already well-known or soon would be. Such famous New York restaurants as Twenty-One and the Stork Club started out in life as Prohibition speakeasies. For habitués, the whole experience was like laughing in church, with no one to cast a stony eye because everyone else was laughing, too.

The booze did not come cheaply. People made jokes about taking out a loan to take on a load. In some speaks, on some nights, a cocktail went for twice what it used to; on other occasions the mark-up could be a factor of ten—it depended on how much beverage was available at a given time and how difficult it was to procure. Sometimes patrons were charged a few bucks just to walk through the doors of their favorite spots, before they had checked their coats or taken their seats or even thought about what to order; this seems to have been the beginning of the now-common cover charge. *Fortune* magazine reported that the more successful speakeasies in the first few years of Prohibition took in half a million dollars in a twelve-month period, an enormous sum in the 1920s, although some places almost certainly made more.

It was not all profit, however. As has been pointed out, "it took money to make money—one New York proprietor put the cost at $1,370 a month. Of this, $400 was graft to federal Prohibition agents, the police department, and the district attorneys. The cop on the beat got another $40 to turn his back whenever beer was delivered."

Speakeasy owners who did not want to pay such overhead, or who were afraid of attracting thieves with their precious inventories, resorted to elaborate security measures, the installation of which required more than just a skilled door fitter. At Twenty-One, for example, "there were four alarm buttons at various points in the vestibule (so that if a raider prevented one of them from being pushed, the doorman could reach another). There were also five separate liquor caches, reachable only through secret doors; complicated electric switches were instantly short-circuited whenever an alarm button was pressed."

No one is certain about the name. Perhaps, as Mencken believed, speakeasy derives from an old Irish word for a drinking place. But whether it does or not, it was an especially appropriate term during Prohibition, when a bartender would often plead for a lower decibel level; the "easier" his customers spoke, the less likely that the cop outside, who had perhaps not been slipped a pair of twenties, would decide to investigate the commotion, or that neighbors would find the cop to complain. It did not much matter in a noisy city like New York, but in other places, and at other times, to drink quietly was to drink safely. "Hush!" said the landlady at Rolliver's Inn in Thomas Hardy's *Tess of the D'Urbervilles*. "Don't 'ee sing so loud, my good man, in case any member of the Gover'ment should be passing and take away my licends."

For all the opulence on the inside, a speakeasy could be a ramshackle place from the street, as it often wore a disguise. It might resemble anything from a tailor's shop to a bicycle repair shop, from an apartment to a synagogue, from a hardware store to a drugstore to a tearoom. There was an undertaking parlor in Detroit that "used its hearses to bring in liquor for the ostensible mourners; in a downtown lawyer's office the receptionist politely told inquirers that Mr. Caveat didn't take such cases as they had in mind, while welcoming people already known into the back room where the bar was. In New York City, the International Hair

Net Manufacturers' Association displayed a sample hairnet in a frame on the wall plus one rolltop desk and a safe containing a few shot glasses and several bottles of disastrous whiskey."

The first step, then, in gaining admission to a speak was to know where it was, to penetrate the facade. This accomplished, the aspiring customer then tapped on the door and waited for a peephole to open. After it did, he waited some more, often nervously, as he was appraised by the eye appearing therein. If he was known to the eye, or if he mentioned the name of a regular customer as a password, the door was promptly unlocked and the gentleman attached to the eye welcomed him as graciously as if the latter were a member of the family. If not, he was told that he had come to the wrong place—no booze here, fella; whatever gave you *that* idea?—and should depart right away.

To many people, this need to be approved was a nuisance; why should they have to await the sanction of a stranger to spend their own money, especially as much of it as a speakeasy charged? To others, it was an unnecessary risk; why should they have to stand in the street and make their case while a policeman or rabid dry strolled toward them or drove down the block, staring at them suspiciously? To still others, it was downright intimidating; what would their companions think if they were turned away?

But to some, the eye at the peephole was a comforting sight, even an invigorating one. It was evidence of a barrier they knew they could cross, and few things in life are more satisfying to those who pride themselves on how others perceive them; few things swell the ego to such reassuring proportions. Approval by the gatekeeper was a means of demonstrating one's status to others; it was like being accepted for membership in an exclusive country club, without having to enlist all the sponsors and fill out all the forms. One could, then, arrive at a speakeasy both literally and figuratively.

Barney Gallant, who owned several New York speaks during Prohibition, understood the dynamic, knew that exclusiveness came to be as much an attraction to his customers as the contents of his bottles. "Take this away," he said, referring to the eye at the peephole and what it stood for, "and the glamour and romance and mystery are gone." Continue to provide those qualities, he might have added, and the customers were already a little high before their first drink.

And once they entered, these members of the anointed in the rocketing years of prelude to the stock market crash of '29, they would waste no time in getting higher, much higher, as if money were but a trifle and the Eighteenth Amendment some ascetic's idea of a joke, as if the world outside the peephole were a desert, a prison camp of the spirit, until, as was the case at Rolliver's, "their souls expanded beyond their skins, and spread their personalities warmly through the room."

And so another of the era's ironies: by forcing people to drink in the luxuriance of speakeasies or the comfort of their homes, Prohibition gave to alcoholic beverages a respectability they had never enjoyed during the heyday of the bumptious and unsanitary saloon.

When President Washington dispatched the troops to western Pennsylvania on behalf of Secretary of the Treasury Hamilton's tax, the Whiskey Rebellion ended. But attempts to evade the law did not; they merely became more circumspect. Some farmers brought their product to smugglers, while others traded it in remote locations under the cover of night and yet others hid it away in places that they thought were secure until the time was right for either consumption or sale. To ensure secrecy even further, a few farmers came up with a different plan. They transported small quantities of beverage in pouches that they concealed in the tops of their boots; then they either sold the pouches or enjoyed the contents themselves in private gatherings with friends. These men were the first American bootleggers. That, at least, is one version of the story.

Another is provided by Alice Fleming, who also dates bootlegging to the early days of the colonial experience.

> Distillers were required to purchase tax stamps and display them on their whiskey barrels. Determined to avoid the tax, some distillers affixed the stamps to the barrels, then removed them after the delivery and used them again on the next shipment of whiskey. Since the tax stamps were concealed in the deliverymen's boots, the illicit whiskey became known as bootleg whiskey.

Regardless of derivation, "bootleg" the adjective and "bootlegger" the noun seem to have dropped out of usage early in the nineteenth century and stayed out for almost fifty years. It was in Neal Dow's Maine that they made their reappearance, when the noun came to describe a man who, like the pushcart vendor of later years, if less blatant in manner, sold his goods in alleys and passageways. He was an important person in his time, this bootlegger, sought out by his fellows and treated as well as, if not better than, other merchants. But once the law was repealed, he was out of both luck and work.

After that, the words went dormant again for another half century, even longer. It was not until the onset of the Eighteenth Amendment that they burst back into the language, showing up in front-page headlines and back-page ads, spoken in a million whispered transactions and providing the focus for an equal number of thirst-addled daydreams.

For it was the bootlegger who supplied the speakeasies. It was the bootlegger who sold to individuals who had the money and wanted their own private supplies. It was the bootlegger who ruled the twenties in the United States, far more than the Anti-Saloon League and the federal government. "In small towns," Stephen Birmingham points out, "the bootlegger gained almost the same respect and social status as the local doctor, lawyer or undertaker. In the cities, bootleggers were invited to all the best parties, and had their pick of the most desirable women."

To Mencken, the fellow who provided the whiskey in this time of national crisis was a hero of the same stripe as the cowboys of the Old West and the soldiers of the Revolutionary War. To others he was Robin Hood, stealing from the dry to ease the plight of the wet. And the kind of man who used to enjoy bragging to his friends about "my caddy" or "my chauffeur" or "my stockbroker," now conversed no less pretentiously or often about "my bootlegger," making him into a possession, a chattel reflecting on the status of his owner. A *New Yorker* cartoon of the period did not go too far when it revealed the pedigree of one young lady's supplier. "Peg's new bootlegger is simply marvelous—tall, small mustache, and just out of Harvard."

Al Capone, the king of Prohibition hoodlums and no one's idea of a hero, provided an updated, if self-exculpatory, definition of his trade. "When I sell liquor," he explained, "it's bootlegging. When my patrons serve it on a silver tray on Lake Shore Drive, it's hospitality."

By stimulating thirst as it did, and denying the time-honored means of quenching it, Prohibition also stimulated an underground economy whose bottom line was the envy of all who ran businesses above-ground. It has been estimated that by the mid-1920s, close to half a million Americans owed their employment, in one way or another, to illegal alcoholic beverages. It has also been estimated that these people earned in the vicinity of a billion dollars a year. "Add the cost of corruption and millions paid to exotic suppliers, and the industry had to gross some $1,400,000,000 to break even," reckons J. C. Furnas. "Since it was fantastically profitable, else the city mobs would not have been in it, assume another quarter billion for profit—total $1,650,000,000. But that is a moderate computation."

About the individual bootlegger's profits, though, there was nothing moderate. He faced much stronger penalties under the law than did his eighteenth-century counterparts, as well as stronger penalties than his twentieth-century patrons, and he took both facts of life liberally into account when figuring what to charge.

Nor was that all. As Mark Edward Lender and James Kirby Martin recount, the bootlegger also had to calculate "costs associated with intercepted shipments (lost either to rivals or to enforcement agents), hired thugs, police payoffs, chemists, distillery workers, ships, trucks, and production equipment." As a result, when the bootlegger finished his arithmetic, the price structure of the alcoholic beverage industry was radically different from what it had been only a few months before; he marked up everything from booze to bottles, labels to labor. No more sixteen-ounce glasses of suds for a nickel; no more free shots for a customer who had already emptied several at the regular price. Instead:

> In Northern cities, cocktails that sold for 15¢ in 1918 were 75¢ by the early 1920s. Domestic lager beer, which sold for about $10.50 a barrel in 1918, cost anywhere from 15¢ or $1 or more a *quart* by 1930 (that is, $160 or more a barrel, depending on the quality of the beer.) Domestic spirits, which averaged $1.39 a quart in 1918, soared to an average of $4.01 in 1930. Prices on imported foreign beverages also rose significantly, and as Clark Warburton pointed out, no doubt a large quantity of American-made liquor was passed off as imported to fetch higher prices. In short, bootlegging activity was less a sign that drinking was rife than an explanation of why it was so hard to drink cheaply.

No wonder that in 1924, J. Chapman wrote in *Outlook* magazine about the Noble Experiment's ability to satisfy the three main passions of the time: "the passion of the prohibitionists for law, the passion of the drinking classes for drink, and the passion of the largest and best-organized smuggling trade that has ever existed for money."

There were three ways for a bootlegger to get his merchandise. He could make it himself in factories that operated openly, assuming there were bribable police in the area; he could make it himself in factories that were done up like other businesses, assuming the local authorities insisted on the law, or at least the appearance of it; or he could bring in his beverages from other countries.

George Remus chose the first two. He also chose not to see Prohibition as a law that went against the American grain—another pun not intended; rather, he saw it as a commercial opportunity on a grand scale, one that could be realized by anyone with pluck and innovation, and what could be more American than that? A lot of other people had a similar view of the Eighteenth Amendment; not even a handful of them succeeded like Remus.

The son of poor German immigrants in Chicago, little George was the only one of his mother's first six children to survive infancy, and she rewarded him with enough love and vigilance for an entire brood. As a result, he was spoiled but charming, a child whose self-absorption was noticeable but worn lightly. Grownups were impressed by him; they liked the way he talked, smiled, commanded attention without actually commanding. He was "talkative, energetic, a book lover, careful in his appearance, and very seldom had to be scolded."

That would change. As an adult, Remus would need frequent scoldings, for he grew up to be a "short, stout, bald man of Napoleonic aspirations," one of Chicago's most successful criminal lawyers, although from time to time he would also represent a labor union or an unhappy spouse or a down-on-his-luck client who could not pay the full freight. "I could easily have become a District Attorney," he said, after he became the target of an entire army of district attorneys. "I was prominent enough politically to secure public office, but have never wanted to take the prosecutor's side in my life." As Prohibition began, Remus was making more than $50,000 a year, and spending it on a wife he did not love and all manner of creature comforts, which he did.

Yet he found himself dissatisfied, restless. Voices nagged at him; they never said anything specific, but they certainly did not suggest that, having already accomplished so much of a material mature, Remus might want to try his hand now at something a little more spiritual. In fact, just the opposite. The voices seemed to egg him on, chanting paeans to greed: you have risen so far and so fast, they might have said; don't stop now, rise further, further. "As compared to the great fortunes other men had amassed in the Land of Opportunity," writes Thomas M. Coffey in *The Long Thirst*, "his $50,000 a year looked puny."

One of those fortunes belonged to Al Capone. It has been estimated that at one point during Prohibition, Capone was grossing between

$60 and $100 million a year on beer alone! Now there, George Remus thought, was a man. His next thought was that he should be a man of the very same kind.

So he stopped practicing law in Chicago and headed for Cincinnati to start breaking it. Having served as attorney for a number of Chicago bootleggers and been as struck by their lack of intelligence as by their sudden wealth, he seems to have decided, like many other outsiders with their noses against the glass, that he could do just as well or better. Entering the illegal alcohol trade with the help of second spouse Imogene, a woman who "took more than routine wifely interest in his business affairs," George Remus soon became the most successful bootlegger in the Anti-Saloon League's home state.

Remus's particular method of doing business was a complicated one, dependent on his early training as a pharmacist as well as on his careful examination of the Volstead Act and his lawyerly belief that he could see a way around it. In 1920, he bought a distillery licensed to manufacture whiskey for medicinal purposes. Then he bought a drug company licensed to sell such whiskey. Then he bought a warehouse that stored whiskey which had been produced legally prior to Prohibition. Remus, in other words, set up a small, tightly controlled, highly proofed monopoly, one that encompassed production, sale, and storage—and no one seemed to notice. Not at first.

What eventually caught the eye of authorities, though, was that something peculiar happened whenever the Remus warehouse interacted with the Remus drug company. Cargo was shipped from the former to the latter on an almost daily basis, but more often than not it failed to arrive, mysteriously disappearing en route. Or not so mysteriously. In simplest terms, what Remus did was steal the medicinal booze from himself and secret it in a place called Death Valley Farm, whence he shipped it out again, this time to bootleggers operating in a five-state area. The trucks carrying *this* liquor, the liquor from which Remus made his profits, were accompanied by well-armed guards and took secure routes and, as a result, *always* made it to their destinations.

Remus became so proficient at this scam that he was soon able to expand his territory to take in most of the eastern half of the United States. He supplied Manhattan speakeasies, Boston cocktail parties, Philadelphia men's clubs. He made weddings in Pittsburgh more festive occasions and wakes in Indianapolis almost as festive as Pittsburgh weddings. Some of his product made it to smaller towns as well, where the gatherings were less formal and the product was as likely to be poured into paper cups as stemmed glasses. Such a reputation did he develop, not just for efficiency but for the quality of his goods, that he soon acquired a clients' list that could have passed for *Who's Who*. It included celebrities of one kind or another; business executives, among them many who had written checks to Wayne Wheeler; and leading figures of government and public service, including many who had received checks and otherwise pledged their allegiance to Wayne Wheeler. One of the latter was Jess Smith, a poker-playing, Prohibition-scorning crony of President Warren G. Harding.

The White House, like much of the rest of the United States, needed a bootlegger to help it through the long, cold nights of the Eighteenth Amendment. The president paid lip service of one kind to the amendment, but of quite another to alcoholic beverages, which he and his pals enjoyed with undiminished frequency; until Harding reformed a bit, later in his term, 1600 Pennsylvania might have been the ritziest speakeasy of them all, and George Remus had more than a little to do with it.

Alice Roosevelt Longworth could not help but notice. Because she "made wine, 'really good beer,' and also 'a very passable gin from oranges,' in a still in her Washington, D.C. basement," the lady knew a little something about illegal beverages. Because she was Theodore Roosevelt's daughter and the wife of Congressman Nicholas Longworth, the lady was a frequent guest at White House functions. On one occasion, she saw waiters pass through the chief executive's study carrying "trays with bottles containing every imaginable brand of whiskey." She was almost certainly witnessing the results of George Remus's relationship with Jess Smith. She did not think the trays should be toted about so casually. It was Prohibition, after all; one should respect the law enough to hide the evidence.

To celebrate his spreading empire, Remus bought an estate on ten acres in a prestigious section of Cincinnati called Price Hill, and turned wife Imogene loose on decoration. She let her imagination, and her husband's checkbook, run wild. For the entrance hall she ordered enough foliage to give the Brazilian rain forest an inferiority complex. For the living room she purchased expensive antiques, early American paintings, and a gold leaf piano. For her bedroom she bought a daily supply of fresh flowers, as well as paintings and statuary and a number of other sumptuous suggestions of the sleeping quarters of Louis XVI.

And then there was the Roman bath, the main feature of which was a sixty-by-twenty-foot indoor Italian marble swimming pool said to have cost $125,000 and ringed by some fifty tables. It was here that the Remuses threw some of the most memorable parties that the Queen City had ever known. They were extravagant, bespangled, free-flowing affairs to which the host invited, among others, the cops and politicians whom he paid to ignore him during business hours, and they slapped one another on the back and filled their glasses to the top and reveled in the spoils of their mutual disdain for the Eighteenth Amendment.

Remus was the biggest of spenders. At one party, he left $100 bills under the plates of his guests as favors. At another, "in front of each couple, a waitress placed a small box which looked as if it might contain jewelry. These boxes, instead of being for the wives, were intended for the husbands, but they did, indeed, prove to contain jewelry—diamond tie pins, diamond cuff links, and so forth. Remus had spent a total of $25,000 on these baubles for his male guests."

Were the female guests jealous? Did they feel neglected? Not for long. After the men had opened their presents, their mates were escorted outside to take a look at theirs: a brand new, 1923 automobile for each and every one of them. A crook George Remus might have been, and a man of monstrously swelled ego, brusque and showy and imperious; no one, though, ever called him cheap.

Even so, the amounts of loot he kept for himself were staggering, enough to convince him that he had done the right thing in forsaking his career as an officer of the court. At the top of his game, Remus was said to be worth $50 million—not a Capone-like figure, to be sure, but more than enough to keep him believing in the American dream. He lived high, drank well, and laughed all the way to the bank—to several banks, actually, because it was too much of a risk to put all that money into just one vault. He had accomplished everything he ever wanted in life, and never quite got over how easy it was. In fact, if he had a regret, and there is no real evidence he did, that might have been it, that it all came *too* easily, that such enormous gains should, by any system of cosmic justice, have been the result of greater struggle, or at least taken longer to achieve.

Then he might have shaken his head. What kind of beef was *that?* Maybe he should buy a car for this fellow Wayne Wheeler. Maybe even a dealership.

But George Remus did not stay at the top of his game for long. People like him never do. The Prohibition enforcers eventually caught up to him, and just as he had found loopholes in the Volstead Act, they found loopholes in his evasions of it. Over the course of the next several years, while his high-priced lawyers haggled and dickered and pleaded with the feds, he went to jail on five different occasions and was fined a total of $11,000. He tried to be philosophical about it. He had realized his goals, reaped his rewards; perhaps the cosmic justice about which he had wondered was now making itself known.

It was, however, something less than draconian. Remus paid the fines, which were a pittance, without complaint; he bore the jail time, which was minimal, with good grace. But something else was happening that he could not bear, neither with good grace nor any grace at all. There were problems on the home front; with the bootlegger away, the wife had begun to play, and her game was inexplicably nasty.

The first thing Imogene did in her husband's absence was steal some of his money. He had so much of it, she thought, that he would hardly miss a little—and besides, he was sitting in a jail cell now; what use did he have for currency? Then she told a lawyer from the Justice Department exactly how Georgie-boy had gotten all that money, gave him juicy details and thorough documentation, much more than the authorities had managed to secure on their own. This sent her husband back to prison yet another time and inspired Imogene to sue for divorce and even try to get him deported. After this scheme failed, she consoled herself by having an affair with the very same Justice Department shyster to whom she had ratted. And then, thinking she had not yet done quite enough to spite that dearly beloved of hers, that there were even more ways to make his life a flaming hell on earth, she decided to go into the bootlegging business herself, hoping to steal some of her husband's customers as well as his dollars—with the Justice Department guy as her partner!

So Remus shot her. Killed her. Gave her a one-way ticket to the end of the world. He got out of jail and picked up his belongings from the warden and then pronounced a sentence of death on his spouse and carried it out himself. As their daughter watched, horrified and weeping, screaming, "Daddy, don't do it! Don't do it!" Remus pulled a revolver out of the pocket of his coat, wedged the business end into his treacherous wife's belly, and pulled the trigger. A single bullet exploded from the chamber and spiraled up into her liver, stomach, spleen, lungs, and associated regions. She whimpered and fell to the pavement in a lump. Their daughter dropped to her knees and tried to comfort her, revive her, shrieking all the while. Someone called an ambulance and Imogene Remus was taken to the emergency room of a nearby hospital, where she did not die until several agonizing hours had passed.

"She who dances down the primrose path," her husband said with remarkable calm, after being told by a policeman that his wife had officially expired, "must die on the primrose path." By this time, he had been arrested, taken to police headquarters, and photographed and fingerprinted and impressed with the gravity of his deed—treated, in other words, not like one of America's foremost purveyors of hospitality, but like a common criminal. He could have used a drink.

But George Remus had not run out of luck, not completely and not yet. This man who had been incarcerated for selling high-quality alcoholic beverages to men and women who paid for them of their own free will with their own legally earned cash was *not* incarcerated for murdering his wife in cold blood in a public place with their hysterical and permanently scarred child virtually in the line of fire. His attorneys, you see, claimed it was not his fault. A good fellow like Remus would never have done such a thing if he were not the victim of "temporary maniacal insanity." It was not as common a plea as it would become later; in fact, one imagines his lawyers stifling a giggle, or at least blushing a bit, as they offered it.

But, to the amazement of all in the courtroom, Remus's lawyers among them, the judge agreed. He even seemed even to feel sorry for the defendant. Terrible thing, that temporary maniacal insanity. The judge pronounced sentence: Remus would be dispatched not to jail but to a mental hospital where the facilities were modern, the treatment humane, and the surroundings something close to posh.

Remus was thrilled. He celebrated the verdict with a party that reminded his friends of the parties he had thrown back in the good old days, before the law got onto him and Imogene turned double-agent. Among the new friends he invited were all twelve of the jurors who had acquitted him. They showed up, emptied a few highball glasses, wished him well. Prohibition not only made strange bedfellows; it sometimes got them soused together.

Then, six months later, more to celebrate. Remus's attorneys persuaded a three-judge panel that their man had regained his bearings, the malady which had struck his gray cells so suddenly having vanished with equal haste. A medical miracle, nothing less. George Remus was no longer insane, no more a threat to society as a whole or any of its individuals. He was set free, bid godspeed, allowed to return to the world he had helped to create, a world of

> booze and bribery, high living and high finance. But, alas for Remus, he . . . had lost his place there. His fortune was gone. His associates had scattered. His flamboyance had faded and even his fame had begun to dwindle. No longer newsworthy, he faced an obscure, lonely, drifting life which would finally end on January 20, 1952, in a "modest" Covington, Kentucky house he was then sharing with a recently acquired third wife.

Modest is the right word to describe the home. Anonymous is the right word to describe the occupant. Obituary writers, in fact, barely knew of George Remus anymore; they had to do some research before they could sit at their typewriters and summarize the accomplishments of a man whose name had once been on the tips of thousands of thirst-cursed American tongues.

Joseph P. Kennedy was the third kind of bootlegger, an importer, although perhaps more of an executive than an actual hands-on handler of illicit merchandise. Sandy-haired and freckle-faced, broad-shouldered and bow-legged, he looked just like what he was, the scion of an Irish Catholic family that had risen out of the mire of nineteenth-century immigrant poverty to the highlands of twentieth-century ease, and then some. "When he walked into a room," a friend of his once said, "he filled it up. His back was straight, his smile was on, his joviality was there. He enjoyed a joke and a laugh." He also enjoyed a stylish and expensive wardrobe, dressing "as nattily as a yacht captain in soft, double-breasted business suits and rakishly-cut stiff sport collars."

Before Prohibition, the Kennedy family, among other pursuits, had traded in alcoholic beverages, and Joe saw no reason to make a change simply because the law had gone whimsical on him. He would stay with what he knew best, at least for the time being, and as a result brought so much Canadian whiskey and scotch into the United States during the years of its illegality that the hooch could have floated the boats that carried it. Peg's new bootlegger, the Harvard gent in the *New Yorker* cartoon? It could well have been Joseph Patrick Kennedy.

Except for one thing. Kennedy would not have sold to Peg. He did not, with but the occasional exception, sell to anyone retail, ignoring the general public altogether. Rather, his customers were fellow bootleggers, and most of a very particular station—not small-time operators, not people who were new to illicit activity. For the most part,

Kennedy dealt with figures in the world of organized crime, and virtually all of them highly placed. According to biographer Ronald Kessler,
"Frank Costello would later say that Joe approached him for help in
smuggling liquor"; through Costello, Kennedy would later have dealings with men like Lucky Luciano, Meyer Lansky, and Dutch Schultz.
Perhaps he chose associates like these because they paid the best, perhaps because he found them efficient and dependable, perhaps because
he felt an affinity to such men, being a criminal himself in his own ways
and very well organized.

Kennedy's bank account grew quickly during Prohibition. It swelled,
overflowed, ran into new accounts and then into more new accounts.
Kessler explains the economics of his operation:

> The best Scotch cost $45 a case on Saint-Pierre and Miquelon, a group of
> eight small, craggy islands in the North Atlantic Ocean about sixteen miles
> south of Newfoundland, Canada. The islands' ice-free ports were perfect
> for whiskey shippers. Since they were under the French flag, the territory
> imposed no high Canadian duty. The cost of shipping the goods . . . added
> another $10 to each case. Overhead, labor, and bribes cost another $10,
> making the total expense $65 a case or $325,000 for a five-thousand case
> shipment. The Scotch was often mixed with other liquids, diluting it by
> half. It was then repacked and sold to wholesalers for $85 a case. Thus after
> cutting, the net profit on an investment of $325,000 could be $525,000, a
> markup of roughly two thirds.

Because of transactions like these, which owed their profitability, in
part, to Kennedy's "intimate familiarity with medicinal permits, sources
of supply and distributorships," he was worth an estimated $2 million
by the mid-1920s. It was a small fortune that became the basis of a
much larger one, not only through continued bootlegging but through
a number of other interests, both during and after Prohibition, and it
led Kennedy to the role of patriarch of a family that would produce
a president of the United States, two U.S. senators, and a multitude
of sons and daughters and other less direct descendants who became
public figures and tabloid personalities. It might have happened without the Eighteenth Amendment. Kennedy might have made as much
money if he had had to do it legally. But it is hard to believe that he
would have made it in such a short period of time. One of the most enduring proofs of the muddle that was the Noble Experiment, at least to
this writer, is the ongoing fame of all persons Kennedy, many of whom,

through their own career choices, seem to be bent on atoning for the old man.

But enough. The world does not need to know more about Kennedys. Too many tales have been told already.

Few, though, have been told about Captain Bill McCoy, who, like the old Joe, brought in his booze from other lands and became exceedingly prosperous as a result. A tall, muscular man, McCoy read American history whenever he could; at other times, he built yachts and speedboats for people like Andrew Carnegie, John Wanamaker, a Vanderbilt or two, and the actress Maxine Elliot, who, according to gossip that most people believed, moonlighted as J. P. Morgan's mistress. McCoy took pleasure in his work, in both the physical and artistic aspects of it; he liked the feel of tools in his hands and salt spray in his face, and he delighted in the sight of a boat coming together according to the vision he had had at the start. He liked to see it slide into the water for the first time, create its first wake, disappear beyond its first horizon. But he was always sad as well as proud when he finished a craft and handed it over to its owner; it was to him as if a lovingly raised child had left home. But he would get over it; he would start on another boat, before idleness could overcome him or melancholy set in too deeply.

Like George Remus, though, McCoy turned sour on what he had and began to want what he lacked. He wanted money, as much money as his customers. He also wanted to make a point.

Bootlegging came immediately to mind. It seemed the perfect vehicle to combine his zest for fortune with his utter disregard for Prohibition. Although not a drinker himself, McCoy opposed the Eighteenth Amendment on what he considered to be philosophical grounds, rating it with the Stamp Act and the Fugitive Slave Law as the most dubious pieces of legislation in the history of the American Republic. Each of the three trampled on the rights of the innocent, he believed, further entrenching a power structure of dubious ethical validity. The Founding Fathers "kicked holes in the laws they resented," he once said to a companion; he would follow their example.

In fact, his hero was a Founding Father who, in McCoy's view, "might stand as the patron saint of rumrunners." It was a man who had himself been a ship owner and had used his vessels more than once to smuggle liquor and other products into the colonies from the West Indies, defying British embargoes. It was a man who spoke publicly, even proudly, of such acts, and urged others to do as he had done. He, too, was making a point. On one occasion, his sloop, which he called *Liberty*, was seized by customs officials for bringing a shipment of Madeira from Africa to the New World. He was sorry to lose the cargo, but defiant about his rights. He would keep trying to import alcoholic beverages, restrictions or not, seizures or not, until such importation was finally legal. The man was John Hancock, an unquestioned patriot who eventually because the first signer of the Declaration of Independence.

McCoy started out in his new line of work not by building a boat, but by buying one, a ninety-foot schooner named the *Henry L. Marshall* that needed a lot of work. He and his brother had to refit it almost completely before McCoy could set sail from his home port of Jacksonville, Florida, to Nassau in the Bahamas. Waiting for him at the docks, the result of a complicated set of arrangements completed just before weighing anchor, were 1,500 cases of whiskey, strapped to the backs of several dozen donkeys who both brayed their discontent at the tonnage and sagged beneath it. McCoy and his crew unburdened the beasts, then hauled the hooch on board and secured it as carefully as they could before heading north toward Georgia.

In fact, McCoy invented something called a burlock to ensure that his cargo sailed both smoothly and profitably. It was "a pyramid-shaped package of six whiskey bottles encased in straw and sewn up in a burlap bag. The burlock gave the bottles as much protection as a wooden crate but took up less space and was easier to carry."

The donkeys, not caring, were just pleased to be free again. They straightened up and neighed a hearty good riddance as the boat drifted out to sea.

"Three days later," we are told, "the *Henry L. Marshall* stumbled through a howling gale into the mouth of St. Catherine's Sound, twenty miles below Savannah, and anchored at the edge of a bayou." The cargo was unloaded in the middle of the night and transported by boat through the bayou to a number of local purveyors. Bill McCoy's take: a reported $15,000.

He went on to make several more Caribbean runs: a few days down, a few days back, a little heavy lifting in between and a lot of profit at the end. Perhaps his most profitable voyage was the one he made in January of 1923, in which he picked up more spirits than usual and sold them for more money than ever. The gross this time was $127,000.

He still had a long way to go to equal the fortunes of Carnegie and Wanamaker, or even Remus and Kennedy, but he seemed on his way. And he was making his point.

McCoy was the originator of what soon became known as "Rum Row," a generic term that described a line of ships anchored in the ocean just beyond the legal limit of American waters, taunting the Eighteenth Amendment with but a narrow margin of safety. Rum Row sold not only rum, but all alcoholic beverages, the ships taking on their cargos in the Caribbean or Canada, several of whose provinces had repealed a national prohibition at about the same time that the United States got started, and had since then greatly expanded its production, fully 80 percent of which, according to some sources, found its way onto American boats. The boats then sailed back to the fringe of U.S. waters and arranged themselves into a line, a gently swaying shopping center for the bibacious middleman or consumer.

After a time, McCoy traded in the *Henry L. Marshall* for the *Arethusa*, later renamed the *Tomoka*, a craft that was the Neiman Marcus of off-shore beverage boutiques, pricey and tastefully decorated, "a floating liquor store, with shelves of samples for visitors. Tasting was encouraged, but only two prospective buyers were allowed aboard at the same time—not so much to prevent law enforcement raids as to deter the hijackers. . . . On deck, a swiveling machine gun emplacement was prominently in view, and every time an unidentified speedboat hove to alongside the *Arethusa*, it remained trained on the visitors throughout their shopping expedition."

When it was over, the shoppers got back into their boats and tried to outrace the Coast Guard to shore. The odds were strongly in their favor. A bootlegger's craft was sometimes capable of speeds approaching fifty miles an hour, and no Coast Guard ship could even come close to that. The attempts were sometimes comical. Picture one as follows: A vessel from what some people are now referring to as Carry Nation's Navy waits just inside the legal limit. A bootlegger approaches from Rum Row. The CNN boat, stationed between Rum Row and shore, starts put-putting, gearing up for pursuit. The bootlegger whizzes by, almost swamping the law enforcers in his wake. The CNN boat finally gets underway and chases for a few knots, but loses ground almost as quickly as if it were standing still. It has no choice but to give up and return to its position again, whence it will be made to look foolish by the next bootlegger sprinting for land.

Sometimes, the Coast Guard crafts worked in tandem. This increased the odds of both a successful capture and a violent outcome. Once in the waters off Louisiana, a Coast Guard cutter named the *Walcott* set out after the Canadian schooner *I'm Alone*. The *Walcott* ordered the ship to stop. "When the Canadian vessel ignored the *Walcott*'s signals," writes Joe Alex Morris, "the cutter opened fire, calling on other Coast Guard boats for assistance. The *I'm Alone* outran the *Walcott*'s 'hot pursuit' but later was caught by another Coast Guard cutter, the *Dexter*, and sunk by gunfire—some two hundred miles off the coast. One crewman was killed and the others were put in irons at New Orleans."

It was a rare occurrence. So was the bootlegger's boat so old and overused that its best days were behind it. But even if they were, the contraband merchant was likely to outrun the gendarmes, although he might have to dump some cargo to make sure. On some occasions after this kind of escapade, particularly along the beaches of Long Island from Coney Island to Montauk Point, cases of rum and vodka, gin and scotch, beer and wine would wash up on shore like sea creatures who had given up the struggle and decided to beach themselves. Sunbathers would run toward the treasure and break into it eagerly. For a few glorious moments on a few summer afternoons in the 1920s, Prohibition was not a ban on alcoholic beverages at all; it was, rather, an almost magical means of providing them, an unexpected bounty from the briny deep.

Usually, though, the Coast Guard watched the bootleggers' boats grow small in the distance as they sped away. Compounding the problem, the maritime guardians had a mere thirty-three cruisers, twenty-five destroyers, and 243 patrol boats in their entire fleet, and these were now required to hunt down countless hundreds of amphibious liquor dealers and cover more than 15,000 miles of shoreline. It was an almost impossible assignment. The Rum Row stood—or bobbed—secure.

And then there was the sheer number of these enterprises with which the Coast Guard had to contend. Rum Rows existed outside every state and almost every city on every coast, from Maine to Florida, along the Gulf of Mexico, and up and down the Pacific shoreline, which was serviced by Vancouver to the north and Mexico to the south. The lights on the boats cut through even the darkest of nights, acting as beacons for those of parched throat and outlawed tastes. Once in a while people would stand on a spit of land, perhaps with binoculars, and peer out at their local Rum Row as they would any other tourist attraction. If they were lucky, they might see a chase, and if especially lucky, they might find the bootlegger putting into shore within hailing distance of them, the sightseers then raising a cheer for the scofflaws and possibly even descending on them to make a purchase, or ask for a free sample, on the spot.

Eventually, or so it is claimed, some enterprising bootleggers went so far as to develop an airborne version of Rum Row. As John Kobler describes it,

> Canadian smugglers, piloting planes fitted with extra 100-gallon tanks, would rendezvous with their confederates' aircraft over American soil and transfer liquor from tank to tank through fueling hoses, thus evading Customs. The replenished planes would then fly back to their base, landing with skids on some frozen lake in the Minnesota woods. There truckers waited to drain off the liquor into barrels and deliver it to Minneapolis and St. Paul.

It was an appalling set of circumstances, said the Anti-Saloon League, and proof positive that Prohibition and disarmament had something in common. Neither would work for the United States unless it were simultaneously embraced by the other nations of the world, virtually all of which happened to be wet and warmhearted and willing to export. This being the case, the league decided that the best thing to do was establish foreign offices. The Woman's Christian Temperance Union, which had lost so much of its clout domestically, also thought it might be a good idea to expand.

It never happened. There wasn't a single country on the globe that wanted either of them.

A seller's market does not inspire the same quality of merchandise as a buyers' market, no matter what the product, and Prohibition was the greatest sellers' market the United States has ever known. Bootleggers took advantage of it not only by slaking the thirsts of the constitutionally deprived at outrageous prices, but by adulterating their beverages, diluting them as much as the market would allow, to increase profits even further. The less discerning the customer, the easier it was to alter his purchase, and many men and women were so desperate during Prohibition that they were not discerning at all. These were people who could not be troubled to make their own or could not afford to go to speakeasies or could not wait to get there before having a few gulps. These were people who would drink anything, anytime, anywhere. These were people whose indiscriminate cravings were the greatest intoxicant of all to unscrupulous bootleggers. A rule of thumb for the latter: one bottle of good whiskey could be "cut" into five bottles of bad.

Most often, the cutting was done in the middle of the night, in plants that were set up in warehouses or storage facilities that looked deserted, and therefore not suspicious, by day. The tools of the cutter's trade were water, flavorings, and alcohol. The water increased the quantities of beverage; the flavorings restored the diluted mixture to something approximating its original taste; and the alcohol replaced the lost pizzazz. Joe Kennedy's scotch, for example, after being watered, might be restored with caramel, prune juice, or creosote, and then spiked back up again with industrial alcohol.

But that was the problem. Actually, it was the crisis. Many were the bootleggers, driven almost as much by a lack of respect for their customers as by greed, who turned to alcohol in grossly unsafe forms, and with no inspection or regulation procedures to check them, their consciences, highly defective mechanisms to begin with, were their only guides. The new pizzazz was, therefore, greater than the old, and in some cases so much greater that it turned out to be lethal.

And few cutters were more lethal than industrial alcohol, a product never meant to be drunk, a toxic substance that had not been banned by the Eighteenth Amendment because it was needed in factories and other workplaces to make chemicals, solvents, insecticides, explosives, fuels, and certain cleaning products—deadly agents all. The Anti-Saloon League did not quarrel with the exemption, but fearful of its misuse, insisted that industrial alcohol be made into an even more deadly compound by requiring that manufacturers add methanol, or wood alcohol, to it. This, reasoned the league in public statements, would ensure that no one, no matter how crazed, would use the product as a beverage base. New labels were printed for containers of industrial alcohol. They read as follows:

POISON

Completely denatured alcohol is a violent poison.
It cannot be applied externally to human or
animal tissues without serious injurious results.
It cannot be taken internally without inducing blindness
and general physical decay,
ultimately resulting in death.

There, thought the league; that ought to do it. There, thought the legislators who supported the new labels; that ought to keep the league happy.

But to bootleggers, some of them at least, the toxicity of industrial alcohol mattered far less than its availability. They stole shipments of the stuff, or forged permits and bought it "legally," then mixed it with scotch or gin or vodka, often the high-quality product they had gotten hold of at a Rum Row. They knew the consequences could be deadly. They did not mind; the consequences were their customers' problems, and the very act of *being* customers made *them* morally dubious, too. Statistics provided by the federal government show that, on an annual basis, twice as much industrial alcohol was turned out in the United States during Prohibition as before—and it was not because twice as many chemicals were being manufactured, or solvents or insecticides or explosives.

Wayne Wheeler was no less indifferent to the situation than the bootleggers. "The person who drinks this industrial alcohol," he declared, ignoring the fact that most people who did so were unaware of the fact, "is a deliberate suicide." It was a statement that recalled the monstrous insensitivity of the liquor industry late in the previous century. And, says Stewart H. Holbrook, it "seemed a notice that the Christian Temperance of Miss Frances Willard had lost out and that an Old Testament God of savage determination had taken over the business in characteristic style."

But there was no public outcry about it, no indignation. Prohibition was too new, too noble an experiment; too many people were determined to give it a chance and Wayne Wheeler was their leader.

Another commonly used cutting agent was antifreeze. Bootleggers claimed it was a flavorful additive, especially when it had been newly drained from an automobile radiator, because the pieces of rust in it gave the solution a rich, full body. Not to mention, one assumes, needed iron. Other cutters used during Prohibition included perfume, cologne, after-shave lotion, mouthwash, hair tonic, shellac—virtually anything made from alcohol, however small the quantities. Eventually, things got so bad that the government stepped in, with the Anti-Saloon League rooting it on, and ordered manufacturers of many alcohol products to add an emetic to them. Officials believed—or claimed to believe—that this would end the illicit use of nondrinkable liquids once and for all.

It did not. Many bootleggers were not only undeterred by the action, they cackled openly at the preposterousness of it. They figured their liquor was so bad to begin with that most of the individuals who drank it were going to throw up anyhow; the emetic just made it certain. Besides, vomiting was probably the best thing a person could do for himself after a few sips of most Prohibition whiskeys. Those people who called them "rotgut" were not insulting them so much as providing an accurate description of the product's effects.

In New York's squalid Hell's Kitchen, bartenders sold a no-frills mixture of raw alcohol and water known as "smoke." At ten cents a slug, most folks could obliterate themselves and still get change for a quarter. Other New Yorkers bought jellied cooking alcohol and squeezed it through a rag to produce a liquid that they either guzzled down themselves or sold to the unsuspecting. Perhaps this is what gave Russian soldiers the idea, many years later, to satisfy their own satanic urges by draining brake fluid from their tanks, filtering it, and chugging down the remainder straight.

A Chicago specialty was Yack Yack Bourbon—main ingredient, iodine—and a Philadelphia favorite called Soda Pop Moon, sold in soft drink bottles, depended for its insidious impact on rubbing alcohol. In Kansas City, Missouri, the undiscerning consumed Sweet Whiskey, "a distillation of alcohol combined with nitric and sulfuric acids that soon destroyed the kidneys." An Atlanta woman arrested for public drunkenness confessed that her undoing had been the almost inconceivable combination of mothballs and gasoline. She just liked to drink, she explained, like to get a different take on reality, and this was the best she could do during Prohibition. Was it her fault that safer beverages were so much harder to find these days, and so much more expensive?

In other parts of the South, people wet their whistles and scorched their esophageal linings with White Mule, a form of clear moonshine so named because it could do as much damage to the unsuspecting as a flying pair of the creature's back legs. It was sometimes taken straight, more often mixed with ginger ale or grape juice, and usually carried around in a fruit jar. "The experienced drinker," says Joe Alex Morris, "kept the fruit jar tightly closed until he was ready to drink. Then he held his breath while he unscrewed the lid and quickly lifted the jar to his lips, gulped the clear liquid, replaced the lid and screwed it tightly into place again. Only then did he attempt to breathe. Frequently this was difficult. For a few moments he coughed and shuddered, and the strained, anxious expression on his face was replaced by an equally strained and anxious smile. He wiped the fusel oil from his lips and, if it was then possible for him to speak, said: 'Boy, that's got a kick—and how!'"

Jackass Brandy, which was not named after the people who craved it, also provided some kicks in the South. This particular by-product of the era's lunacy was "supposedly made from peaches and sold for four dollars a quart. A few drinks usually caused severe intestinal pains, and sometimes internal bleeding." There were druggists who sold wood alcohol milkshakes and bootleggers who offered the same poison to customers without the ice cream; the wood alcohol was referred to, sometimes even by people who were drinking the compound knowingly, as a Coroner's Cocktail. "Farm hands in the Middle West," writes Herbert Asbury, who has made quite a study of Prohibition's most dangerous libations, "drank a fluid drawn from the bottom of a silo, where silage had rotted and fermented for perhaps several years. No viler beverage can be imagined."

Yes, it can. Squirrel Whiskey—and it did not have to be imagined; it actually existed. The recipe is a secret that has withstood the ages, to the certain benefit of the common weal, but the name, it is believed, comes from the tendency of people who had taken a few sips to try to dig their feet into the sides of trees and try to run up to the top branches. Some, it is rumored, having attained the height, even tried to leap from branch to branch.

The ingredients of Goat Whiskey, popular in Indiana and South Dakota, are another secret, although rumor had it that the title creature, especially one who had grown old and ill-mannered and terribly infirm, was one of them. Nor has it ever been revealed how bootleggers cut Old Crow whiskey, only that, once they did, customers referred to it as "Old Corrosive."

Then there was Jamaica gin, or Jake: 90 percent alcohol, 180 proof, a decoction that was not so much a beverage as a virus loosed on society in liquid form, a small-scale plague on the verge of getting larger all through the twenties. In most states, Jake was legally obtainable by prescription because, in minute doses, it could help to relieve an upset stomach. But, inevitably, bootleggers bought up supplies of Jamaica gin, or made their own mutations, and sold them to people constitutionally incapable of drinking minute doses of anything alcoholic.

According to a joke that was sometimes whispered in corners, sometimes shouted across rooms in public, a fellow was advised to drink his Jake as soon as it was poured.

To get the pleasure as quickly as possible?

No, to empty the glass before the beverage ate through the bottom.

A joke, yes, but the person who told it was not kidding. In fact, the warning came as close to truth-in-advertising as many bootleggers were ever willing to get. Jamaica gin did not just make a person sick, not just threaten recurring ailments of the stomach or bladder; it affected his ability to use his hands and feet, even, in many instances, giving him a permanent limp. William G. Shepherd described the ailment in the July 26, 1930 issue of *Collier's Weekly*.

> The victim of "jake paralysis" practically loses control of his fingers. . . . The feet of the paralyzed one drop forward from the ankle so that the toes point downward. The victim has no control over the muscles that normally point the toes upward. When he tries to walk his dangling feet touch the pavement first at the toes, then his heels settle down jarringly. Toe first, heel next. That's how he moves. "Tap-click, tap-click, tap-click, tap-click," is how his footsteps sound.
>
> The calves of his legs, after two or three weeks, begin to soften and hang down, the muscles between the thumbs and index fingers shrivel away.

The condition was called Jake foot, and the victims were Jake trotters or Jake steppers, men who got around as best they could with their deformities, footsteps echoing asymmetrically as they struggled down the streets of Prohibition America, probably its most visible victims. And their hands, their poor hands; no longer could they easily hold a glass or bottle, even if there was water in it, even if it contained medicine to alleviate the pain in their limbs for a few minutes. To some people of the period, the malady was the just deserts of a wanton disregard for the law; to others, it was pathetic evidence that the law had gotten a divorce from common sense, something not to be expected in a place like the United States.

At one time or another during the twenties, there were several hundred cases of Jake foot in Rhode Island, Connecticut, and Massachusetts, several hundred more in Cincinnati, at least 500 in Wichita, 800 in southern Tennessee, 1,000 in Louisiana, and according to estimates that have the ring of plausibility, between 15,000 and 20,000 in the entire country, all these people tap-clicking, tap-clicking their way slowly from place to place, often bent to the side and refusing to meet the eyes of passersby, shriveled hands hidden in their pockets. No one ever died from Jamaica gin, at least not as far as the histories record, but no one ever recovered either.

In fact, so vicious a poison was it that, in researching its origins, government scientists learned some of the principles that would lead their German counterparts to develop nerve gases in World War II. It is an appalling thing to say about a substance that human beings willingly, and so frequently, put into their bodies a couple of decades earlier.

Even beverages that were not adulterated, not cut with one deadly ingredient or another, could be dangerous to a person's health when they were made outside the law. A government inspector found a brewery operating in a rundown barn somewhere in the Midwest; there were no cows or pigs or horses inside, no signs of any kind that the barn had recently been used for an agricultural purpose except for the hayloft overhead. But the hayloft was a cloud of pestilence. "Floating around on top of the ale in the vats," the inspector told his superiors, "were all sorts of refuse and filth—straw, hay, seed, mice, bugs, flies and other things not calculated to add to the potability of the ale. I found floating in one vat a large dead rat, almost as big as a fair-sized rabbit." Other foreign objects found by inspectors in impromptu breweries and distilleries include almost everything animal, vegetable, and mineral that was indigenous to the United States at the time.

There is no way of knowing how many people died of adulterated booze during the reign of the Eighteenth Amendment; wets exaggerated the number for their purposes, drys minimized it for theirs. But some statistics are available, and they are parts of a depressing whole. In 1925, a reported 687 New Yorkers went to their eternal rewards long before they had intended because of venomous beverages; a year later, the total seems to have climbed to 750. It is seems fair to assume that comparable percentages of the population became fatalities in other cities. "In 1927," writes Ethan Mordden of the entire nation, although it is not certain how he arrived at his figure, "the death toll from the imbibing of 'liquor' containing poisoned alcohol stood at 11,700." But even before this, Will Rogers had been moved to say that "governments used to murder by the bullet only. Now it's by the quart."

Those who opposed Prohibition were aghast. Those who supported it were unbelieving. Editorials appeared in newspapers and debates began in legislative chambers. So many heads shook in amazement, yet so few should have, for a horrifying preview of the Eighteenth Amendment's effect on those who disregarded it had already been provided, even before the ban took effect.

It was a few days before Christmas, 1919. Prohibition would begin in less than a month, and people in the towns of the Connecticut Valley, such as Oxford, Seymour, and Waterbury, had begun to buy up supplies of legal spirits, stashing away their favorite brands in secure hiding places the way a later generation of Americans would stockpile canned goods for air-raid shelters. So much good liquor had disappeared from the stores even before Santa came down the chimneys that many of those who had not stockpiled the good saw no choice but to turn to the bad. It was wood alcohol that went into the eggnog that year, not brandy; it was Coroner's Cocktails for all who wanted to quench an adult thirst around the Yule log. As a result, more than seventy citizens of the Connecticut Valley died over the holidays, and dozens more were blinded, some temporarily, some forever. Everything that happened after that around the country, the deaths and disfigurements and the mind-wracking illnesses, followed as logically as thunder after lightning.

Poisoned booze was the great, unsung tragedy of Prohibition. People today know about bootleggers and speakeasies; they are familiar with the names Capone and Kennedy; they have a general impression of casual lawbreaking and wild times kindled by spirits that were not supposed to be so readily available. But they do not know about Yack Yack Bourbon and Jackass Brandy and Squirrel Whiskey. They do not know about cooking alcohol squeezed through a rag and mothballs dropped into a steaming mug of gasoline. And they do not know about Jamaica gin and the men who drank it in doses that were so much more than minute, thereby getting rid of their thirsts for a few minutes as they turned into cripples for the rest of their lives.

Even men and women who could afford better were sometimes the victims of deadly drink; it could find its way into the best of night spots, the most soigne of private parties, the most respectably labeled and highly priced bottles, the finest crystal. Anyone, at any time, could be fooled by a bootlegger.

And when the booze was malignant, it could kill in clusters. During a single four-day period in 1928, thirty-four people died in New York City alone from unwittingly drinking wood alcohol. Just four days. Just New York City. Just wood alcohol.

But the problem was known at the time, known so well, in fact, that among other things it led to the increased popularity of cocktails. They had been a staple of the drinking person's diet since colonial times, of course, but were often looked at with a dubious eye. Real drinkers, it was thought by men and women who liked to consider themselves that, did not mix with gin with tonic or rum with cola any more than a gourmand would put sauce on a steak or ketchup on scrambled eggs. Some tastes could not be improved; some pleasures were best taken as given.

Now, though, all of that changed. "Recipes were invented," writes Stephen Birmingham, "sampled, and quickly passed around. Into the shakes went whites of eggs, yolks of eggs, milk, honey, Worcestershire sauce, orange-flower water, wines, herbs, spices, and mixes of every and the most incomparable variety." All of them to mask the taste and dilute the deleterious effects of booze which had itself been diluted in more virulent fashion, booze which was like none that had ever been poured before, beverage that skipped the high and went straight to the hangover—and then, in too many cases, even beyond.

In fact, things reached such a pass that at one point the humorist E. B. White was moved to offer a solution, proposing that the federal government nationalize speakeasies. This way, he said, "the citizenry would be assured liquor of a uniformly high quality, and the enormous cost of dry enforcement could be met by profits from the sale of drinks."

It was a tongue-in-cheek comment. It was not a tongue-in-cheek time.

Meyer Lansky, the bootlegger who was a client of Joe Kennedy's, and who would one day be known as the Godfather of Godfathers, the J. P. Morgan of organized crime, the money man behind all the other money men, would not sell adulterated alcohol. "Partly," writes Birmingham, "it was his snobbish nature. But also, he reasoned, dealing in cut, ersatz liquor—in which a bottle labeled 'Scotch' might be only colored water, raw alcohol, and a splash of real Scotch for flavor—meant that one's clientele would consist mostly of skid-row bums and the sleaziest bars; there would be little repeat business."

George Remus was of similar mind. "I never poisoned anybody," he boasted more than once. "That's something they can say for Remus."

As they could for Bill McCoy. The captain did not stay in the bootlegging business long, however, not nearly as long as some of his colleagues. The authorities nabbed him early on; he pleaded guilty to charges of violating the Volstead Act and was shipped off to a low-security federal prison in Atlanta for less than a year. It was closer to a vacation than to serious time behind bars, but when he got out, he was a changed man.

His friends assumed he would return to the business that had made his fortune, simply being more careful in his procedures, perhaps more selective in his customers. He did not. McCoy no longer wanted anything to do with Rum Row, and in fact his creation would not long survive him as a prosperous entity. After four years, writes Andrew Sinclair, "over-competition, murders by hijackers, the harrying of the Coast Guard, and long months at sea with too much liquor on board reduced the ships on Rum Row to a desolate line of vessels which barely paid their way."

But it was not just Rum Row upon which McCoy turned his back; he wanted nothing to do with bootlegging in any form. He surprised everyone, perhaps even himself, by becoming a realtor: buying houses, selling houses, going boringly but thoroughly legitimate. When people asked about the dramatic career change—and many did, unable to believe what they had heard—he replied that it was not as peculiar as it seemed. Too many undesirables had gotten into his old field, he said. He was sincerely troubled by this; he did not want to associate, even indirectly, with lowlifes. And worse, people guilty of murdering or maiming their customers. From the start, McCoy had considered himself a patriot, not a criminal. He was providing a product to men and women who were being denied the product by unjust means. He, not the officers of the law who had lain in wait for him, was the true public servant.

His customers, too, considered him a patriot. As a result, they trusted him completely; that was why they were so sorry to see him go. They knew that he never cut his booze with water, never brought it back with poison. You might pay a little more for Captain Bill's stock, but you would never get sick from it, never lose control of your hands or your feet, never find any of your bodily functions impaired. According to at least a few historians of Prohibition, this is why people always referred to his beverages—and why, later, others would refer to anything of known and superior quality—as "the real McCoy."

9

Executive Softness

n 1924, a revolutionary named Plutarco Elias Calles became
president of Mexico. A former army general with a quick
temper and a fondness for imposing his will on others, a
thoughtful man but in a primitive, sometimes vicious kind
of way, Calles "brutalized the Church, repressed the Left,"
and committed various other offenses against various other
political opponents. He was also hell on drinkers. Several
years earlier, as governor of the state of Sonora, he had had
to enforce a ban on alcoholic beverages, and did so with
remarkable effectiveness. The liquor interests went out of
business; very few bootleggers stepped into the void; consumption dropped dramatically.

Several years after the Eighteenth Amendment took effect
to the north, a reporter from a U.S. newspaper, looking for
some kind of new angle on the story, asked Calles the secret
of his success with tippling. El presidente responded without equivocation. "I blew up all the breweries and distilleries
with dynamite," he said. "Then I arrested a few smugglers
who were taking contraband across the border from Arizona
near the Cananea pass. I had them all shot the next morning." He stopped, allowed the reporter to finish writing—
perhaps with a suddenly quivering hand—before summing
up. "After that, the law was generally observed."

Calles called this philosophy of law enforcement "executive firmness," and, learning of the problems that Americans
were having with their own attempts at banning alcohol, he
wondered why they did not adopt similar means.

So did some Americans. An unidentified essayist of the time, entering a contest on "law observance" sponsored by the automobile magnate W. C. Durant, suggested that all violators of the Eighteenth Amendment be sent to concentration camps in the Aleutian Islands. Others thought the Aleutians were too close to home; they recommended Siberia, Tierra del Fuego, the South Pole, another planet. Then there were the old-fashioned types, advocates of tarring and feathering, drawing and quartering, stocks and pillories; this kind of thing was good enough, after all, for our ancestors. Another rabid dry pointed out that the Aztecs had made drunkenness a capital offense, and of course everyone knew that the Aztecs were among the most advanced people of their time. Not to mention the most sober.

It is not certain that the Commissioner of Internal Revenue, David Blair, had any knowledge of the Aztec legal code, but it is possible. In a speech one day, he recommended that all American bootleggers be lined up in front of a firing squad and shot to death. The site of the speech was a Presbyterian church in Philadelphia.

In addition, Blair had the government print leaflets urging drys to spy on their wet neighbors and report their intelligence anonymously, using telephones outside their neighborhoods so they would not be seen or overheard. John D. Rockefeller was also a proponent of espionage, and at one point hired private detectives to look into the habits of his friends and business associates; if they turned up evidence of improper thirst quenching—some people said that even hearsay would satisfy the old man's curiosity—they were instructed to tell Rockefeller so that he could terminate the relationships and then report his former friends to the authorities.

And John D. Meyer, the United States attorney for the Western District of Pennsylvania, pleaded with the young men and women at the Carnegie Institute of Technology, for their own good as well as that of the entire nation, to tattle on their fellow students. People who are swilling beer or whiskey, he said, should not be your friends in the first place, regardless of other, more socially responsible qualities they might possess. When Meyer was criticized for such a position, by those in his audience as well as by local journalists, he refused to back down. "If necessary," he said, "I will put a spy on every doorstep in Pittsburgh."

But Henry Ford, who would later threaten to shut down his automobile assembly lines if the Eighteenth Amendment were ever repealed, thought that even more drastic steps were necessary. Forget spies, he said; bring on brute force. Ford wanted the army and navy to regulate compliance. And Clarence True Wilson, founder of the Methodist Board of Temperance, Prohibition and Public Morals, as well as an advocate of mandatory five-year jail terms for anyone who purchased so much as a pint of bootleg liquor, was on the same wavelength. Call out the marines, he told the totally unsympathetic Harding administration; arm them to the teeth and send them to the speakeasies. Give the people inside a few minutes to depart, and if they choose not to, open fire anyhow. Then Wilson explained, albeit in somewhat muddled fashion, why he felt as he did about demon rum. "It is not the individual poisoning which constitutes the chief menace of alcohol," he said. "It is the chronic and racial poisoning which strikes at the root of future generations and lowers the level of citizenship. Better hundreds sent to their graves by wood alcohol which they were under no compulsion to drink rather than millions cut short of their full possibilities by alcohol which perhaps they never drank at all."

Blair and Rockefeller and Meyer and Ford and Wilson might have been overreacting, but at least they had a realistic view of the problem. They knew that the Noble Experiment was turning out ignobly; the available manpower could not cope with the ongoing American thirst and the thirst was showing no signs of lessening, law or no law. They knew that extraordinary steps were required. They simply got a little *too* extraordinary in their suggestions.

Several years later, President Herbert Hoover would appoint the National Commission on Law Observance and Enforcement, usually referred to as the Wickersham Commission, after its chairman, a former attorney general of the United States, and in January of 1930 it released a report concluding that the numbers had been against Prohibition from the start. It was "a police regulation over 3,5000,000 square miles of territory, requiring total abstinence on the part of 122,000,000 people who had been accustomed to consume 2,000,000 gallons of alcoholic beverages per annum." In 1920, there was one agent for every 2,327 square miles, one for every 69,546 Americans. More agents were hired as the Eighteenth Amendment ground its way forward, but the number never exceeded 3,000. Each one of them was a David. The bootleggers and bartenders were Goliaths. What happened in the Bible was a fluke.

Obviously, if the law were going to make an impression, if it were going to change habits so deeply embedded in the past and lay the foundation for a future free from alcohol abuse—or, more ambitiously, use—a special breed of man would have to be employed to insist on obedience. Not an ordinary cop, who would lack the commitment; not a run-of-the-mill reformer, who would lack both toughness on the streets and legal training; and not a reformer-bankrolled politician, who would not even know where to begin. Among other things, it would take some-one strong enough to withstand large helpings of hostility. Max Lerner has written that the attitude of many Americans toward the dry forces was "very much like that of a Resistance movement toward an army of occupation." Defiance, in such cases, becomes a civic duty, and those who attempt to quash it, like the revenuers who tried to collect taxes from their neighbors during the Whiskey Rebellion, are pariahs of the worst sort.

In addition, the Prohibition enforcer would have to be honest, coura-geous, tireless, savvy, and, of course, dry. He would have to be able to turn the other cheek, keep a stiff upper lip, apply his nose to the grind-stone and keep it there, regardless of either temptation or reprisal. Did such mortals exist? Yes. One of them was Eliot Ness, Al Capone's neme-sis, an earnest man who headed up a special Justice Department unit in Chicago known as the "Untouchables." Capone tried to bribe Ness on a number of occasions; Ness declined. Capone tried to kill Ness on three occasions; Ness survived. Writes Geoffrey Perrett of the lawman and his posse:

> The Untouchables located and shut down more than thirty [of Capone's breweries] and arrested more than one hundred people . . . seized more than fifty trucks, nearly all brand-new; and smashed millions of dollars' worth of brewing equipment. Beer had been trucked openly through the streets of Chicago in the Twenties. In 1930 it was becoming hard to find and was delivered in passenger cars a couple of barrels at a time.

But were there *many* mortals like Eliot Ness? No, not in Chicago or anywhere else, and of their number the Internal Revenue Service ended up hiring but a fraction. Most of the people it recruited, far from having Ness-like attributes, were misfits, a collection of bunglers and bumblers and low-rent scofflaws as uninspired, although not nearly as innocent, as the Keystone Kops.

They were called, simply, Prohibition agents. They were employees of the of the newly created Prohibition Bureau, under the jurisdiction of the Treasury Department, and someone who watched them in ac-tion, a person not so much cynical as perceptive, described them as "the inadequate . . . forced by their country to pursue the prepared." But it was worse than that. Not until 1927, the eighth year of the Noble Experiment, was legislation passed that required prospective agents to be vetted through Civil Service. This did not guarantee their competence, but it was at least an attempt to identify and screen out the worst of the applicants. Questions like the following, a sample question from the first Civil Service exam for prospective agents, are an example of the process:

> Assume that you are a Prohibition officer working occasionally with Agents Jenkins and Thompson, both of whom you have known for about six months. During the progress of an important investigation, upon which all three of you are engaged, Agent Jenkins approaches you with the statement that Thompson is "crooked" and is associating regularly with violators of the National Prohibition Act. Assume such facts as you may desire, not inconsistent with those given here, and state, in approximately 150 words, what, in your opinion, you should do under the circumstances.

Furthermore, not until 1930 did Treasury hand over supervision of the agents to the Justice Department, a much more logical home for them. Before that, and before the Civil Service exam, men could "qualify" for the position of agent simply by having been lickspittles for second-string politicians and ward healers. That was the deal the Anti-Saloon League had to make with the politicos; if the latter were going to give their approval to the Eighteenth Amendment, and thereby risk alienating huge numbers of voters, they were also going to assume control of the employment opportunities, enriching themselves with the power of patronage, and using it, at least in part, to win back some of their thirst-cursed constituents.

And, naturally, the man that the pols chose was a different breed from the man the League would have preferred, a man to whom something was owed for services rendered, or from whom something would be desired in the future, rather than a fellow who believed in the deepest recesses of his heart that alcoholic beverages were the curse of the ages. It was for this reason that a GOP boss in New York was able to put a toady on the Prohibition payroll merely by writing a note that said, "This is to certify that Samuel Gross is an enrolled Republican." Old Sam presented the note at the office of the New York Prohibition administrator, and with no questions asked, was able to walk away with a badge on his vest and a smile on his lips.

On the surface, though, it seemed a small favor. An agent's duties were inglorious, his hours long, and his salary minimal. He made $1,680 a year to start, and the amount almost never grew to more than $3,800.

In today's terms, that is at best a range of from $15,456 to $34,960, hardly the kind of income that most men covet, not at all worth agonizing about the charge that Jenkins made of Thompson and what should be done about it.

But there were perks aplenty, unstated benefits and private bonuses and secret retirement programs that were available to almost every agent who was willing to cross his fingers when he took his oath. In return for ignoring George Remus's factories or Bill McCoy's boats, in return for protecting the route of a designated shipment of whiskey, for allowing beer to be transported in the guise of cereal beverages, for not inspecting the backs of certain trucks, for seeing to it that certain speakeasies were warned prior to a raid, or merely for looking the other way when instructed, a Prohibition agent could multiply his earnings many times. Mabel Walker Willebrandt, the assistant attorney general in charge of Prohibition enforcement, was appalled by the situation. Most agents, she said, are "as devoid of honesty and integrity as the bootlegging fraternity . . . no more to be trusted with a commission to enforce the laws of the United States and to carry a gun than the notorious bandit Jesse James."

And like a fellow who stuck up banks and trains, an agent could sometimes get rich beyond his wildest dreams. Take the case of Edward Donegan, about whom little is known except that, in the year before Prohibition began, he was as far down on his luck as a man could be, the next thing to a pauper, having no source of income other than the driftwood he collected along the banks of the Gowanus Canal in Brooklyn and sold to people for their fireplaces. "Woodchucks," men like this were called, and "few New Yorkers ever pursued a humbler trade." Making matters worse for Donegan was his need to support a wife and three children on his meager, and sporadic, earnings. None of them ate regularly, dressed warmly or had any faith that tomorrow would be a better day.

Then, in 1920, Donegan got a job as a Prohibition agent. Did he have a friend in high places? Did he secure the position on his own? There is no evidence either way, but that Donegan put his mind to work on the new set of opportunities before him and refused to be daunted by his unimpressive background is clear. Within a few weeks of beginning his new duties, he came up with a swindle of near-miraculous proportions, one that took in not just the city of New York but the entire state. A man of irresistible charm when the right occasion arose, he had been unable to show this side of his personality along the Gowanus, where his only companions were real woodchucks. Now, however, he could bat his eyes, click his tongue, and whisper sweet nothings to all those female clerks in the office of state Prohibition Director Charles R. O'Connor. Or, as a judge would later put it when the swindle finally came to light, Donegan "debauched" them.

The women, whom one feels certain would have used a less judgmental verb, thanked Donegan for his attentions by providing him with phony permits to withdraw supplies of such legal liquids as industrial alcohol and near beer from government storage facilities. Donegan then sold the permits to bootleggers at scandalously inflated prices. Actually, there were a few more twists and turns to the scheme than just those, but suffice it to say that within four months, Donegan was able to deposit more than a million and a half dollars into the first savings account of his life. As a rough guess, that is eight centuries' worth of driftwood collecting. No longer was he the owner of a single, crumbling home within walking distance of a modest Brooklyn waterway; now he was the master of two residences, both in the grand style, his family ensconced in one and his mistress in the other.

There were few Edward Donegans in the world. But rewards of some denomination were there for almost any agent's taking. Henry Lee writes of "one inspector [who] was able to bank $193,553.22 and another $102,829.45. One captain had deposited $133,845.86, two more had more than $60,000 each and seven others had put aside nest eggs ranging from $14,000 to $32,000 apiece." So common was this kind of thing that Donegan's supervisor, the head of the New York City Prohibition Squad, "in time wearied of seeing his $2,000-a-year men arrive [for work] in chauffeured limousines." Determined to do something about it, he called a meeting one day, cramming every agent in his command into one room. They looked around at one another, bewildered. When they were ordered to put both hands on the tables in front of them, they were even more bewildered. The supervisor, it turned out, wanted to look at their fingers. He said, "Every son of a bitch wearing a diamond ring is fired!" According to one account, half the room emptied.

Corruption was everywhere during the 1920s, far more prevalent than, say, the rejection of alcoholic beverages. A dirty little secret at the start, it soon became common knowledge, the stuff of knowing winks, casual references, sardonic jokes: the stuff, in other words, of everyday chitchat. "Barely two months after the start of Prohibition," writes Eliot Asinof, "the first two agents were arrested in Baltimore for taking bribes. Warrants were issued in Philadelphia for the arrest of federal agents for conspiring to withdraw $15 million of liquor from distilleries by means of fraudulent permits. . . . One hundred agents in New York City were dismissed after an investigation into the abuse of permits for the use of intoxicating liquor and so on and so on, ad nauseum."

But it was not just agents. A former Prohibition Enforcement Department head, a state treasurer, several customs inspectors, mayors, police chiefs, fire chiefs, presidents of city councils, aldermen, and country commissioners—people holding these and numerous other positions of responsibility were arrested for violations of the Eighteenth Amendment, the law in which so few Americans could believe, even those who had agreed to apply it to earn their daily bread.

Agents, though, were the biggest problem, sometimes as insensitive and even savage as they were underhanded. On one occasion, some agents pumped so much ammo into a rumrunner's boat that it ricocheted off another boat, and then banged into a store and a couple of houses before finally coming to rest within inches of a petrified onlooker. In addition, there were reports of agents breaking into homes without warrants, lobbing mustard bombs through windows without cause, and patting down women on the hips and thighs and buttocks, looking for cheap thrills even more than for hidden intoxicants.

"One of the most shocking cases," Henry Lee believes,

> involved Charles P. Gundlacht, a hospitable farmer with a German weakness for beer, who liked to press a glass of home brew on strangers passing his farm near Leonardstown, Maryland. One thirsty wayfarer, a Washington Prohibition agent, repaid the old man's kindness by returning later and destroying all the brew he found. Even that act of vandalism did not assuage his noble responsibility "to enforce the laws (that) rests upon every public official," as Herbert Hoover once said. With three other agents but without a search warrant he returned a second time to the farm. This time, old Gundlacht was ready. He met the agents with a shotgun.
>
> "I know who you are," he said when they identified themselves, "and I don't give a goddamn."
>
> He warned that he would shoot and, as they continued to advance, fired a blast that wounded one agent in the knee. Returning the fire, they dropped him with a shot in the foot. *Then, according to the sworn statement of Gundlacht's widow, they ignored his pleas and shot him through the head as he lay on the ground.*

> For this atrocity, one agent won a federal acquittal on the plea of self-defense, while the cases against the other three were nol-prossed.

This kind of thing was an aberration, both the behavior by the agents and the leniency of the courts. But neither was the Prohibition Bureau lenient in reacting to the outrageous behavior of its employees. In fact, in its first four years of existence, the bureau fired a thousand employees, not just agents but lawyers and clerical workers, all sorts of people. And during a six-year period, the bureau had to hire more than 10,000 persons to fill 2,200 positions, such turnover was there for malfeasance or ineptitude or a combination of the two. Said Seymour Lowman, assistant aecretary of the treasury in charge of Volstead implementation, more than a little woefully, "Some days my arm gets tired signing orders of dismissal."

Yet few of the dismissed agents remained unemployed for long. A large number promptly provided their services to the other side of the law, which welcomed them as warmly as an evangelist welcomes a repentant sinner, or the devil a repentant do-gooder. Actually, agents were often courted while still on the government's payroll, receiving notes, phone calls, and visits, and being offered gifts, flattery, and assurances of a life without financial care or extreme thirst. All they had to do, like today's professional athletes, was declare themselves free agents and sign on with a new team. Ira L. Reeves, in charge of compliance to the Eighteenth Amendment in New Jersey, where there was no more compliance than anywhere else, said the move made perfect sense. "The prohibition service," he explained, and as Willebrandt had hinted earlier, "has proved to be a training ground for bootleggers. While in the service, the agents, investigators, and inspectors naturally learn all the ropes of the underworld, as well as the government's methods in attempting to apprehend and convict violators. Naturally, when leaving the service of the prohibition forces, they are sought by those engaged in illicit business."

Perhaps no one was less sanguine about Prohibition's chances than Congressman Fiorello La Guardia, the little old brewmaster who had defied the Eighteenth Amendment a few years earlier from the seat of national government. He said it simply could not be done. There was no way. It would take 250,000 agents to impose Prohibition on New York City alone, he swore, and another 250,000 to "police the police."

And speaking of the police—that is, the members of the numerous local constabularies, as opposed to federal Prohibition agents—they were, on the whole, even less willing to devote themselves to the Eighteenth Amendment than were the agents. It was not supposed to be that way. The police were supposed to lend a hand, to assist the agents by making arrests, imposing fines, impounding caches of spirits, and generally seeing to it that the United States became as free from the depredations of alcohol as the law demanded. In fact, because of their superior numbers, they were supposed to do even more for the cause of a drier America than the feds. And perhaps, ultimately, they did. But the police were also responsible for enforcing all the other laws in their communities, from jaywalking to manslaughter, from burglary to vandalism; as a result, they were even more lax than the agents in tending to the requirements of Prohibition.

They were no less eager, though, to sell themselves to the highest bidder, and in some cases to any bidder at all. Chicago Chief of Police Charles C. Fitzmorris said at one point that "sixty percent of my police are in the bootleg business." Similar complaints, and similar percentages, came from officials in other cities.

Nor were the police any less capable than the feds of displaying a spectacular degree of maladroitness. The following article, reprinted in full, appeared in the *New York Times* midway through 1921. The *Times* was obviously a more whimsical publication then than it is at present.

> An alleged dry law violator was freed yesterday because the bottle of whisky in his possession failed to survive the exhaustive experiments which five arresting policemen made to determine whether the whisky was whisky.
>
> The prisoner was William Manning, who has a saloon at 1662 Third Avenue. The raiders were Lieutenant Steinkamp and four policemen. They found a bottle behind the bar. But when they got to court, the case of the people of the State of New York consisted only in an empty bottle and a strong impression on the minds of the five policemen that it had contained whisky of most unchallengeable characteristics.
>
> It was observed by all when the bottle was seized that it contained a reddish liquid with a whisky smell. But the police have been repeatedly directed by Magistrates to disregard the rumors which the inaccurate organs of sense and smell convey to the brain and to depend only on the trustworthy palate.
>
> Consequently, Lieutenant Steinkamp, after the confiscation, ordered every man to do his duty. It was reasoned that if one or two witnesses make a good case, five make a better one. When the case against Manning was ap-

parently iron-clad and copper-riveted, they arrested him and the bartender, John Reilly.

"But where is the corpus delecti?" demanded Magistrate Edgar V. Frothingham in Harlem Court after hearing the testimony.

"There's the bottle," said Lieutenant Steinkamp.

"But there's nothing in it. What has become of the contents?"

Lieutenant Steinkamp looked puzzled, and scratched his head.

"Well, we tasted it," he said finally.

"What for?"

"So that we would have a good case."

"Why taste it all?" demanded the Magistrate. "Why not send it down to the chemist to have it analyzed? We can't hold defendants on evidence that has been verified into a state of nothingness. Defendants discharged."

It was not an isolated event. Sometimes it seemed as if the halls of justice were as common a site of liquor law violations as speakeasies. There were reports at the time of judges showing up for trial with booze on their breath, of bailiffs tripping over perfectly level floors on their way into the courtroom, of attorneys hopelessly slurring their opening remarks, of stenographers hiccupping as they took them down, and of jurors dropping half-pints from their pockets as they retired to deliberate. In fact, in 1928 an entire jury in San Francisco was put on trial for drinking the evidence in a case it was hearing. As a result, this defendant, too, was set free. It would not be surprising to learn that he celebrated by heading for a grogshop and working his way up to a princely hangover, or that some members of the jury had situated themselves on adjoining stools.

Another irony of the period was that Isidor Einstein looked like a beer keg. He stood five feet, five inches tall, weighed 225 pounds, and was thickest in the middle, tapering back a bit both above and below the waist. As he walked, he listed from side to side, a rolling gait that made him appear unsteady, even slightly inebriated. Seen from the front, "his noble paunch, gently wobbling, moved majestically ahead like the breast of an overfed pouter pigeon."

More often than not, Izzy, who simply cannot be called by his last name, as is the authorial convention, nor by the formal version of his first, had a smile on his face. It was a subtle one, though, even a little sly; it seemed as if he had just recovered from, or was about to begin, an uproarious fit of laughter, not that he was in its midst. But as the Noble Experiment got underway, Izzy found himself employed as a clerk in a branch post office on New York's Lower East Side, where he was plagued with monotonous duties, a drab workplace, and a salary that seemed a weekly insult. Yesterday blended into today, today into tomorrow—nothing to smile about at all.

He was not, in the traditional sense, an educated man. He had not spent much time in school, did not turn to books in his spare hours. But he had a marvelously tuned ear for languages, and the Lower East Side, with the greatest, and probably most diverse, population density of any neighborhood in the United States, was a teeming, swirling, raucous center of immigrants, most of whom still spoke in their native tongues. Simply by walking the streets and watching and listening, Izzy picked up German, Polish, and Hungarian fluently; Russian, Yiddish, French, and Italian passably; and even a few words of Chinese. He sometimes entertained friends with his dialects, doing funny bits of improvised palaver for them. He was great at parties, or with co-workers on his lunch hour, but he despaired of ever being able to use his gift for a worthwhile purpose. He was certainly never going to be a linguist in any kind of official capacity. Did he have other gifts he was not using, other interests, other instincts? He didn't even know—that's how bad things were for him. Like George Remus and Bill McCoy before him, Isidor Einstein had reached a crossroads in his career.

Then one morning he read in the newspaper that Prohibition agents were getting five dollars more a week, just to start, than he was making after several years at the post office. Five bucks a week! And an agent didn't have to do exactly the same things in exactly the same places for exactly the same amount of time whenever he showed up at work. An agent got out and about, perhaps even flirted with danger and intrigue; at least he got to meet different kinds of people. Izzy put down the paper for a moment, then quickly picked it up and read the article again. It was the first day of the rest of his life.

Isidor Einstein went on to become the most famous Prohibition agent of them all, a "master hooch hound," as was written by a contemporary, "alongside whom all the rest were pups." Never mind that no one remembers his name today; earlier in the century, he was better known than Eliot Ness and all the Untouchables put together, and he did his job as if he were a combination of Ness, Fatty Arbuckle, and Lon Chaney. He and his partner Moe "The Peerless" Smith, a former cigar store owner and an even larger physical presence than Izzy, "probably made the front pages more often than any other personages of their time except for the President and the Prince of Wales." Prohibitionists cheered lustily for Izzy; he gave them hope that this whole, crazy scheme of theirs just might work.

Bootleggers, on the other hand, virtually spat his name, and bartenders quaked when they thought of him, dreading him for his dedication and cunning. Some of them got photographs of Izzy, blew them up, and hung them next to their cash registers, sometimes even draping them in black crepe. Signs above the photos read: LOOK OUT FOR THIS MAN! or THIS MAN IS POISON!

But that was the problem: the picture. For all the good it did in identifying him, it might have been one of those new kinds of paintings by Picasso or someone like that, one of those so-called works of art whose subject was a total mystery because you could not make out any of the individual features. Izzy Einstein, you see, never looked the same way twice. Nor did he sound the same way twice, not on the job, at least, because to Izzy every working day was Halloween, or even better, an international festival, a chance to display his knack for languages as he had never done before. He would don a costume, sharpen his accent, and set out in affable pursuit of all those who did not kneel before the shrine of the Eighteenth Amendment.

He arrived at some drinking establishments as a German pickle packer, at others as a Polish count, at others as a Hungarian violinist. He also became, for a few hours or days here and there, a Yiddish gravedigger, a French *maître d'*, an Italian fruit and vegetable vendor, a Russian fisherman, a Chinese launderer, and an astonishing variety of Americans: cigar salesman, football player, beauty contest judge, streetcar conductor, grocer, lawyer, librarian, plumber—all of them so that he could fool bartenders into thinking that he belonged in their joints, was just another customer waiting to be served just another drink.

Once he did, he collected evidence ingeniously. He "sewed into his breast pocket a funnel connected by a rubber tube to a concealed flask. He would hand the bartender a bill to change and, as he went to the cash register, toss the drink down the funnel." When the bartender gave Izzy his money, the agent gave the bartender a set of handcuffs, slapping them across his wrists and setting them securely. The concealed flask went to the lab for confirmation of contents.

It was the best job Izzy ever had or ever would have, and he knew it. If he felt himself taking it for granted, or getting a little restless, neither of which happened very often, all he had to do was think of the post office, and all those letters he had sorted into all those slots that gaped at him like a million mouths he would never be able to feed. He could think of co-workers as bored as he, of the same walls and same floors and same dim lights from morning to night, every day of the week. The same smells, the same sounds, the same clock on the wall, ticking away indifferently. It made him shudder. It made him appreciate.

But the new job had not been easy to land. The chief agent of the Federal Prohibition Bureau, Southern New York Division, James Shevlin by name, was dubious about Izzy when he came in for an interview, and grew more dubious by the moment. Shevlin asked questions; Izzy gave answers in his own inimitable manner. Finally Shevlin said, "You're not the type," and added a little emphasis by standing up and gesturing toward the door.

"Why not?" was the response.

"Because you don't look like a detective."

To which Izzy replied, after a few moments of considering the point, "There might be some advantage in not looking like a detective. I could fool people better."

And fool them he did, time after time, at crime scene after crime scene, although never more successfully, nor against greater odds, than the day he disguised himself as a Negro and made his way up to Harlem.

Izzy and Moe prepared for the journey by practicing their deep-molasses drawls on each other until they sounded just right—at least to each other—then secreting themselves in the men's room of the federal building and smearing their faces with burnt cork, touching up a little here and there to get the tones as even as possible. They looked at each other, sighed, and dashed down the stairs, hopping into an unmarked vehicle and driving to a grocery store in the heart of black New York, which, they had reason to believe, sold bootleg liquor on the side. The two agents found a parking place right in front, got out of the car, and strutted across the sidewalk. So far, so good.

Inside the store, they began to browse the shelves. Once or twice they nodded to their fellow customers, being as friendly as they could without getting too close or standing directly in the light; burnt cork, seen from a few inches away, fools no man or woman of any race.

After a few minutes, Izzy and Moe, casual as could be, proceeded to the counter, where Izzy, with his head down and eyes off to the side, asked the clerk for a small can of tomatoes and a large can of beans.

That, he had been tipped, was the code: the tomatoes were gin, the beans whiskey; a small can was a pint, a large can a quart.

The clerk winked at the two men, then ducked into a back room and emerged a few seconds later with the booze. Izzy thanked him, then whipped out the cuffs. "There's sad news here," he said, in the phrase that would become the signature of his busts, and probably dropping the black dialect. "You're under arrest."

The clerk was dumbfounded. So were several customers who saw the collar and dashed outside to tell passersby what was happening. The result: near pandemonium on the street. As Thomas M. Coffey puts it in *The Long Thirst*, "Hundreds of actual Harlem residents gathered outside the delicatessen, pushing and shoving in an effort to get their hands on the two simulated blacks inside. Once again, Izzy and Moe were in deep trouble, but before the infuriated crowd could enter the store and drag out these phony 'brothers,' the sound of sirens announced the arrival of the police from the West 135th Street Station."

The "brothers" were saved. But it was a close call and a harrowing one; although Izzy repeated many of his disguises in different places at different times, never again would he and Moe dress up like the opening act of a minstrel show.

On another assignment, this time working without either his partner or an elaborate disguise, Izzy looked into the tippling habits of doctors at Mount Sinai Hospital. The account is the agent's own, included here not because of its accuracy, which is suspect, but because of the glimpse it provides of the narrator's personality.

> Hanging around there as requested, I noticed that fellows in white coats were slipping out of the hospital on mysterious errands to a place in the neighborhood. Next day I had on a white coat myself, and followed the trail. The place was just an ordinary speak, but so partial to us White Coats that the only question asked was, "What's yours?"
>
> I said, "Gin."
>
> Evidently this was less in demand than whiskey, because the bartender had to go into a back room, from which he returned with a pint flask and poured me a drink. I was about to do *my* little pouring act, into my pocket funnel, when I noticed the smell of the stuff. It was enough to take the tin off a tin can.
>
> "Whew!" I said. "What kind of bathtub was this born in?"
>
> He took a smell of it himself and his jaw dropped.
>
> "Gee!" he gasped, "I hope you didn't drink any of it because I made a terrible mistake." Explained that this was his first day on a new job and that he was still a little mixed as to what was what. By an unfortunate error, he

had given me stuff intended for cleaning the brasses, under the impression
it was gin.

"Gosh!" he repeated, "it's lucky you didn't drink it."

I accepted his apologies and a glass of the genuine. Then I arrested him.

"I wish you'd drunk what I gave you first," he said.

Which was hardly polite. But I was willing to overlook it.

As a Jew, although not an especially devout one, Izzy took special
pride in nabbing bootleggers who trafficked in sacramental wine. Under the Volstead Act, each Jewish family was permitted one gallon per
year per adult. For an entire synagogue, that meant hundreds of gallons, which in turn meant that a lot of crooks had decided to claim
to be the spiritual leaders of a lot of phony places of worship. One
was really a laundry, another a delicatessen, a third a post office box;
Izzy and Moe retrieved wine from all of them. They also cracked the
case of the Assembly of Hebrew Orthodox Rabbis of America, which
turned out to be not an organization but an individual, not an orthodox
Jewish scholar but a red-nosed Irishman named Sullivan. During Prohibition, it was believed that fully "three quarters of sacramental wine,
legally delivered to churches for religious purposes, had been stolen and
bootlegged."

In his first two years on the job, either alone or in the company of his
peerless partner, Izzy accounted for the phenomenal total of 20 percent
of all Prohibition-related arrests in New York City, a figure that indicates not only his own diligence, but the indifference or incompetence
of most of his colleagues. By the five-year mark, Izzy and Moe had introduced almost 5,000 tippling Gothamites to the specific penalties of
the Volstead Act, an average of more than three per working day.

Even more remarkable was how well their methods, unusual though
they were, held up in court. Nine out of every ten sellers or manufacturers or thieves of alcoholic beverages nabbed by Izzy and Moe were
convicted; no other agents came close to that figure. Further, the two
men personally confiscated almost 5 million bottles of beer and wine
and liquor, a haul worth more than $15 million. And they did it all with-
out resorting to weapons. Izzy was afraid of guns and neither owned nor
carried one; Moe packed a revolver every once in a while, but fired it
only twice. "Once," writes Herbert Asbury, "he shot out a lock that had
resisted his efforts, and another time he shot a hole in a keg of whiskey."
The two men might have been "a pair of zanies," as people said of them,
but their efficiency was the stuff of legend.

Moe did not seem to care. He was a retiring sort, the kind of man who did his job, went home to his family, and had no interest in how others might regard him or whether they regarded him at all. Izzy, on the other hand, garrulous to begin with, took to the limelight as avidly as his victims took to barstools. He became a celebrity, not only to the public at large, but to Prohibition administrators in other cities, who, reading or hearing of his exploits, asked New York officials to spare him for consultations—guest shots, so to speak. Usually the New Yorkers agreed, thinking of their man as a good-will ambassador, and of his fame as a reflection of the skills with which they ran their departments.

As for the star of the show, he was delighted to hit the road, to perform in front of new audiences, to vary his days even more. So he became, among other things, a Mexican laborer in El Paso, Texas; a member of a construction crew in Providence, Rhode Island; and an out-of-work mechanic in Detroit.

The latter was a special case. At one point during Prohibition, the manufacture, sale, and importing of illegal beverages from Canada became Detroit's second most lucrative industry, surpassed only by the manufacture and sale of automobiles. The city's bootlegging business "was three times larger than her chemical industry, eight times the size of her stove and heating appliance industry, ten times the size of her cigar and tobacco industry. . . . The annual liquor turnover in Detroit, according to the New York *Times*, was valued at $215 million."

Dropping into a saloon in the vicinity of one of the auto plants, Izzy found that his reputation had preceded him, even this far from home. It seemed that "the bartender refused to serve him because, he said, pointing to a black-draped photograph of Einstein, 'Izzy Epstein's in town.' 'You mean Einstein, don't you?' Izzy asked. When the bartender insisted it was Epstein, Izzy bet him a drink. The bartender poured him a shot of booze, Izzy emptied it into the secret funnel. . . . Then Izzy announced in his usual plaintive manner, 'There's sad news here. You're under arrest.' "

After he had been traveling for a while, and enjoying the stimulation of places he never imagined he would see, Izzy boasted that he could step off a train in any city in the United States and locate illegal alcohol within thirty minutes, no matter how carefully guarded the local operations were. Only once did he fail; in Washington, D.C., it took him a full hour to quench his assumed thirst, and he succeeded then only because a policeman took pity on him and gave directions to the nearest taproom.

But in Chicago and St. Louis, he claimed, he found liquor in twenty-one minutes, in Atlanta in seventeen, and in Pittsburgh, where he had done himself up like a steelworker and paraded around with a grimy face and a rusty lunchbox, in a mere eleven. In New Orleans, though, he made even these achievements seem like dallying when he waddled off the train from New York and slid his bulk into the back seat of a waiting cab. Before even giving the driver his destination, he asked where he could cure his thirst.

You need look no further, the man said to Izzy, or words to that effect, and reached under the front seat for a bottle. Four bits for a good, healthy swallow.

Izzy shook his head. "There's sad news here . . ."

Elapsed time: thirty-five seconds.

To newspaper columnists, Izzy was a dream come true, manna from heaven, a comic-novel character plopped down in real life. The crooks, they had found, were easy to write about, what with their outrageous lifestyles, their daring escapades, their open and haughty defiance of the law. They were always good for an attention-grabbing quote, an eye-catching photo. But on the law-abiding side of Prohibition, things were different. Chicago writers, for instance, found that interviewing Eliot Ness was like talking to a roll of wallpaper, and the other Untouchables were equally unengaging. They were decent men, but had nothing to say; virtuous, but almost completely without style. The only great copy on the dry team was the old postal worker from the Lower East Side.

The *New York Times*:

> Izzy Einstein . . . holds the record in the United States for the largest number of liquor arrests.

The *Brooklyn Eagle*:

> Izzy does not sleep. He's on the job day and night, and accomplishes more for the drys than half a dozen anti-saloon leagues. It's getting so now that a saloon-keeper hesitates in serving the wants of his oldest and best-known customer, for fear that he may suddenly develop into Izzy.

The *New York Tribune*:

> [Izzy Einstein is] the master mind of the Federal rum ferrets.

Syndicated columnist O. O. McIntyre:

[Izzy Einstein has] become as famous in New York as the Woolworth Building.

Wayne Wheeler, in a letter to Einstein widely quoted by journalists:

The bootlegger who gets away from you has got to get up early in the morning.

Maybe, Izzy began to think, his father would finally forgive him for not having been a rabbi. Maybe his wife would finally apologize for what she said when he changed jobs, telling him that chasing bad guys was no line of work for someone with four young children. Maybe those children would have someone to look up to now, after all.

But as Izzy's fame increased, so did the resentment that other agents felt toward him, and to a lesser degree his partner. The two of them got it from both sides. The honest agents were offended because they were trying just as hard, albeit with less success and panache, to perform the same thankless tasks as the dynamic duo, and agents on the take were offended because the pair were setting such a bad example. Not only that, they were sometimes arresting the very people who had paid off other law enforcement officials precisely so they would *not* be arrested. When those officials dropped hints to Izzy and Moe about their overzealousness, the two refused to take them, unwilling to yield to the law's lawlessness. They went about their business, leaving increasing tensions in their wake, either not knowing how to deal with them or, more likely, not caring.

In the end, then, at least in retrospect, it seems there was no choice: Izzy and Moe had to go; flamboyant success could not compete with inconspicuous turpitude. "The service must be dignified," said an IRS spokesman, trying to explain the decision to a baffled press corps, to men who were so amazed at what they were hearing that they could barely make their pencils work. "Izzy and Moe belong on the vaudeville stage." They were fired in 1925, at the height of their productivity.

The decision made headlines. It brought joy to bootleggers and crooked agents and dismay to drys as well as to people of all thirst-quenching persuasion who simply enjoyed a good show. More than one person called this Prohibition's darkest day yet, as law enforcement in the nation's largest city had in one terrible swoop gotten both duller and less efficient.

Izzy and Moe went on to careers as life insurance salesmen, and although they did not work together, each did quite well for himself, accounting for more than $400,000 worth of business in his better years, "selling policies in numerous cases to the men they had raided." They spent more time with their families, more time with newly made friends and admirers. They also became members of one of Mayor Jimmy Walker's favorite groups, the Grand Street Boys Association, which raised money for a number of New York charities. Both would take an occasional drink, a cocktail or a beer; unlike hizzoner, neither would flaunt it.

But their new lives did not interest them, certainly not to the extent that their old ones had. Moe quickly, and willingly, faded from public view, much more comfortable in the spotlight's absence. Izzy fought against such a fate. Foreshadowing today's media darlings, he sort-of-wrote a book. He called it *Prohibition Agent No. 1*, and dedicated it to "the 4,932 persons I arrested, hoping they bear me no grudge for having done my duty."

Some of them did. Most, it seems certain, did not. "In my work I never resorted to violence," the agent declared a few chapters later in his volume, "never got flustered and called out the police and state troopers, never pulled a gun on anybody. I showed I meant business, that was all. And I let the fellows I arrested see that I was a human being."

On the day the book was published, the author invited reporters to a party. After regaling them with tale after tale of his adventures—some from the book and at least partly verifiable; some, no doubt, from the deep wells of his imagination—Izzy was interrupted by a young journalist, the kind we would today call "investigative." It was not enough for this person to know the facts; he wanted to get behind the story, to understand the motivations of those involved, the yearnings and the dark secrets. He said, "But Mr. Einstein, do you believe in the moral principle of Prohibition?"

Izzy's jaw dropped as if it had been attached to his cheeks with a screw and the screw had just fallen out. The room got suddenly still. *Moral principle of Prohibition?* Izzy scratched his head. He never knew there *was* such a thing. It was a job, Prohibition, that was all, except that he could use his languages and dress up in all kinds of nifty costumes and become feared and famous and so, better than a job, it was a game—but in a meaningful sense, as a sport is a game to a professional athlete.

In other words, being an agent was fun, fun that paid better than the post office, if not as well as selling insurance. What more could a man want from his employment? There was no reason to get philosophical about something if it was fun, was there? You damn well never thought about such a thing as the *moral principle of Prohibition*.

The reporter waited.

The room stayed silent.

The greatest dry enforcer of them all lit a cheap cigar. He sucked in hard a time or two, blew out some small black clouds, and, without removing the stogie from his lips, finally spoke to the young man. "I don't get you," he said, and took the next question.

Isidor Einstein outlasted Prohibition by a mere five years, dying in 1938 of an infection after his right leg was amputated. To some, the amount of space given to him in newspapers of the time seemed out of proportion to his significance in the larger scheme of things. Perhaps the same objection has occurred to readers of this book. It is probably valid in both cases. But Izzy brought so much energy to the Eighteenth Amendment, so much mirth to righteousness; he is, to this author as well as to all those reporters of an earlier generation, an irresistible kind of guy, the kind who cannot help but spill over into a few extra paragraphs.

In 1920, Congress allocated a little more than $2 million to the war against alcoholic beverages. Wayne Wheeler thought it was plenty. In fact, he went so far as to say that Prohibition might even be a profit-making venture for the federal government, because what it collected in confiscated goods, forfeited bonds, and fines would be more than the cost of enforcement. And he smiled that smile of his, the one that was so very different from Izzy Einstein's.

But Wheeler was wrong, and might have known it even as he spoke. The $2 million allocation proved as effective against the great American thirst as a pair of galoshes would have been against a monsoon.

In fact, so disastrous were the first year's efforts at enforcement that in year two, 1921, the budget almost trebled to $6,350,000. Actually, it was even greater than that if the amounts of money spent by the Coast Guard and U.S. Customs are taken into account, in addition to the Prohibition-related expenditures of local police departments. As a result, there seemed to be some progress; according to various early estimates, Americans were drinking either a little less or a lot less than before, or somewhere in between—it depended on who was doing the estimating. But they were drinking still; no one could deny that, and the quantities they were drinking remained substantial. Thus, by 1930, the total amount spent on agents and equipment and court proceedings had risen to more than $12 million, although things had come to such a pass by then that Commissioner of Prohibition James M. Doran was estimating it would not be possible to dry up the United States for a penny less than $300 million. Other people threw out even higher figures. $350 million. $400 million. Half a billion!

Such amounts were not possible, and Congress would not have considered them even if they were. The House and the Senate seemed to be wanting it both ways; having approved Hobson-Sheppard, America's elected officials now set out to atone for it by voting too little money to carry out the law properly.

Wets, of course, were delighted with the small allocations; they meant that Prohibition would be easy to ignore, and that the constant violations, reported almost daily in the press and freely discussed among citizens in all sorts of forums, would be a constant reminder of the law's irrationality.

But, yet another irony: drys were also pleased, and not just Wayne Wheeler, for they saw the disbursement of funds not as a matter of finances so much as of image. They believed that if the government spent a lot of money on the Eighteenth Amendment, it would be tacitly admitting that abstinence was an unnatural state, one that had to be forced upon Americans. To the contrary, the Anti-Saloon League's position was that people were as hungry for Prohibition as they had once been thirsty for alcohol, and that once exposed to it on the grand scale would readily concede its virtues.

As a result, the drys claimed not only that the enforcement dollars were sufficient, but that, all evidence to the contrary, the law was being welcome like the overdue promise of eternal life. Roy Asa Haynes, the Prohibition commissioner before Doran, a man known to many as "Wheeler's puppet," provided unceasingly optimistic updates to the public.

January 1922: "The Amendment is being enforced to an even greater extent than many of its devoted friends anticipated."

December 1922: "[The] home brew fad is taking its last gasp."

April 1923: "Bootleg patronage has fallen off fifty per cent."

December 1923: "There is little open and above-board drinking anywhere."

Whether Haynes believed any of this or just wished it so or had simply been told to speak the words by Wayne Wheeler, no one can say. The same doubt arises over the statement of a man who was not in the service of the government, a private citizen who took quite seriously his life's work of making women look better. He also took seriously the dry law's contribution to his work. "It is very easy to trace the growth of beauty salons to Prohibition," this fellow said to a reporter from the *Washington News*. "When men drank, they were not critical. Their wives and sweethearts looked attractive to them without the assistance of beauty parlors. Now men remain clear-eyed at evening and notice wrinkles, pallor, straight hair and unsparkling eyes. As a result, women flock to beauty parlors and we have to turn them away each day."

In fact, according to the chairman of the Republican Party in 1928, the ban on booze had a lot to do with people of both genders flocking to all sorts of businesses. "Most of the present prosperity is due to Prohibition," Hubert Work declared. "There is more money in the savings banks, the children wear better shoes."

Perhaps. But bootleggers were wearing the best shoes of all. The economy was booming, all right, and for all manner of reasons, virtually none of which was the Eighteenth Amendment. But crime statistics were soaring to bull market heights as well. In the first four years of Prohibition, authorities confiscated almost 700,000 stills. Even more kept operating, many more, with Prohibition Administrator General Lincoln C. Andrew telling a Senate committee that he thought his men were finding fewer than one of every ten of the illegal machines. Stills were everywhere at the time, in houses, factories, churches, schools, stores, municipal buildings, warehouses, private clubs, parks, pastures, silos, forests, backyards, and even, in the most memorable case of all, in a redwood tree near Dyersville in northern California.

It was a sight that few people saw, but those who did never forgot it. The tree's trunk had been hollowed out, although with a diameter of twenty-four feet, it was no easy task. Then a still was hidden inside. The opening through which the drilling had been done and the machinery installed was covered with a piece of canvas that had been painted the color of bark, so that the tree, at least from a distance, resumed its original appearance. Squirrels and birds did not seem to be fooled; the humans who caught a glimpse of the redwood, though, thought it just another tree in the forest, although they might have wondered why trails of steam occasionally seeped out of cracks in the trunk.

For several months, the cleverly concealed still poured out its product. Then, somehow, federal agents found out about it and moved in. They stormed the tree, surrounding it, unholstering their weapons and standing vigilant. They yelled for those inside to come out; no one did. After a while, the agents went into the trunk themselves and found only the still, no operators. They considered dismantling the apparatus and removing it, but decided instead on a different course. They threw a chain around the tree, padlocked it, and posted a sign that said: "Closed for One Year for Violation of the National Prohibition Act." The bootleggers seem never to have returned, and despite the agents' best efforts to find them, were never caught. The tree took the rap alone.

Then there was the still found on a farm just outside of Austin, Texas, a few months after Prohibition began. For a time, federal agents said, it was churning out 130 gallons of top-quality, 100 percent illegal moonshine every single day. The owner of the farm, and the illegal beverage it produced, was Senator Morris Sheppard, Lone Star Democrat.

While bootleggers hid stills, their customers hid the spirituous beverages that the stills manufactured. Most often, it seems, they poured them into hip flasks, which rode on the body in the designated location and also fit unobtrusively into briefcases and purses and overnight bags. In addition, they stored their libations in books that had no pages, briefcases that had no briefs, "boots expansible at the ankles, hollow canes, ladies' muffs, baby carriages with storage space beneath the baby, pants with extra large pockets." The Eighteenth Amendment might not have inspired abstinence, but it was a boon to creativity in both product design and attire.

It also led to a certain resourcefulness in the use of nature's bounty. "At the Buffalo end of the International Bridge, spanning the Niagara River," it was revealed at the time, "Customs officials once caught a returning citizen with two dozen eggs which he had emptied through small holes, refilled with Canadian whiskey, and sealed." Caught elsewhere at the time was an individual who had emptied the contents of a coconut and then filled it up with newly purchased liquor.

Alcoholic beverages were stashed in bras and corsets and bloomers, in trumpet cases and violin cases and pianos, and even in tiny containers that fit between the toes of people wearing oversized shoes. "One Detroit mechanic," writes Larry Engelmann, accommodated bootleggers on the highway. He "made a small fortune by altering gasoline tanks so that half of the tank could carry gasoline and half could be filled with booze."

And there were more violations of the law, many more, either the letter of it or the spirit of it or both, violations unceasing and innovative and witty.

H. L. Mencken drank all through the era, and not just Methodist-brau. He drank anything he could get his hands on, at any time it was available. "I shall make dandelion wine if I can find a dandelion," he said. "But down here they are not to be trusted. Dogs always piss on them. And, now and then, a policeman."

The comedian W. C. Fields drank all through the era. His favorite cocktail was something he called a martini; what he meant was that "he had a bottle of gin in one hand and a bottle of vermouth in the other, and he took alternate pulls, favoring the gin."

Visitors to the United States from England drank all through the era. In New York, as one source has it, no sooner did they check into a hotel than they "had a card pushed into their hands by a bell-hop which said 'Sam Mordecai, Interior Decorator'—and you knew, of course, that it was *your* interior Sam wished to decorate. Sam then delivered bottles in brown paper parcels."

The patients of doctors drank all through the era, and not just when they happened to be ill. In the Eighteenth Amendment's first six months, 15,000 physicians and 57,000 pharmacists applied for licenses to prescribe booze. By 1929, 11 million prescriptions a year were being filled, and as Jules Abels points out, "The Prohibition Bureau could not spare the manpower to make even a token inspection of their validity."

In Massachusetts, authorities arrested 20,000 people a year for illegal transactions of one sort or another with alcohol.

In Kentucky, alcohol played a part in 75 percent of all arrests during the era.

In Iowa, there were as many as 430 liquor law cases awaiting trial at any one time.

In Chicago: 600.

In New York, the number of drinkers and suppliers being nabbed was so great that, had the state decided to prosecute all of them in a single year, the cost to taxpayers, even if the cases had been settled without a jury, would have been $20 million. With a jury: $70 million.

In the southern district of Alabama, the heart of moonshine country, a place where stills sprouted in the countryside like wildflowers, United

States attorneys were spending 90 percent of their time trying to enforce the Eighteenth Amendment.

North Carolina: 70 percent.

West Virginia: 70 percent.

Northern Florida: 60 percent.

Minnesota: 60 percent.

Arkansas: 50 percent.

Nationally: 44 percent, and according to the office of the Attorney General, in the first forty-one months of Prohibition, the federal government initiated 90,330 liquor law prosecutions.

Never before had the American legal system been so thoroughly, and unmanageably, congested. It was a quagmire, and into it sank all hopes of speedy justice, or even of speedy resolution without the justice. In 1916, the federal courts handled a grand total of 20,432 cases. Thirteen years later, the number had more than quadrupled, and virtually all of the increase was attributable to the demands of the Volstead Act. "In 1928 and 1929," according to Justice Department reports, "prohibition cases accounted for nearly two-thirds of all federal district court criminal cases (as well as over half the civil suits against the government.)"

The legal system was too chaotic these days to be called a system. Men and women with alcohol on their breath or in their possession were being herded into police vans, crammed into holding cells, forced to stand in long, unmoving lines to be fingerprinted and photographed, and the careful observer, trying to make sense of it all, could not help but note the unmistakable stench of vice. The United States attorney for the southern district of New York was quoted as saying that he found "the fifth floor of the Federal Building a seething mob of bartenders, peddlers, waiters, bond runners and fixers. Federal judges have told me that the whole atmosphere of the Federal Building was one of pollution . . . and reports were made to senior judges of attempts to bribe jurymen even in the toilets of the building."

Finally, to clear the air as well as to save both time and money, the Justice Department decided to compromise its standards of punishment and establish "bargain days," otherwise known as "cafeteria courts." One day a week a lawbreaker could present himself before a judge and, provided he was not a bootlegger of the magnitude of Remus or McCoy, be assured of a reduced fine and no jail term in return for a quick plea of guilty. Almost immediately the backlog began to ease. Few judges reported actually getting caught up with their caseloads, but most made progress and the burdens were consequently lightened as well on agents and members of the local police.

Bargain days were especially popular among speakeasy owners, because more often than not the fines they were assessed added up to less than the yearly license fees they had had to pay before the Eighteenth Amendment took effect. And so yet another of the era's many, unintended ironies: if a fellow could manage just one arrest a year, he might be able to operate his watering hole more cheaply now than he could when it was legal to do so.

It took a long time for Wayne Wheeler's influence to disappear. His luck, on the other hand, ran out in a matter of weeks.

It was the spring of 1927, and rumors were circulating, both inside temperance circles and without, that Wheeler had become ill, perhaps dangerously ill. He was on his last legs, would not survive the month, would not survive the day. Wheeler not only denied these stories, but attributed them to the enemy. "This is unmitigated bunk," he said. "I have been thirty-three years in this fight and will never quit as long as God gives me breath to fight the lawless contraband. My health is better than the wets wish it and it is getting better every week."

But it was not. If anything, the heart disease and kidney problems that had been troubling him for a long time were getting worse. "His incessant activity," wrote biographer Justin Steuart, "had worn out his tremendous vitality." Eventually, even Wheeler had to admit that his health was not what he wanted it to be, and in an attempt to regain at least a small measure of vitality, this man who had once been known as a "locomotive in trousers" went off for the summer to a cabin in the woods of western Michigan, far from civilization and its beverages.

He still did the league's work, but not as much of it as before. He still "loved the limelight," as Steuart put it, but allowed it to shine on others in the movement now and then, and did not seem to be troubled. And as the spring of '27 lazed its way into the summer and the summer slunk toward fall, Wheeler began to show improvement. He worked a little harder without ill effects, took a daily stroll at better than a snail's pace, and gained some color in what had become a ghostly complexion.

Then on August 13, another in a long series of hot, damp backwoods days, Wheeler was resting in his upstairs study, having perhaps overdone it a bit that morning on various projects for the league. His eyes were closed, his mind drifting; he was within a few seconds of dozing off. He never made it. He heard a scream from the kitchen, a sudden eruption of sound that jarred him in an instant to complete wakefulness. Rushing downstairs, almost stumbling in his haste, he found that the gasoline stove in the kitchen had exploded. His wife, who had been standing next to it, was now "engulfed in flames like a human torch."

Wheeler did not panic. He yanked the rug up from the floor and wrapped it around his wife as quickly as he could, smothering the fire but not the pitiful cries that continued to escape from her mouth. Holding her in his arms, the rug warm and foul-smelling but the blaze apparently extinguished, Wheeler told her to be calm; everything would be all right, he knew it. He squeezed her tightly and she closed her eyes and exhaled with a groan, but there was no way for him to know what it meant. He held onto her, just held on. She had been his life almost as much as the cause had been.

Then he remembered his father-in-law. Where was he? He had been keeping Wheeler's wife company while she cooked, but seemed now to have disappeared. It made no sense. Still embracing his wife, Wheeler backed up a few steps and leaned around a corner of the kitchen. He gasped. His father-in-law lay in a silent heap on the floor, curled almost fetally at the foot of a chair. Seeing his daughter catch fire had been too much for the old man; he had suffered a heart attack, his second in a matter of weeks.

Wheeler called the hospital. An ambulance came in a few minutes and picked up his wife and rushed her away, but the best efforts of doctors and nurses and other emergency room personnel could do nothing to save her. She died later that night. Wheeler's father-in-law, whom he considered one of his best friends, did not have to be rushed anywhere. He was pronounced dead in the kitchen.

Wheeler did his best to carry on. He prayed for guidance and understanding; refusing to believe that the tragedy was the random, senseless event it seemed, he vowed to find the meaning of it, to learn what his Maker wanted him to learn. He even kept a speaking engagement nine days later, despite being urged by friends and his physician to cancel. But as Thomas Coffey says, "his voice was so weak that only those in the front rows could hear him. Realizing that he lacked the strength to deliver his entire address, he gave a short summary of it and asked his listeners to read the rest from copies which had been printed in advance." He received a huge ovation for the enormity of his effort, but it did not seem to register; his face was glazed and pasty, his eyes unfocused. He was taken home and put to bed, too exhausted even to resume his dialogue with the Almighty.

Before long, he was admitted to a sanitarium in Battle Creek, and he seemed to rally, showing his nurses an occasional smile, an occasional spurt of energy. But these were tricks of the body, final spasms; they were not signs of returning vigor. One evening, "after recovering sufficiently to be able to sit up in a chair, he reached out for a book but, without touching it, lurched forward, dead." He was mourned by friend and foe alike, although the former had a distinct edge in sincerity.

By that time, Americans had been living under Prohibition for seven and a half years. The late Wayne Wheeler was a smart man, well-attuned to his time. He must have known that there would not be another seven and a half.

10

The Hummingbird
Beats the Odds

"There is as much chance of repealing the Eighteenth Amendment," said its co-sponsor, Senator Morris Shepard, Democrat from Texas, speaking on the record and for the ages and not acknowledging the fact that, by putting up a still on his property, he had already enacted his own, personal repeal, "as there is for a hummingbird to fly to the planet Mars with the Washington Monument tied to its tail."

A year and a half after Prohibition began, the Nineteenth Amendment to the Constitution followed it into law. It ended a decades-long struggle that never should have been necessary in the first place and gave women full membership in the American electoral process.

> Section 1. The right of citizens of the United States to vote shall not be denied or abridged by the United States or by any state on account of sex.
> Section 2. Congress shall have power to enforce this article by appropriate legislation.

It was believed that one of the first things women would do with the vote was solidify Prohibition. They would ensure that dry legislators stayed in office and dry laws remained on the books; they might even vote in tougher men and stricter laws. They were upset that some drys, the more conservative among them, had opposed the Nineteenth Amendment, fearing that it threatened the traditional, male-dominated structure of the family. And they were pleased that some wets, the more liberal of the breed, had worked for the amendment, believing that a male-dominated family was a problem of the same kind, if not magnitude, as a male-dominated society.

But these were exceptions. In most cases, women and drys were natural allies. They went back a long way together. In fact, had it not been for the former, the latter would not have become the power brokers that they turned out to be.

Further, there was a precedent for women to vote in favor of Prohibition. In New Zealand, females had won the right to vote in 1893, and shortly afterward proved instrumental in approving a ban on alcohol on a local-option basis. They went to the polls in large numbers and voted in near-unanimous fashion. Their unity made them an overnight force in their country's politics.

It did not happen in the United States. What did happen was something no one foresaw, something that, even in retrospect, left most observers puzzled, especially those who had hoped for a stirring affirmation of the Eighteenth Amendment and more teeth in the Volstead Act. Women, it seems, showed less of a concern for the provisions of the Nineteenth than for what they perceived to be its symbolism, which is that they were now, more than ever before, the equals of men. Thus they did not flock to the voting booths as a single entity to express their support for abstinence. They did not flock to the voting booths as a single entity to express their support for anything. They remained, as women had always been, a collection of individuals, many of whom, in the wake of suffrage, now demanded that they be allowed to titillate themselves with the same pleasures as men. Some of them took up tobacco for the first time. Others, noted Frederick Lewis Allen, "were drinking—somewhat less openly [than males] but often all too efficaciously. There were stories of daughters of the most exemplary parents getting drunk—'blotto,' as their companions cheerfully put it—on the contents of the hip-flasks of the new prohibition regime, and going out joyriding with men at four in the morning."

In other words, a surprising number of American women decided not to use the privilege that the Nineteenth Amendment gave them to cancel out the satisfaction of joining the men in abusing the Eighteenth. Among them were "the feminist journalist Rheta Childe Dorr [who, in 1929] published *Drink: Coercion or Control?* endorsing government regulation of liquor sales. She contrasted the lawlessness and discord of the American system with rational Scandinavian government controls. Two congresswomen, Florence P. Kahn of San Francisco and Mary Norton of Newark, New Jersey, opposed Prohibition publicly throughout their tenures."

To some observers, it seemed that women were simply responding to the lure of the forbidden. To others, Allen among them, World War I had more than a little to do with it. Women, he said, seemed to have "been infected by the eat-drink-and-be-merry-for-tomorrow-we-die spirit which accompanied the departure of the soldiers to the training camps and the fighting front."

So infected, in fact, that they showed the spirit in another, perhaps even more insidious, way. Or so the Anti-Saloon League believed. As early as 1913, one of its posters declared that *alcohol inflames the passions,* thus making the resisting of temptation especially difficult. . . . *Avoid all alcoholic drink absolutely.* The control of the sex impulses will then be easy, and disease, dishonor, disgrace, and degradation will be avoided." The league now believed that too many women were not avoiding drink and were as a result suffering a variety of consequences, uncontrollable sex impulses among them.

In time, with more and more women joining the fight for repeal, their ranks came to be headed by Mrs. Pauline Sabin, a woman known for "her grace and delicate beauty, her fine taste in clothing, and her prominence in New York society." She was the wife of a Morgan banker, the daughter of Theodore Roosevelt's secretary of the navy and, through him, heiress to the Morton's Salt millions, and the granddaughter of Grover Cleveland's secretary of agriculture. It was she who first organized the anti-Prohibition women, she who vowed to undo the deeds of her sisters a generation or two back, she who bore the vilification that followed in torrents.

Sabin was an unlikely choice for such a role, and not just because of her pedigree. Initially, she had supported Prohibition, seemingly without reservation. The mother of two young sons, she often said that she thought "a world without liquor would be a beautiful world" for them. It would ensure their health, both mental and physical, would increase the odds of their finding worthwhile companionship, and would provide more opportunities for them, vocational and otherwise, in the future. She did not work actively to pass the Eighteenth Amendment, but she admired those who did, thinking of them as allies in her children's future. Once the thirty-six states had ratified, Sabin settled in to enjoy the results.

Like a lot of others, she seems to have become disaffected gradually; we are not aware of the steps. But they were steps taken by many Americans, mothers and fathers, at the same time. "By the beginning of 1927," writes Gerald Leinwand, "five states with a total of 20 million people—New York, Illinois, Wisconsin, Montana, and Nevada— held referendums urging some substantial changes in prohibition." And a year later, Sabin announced her own change in a magazine article that startled those who thought they knew her. She called it simply, "I Change My Mind on Prohibition," with the subtitle stating that "a former advocate of prohibition finds that she made a mistake and has the rare courage to admit it."

In the article, Sabin declared that the Eighteenth Amendment was not a good thing for children after all, neither hers nor anyone else's, because they were "growing up with a total lack of respect for the Constitution and for the law." They could make up their own minds not to drink, she now believed, and those who had been properly raised would surely do so. A piece of legislation that insisted on abstinence but was everywhere defied was doing far greater harm—to kids, grownups, the entire society—than alcohol. It might have taken her a while to come to this conclusion, she admitted in the article, but the length of time simply gave her modified views a more solid foundation.

A few months later, when the Republicans chose Herbert Hoover as their presidential candidate, Sabin sat on the party's National Committee, the first woman ever to do so. She thought highly of Hoover, agreeing with him on most issues, speaking publicly on his behalf at several functions, and even helping to raise money for his campaign. But when he refused to denounce Prohibition, as she had many times urged him to do, when he in fact gave it one of its most enduring, if ludicrous, nicknames, by calling it "a great social and economic experiment, noble in motive and far-reaching in purpose," she was on his side no longer. She quit the committee, quit the Republican Party, and in a chic and polished private room at the Drake Hotel in Chicago, she formed a bipartisan group of kindred spirits to oppose the Eighteenth Amendment and all that it stood for. "At an earlier meeting to select a name," writes David E. Kyvig, "the merely awkward Women's Organization for National Prohibition Reform (WONPR) won out over the truly dreadful Women's Legion for True Temperance."

Those who joined the WONPR were asked to make a pledge, much as women on the other side of the issue had done in the previous century.

> Because I believe that prohibition has increased crime, lawlessness, hypocrisy and corruption; because I believe that the cause of real temperance has been retarded and that sumptuary laws have no place in the Federal Constitution, I enroll as a member of this organization, which is working for some change in the law to bring about a sane solution of the problem without the return of the saloon.

It might be too late for Sabin and her new allies to make a difference in the 1928 elections, but they were determined to do what they could in the future.

Proper drys were appalled. That a lady of Pauline Sabin's background would write the article she had written and then found the coalition she had founded was barely to be believed, and not at all to be countenanced. The Anti-Saloon League's Bishop Cannon railed at her and those she had enlisted. He said that, morally, there was no difference between these women and "prohibition's criminal offspring, the bootleggers, smugglers and racketeers." Both, he went on, "will continue in their everyday lives deliberately and completely to disregard the law's very existence."

To the *American Independent*, a temperance newspaper, the members of the WONPR were, despite their social standing, "the scum of the earth," an unsavory batch of so-called ladies "possibly late at night flirting with other women's husbands at drunken and fashionable resorts."

To the ardent prohibitionist Dr. Mary Armor, "Mrs. Sabin and her cocktail-drinking women" were the foes of other women, decent women, everywhere, and "we will out-live them, out-fight them, out-love them, out-talk them, out-pray them and out-vote them."

And to Fletcher Dobyns, who wrote a study of Prohibition published by the Woman's Christian Temperance Union's Signal Press, it was unthinkable "that the women of America had transferred their intellectual and spiritual allegiance from women like Frances E. Willard, Jane Addams, Evangeline Booth, Carrie Chapman Catt and Ella Boole to such women as Mrs. Sabin."

Unthinkable it might have been, but in the case of Boole, perhaps not such a bad idea. In 1929, it was reported that six Prohibition agents had broken into the home of a suspected bootlegger, beaten him with

clubs, and as his wife tried to rescue him, or at least deflect the impact
of the blows, blasted her with a shotgun from point-blank range, killing
her on the spot. Wets and drys alike were horrified at such violence,
such excess. Ella Boole, the head of the WCTU and a Ph.D.-holding
member of Phi Beta Kappa, the national honor society for people of
high academic accomplishment, was not. When told of the incident,
she responded through lips tugged back at the corners in disdain. The
bootlegger's wife "was evading the law, wasn't she?" Boole replied, and
found no further comment necessary.

Sabin was dismayed by such callousness, and no less so by what she
perceived to be the ignorance she was also encountering now. "The
WCTU has always been a Total Abstinence organization," Boole liked
to say, ignoring the meaning of "temperance" as had so many other
reformers over the years. She was also a little fuzzy on the meaning of
"debate," instructing WCTU officials that they should not participate
in such things "unless only the dry position were offered." Sabin could
only shake her head.

She was dismayed as well by the way people reacted to her. She had
expected her old friends to be disappointed at her rejection of the Eighteenth Amendment, but not to express their feelings so vituperatively, to
make things so personal, to refuse to admit that a woman could disagree
with dry views, even a woman who had once espoused those views, and
still be honorable, decent, forthright. Not a bitter person, Sabin could
not understand the bitterness of others, especially when it came to a
matter like Prohibition, which, in her view, presented so much evidence
for the one side, so little for the other.

But she would not be discouraged, and in fact found herself cheered
by the fact that so many others, former foes, now applauded her. "When
I said . . . I was going to fight Prohibition," she told a newspaperman in
the WONPR's early days, "the letters began pouring in from all over
the country. . . . I found I had spoken for thousands of other women.
There was a large group ready to be organized, waiting to be organized. . . . I could not turn back from it."

Sabin's group began holding meetings in 1929 with seventeen charter members, but it grew faster than any other organization on either
side of the issue had ever grown before. Within a few months, 60,000
women had joined the WONPR; by 1932, the total had leaped to more
than 1,100,000, at least according to figures provided by a Sabin associate, and among them were some of the most influential ladies of their

day. Mrs. Archibald B. Roosevelt, Mrs. Caspar Whitney, and the statesman Elihu Root's daughter-in-law, Mrs. Grace Root, signed up with Sabin in New York. Mrs. Pierre Du Pont agreed to head the Delaware branch of the WONPR; Mrs. R. Stuyvesant Pierrepont enrolled in New Jersey; and such lady Brahmins as Mrs. William Lowell Putnam and Mrs. Lothrop Ames came aboard in Massachusetts. These were the opponents of what Frances Willard and Carry Nation had wrought. These were the new crusaders. None had previously been referred to as the scum of the earth.

Perhaps, as has been suggested, the ladies were now tolerant of alcoholic beverages not just because *in*tolerance was so unworkable, but because women of Sabin's wealth and position had traveled so extensively abroad. In Europe, in particular, they had seen the fair sex drink freely, both in the company of men and by themselves, and seem none the worse for it. They had seen citizens of both genders consume spirits without cultures crumbling or even showing signs of strain. What they did not see were attempts to pass laws that would restrict such behavior. They could not help but wonder how their own nation, supposedly so progressive, had gotten itself into such a fix.

But not every member of the Women's Organization for National Prohibition Repeal was an imbiber. It may even be that a majority were not, or were at least not women who drank with any frequency or lustiness. In fact, Mrs. Fred A. Alger of the Michigan WONPR probably spoke for many when she said that she had signed up in the hope that the group's success would lead to *less* drinking. She and her fellow members were "not trying to make it easier to obtain liquor. We are trying to make it more difficult; we are trying to regulate and control the sale of liquor, trying to wipe out the dives that infest Detroit and the rest of the state." By legalizing alcohol, she believed, "we can at least see what is going on and apply intensive restrictive measures."

Speaking for yet others in the WONPR, Grace Root, whose father-in-law had been secretary of war, secretary of state, a presidential candidate and the 1912 recipient of the Nobel Peace Prize, stated that there was a principle involved here which had nothing to do with beverages of any kind. Prohibition was "an invasion of property rights, personal rights," she insisted, and she opposed it on those grounds.

Whatever their reasons, the members of the WONPR were united in their goal, and they published leaflets, made speeches, gave teas, reasoned with legislators. And Root went even further, stepping out of character on one occasion to do something as pitiless as it was clever. In a book she wrote entitled *Women and Repeal*, she included a pair of photographs side by side. There was "Mrs. Sabin of the Women's Organization for National Prohibition Reform, her well-groomed socialite good looks enhanced by the lighting and printing techniques used at that time also in portraits of motion-picture stars, contrasted most cruelly with Mrs. Boole of the Woman's Christian Temperance Union, whose robust countenance—split by a wide and toothy grin—branded her as the stereotype of the Eternal Frump." The photo's caption merely identified the two women; it neither said anything else nor needed to.

In the long run, the Women's Organization for National Prohibition Reform did not prove to be as calculatingly effective an organization as the Anti-Saloon League; it was more refined in its actions for reasons both of gender and breeding, and it seldom took dramatic, attention-getting or coercive steps. The steps it did take were as likely to be reported on the society pages as on the front pages of most newspapers. But it did exert a steady stream of pressure, and the pressure came to be felt by men at all the decision-making levels of American society. As well it should have been; the WONPR were their wives.

Sabin's husband Charles, the president of J. P. Morgan's Guaranty Trust, also served as treasurer of the mostly male Association Against the Prohibition Amendment. It was the first wet citizens' lobby of any stature in the United States, founded in 1920 by men who, truth to tell, did not normally show much interest in matters other than trade, taxes, and investment strategies. They were reasonable people, as they thought of themselves, "individuals of irreproachable reputation" who were forced to act in this arena because so many men had acted so unreasonably before them—men like Ford and Carnegie and Frick and Swift and McCormick and the Rockefellers, who had been so smart and so perceptive about so many things but were wrong, dead wrong, on the crucial question of employee thirst-slaking. The AAPA believed in temperance as the dictionary defined the word, not as Ella Boole did. "Beer and Light Wine now," read the group's letterhead, "But No Saloons even."

The association's founder, William H. Stayton, was a lawyer and businessman, working at the time in Washington, D.C., for the Navy League of the United States. A legal halt to alcoholic beverages had made no sense to him when it was in the talking stages, and he "watched with growing alarm the inexorable progress of the Eighteenth Amendment through Congress and the state legislatures." In the first few months after passage, as Stayton noted the blatant disregard it inspired, it made even less sense to him. He believed, in fact, that the amendment was less a law than "a symptom of a disease," which he identified as "the desire of fanatics to meddle in the other man's affairs and to regulate the details of your life and mine." And when Stayton concluded, as he did early on, that Prohibition was increasing his taxes, mucking up his investments, and interfering with trade by denying the U.S. a valuable item of export, all of this at the same time that it was giving the federal government unprecedented power, his disfranchisement was complete.

Before the AAPA came along, wets were virtually powerless. They had no leaders so there could be no followers. They had no organizations so there could be no plans, no goals or steps to reach goals or alternate steps to take when the first ones fell through. There was no one collecting money, no one disbursing it. The brewers and distillers had been pooling their resources for decades, but so vested were their interests that few people took their view of Prohibition seriously. What wets needed was a partnership of people who were disinterested, a solid core of citizens who objected to the Eighteenth Amendment not for selfish reasons but because it was bad for America, all of America. There were almost surely more wets than drys in the United States at any given time during the 1920s, but numbers alone do not make a cause, at least not an effective one.

The AAPA would change that, but gradually, so gradually in fact that its first few years seemed to show no progress at all. By 1921, the group had been able to attract only about 100,000 members nationwide, and its treasury, most of it personally donated by Stayton, was more the size of a petty cash fund. Few people knew the AAPA existed; fewer still paid it any mind.

But the longer Prohibition lasted, the more obvious its unworkability became, and the more obvious its unworkability, the more the AAPA prospered. After all, for most of the decade it was the only group of its kind; if you were troubled by the Eighteenth Amendment and wanted to work for its modification or repeal, there was only one place to go. By mid-1926, AAPA membership had climbed to 726,000, "scattered fairly evenly across the United States but with the greatest numbers in New York, Ohio, Illinois, and California."

The members of the Association Against the Prohibition Amendment were eager to make a difference, and knew just how to go about it, for as Andrew Sinclair writes, they had studied at the feet of the masters and taken notes carefully.

> The Association used precisely the same threats and organization at the grass roots as the [Anti-Saloon] League had. It supported all wets in elections, regardless of their party or their personal morality. It kept records of the votes of Congress on wet and dry measures, and circulated these records to its members. It subsidized research studies and put out propaganda to show the failure of prohibition. It encouraged the support of businessmen for economic reasons. It tried to place favorable articles in the newspapers and magazines. Indeed, in every action, it was the Siamese twin of the Anti-Saloon League.

Among the AAPA's notable inductees was Irvin S. Cobb, author of some sixty books and a frequent contributor to the *Saturday Evening Post* and *Cosmopolitan*. Cobb had refused to join the group at first because he was skeptical of its chances. There were too few members, he believed, and there was so much momentum against them. The same was true of ex-New York Mayor Seth Low and railroad tycoon Stuyvesant Fish, but they eventually followed Cobb's lead, as did Charles Sabin, publisher Charles Scribner, financier John J. Raskob, civic leader and philanthropist Marshall Field III, and chemical tycoons Irenee and Pierre Du Pont. But in time they all came around, all deciding to buck the momentum, with Pierre Du Pont joining up, he said, because "the great error in the Prohibition movement is failure to distinguish between the moderate use of alcohol and drinking to excess."

Among others who came to agree were senators and congressmen and governors and mayors, federal judges and diplomats, military leaders and business executives, including men who held more than a hundred directorships on the boards of companies with a total of two million employees and some $40 billion in assets. Influential men all, and now all brothers-in-arms under the banner of William H. Stayton's Association Against the Prohibition Amendment. In fact, the AAPA gained, not just in membership but in prestige, precisely as the Anti-Saloon League lost. Perhaps they were not so much Siamese twins as mirror images of each other.

And Eric Hoffer knew the reason, or one of them, at least. Although his book *The True Believer* would not be written for many years and its subject would be an altogether different one, it contains the following passage relevant to the demise of the Noble Experiment: "It is a perplexing and unpleasant truth that when men already have 'something worth fighting for,' they do not feel like fighting. . . . Craving, not having, is the mother of a reckless giving of oneself."

As of January 16, 1920, at 12:01 a.m., drys no longer had a reason to crave. This is not to say that they suddenly became complacent about the issue of alcohol use, only that their fires, which had burned so hot for so long, naturally began to cool. As they did, so did the willingness of drys to contribute time and money to the cause. Between 1921 and 1925, the Anti-Saloon League went from being the most prosperous group of lobbyists in America to one that operated on a constantly tightening budget, forced to count the pennies rather than rake in the dollars, as well as to lay off workers or reduce their salaries. As the decade moved ahead further, the league became less and less able to determine the outcome of political campaigns, and thus less and less able to purchase the candidates.

Wets, on the other hand, had become officially enraged. They were the outsiders now, the ones doing the craving; drys were the new status quo. As such, they assumed the support of the multitudes, whereas the wets sought to organize themselves into a multitude. They sought out one another and joined together in anti-Anti-Saloon League leagues, their goal to persuade people to defect from the ranks both of the uncommiteds and the previously committed to the other side. It was the only way they could realize their goals. It was also precisely what happened.

The American Bar Association was among the first, and most respected, of the formerly neutral groups to take a stand against the Eighteenth Amendment. Polling its members in 1930, the ABA found that 13,779 of them wanted to see the amendment repealed, while fewer than half as many favored its continued existence. Another attorneys' association, New York's Voluntary Committee of Lawyers, had previously announced its opposition to the amendment on the grounds that it was "inconsistent with the spirit and purpose of the Constitution."

Before long, the American Legion came to the same conclusion, as did the Veterans of Foreign Wars and the National Republican Club, each of them a pillar of respectability, a bastion of the establishment, with the latter disregarding the wishes of its own president, Hoover, and going on record for repeal by a tally of 461 to 367. Among members of the Women's National Republican Club, the margin was even greater;

fully 85 percent of them, as Pauline Sabin reported in her magazine article, wanted Prohibition to end. The percentage was not so high, although still impressive, in a poll of Americans from all walks of life taken by the prestigious *Literary Digest*. It drew 4,668,000 responses, one of the highest totals ever for its surveys, and almost three-fourths of them wanted the return of legal booze.

Even some of the labor unions which had previously accepted the William Allen White line on abstinence, that it was in the long run the best thing that had ever happened to the American working stiff, rethought their positions. It was back to the attitude of colonial times, when alcoholic beverages were the "good creature of God"; it was back to the attitude of the mid to late nineteenth century, when a working man was entitled to ease his burden by emptying a glass.

One leader, though, did not rethink his position. Although a teetotaler himself, Samuel Gompers, the cigarmaker who founded the American Federation of Labor, had never believed in forcing others to abstain. He believed that each human being should choose for himself whether to drink or not; it should be a matter of personal freedom, not national policy. People were entitled to look forward to something, and if that something happened to be the occasional, or more than occasional, belt after work, then it should not be forbidden by law. Their workday, their choice. Perhaps, Gompers liked to think, on some future workday it would be a larger check or better working conditions to which they looked forward.

Assistant Attorney General Mabel Walker Willebrandt, who had railed against the corruption of Prohibition agents, agreed. "No one who is intellectually honest will deny that there has not yet been effective, nationwide enforcement. Nor will it be denied that prohibition enforcement remains the chief and in fact the only real political issue in the whole nation. No political, economic or moral issue has so engrossed and divided the people of America as the prohibition problem, except the issue of slavery." It was not, given the tenor of the time, a controversial statement, even for someone in her position.

But it would be followed by a controversial action, one that shocked her friends and co-workers and sent tremors down the spine of every Eighteenth Amendment acolyte who heard of it. Willebrandt announced that she was quitting her job with the Justice Department and going to work for Fruit Industries Incorporated—an organization, which, despite the general name, had a membership specifically composed of grape growers. Willebrand helped to arrange a series of government loans for them, a form of price supports because of poor harvests, and then stood by with a smile as the growers announced the introduction of a brand-new product, a liquid grape concentrate called Vine-Glo, "which was available in sherry, port, tokay, muscatel, reisling, moselle, sauterne, burgundy, and champagne flavors." It contained no alcohol, but if water and sugar were added to the concentrate and the resulting liquid were allowed to stand for two months, the alcohol content would be 12 percent, which is to say that it would have turned into a passable wine, "a fine, true-to-type guaranteed beverage ready for the Holiday Season."

Fruit Industries Incorporated wanted someone with Mabel Walker Willebrandt's expertise and good name to help with the Vine-Glo launch. She surprised the growers no less than the rest of the world by agreeing. She thought Vine-Glo had an exciting future. She wanted to be part of it. The Noble Experiment, she told her friends, and not with any particular regret or even a desire to explain her previous support, was too experimental, not noble enough, and would soon be a thing of the past.

But this did not mean that the government was giving up on it, not at all. In fact, in 1929, Congress somehow got up the nerve to pass something known as the Jones Law, aka the Five and Ten, because it raised the maximum jail term for first-time offenders under the Volstead Act from six months to five years, and the maximum fine from $1,000 to $10,000. Previously, these had been the penalties for a repeat offender.

Toughening a law against which vast numbers of people have been rebelling in its weaker form is not normally a prudent step. Morris Sheppard, more than most people, should have realized that. But if he did, he kept it to himself; what the sneaky senator with the secret still said publicly was that Volstead should be altered again, this time to get to the heart of the matter by punishing not the bootlegger and not the bartender and not the speakeasy owner and not the crooked federal agent, but the person who makes the preceding vocations possible, who not only provides so many people with a livelihood but ensures their wealth. That person, Sheppard huffily declared, is the customer.

It was enough to make William Randolph Hearst reach first for a bottle, and then for the throat of the nearest member of the Senate or House of Representatives. The newspaper publisher had long been an ally of the Anti-Saloon League; like his fellow corporate barons, Hearst preferred his workers sober, and reporters had a well-deserved reputation for disdaining the condition. Yet the reporters in Hearst's employ wrote editorials praising the Eighteenth Amendment, feature stories glorifying its promoters, and news stories recounting arrests and convictions; their boss demanded it, and it was he, after all, who signed the paychecks that were so often cashed in watering holes.

But Hearst had begun to waver in recent years, surveying the social wreckage around him, and the provisions of the Jones Law were the last straw. "I am against Prohibition," he now affirmed, "because it has set the cause of temperance back twenty years; because it has substituted an ineffective campaign of force for an effective campaign of education; because it has replaced comparatively uninjurious light wines and beers with the worst kind of hard liquor; because it has increased drinking not only among men but has extended drinking to women and even children."

Henceforth, the Hearst papers would have a new editorial position, and people like the Sabins and William H. Stayton would show up in the profiles, their character and convictions glowingly rendered. And if the men and women who wrote the profiles wanted to have a few sips of something-or-other when they finished writing them, or even between paragraphs, they should be entitled, as long as they remained factual and grammatical and did not make a mess at their desks.

But the most significant defection from the antialcohol forces was that of John D. Rockefeller Jr., the old man's son, and it is difficult, so many years after the fact, to convey the impact of his announcement. Perhaps if Ralph Nader were to ask for fewer restrictions on corporate America, or Bill Gates were to lobby for higher capital gains taxes, or Pat Robertson were to decry the weakening of the wall between church and state. No one had seen the Rockefeller shift coming; when it did, more than one dry acknowledged, at least privately, that it was the beginning of the end for all who sought a dry America through legislation.

The shift was foreshadowed by his wife. "Mrs. John D. Rockefeller Jr., as early as 1924, asked, 'Have [we] not come to the time when we must honestly enforce our prohibition law or honestly try to change it?'" Perhaps the question got her husband thinking. Or perhaps some doubts that he was already feeling led to his mate's question in the first place. Either way, in a letter announcing his new position and the reasons for it, Rockefeller traced a lineage that should have been resistant to even the slightest hint of repeal. "Neither my father nor his father have ever tasted a drop of intoxicating liquor," he said, "nor have I. My mother and her mother were among the dauntless women of their day, who, hating the horrors of drunkenness, were often found with bands of women of like mind, praying on their knees in the saloons."

Initially, Rockefeller said, he had hoped that Prohibition would be "generally supported by public opinion and thus the day would be hastened when the value to society of men with minds and bodies free from the undermining effects of alcohol would be generally realized." But Rockefeller could delude himself no longer. He continued:

> That this has not been the result, but rather that drinking has generally increased; that the speakeasy has replaced the saloon, not only unit for unit, but probably two-fold if not three-fold; that a vast array of lawbreakers has been recruited and financed on a colossal scale; that many of our best citizens, piqued by what they regarded as an infringement of their private rights, have openly and unabashedly disregarded the Eighteenth Amendment; that as an inevitable result respect for all law has been greatly lessened; that crime has increased to an unprecedented degree—I have slowly and reluctantly come to believe.

Rockefeller's critique is a perceptive one in many ways, but it needs a point of clarification and another of rebuttal. He refers to a "vast array" of lawbreakers, a phrase which reminds one generation of the television show about Eliot Ness and his men called *The Untouchables*, and reminds a later generation of the movie of the same name. These, in turn, call to mind gangland hits and bloody assassinations and gun battles raging in the streets, with desperate thugs hanging onto the running boards of cars as they fire automatic weapons at their fellow thugs while innocent men and women duck for cover on the sidewalks.

It was not like that at all, at least not very often and not in many places. Prohibition gave rise to far less violence than is commonly imagined. It is true, though, as popular accounts have it, that Ness's Chicago was the mecca for the era's brutality, the place "where a tough on the rise went to make bad, as young Alphonso Caponi did." And it is true that Chicago was the home of the first Prohibition crime; three of them, in fact, were committed within an hour of the law's taking effect. Six armed men stole two freight cars of whiskey for medicinal use; another gang hijacked a truck full of the stuff; a third swiped four barrels of grain alcohol from a government warehouse—all of this before the Eighteenth Amendment had seen its first dawn. No one knows precisely how many hijackings or thefts or illegal shipments of booze there were, either in

Chicago or the United States as a whole, although the number was certainly vast.

What is not true is that the majority of them were perpetrated in violent fashion. With regard to murders in particular, the estimates vary wildly. According to figures released by the federal government in 1929, 135 criminals and 55 Prohibition officers had given their lives to that point. Another study, this one in 1931, put the total of deceased agents at 60, while further reporting that 144 civilians had been killed. Yet another reckoned the toll at 92 agents and 178 civilians. Some historians believe that the total number of deaths attributable to the dry laws, including bootleggers and their cronies, was as low as 286, others that it was as high as 1,360, perhaps even higher. Whatever the truth, and it will never be known, the number of fatalities does not square with John Rockefeller Jr.'s impression, nor the impression that so many others have come to share over the years.

Neither does it compare to the number of individuals who died as a result of toxically adulterated beverages. Here was the real inhumanity of the era, the true violence, the most emblematic of its many misdeeds, which probably led to more victims in a single year than guns could claim for the entire period. And it was the law that made it happen, the law that took the manufacture of beer and wine and whiskey out of the hands of people who were for the most part respectable and turned it over to hoodlums. "The Prohibition experiment," believes Henry Ford biographer Robert Lacey, "transferred some $2 billion a year from brewers, distillers, and their shareholders into the hands of murderers and crooks, making possible the extraordinarily embedded role that organized crime plays in modern American life."

But Prohibition did not create organized crime. It did not, as Rockefeller seemed to believe, give birth to syndicates of murderers and crooks and shredders of the social fabric. That distinction might belong to the gambling syndicates that formed in New York, Chicago, and New Orleans more than half a century earlier as a means of protecting their interests from various reform groups. Or it might be that organized crime grew out of the illicit behaviors of saloons and whore houses. Or perhaps it grew, no less organically, in corporate boardrooms, where thuggery was sometimes planned against unions, and in union halls, where reprisals were sometimes planned against management. Perhaps, as wiser historians suggest, it was a combination of all.

Regardless, it is true that Meyer Lansky, Lucky Luciano, and Bugsy

Siegel, to name but a few of the era's blacker hearts, ran small-time gambling operations well before Prohibition began, which is to say that they were perfectly placed when the Eighteenth Amendment dropped into their laps and provided the means for them to switch product lines and go big-time. Whether organized crime would have reached the same heights without the law's impetus cannot be known. It certainly would not have reached those heights as quickly, if for no other reason than that the enormous profits of Prohibition were the seed capital for numerous other underworld activities, an expansion of numbers and prostitution, of loan-sharking and protection, and, in later years, drugs.

The seldom impartial Fletcher Dobyns may, for a change, be taken without reservation in his paraphrase of a report issued by the Illinois Association for Criminal Justice in 1926. Dobyns says it concluded that "crime had been steadily rising for years and that the characteristic features of the crime situation existed before the adoption of the Eighteenth Amendment." He goes on to list some of the features.

> The bitter racial hatreds and conflicts that have followed the movement of large numbers of Negroes to northern cities; the wars between rival gangs that sought to control the vast revenues derived from gambling, vice and dope; the alliance between politics and crime and the use of gunmen and sluggers to control elections; the use of sluggers and bombers by small business enterprises to get rid of competitors; the development of a large body of professional gunmen and sluggers in the war between laborers and employers; the fact that men of this class have obtained control of many labor unions and also levy blackmail upon many kinds of legitimate business; the organization of criminals for the purpose of intimidating the police, public prosecutors, juries and witnesses. These are only a few of the causes of crime set forth in the report.

However, all of this acknowledged, it must be admitted that Prohibition had "greatly lessened" the regard of Americans for their legislative bodies, and Rockefeller was not alone in realizing it. As far back as 1923, Justice John H. Clarke of the Supreme Court of the United States, speaking to the alumni of the New York University Law School, was ruing the consequences of the Eighteenth Amendment. He believed that the disrespect Americans were showing for Prohibition was metastasizing into a disrespect for all laws, and that the end of this sorry and perhaps irreversible process was nowhere in sight.

And in fact, the longer the Noble Experiment dragged on, the greater the strain. According to reports at the time, a mere 22,000 persons were convicted of violating the Volstead Act in its first eighteen months of existence. In 1926 alone, the total was 37,000. "Every available index," as Kyvig has shown, "registered growing rates of violation rather than an increasingly effective law." It was not just that Americans had a long tradition of drinking alcoholic beverages; it was that they had a long tradition of independent thought and action, and as a result did not believe that anyone, not even the people who represented them in public office, or perhaps *especially* the people who represented them in public office, had a right to dictate their pleasures.

So much was called into question by the Eighteenth Amendment; so many Americans were left wondering. Was democracy a less viable form of government than they had always thought? Less competent, less responsive, less sensible? It was, after all, a minority of citizens who wanted a complete ban on alcoholic beverages; how did their will manage to subvert that of the greater number? And why did the minority, with but a few exceptions, not learn the error of their ways from the resulting chaos? Others would concede the benign intentions of the drys; could *they* not concede the horrible effects of their miscalculations? The so-called lost generation, about which Hemingway, Fitzgerald, Stein, and others had begun to write, might have been created by the shattered idealism of World War I, but it was nurtured by the skewed morality of Prohibition.

Another convincing argument for repeal was financial, and Senator Arthur Capper of Kansas made it both emotionally and statistically. Capper's constituents were farmers, the very people who, for their variety of reasons, had endorsed dry laws with such heartiness a decade or more earlier. Now they were losing so much money because of them that their very livelihoods were in question. They should have known it would happen; either they did not, or they refused to admit to themselves the truth.

It was left to Capper to reveal their plight well after the fact, in an article for the January 24, 1925 issue of the *New York Times*. In it, he claimed that from the start of Prohibition to the present, America's men and women of the soil had gone $20 million into the red. It happened, he said, because they had previously devoted so much of their land to crops that were used in the production of beer, "the billions of pounds of barley, rice and hops." But, he went on, they "were compelled to seed their lands to other crops after Prohibition went into effect. Within a year," he revealed, "the price of wheat dropped from nearly three dollars a bushel to less than one dollar; a large part of the barley lands were seeded to wheat, causing an overproduction and therefore a surplus of between ten and twenty percent of the wheat crop, demoralizing the price until a short crop in Canada boosted the world price of this grain."

And the government was in worse shape than the farmers. Once the Eighteenth Amendment was repealed, the Justice Department did some calculating and decided that the total price tag for enforcement, haphazard though it had been, had still managed to soar to $129 million. Another source, perhaps more objective, had the figure at almost twice that. And neither included the costs of trying and convicting half a million barkeepers and suppliers and manufacturers in federal courts, nor the costs associated with the courts' backlogs and their inability to prosecute more serious crimes because of them. Even after collecting more than $56 million in fines for Volstead violations, the feds were still well in arrears on their investment.

Meanwhile, Uncle Sam was missing out on many more millions of dollars in taxes. Wayne Wheeler's assurance to President Wilson that the income tax would make up the difference was not even close to being accurate. One group of researchers determined that the government took in $1,350,000,000 from the income tax in 1925, but failed to collect $1,874,000,000 in levies on beer alone. And the former amount would have been higher were it not for the fact that more jobs had been lost during Prohibition than gained—legal jobs, at least. The census of 1910 had listed 70,000 people employed in the production of alcoholic beverages and another 169,000 owning or working in saloons. The people who took their places in clandestine breweries and distilleries and speakeasies paid no taxes at all, or at least far less than their share.

In studying 1933, Prohibition's last year, Mark Edward Lender and James Kirby Martin determined that tolls on distilled whiskey would have added $500 million to the Treasury. And Jouett Shouse, a longtime dry who, like John D. Rockefeller Jr. and others, had reluctantly come to the opposite conclusion, believed the total benefit to federal coffers from the repeal of Prohibition would be $1 billion. Several other sources arrived at figures somewhere between the two amounts.

Most Americans, although unaware of the specific figures, certainly had the sense of things. They felt the waste of the Eighteenth Amendment as clearly as the duplicity, and they became increasingly restive. They broke the law ever more flagrantly, and so often that they seemed no longer to think of their actions as illegal; the *law* was illegal, or should have been. They wrote more and more letters to their legislators, whether prodded by the AAPA or the WONPR or not. In New York, men were seen on the streets wearing "Beer for Prosperity" neckties. In Detroit, thousands of people of both sexes marched in the Michigan Civic League's repeal parade, many of them carrying banners that read:

Billions Spent
Or
Billions Saved

And:

Prohibition and Poverty
Or
Beer and Business

And:

Bring Back Beer
To Bear the Burden

Many of the people who marched in the parade were unemployed. Many of the people who stood along the route and watched the marchers were unemployed. Many people who knew nothing about the parade and would not have cared one way or the other even if they had known were unemployed. For the United States had begun to sink into the Great Depression, the deepest economic misery in our history. It was, as Alistair Cooke writes,

> not just a blow to the extremes of the millionaire and the coal miner. It blighted everybody, except the very poor who had nothing to lose. When steel stocks went from ninety down to twelve, the automobile manufacturers simply let half their workers go. There were skyscrapers just finished that lacked tenants. A secretary was a ridiculous luxury. There were truckers with nothing to truck, crops that went unharvested, milk that went undelivered to people who couldn't afford it.

Which is to say there was something else that could no longer be afforded: Prohibition. Or so a good many Americans had begun to think. Just as drys found a compelling argument for their cause in World War I, so did the financial woes of the 1930s provide justification for the wets in even stronger terms. They believed that "if the production and sale of liquor were legalized, more people could be put to work, the government would gain revenue, unemployment would be alleviated, and the depression could be reversed." They had a lot of evidence on their side.

Another of the Detroit parade banners described the event this way:

The Procession
To End Depression

Newspapers, both in Detroit and elsewhere, wrote a lot about the parade and the conditions that had inspired it. So did papers in other cities, of which there were more than ever before, as well as the more topical magazines, which had also become a thriving enterprise. There were conversations about the parade on the radio, and newsreel pictures of it, narrated in stentorian voice and accompanied by melodramatic music, played in movie theaters. For this was the time when the media were becoming mass in the United States, and although a significant number of journalists seem to have supported Prohibition at the start, most were now rethinking their position, especially those who wrote for the tabloids, which emphasized tales of crime, insensitivity and injustice. As a result, headlines like the following became common:

Dry Agent Accused
Prohibition Graft
Enforcement Farce
Drunken Children

And the media campaign against the Eighteenth Amendment, although it was in truth not so organized as truly to be a campaign, went further. "The plot of the first all-talking motion picture," as John C. Burnham says about *Lights of New York*, released in 1928, "revolved around bootleg whiskey." He further relates that a survey of films conducted in 1930 showed drinking played a part in four-fifths of them, and in virtually no cases was the portrayal a negative one. Another survey indicated a positive portrayal rate of three-fourths, and went on to attest that the hero drank in two of five films and the heroine in one of five, whereas the villain wet his whistle in only one of ten.

A few years later, Clarence Brown, a director at MGM, said that in his view, as well as that of most others he knew in Hollywood, "motion pictures should depict and reflect American life, and cocktail parties and speakeasies were definitely a part of that life. We were able to prevail to a large extent, and I believe that it was the motion picture, showing that in spite of prohibition, liquor was an immense factor in American life, that had a great deal to do with changing people's sentiment on the question." More likely, given the general timidity of moviemakers in those days, it was the other way around: the changed sentiment led to the positive movie depictions.

Regardless, wets were no less eager than drys had been to make their point, and no less willing to use all the means at their disposal. Thanks to the newspapers and magazines and radio shows and movies—which is to say, thanks to the Big Bang of what is now being called the Information Age—the new generation of repealers had more of those means than the old generation of abstainers could ever have imagined.

Yet there is something else to say about the Noble Experiment, something that has received even less publicity than poisoned hooch, something that seems even less credible to many people than the notion of minimal violence in the era, something that is almost . . . well, noble. There are, in other words, two sides to the story of the national dry laws, and the one presented so far in this chapter, although accurate, is far from complete.

Prohibition did not prohibit, of course, but despite what John D. Rockefeller Jr. and William Randolph Hearst and many others believed, it *did* reduce—and given the amount of alcohol consumed by Americans prior to 1920, and the familial and societal disruptions that resulted, this was an accomplishment of no small significance. It is also a fact which, crucial though it is to any study of the life and times of the Eighteenth Amendment, has become widely accepted only in the past two and a half decades. Before that, most historians, beginning with those who wrote during the period itself, claimed that more booze was consumed during Prohibition than before.

It is hard to understand why. Were these chroniclers guessing? Hoping? Demonstrating their own anti-Eighteenth bias by trying to make a point rather than digging out the truth? Were they allowing themselves to be misled by occasionally ostentatious displays of tippling and all the notice they received? Did they just assume, the perversity of human nature being what it is, that anything proscribed would ipso facto be more desired and therefore partaken of more greatly? Or did they know something about Oglethorpe's Georgia and Dow's Maine, where drinking really *did* seem to increase when it was prohibited, and deduce that the same must be true now of the entire nation? If so, they should have read more carefully, realizing that neither Georgia nor Maine put even a modest amount of time or money into enforcement, and that each was a dry state surrounded by wet ones, so that it was not difficult to procure an alcoholic beverage that was both safe and tasty.

Even journalist Walter Ligget, who has been called "probably the greatest expert on the subject," proved guilty of misrepresentation. In testimony before the House Judiciary Committee in 1930, Ligget claimed that he had in his possession "a truck load of detail and explicit facts" that proved beyond a doubt that "there is considerably more hard liquor being drunk than there was in the days before Prohibition."

Mencken agreed, although without going so far as to cite spurious evidence. "I believe," he declared, "there is more bad whiskey consumed today than there was good whiskey before Prohibition." There was not, but people were saying this kind of thing in their frustration, one fellow complaining to another about the absurdities of the law, perhaps filling a glass for his mate and himself as they mutually commiserated. Yet the hyperbole somehow became the conventional wisdom, and remained in that exalted position for many years.

Not until the 1970s does the truth of the Eighteenth Amendment seem to have been conclusively established, and David E. Kyvig is one of the persons responsible. In his book *Repealing National Prohibition*, he provides the following analysis:

> During the period 1911 through 1915 . . . the per capita consumption by Americans of drinking age (15 years and older) amounted to 2.56 gallons of absolute alcohol. . . . In 1934, the year immediately following the repeal of Prohibition, the per capita consumption measured 0.97 gallons of absolute alcohol distributed as 0.64 gallons of spirits, 0.35 gallons of wine, and 13.58 gallons of beer (4.5 percent alcohol after repeal). Total alcohol consumption, by this measure, fell by more than 60 percent because of national Prohibition. Granting a generous margin of error, it seems certain that the flow of liquor in the United States was at least cut in half.

So it seems as well to historian Norman Clark, who in 1976 "reviewed the literature and concluded that estimates that placed the annual absolute alcohol consumption rates at between 50 and 33 percent less than those of the preprohibition years were essentially correct."

Jules Abels comes to a similar verdict not by reviewing the literature, but by comparing government figures for alcohol use in 1918, when a majority of states had banned alcoholic beverages, and in 1935, almost two years after the Noble Experiment had ended. He finds a 17 percent drop in the amount of spirits imbibed, a 30 percent drop for beer and malt liquors, and a 37.5 percent drop for wines. He reasons that there would not have been any decline at all, certainly not as early as 1935, if drinking had actually increased during Prohibition.

Abels seems certain about his numbers. And Clark seems certain about his and Kyvig about his. This author, however, finds that the nation's health records provide a more accurate portray of Prohibition's partial efficacy than its records of consumption. For instance:

> In 1943, Forrest Linder and Robert Grove compiled mortality figures for the Census Bureau in *Vital Statistics Rates in the United States.* They found that from a high of 7.3 deaths from chronic or acute alcoholism per 100,000 population in 1907, the rate fell gradually (possibly as a result of state prohibitory laws and war prohibition) to 1.6 per 100,000 in 1919 and then to 1.0 in 1920, the first year of National Prohibition. The rates then climbed slowly again, probably reflecting the gradual increase in illegal (and often poisonous) liquor supplies . . . peaking at 4.0 per 100,000 in 1927—although in 1932, the last full year of Prohibition, the figure was down once again to 2.5.

In addition, fewer people died from, or even contracted cases of, cirrhosis of the liver. Other diseases, either caused or exacerbated by heavy drinking, also became less common and less fatal. There were fewer deaths, and fewer admissions to hospitals, due to alcohol-related violence. And it appears, although it is not definite, that alcohol played less of a role than it did in the past in accidents, both on the road and in the workplace.

Even more informally, a majority of college administrators surveyed at the time said their students were more sober than they used to be, and many were the business executives who told pollsters that their employees seemed more clear-headed and quick-witted after lunch than had previously been the case.

Sales of Coca-Cola and Canada Dry ginger ale skyrocketed during Prohibition. So did sales of orange and grapefruit juices. "The Welch Grape Juice Company," Lender and Martin tell us, "sold a million more gallons of juice annually during the 1920s than it had in 1914." One of the reasons, admittedly, was that these were common ingredients in cocktails, blunting agents for the rotgut. But another reason was that people were drinking them straight, in greater numbers than they had in the past. They were so much easier to obtain, and so much less dangerous to imbibe, than bootleg hooch.

In retrospect, it seems inevitable. The wonder was not that Americans drank less under the Eighteenth Amendment, but that historians took so long to admit it. The consumption of alcoholic beverages was simply too inconvenient an activity for too many people. "Prohibition," said the oft-inebriated Wall Street magnate Jesse Livermore, "was a condition for those who didn't have 'connections.' "

Livermore had them. But a lot of others, the kinds of people he referred to derisively as "minnows," were lacking connections, and simply could not indulge their thirst for alcohol as often as they used to. Some did not have the time or patience or skill to brew or distill or ferment as much beverage at home as they would have bought at the store. Some did not enjoy the speakeasy as much as the saloon, finding it a stuffier, more status-conscious, less neighborly place. Some did not have the money to drink as much whiskey at the speaks as they had at saloons. There were reports from social workers of the time that the attitudes of their clients about alcoholic beverages were changing. One woman said that the people with whom she dealt were no longer winking at the custom; now they were scowling, and, having been forced by circumstance to become abstainers themselves, they were trying to make a virtue of their plight by helping others to see the wisdom of abstaining as well.

And there were reports of men and women not so penurious who, while perhaps not respecting the Eighteenth Amendment and the motives of the people behind it, feared it enough either to stop boozing or cut back on amounts or frequency. This was especially true of the casual drinker, the person who had always been able to take or leave his liquor; why run the risk of a fine or jail term, he now asked himself, for so small a pleasure? A law, no matter how unpopular it is or how unreasonable it seems, will always discourage some people from the proscribed behavior; others will be fined or incarcerated and for that reason, some of them, too, will begin to act in a different manner.

It is, to repeat, a mystery that so many analysts of the period could suppose for so long a time that a nationwide ban on alcoholic beverages, however absurd in conception, however inefficiently imposed, could somehow make them more attainable for more people. Yes, what is prohibited takes on a cachet that it did not have when it was allowed, but only to certain people, and the same law that giveth the cachet taketh away the ease of access.

Drys, of course, greatly exaggerated the new American dryness. They undercounted speakeasies, scoffed at home brewing, minimized crime. On at least one occasion, the absurdity of their optimism led them to do something that would later have to be undone. Within a week or two of the start of Prohibition, a mere fourteen days or less, the New York commissioner of public charities was crowing, "There are so few patients in the alcoholic ward of Bellevue Hospital . . . that the Hospital Committee has just approved its abandonment." As journalist Mark Sullivan comments, "The action was premature. Long before prohibition was ended Bellevue again had need for an alcoholic ward."

The Anti-Saloon League also touted the Eighteenth Amendment's ripple effects. It claimed that people were putting more money than ever before into savings accounts, as well as spending a higher percentage of their disposable income on the necessities: food, shelter, and clothing. In many cases it was true, although there were other factors involved, the most notable of which was the general American prosperity of the 1920s. There was, in other words, more money available for people to spend and save wisely than there had been before the dry law took effect.

In addition, the league declared that Prohibition lessened the amount of strife in American households, something it had no possible way of measuring or even intuiting. And then it got completely carried away and insisted that the Noble Experiment, because it took such a high moral ground against such deeply entrenched opposition, actually *increased* respect for the law in America. If ever there were a time to suspect the dry forces of sneaking a nip or two on the side, thereby scrambling their perceptions irredeemably, this was it.

On the other hand, it is important to point out that quantity of drinking is not the same thing as quality, and the nobility of the experiment cannot be measured in terms of the former alone. A friend of Winston Churchill visited the United States during its dry years and Churchill later wrote that the man was not impressed. "There is less drinking," he noted, summing up his friend's position perfectly, "but there is worse drinking."

In 1932, Franklin Delano Roosevelt ran against Herbert Hoover for the presidency of the United States. Prohibition was not an issue. The incumbent did his best to avoid the subject and the challenger brought it up rarely, and then only to denounce it.

At one point, in an open letter to New York Senator Robert Wagner, Roosevelt quoted in part from a declaration of the American Legion, writing that "the Eighteenth Amendment has not furthered the cause of a greater temperance in our population, but on the other it has 'fostered excessive drinking of strong intoxicants,' and has 'led to corruption and hypocrisy,' has brought about 'disregard for law and order' and has 'flooded the country with untaxed and illicit liquor.'"

Later, at a campaign stop in St. Louis, Roosevelt told a gathering that, as president, he would add several hundred million dollars annually to the federal budget by taxing beer. The people in his audience cheered, but only for a few seconds, a few decibels. They knew that the Eighteenth Amendment was breathing its last. Nothing mattered now but the Depression, and most people had already concluded that it would take more than just the demise of the Eighteenth Amendment to bring about a solution.

Two weeks before Roosevelt was inaugurated, the Senate voted sixty-three to twenty-three to bring the issue of repeal before the American public. Four days later, the House agreed by a count of 289 to 121. But they were not done. The two chambers then modified the ratification process, eliminating various bureaucratic demands to allow the states to vote on the dry laws virtually without delay. Never before had the two chambers of national government speeded up the process of legislative reform like this, and it has not happened since.

And furthermore, the states that did the voting were not the states as they existed in 1920. "Congressional voting districts," we learn from Catherine Murdock Gilbert, "were finally reapportioned, now reflecting the urbanization of America and the decreasing voting power of the dry rural districts."

But the Noble Experiment ended even before that voting power could be loosed upon it. Little more than a week into his presidency, Roosevelt demanded immediate modification of the Volstead Act to permit the manufacture and sale of beer and light wines, even as the Eighteenth Amendment remained in effect, awaiting the verdict of the states. The Senate passed the measure two days after receiving it. The date was March 16, 1933.

And then, on December 5, whiskey also rejoined the marketplace of permissible refreshments as Prohibition was put to death by ballot some thirteen years, ten months, and nineteen days after it became the law of the land. It was Utah that made the decision official at 3:32 P.M. local time, when it became the thirty-sixth state to ratify the Twenty-first Amendment to the Constitution: "Section 1. The eighteenth article of amendment to the Constitution of the United States is hereby repealed."

Simple as that.

An hour and a half later, Franklin Roosevelt, nine months into his first term in the White House, signed Presidential Proclamation No. 2065, and alcoholic beverages in all their infinite variety and regulated potency were once again legal commodities in the United States.

Some states, however, kept dry laws of their own on the books—in the case of Oklahoma, for another two and a half decades. And to this day there are towns and townships and counties in which alcohol cannot be purchased, or is available only at certain times, in certain establishments, after certain formalities have been observed. But as a national phenomenon, a coast-to-coast exercise of self-denial and consolatory delusion, Prohibition was over evermore.

Perhaps the only person in the entire land to be surprised by it all was Frederick Neal Dow, the son of the man from Maine. "Happily for the welfare of the country," Dow had stated in 1931, the handwriting on the wall obvious to so many others but invisible to him, "the probability is that the Amendment will never be rescinded. To accomplish that, Congress, by a two-thirds vote of both houses must oppose it. That vote is not probable because it could only be had after a political revolution unparalleled in the history of the country."

In fact, there *was* something unparalleled about the Eighteenth Amendment. To this day, it remains the only one of twenty-six constitutional amendments ever to be repealed.

Yet the rejoicing was not as great as some people had expected, neither as raucous nor as long-lasting. One reason was the certainty of the outcome. Another was weariness from the battle. Still another was that the Utah vote came so late in the day in the Eastern time zones that trucks carrying officially approved liquor could not make their deliveries to clubs and restaurants before they closed. Even if they had, a majority of purveyors probably would not have accepted the contents and prepared them for sale. As John Kobler relates, they had suddenly gotten law-abiding. "Most speakeasies," he writer, "having survived a decade of illegality, declined to risk a penalty now by operating without a license, but the licensing officials could not handle all the paper work. The chairman of the New York State Alcohol Control Board, Edward P. Mulrooney, stayed at his desk all night, managing to validate barely 1,000 licenses."

For these reasons, the celebrations tended to be small and private and spread out over a period of many days, some of them after December 5, a few well in advance. People were relieved more than elated, musing over the improbability of what they had endured; rather than pumping their fists in victory, they seemed to be wondering why there had ever been a contest in the first place. It was, to some extent, the reaction of people awakening from an unpleasant dream, the details of which are already getting hazy.

There was, however, one celebration of note, an event that had been in the planning stages for a long time and so was ready to begin within a few hours of the Utah bulletin. It took place at the Waldorf-Astoria Hotel in New York City and was attended by almost all of the directors of the Association Against the Prohibition Amendment.

They seated themselves at their tables, unfolded their linen napkins, and waited with a kind of subdued expectancy. A few minutes later, "waiters wheeled in a hammered-silver, six-gallon punch bowl, brimming with cocktails. With the bowl were a matching tray, two ladles, and twenty-four elegant silver goblets." The bowl was not just a vessel for spirits; it was a present. On the side was an inscription which read:

> To
> Captain William Henry Stayton
> who from November 12, 1918, until December 5, 1933
> led the Association Against the Prohibition Amendment
>
> From
> The Directors of the Association
> as a mark of their affection and appreciation
> on the occasion of their Victory Dinner
> held in New York City, December 5, 1933

The Women's Organization for National Prohibition Reform also had a victory dinner, the festive nature of which owed nothing to the potency of refreshment; the ladies served not a single drop of alcohol.

President Roosevelt acknowledged the Nineteenth Amendment in more private fashion, pouring himself a victory cocktail in the White House living quarters. It was said by some to have been the first legal martini mixed in the United States in well more than a decade.

Mencken, as was his way, observed the occasion perversely, by swilling down a tall glass of water, which he emptied in a single gulp. "My first in thirteen years," he swore, and wiped his lips with his sleeve.

Even Henry Ford, once so adamant a foe of beverages with bite, jumped onto the bandwagon. "A day after repeal," writes Ralph

Blumenthal, "[he] astounded luncheon guests at the Dearborn Inn by serving beer."

Eugene Johnson, as might be imagined, did not celebrate at all. "The devil often gets the best of it," Pussyfoot lamented, and retired from the dry cause almost as soon as the Twenty-first Amendment pushed the Eighteenth into history's voluminous dustbin.

And so as things turned out, the Washington Monument had not been too great a weight for the hummingbird to carry, nor the planet Mars too much of a distance.

Epilogue: Strange Bedfellows

The years went by in fits and starts, and Americans turned their attention to matters other than the satisfying of thirst. Bruno Richard Hauptmann was arrested for kidnapping the Lindbergh baby. Bonnie and Clyde were gunned down in Texas, Ma Barker in Florida, and John Dillinger outside a theater in Chicago. Adolf Hitler denounced the Treaty of Versailles and decided that he was the man to right its wrongs; so did a lot of his countrymen. Dust storms swept the Midwest, and they might have been the worst ever, forcing thousands of farm families to pack up their possessions and pile into their cars and trucks and drive into the sunset, heading for ground that was not so quick to blow away. And, in 1933, California became the first state to have a minimum drinking age of twenty-one; other states would follow, but it would be fifty-five years before Wyoming became the last state to pass such a law.

Hauptmann was put to death, swearing his innocence. Lucky Luciano, one of the kings of organized crime, got thirty-to-fifty in a federal pen. Babe Ruth retired, hitting a home run in his last game. FDR was reelected. Howard Hughes flew across the country in less than eight hours. The *Hindenberg* flew across the Atlantic and crashed in New Jersey, the flames devouring thirty-eight people, the newsreels running the footage over and over. Amelia Earhart flew across the Pacific and vanished, never to be seen again. Edward VIII, king of England, fell irretrievably in love with the American divorcée Wallis Warfield Simpson, and would give up his throne and would never regret it. The stock market plummeted another time.

But it did not fall as far as it had in 1929, and it rose much more quickly. The Great Depression was finally coming to an end, helped in small measure by increased employment in the liquor trade. In 1940, when Roosevelt was elected a third time, the Distilled Spirits Institute estimated that 1,229,000 men and women were paid $1 billion to manufacture and sell alcoholic beverages in the United States. And millions more Americans could now afford to buy.

A year later, the Japanese attacked Pearl Harbor, and the country's mobilization for war put the Depression out of business for good. This time, though, there were no calls for a ban on booze, no revival of the temperance movement or even much expression of temperance sentiment. Booze was too valuable to the economy, at last providing that several hundred million dollars a year that Roosevelt had promised in 1932. In fact, by the time World War II ended and Jackie Robinson integrated baseball and a Twenty-*second* Amendment was added to the Constitution and Americans took up arms again in Korea and television went from black-and-white to color and movies went all the way to 3-D and the U.S. started sending military advisers to South Vietnam and the number of cases of polio began to drop because of the Salk and Sabin vaccines and Elvis Presley hit the top ten for the first of many times and the Soviets scared the hell out of Americans by launching the satellite called *Sputnik*—by 1957, in other words, the federal government had taken in more tax money on alcohol than even the most optimistic of wets would have guessed: $59,500,000,000 in less than two and a half decades. There was no evidence that the United States was a less sober or less healthy or less productive nation as a result.

Since then, a few more decades have passed and an entire century has turned and, to some people, Prohibition and the events and attitudes that led up to it have come to seem quaint, the artifacts not of the bustling American culture that we know today, but of a different one, a culture more naïve, even charmingly primitive. People no longer believe in the spontaneous combustibility of drunks, nor in the efficacy of praying in front of saloons. The city and the country have become harder to distinguish from each other both geographically and ideologically. The Anti-Saloon League does not exist anymore, and only in footnotes do the history books mention the Prohibition Party and the fellow it nominated for president in 1904, the unfortunately named Silas Swallow.

Other footnotes include Frances Willard and Wayne Wheeler. Neal Dow, Diocletian Lewis, Howard Hyde Russell—these individuals are virtually forgotten; for them, a footnote would be a promotion. Only Carry Nation, of all the nineteenth-century dry evangelists, still inspires a nod of recognition today, and sometimes that does not even come until her modus operandi has been described. "Ah, yes," someone will say, "wasn't she the woman with the hatchet?"

But there are new groups now, new reformers of an entirely different sort, and their approaches are much more focused, limited, modest.

In 1935, a stockbroker from New York City known as Bill W. and a surgeon from Akron, Ohio, called Bob S. made an important discovery. They found that they could solve their drinking problems, or at least cut back significantly on their intake, merely by talking to each other, one man confessing the extent of his dependency, the other offering counsel based on his own experiences, the two of them providing support through mutual companionship and understanding. They sat and listened, sympathized and reinforced, got more and more sober. So pleased were they with their recoveries that they decided to expand on their methods and share them with the rest of the world, to spread the gospel of abstinence through fraternization.

With assistance from John D. Rockefeller Jr., who provided an initial donation of $5,000 and assigned some of his top aides to help Bill and Bob get started, the two men formed Alcoholics Anonymous, basing it on a twelve-step method of recovery that begins with an admission of powerlessness, works its way up through a reliance on God and His beneficent powers, and ends with the alcoholic's vows to make amends to his victims and spread the gospel even further.

The group now has almost 2 million members in a number of countries, more than half of them in the United States. They are of all ages and occupations, although almost 90 percent are white and two-thirds are male. Half of them claim not to have taken a drink for at least five years, this despite the fact that they could barely keep their lips together for five minutes previously, and many of the rest say they will get to the five-year mark themselves at some point, and then, one day at a time, one step at a time, move as far beyond it as time will allow.

Yet Alcoholics Anonymous does not work miracles, and in fact does not believe as a matter of policy that miracles are possible. In its early days, according to a disappointed Bill W. and Bob S., only 5 percent of the group's members gave up their seats at the bar. At present, AA does not discuss its success rate, but experts in the field of alcohol treatment and rehabilitation say that even the best programs cure somewhere between 25 and 50 percent of those they treat. Other experts, however, say those figures may be high; it is not clear whether they take into account, or even precisely how they define, recidivism.

Alcoholics Anonymous does not make promises, does not raise false hopes. It says that it is not for everyone; it can help only those who sincerely *want* help. In others words, it can teach hymns but only to those who already belong to the choir. Yet a person like this, a man or woman who sincerely wants to change his or her behavior, is likely to do so regardless of whether or not one particular agency or method of treatment exists; it is the determination to heal oneself, that is to say, which is the crucial ingredient, not the trappings of organization. It is the will that matters, not the setting.

But what about people who lack the will? What about the drinkers who do not admit they have a problem, or believe that alcohol is the solution that life has provided for other problems? These are the people who threaten their families, their friends, and the larger society, and these are the people who remain beyond the reach of Alcoholics Anonymous or any other providers of aid. It is, of course, unfair to blame AA for the men and women who eschew its services; it is, however, important to note that the group's reach is not extensive.

According to the most recent numbers of the National Council on Alcoholism and Drug Dependence, alcohol "contributes to 100,000 deaths annually, making it the third leading cause of preventable mortality in the U.S., after tobacco and diet/activity patterns." Almost 14 million Americans, or 7 percent of those above the age of eighteen, "have problems with drinking." This includes slightly more than 8 million who are considered alcoholics. Of the latter, men outnumber women by almost three to one. These numbers have remained constant for almost thirty years, which further reinforces the point that, despite the good it has done for individuals who are eager to be cured, Alcoholics Anonymous has had little or no impact on the drinking habits of Americans on the whole.

"It has even been suggested," writes Andrew Barr, an abiding skeptic, "that attending AA is less effective than allowing the abusive drinker to get over his problem on his own. Those who join AA are told that they can never drink again. This prohibition encourages many AA members to switch their fixation from alcohol to cigarettes, coffee, and high-calorie desserts without dealing with the underlying problem that led to the abusive drinking in the first place."

Another reform group has been founded more recently, its goals of an entirely different nature.

In the spring of 1980, a thirteen-year-old girl named Cari Lightner was walking along the side of a road in northern California, on her way to a school carnival in the town of Fair Oaks, a few miles from Sacramento. She might have been thinking about one of the rides. She might have been thinking about the games of skill along the midway. She might have been thinking about the girls she would meet, and the boys who would look at them with secret adoration, once she arrived.

But she never did. Forty-seven-year-old Clarence Busch saw to that. Filled to the brim with booze, more booze than the law allowed and certainly more than he could handle, Busch was speeding down the road in his car, swerving right, swerving left, and at one dreadfully unfortunate moment, swerving onto the shoulder and striking Cari Lightner. The girl bounced off the right front fender of Busch's car and fell to the ground, the impact killing her instantly. The driver did not know that, however; he could have stopped, tried to help. Instead, he hit the gas and drove away even faster than he had approached.

At the time, Clarence Busch was out of prison on bail, awaiting trail on another charge of hit-and-run driving, this crime also committed while under the influence. Before *that* incident, Busch had been arrested two other times for drunk driving. He was an admitted alcoholic, a menace to all in his life and all in his path, and yet on the day he ran over Cari Lightner, he was the possessor of a perfectly valid California driver's license.

Busch was arrested in Cari's death, charged with vehicular homicide, and sentenced to an unpardonably minimal two years in jail. Yet he ended up serving only eleven months, and not a single one of them within the confines of a cell; he divided the stretch almost equally between a work camp and a halfway house. When he was released from the latter, he moved to Wisconsin, where he applied for, and was through proper channels issued, a license to drive a car. It would later be revoked—not, strictly speaking, because of his record, but because of the technicality of his having lied about his record on the Wisconsin application.

Out of that tragedy, and the raging ineptitude of the law enforcement agencies that virtually encouraged it to happen, came Mothers Against Drunk Drivers, or MADD, which today boasts more than 2 million members and active supporters in 600 affiliates in the United States, Canada, and Puerto Rico. Founded by several women, among them Cari's mother Candy, MADD has worked over the years to accomplish a number of legislative goals, such as ensuring that victims of drunk drivers are provided the same kinds of compensation that are offered to victims of other crimes, in addition to increasing incentives for states to enforce drunk-driving laws. Both measures were part of the Omnibus Anti-Drug Abuse Act of 1988, the passage of which was the completion of a long and successful campaign for MADD, a lobbying effort that won the group the respect of the act's foes no less than its supporters.

MADD also helped to establish an annual "National Sobriety Checkpoint Week," when police officers from one end of the country to the other pull over motorists and make sure it is the vehicles that are fueled, not those behind the wheel. And, in conjunction with Saturn automobile retailers, MADD has come up with something it calls the "Tie One On For Safety" campaign, which urges drivers to tie a red ribbon onto the antennas of their cars to indicate they will serve as designated drivers, especially over Christmas and New Year's.

These days, MADD likes to call itself the largest crime victim's assistance organization in the world, and it has recently had reason to lament the extent of the crime that concerns it most. In 2000, the latest year for which figures are available as of this writing, more than 16,650 Americans were killed in crashes involving alcohol. That is an increase over the preceding three years and represents about 40 percent of the total number of people killed in all 2000 traffic accidents. Says Millie I. Webb, MADD's national president, in one of the organization's press releases, "Each of these deaths—the deaths of our precious loved ones—was 100 percent preventable."

In the hope of preventing at least some of them, the group continues to lobby state legislatures to pass antidrunk driving laws, and its success here has been impressive. At the end of 2001, twenty-nine states and the District of Columbia had made changes in their legal definitions of drunkenness, lowering blood alcohol limits from 0.10 to 0.08.

MADD also lobbies the media, and according to sociologist Barry Glassner, it has had an impact here, too. In *The Culture of Fear*, Glassner writes that MADD was partly responsible for forcing journalists to report on "the issue of drunk driving in a sound and sustained way throughout the 1980s and early 1990s. Thanks in part to that coverage, the number of alcohol-related deaths plunged by 31 percent between 1982 and 1995. Fatality rates fall twice as rapidly, studies find, in years of high media attention compared to those of relatively little attention."

Hence, perhaps, the high rates in 2000, when this author's study finds the media were inattentive.

Among the most recent of MADD aims is the elimination of drinking by minors, whether they get into a car afterward or not. There is no evidence that the group is as yet succeeding with this particular mission; nonetheless, more than any other assembly of alcohol reformers, going all the way back to Elizabeth Jane Trimble Thompson and the first Women's Crusade, Mothers Against Drunk Drivers has realized its goals, primarily because those goals have been so wisely conceived, directed toward abuse rather than use.

One of the old associations, and only one, continues to exist.

The Woman's Christian Union was not heard from much during Prohibition; it neither received much credit for the Eighteenth Amendment, nor much blame for the aftermath. In 1923, its members "poured $5,000 worth of 'fine whiskies and cordials' into a Cleveland, Ohio, street. After the Pennsylvania state legislature refused to fund an enforcement law, the state WCTU donated $250,000 to Governor Gifford Pinchot 'to use as he saw fit for enforcement purposes.' New York WCTU members dominated lobbying for state prohibition and enforcement laws." Other than that, the ladies dwelled in the background of the 1920s; by the time their objective of a nominally dry nation had been achieved, the WCTU had become an anachronism, a reminder of the days when the temperance movement dwelled more on the periphery of events than in the center.

But the group has refused to die or disband or give up; its members carried on through Prohibition and they carry on today. At present, the WCTU claims a total membership of about 5,000 persons in thirty-three state associations and 450 local branches across the country. Its nineteenth century members prided themselves on being up-to-date because they used the new dictaphones and type-writing machines; with the twenty-first century now underway, there is a Woman's Christian Temperance Union website and an increasing volume of correspondence by e-mail. All these years after its heyday, the WCTU is a dinosaur that refuses to consider extinction for the obvious reason that it feels too frisky.

But there is more on its mind in the new millennium than temperance, much more, and one suspects the reason, at least in part, is that the ladies no longer believe they can have a significant impact on American drinking habits. They would never admit such a thing, of course; unfailingly good-natured, they keep on believing in the perfectibility of others and keep on defining perfection by their own lights. And so, as they go about their chores, which these days include a campaign to encourage restaurants not to serve alcohol with their meals, their hearts are as committed as ever and they say all the right things.

Their hearts, though, seem equally committed to other causes, especially pornography, and the ease with which children can avail themselves of it. The WCTU lobbies libraries to prevent access to pornographic material on their computers, and it lobbies communities to close down shops that sell adult videos. It is opposed as well to drugs and tobacco, and devotes more attention to them than it did in the past. It lobbies on behalf of equal pay for women who do the same jobs as men, and, like Carry Nation, its only true superstar, it supports the establishment of shelters for abused women and children.

And, as strongly as ever, it believes in education. The WCTU continues to publish materials for America's schools, public and private, elementary and middle and high. But they are very different kinds of materials from what the group published in its early days, at once more accurate and less strident. They are also not as pervasively taught; the WCTU itself says it does not know how make schools make use of the information it provides, nor how seriously the information is taken.

Among its current teachings are the following:

- Ninety-one percent of high school seniors have tried alcohol.
- The average age for taking the first drink of alcohol is eleven and a half years.
- There are more than 3.3 million teen alcoholics in the United States.
- Alcohol "harms virtually every organ and system in the body." [The

finding is that of the National Institute of Alcohol Abuse and Alcoholism.]

- Alcohol has been implicated in up to 75 percent of all rapes, 70 percent of domestic violence incidents, and 20 percent of suicides.

But for the most part, the WCTU seems less didactic than it used to be, sponsoring contests as much as issuing warnings, emulating *Sesame Street* more than Miss Grundy. Recently, it shipped off to the schools a picture of a nervous-looking clown walking a tightrope over a net. Under the net were booze, drugs, and tobacco. ABSTINENCE—THE ONLY SAFETY NET, was the message of the scene; students in grades one through three were invited to color it in and submit it for a top prize of between $15 and $25 dollars, depending on the entrant's grade. The judging was to be done on the basis of "originality, appropriateness of color selection, neatness and instant appeal."

For older children, the WCTU offers prizes for drawing posters and writing essays, the purpose of the latter being "to offer an opportunity to students to research the subjects of alcohol, illegal drugs, and tobacco with emphasis on total abstinence."

And students of all ages are asked to sign a pledge, as temperance has asked of its recruits from the very beginning. They are to "promise, with God's help, never to use alcoholic beverages, illegal drugs, or tobacco."

The more that science learns about illegal drugs and tobacco, the worse they seem; it is, thus, not unreasonable for a temperance society to insist that its adults as well as its children pledge to avoid them. Alcoholic beverages, though, are different. In moderate amounts, they do no harm. In fact, in moderate amounts, they seem in many cases to be salubrious, with most alcohol researchers defining "moderate" as no more than two drinks a day for most men and one for most women. As for the definition of "drink," it is twelve ounces of beer, five ounces of wine, which is about half a cup, or one-and-a-half ounces of spirits, all of which contain approximately the same amount of alcohol: half an ounce, or twelve grams.

Another important factor, it seems, is the constancy of moderate drinking. "Even relatively modest amounts of alcohol may be protective if consumed frequently," writes Dr. Kenneth Mukamal of Beth Israel Deaconess Medical Center in Boston, after studying more than 38,000 men over a period of twelve years.

Mukamal says that frequent, moderate consumption is most protective against heart disease. A variety of studies support him, showing that moderate imbibers are less likely to suffer coronary disease than teetotalers and less likely to die from it when they do contract it. They are less likely to die from ischemic stroke than teetotalers, and, says the *Journal of the American Medical Association,* "this protective effect of alcohol consumption was detected in both younger and older groups, in men and women, and in whites, blacks, and Hispanics." In fact, moderate drinkers are less likely to die, period—or, more properly put, they have a better chance of living longer. According to data from the Physicians' Health Study, which was collected at Harvard University and involved more than 22,000 men, "the difference between consumption of small and large amounts of alcohol may mean the difference between preventing and causing excess mortality." More specifically: "Compared to men who consumed less than one drink per week, the risk of deaths from all causes was 28% lower for a man who had 2 to 4 drinks per week, and 21% lower for one who had 5 to 6 drinks per week."

Those who drink in moderation also reduce their likelihood of getting hepatitis A from raw oysters by 90 percent. Of course, as a benefit of restrained tippling, this is a bit of a stretch; abstinence from raw oysters, which is an eminently achievable condition, reduces the likelihood 100 percent.

According to another study published in the *Journal of the American Medical Association* involving 983 diabetics, those who took one or more drinks a day had a 79 percent lower risk of dying from heart ailments than did nondrinkers. Diabetics also seem less likely to die from a number of other maladies, such as chronic obstructive pulmonary disease. Scientists in Japan, whose work was detailed in the *Journal of Studies on Alcohol* in 2001, even found a relationship between the restrained use of alcohol and more acute vision. "Whereas heavy drinking is associated with a variety of eye diseases, [such as cataract, keratitis, and color vision deficiencies]" the scientists write, "moderate consumption of alcohol has been reported to be possibly protective against age-related macular degeneration (AMD), cataract and diabetic retinopathy." And, states a Swedish team of researchers, "Alcohol consumption has a weak inverse association with risk [of hip fracture among postmenopausal women]."

In some cases, the kind of beverage does not matter; beer, wine, and spirits all tend to produce the same effects. Wine, though, seems the best of the three in lowering blood pressure and cholesterol levels; beer and whiskey also make a contribution, but not as great.

Scientists at the University of Milan in Italy have concluded that a glass and a half of wine very day might help prevent, or at least delay, such neuro-degenerative diseases as Alzheimer's and Parkinson's. Experiments at Erasmus University in Rotterdam, the Netherlands, support the Italian findings, but indicate that brewed and distilled beverages also have a salutary effect on such ailments. And a 1998 issue of the *European Spine Journal* reports that "intake of wine was found to be strongly associated with a good prognosis after first-time lumbar disc surgery."

More specifically: red wine, according to a study conducted at the University of North Carolina at Chapel Hill, contains a chemical called trans-Resveratrol, which helps to fight cancer. Other studies indicate that frequent doses of cabernet sauvignon or merlot or pinot noir inhibit the body's production of endothelin-1, which makes blood vessels contract and thereby leads to heart disease.

As for white wine, it seems to assist the proper functioning of the lungs, in particular, improving the volume of air they can expel in a single breath.

As far as the Finns are concerned, beer is the beverage of choice for kidney stones, with a bottle a day lowering the odds by as much as 40 percent. Wine and distilled spirits had no effect on kidney stones one way or the other, the Finns say; neither did coffee, tea, milk, or water. It is also claimed that beer is a kind of health food, certainly an improvement on Diet Pepsi or high fructose-laden fruit drinks. "For moderate drinkers," says an article some years ago in the *American Journal of Clinical Nutrition*, "beer provides 11% of dietary protein, 12% of dietary carbohydrates, 9% of dietary phosphorus, 7% of dietary riboflavin, and 5% of dietary niacin."

Even dogs, it seems, can improve the quality, and perhaps even the length, of their lives with alcohol, reducing their risk of blood clots. And cardiac researcher John Folts at the University of Wisconsin found that canines who drank dark beer experience even fewer clots than those fed lighter brews. The breed of dog did not matter. The brand of beer did. Guinness Extra Stout was much more likely to produce the desired effect than Heineken lager, and both, one assumes, are medicinally superior to Bud Light. There is no word on what the Society for the Prevention of Cruelty to Animals thought of the study.

All of this, to make the point again, is the result of minimal drinking: sips as opposed to swigs, a glass or two as opposed to a bottle or two. Drinking to excess, science has proven, increases one's likelihood of suffering all manner of malfunctions: cirrhosis of the liver, pancreatitis, and cancers of the liver, mouth, larynx and esophagus. It can lead to sleep apnea, loss of appetite, vitamin deficiencies, stomach ailments, digestive problems, skin problems, obesity, memory loss, heart and central nervous system damage, and psychological disorders of virtually every type.

The findings about alcohol in moderate quantities, though, are a remarkable mass of information, making lies of old truths and wives' tales of what were once considered words to live by. And, perhaps finally, it points out the wisdom of temperance as the word was originally defined, as the first of the reform groups believed it should be practiced, as the modern medical community believes it may safely be practiced again.

People in Oklahoma got wind of all these developments at the same time as people in the rest of the country. They read the same newspaper and magazine articles, heard the same reports on TV and radio. One wonders, though, what might have happened if they had known earlier. Would things have been different for them? Would they have taken action at the polls long before they did? Or would they have ignored reason and held onto their previous ways out of habit? Oklahoma, you see, was one of a handful of states to revert to prohibition within its own borders the minute the national law was repealed in 1933. In fact, it had never known so much as a single wet day of statehood, having entered the union dry as a bone in 1907.

Not that all Oklahomans thought it was a good idea. There had been angry debates among lawmakers even before statehood; citizens had fought with one another in the old territorial days with both words and guns, and as was the case in other states and localities, the lobbying groups for the drinkers had tried to outmanipulate the lobbying groups for the teetotalers. In the Sooner State, they never did.

But one of the reasons that dry laws stayed on the books in Oklahoma for so many years was that they were so easy to avoid—so very easy, in fact, that an effort at repeal seemed to many a waste of time; why spend both hours and dollars beyond counting to make a change on paper that has already been made in daily life? "It never was difficult to get liquor," said a newspaper report that looked back over the twentieth century and into the nineteenth. "Cocktail parties for a visiting dignitary were held without shame in hotels, visible to anyone who cared to look." On one occasion, it has been reported, the dignitary was Richard Nixon, the vice president of the United States. He lifted a glass or two, seemed to enjoy it, did not act like a man who was doing anything wrong.

Nor was there any shame in tippling for a person who had not achieved the rank of dignitary. "A newcomer to the state soon learned that a 'business' card containing only a telephone number and left in the doorway was the key to a plentiful supply of liquor and deliveries were made anytime—in the middle of the night, on Sundays and holidays, and to the front door of a home." It was a welcome wagon of sorts, especially designed for people wanting to get *off* the wagon.

Perhaps to regulate the liquor traffic, perhaps to close the gulf between word and deed in the state, the legislature decided to place the subject of repeal on the ballot in 1959. *Sputnik* had fallen to earth by this time and the Supreme Court had ordered the states to hurry up and desegregate and now two more states called Alaska and Hawaii had joined the union and Xerox had produced its first commercial copying machine and Ayn Rand had published a monumental novel of ideas called *Atlas Shrugged*. And Oklahomans were going to vote on a referendum to make booze legal in their state. It was the fifth time they would do so in fifty-two years; the previous four had resulted in a continuation of the status quo.

To some people, both inside the state and elsewhere, this was a mystery. Why keep voting one way and drinking the other? The humorist and native son Will Rogers explained as best he could. "Oklahoma will be dry," he drawled, "as long as its citizens can stagger to the polls."

The opposition to legalized alcohol in 1959 was led by two groups. One was preachers. The other was bootleggers. The preachers wanted prohibition to continue for moral reasons, the bootleggers for economic ones. The preachers sponsored prayer meetings; the bootleggers, not wanting their opposition to repeal to make headlines, sneaked into the back pews and moved their lips. The preachers lobbied the politicians during office hours; the bootleggers saw them at night. The preachers solicited money; the bootleggers donated as much as they could spare, although "by indirect and circuitous routes."

It was all to no avail. Neither the Almighty nor the electorate was sympathetic to the dry cause in Oklahoma as the 1950s drew to a close. The final vote was 396,845 people in favor of repeal, 314,380 against. Even a local-option provision failed, by the even larger margin of 469,503 to 221,404.

The clergymen and the bootleggers commiserated separately.

Acknowledgments

I am not, by training, a historian, but I play one in the preceding pages and have been well prepared for the role.

The most notable guidance was provided by W. J. Rorabaugh. First came his book, *The Alcoholic Republic*, which I read upon its publication in 1979 and as a result of which I was inspired to learn more about the role of spirits in American life. Second came his direct input in *this* book; Rorabaugh read the manuscript, fine-tooth-combed it, and provided me with many pages of notes and suggestions. I am immensely grateful.

As I am to the reference staff at the Westport Public Library, which was able to locate some of the most arcane volumes ever written on either alcohol or anything else. The staff includes Kathy Breidenbach, Marta Campbell, Debbie Celia, Tilly Dutta, Marjorie Freilich-Den, Sylvia Schulman, Sheri Szymanski, Joyce Vitali, and George Wagner. Also: Carole Braunschweig, Suzanne Bush, Beth Dominianni, Judy Hinkle, Jackie Kremer, Beth Paul, and Janie Rhein.

Rachel Rice arranged my interlibrary loans. Sometimes the books took a few weeks to arrive. Sometimes I asked whether she could cut the time to a few hours. She did not seem annoyed.

My thanks also go to William Beatty, the librarian-archivist of the Woman's Christian Temperance Union, who took a dozen or more phone calls from me and never failed to answer my questions or lead me in the right direction.

301

In the course of researching this book, I visited the homes of Neal Dow and Carry Nation, as well as WCTU headquarters in Evanston, Illinois, where the staffs cheerfully provided me with detailed information and lengthy tours.

No less am I grateful to Micah Kleit, Jennifer French, Ann-Marie Anderson, and Gary Kramer of the Temple University Press, and Carol Bifulco of BookComp. All made the book read better, look better, or sell better than it would otherwise have done.

One of the many authors cited in the text, besides Rorabaugh, is the estimable Gilbert Seldes. His son, Tim, is my literary agent and seems to think I have brought no dishonor to the family by including his father in the preceding pages. For that, as well as for his formidable presence in my writing life, I am appreciative.

Notes

Introduction

page 1   "senior dignitaries," Tannehill, p. 63.

    2   "the lady who fills the mouth," quoted in ibid., p. 63.

    2   "Then [the Egyptians] kneaded [it]," David, Rosalie, *Handbook to Life in Ancient Egypt* (New York: Facts on File, 1998), pp. 289–90.

    2   "Banquets frequently ended," quoted in Kyvig, *Law*, p. 169.

    2   "was considered a suitable subject," ibid., p. 169.

    2   "Do not get drunk," quoted in Tannehill, p. 64.

    2   "the spirits of their dead warriors," Fleming, p. 6.

    2   "drinking rivers of beer," Durant, *Caesar*, p. 478.

    3   "some authorities regard," Fernández-Armesto, p. 96.

    3   "a strange-tasting dark purple juice," Fleming, p. 8.

    4   "She wandered down," ibid., p. 8

    4   "does of a truth," quoted in Durant, *Greece*, p. 366 n.

    5   "scenes of bibulous merriment," quoted in Durant, *Caesar*, p. 7

Chapter 1

page 7   "the great gathering place," McCullough, p. 81.

    8   "a Southern counterpart," Halliday, p. 44.

    8   "disgruntled artisans," Phillips, p. 6.

    8   "and either applauding," Hallahan, p. 75.

    8   "the gods who are most interested," quoted in Getz, p. 23.

    8   "William Bradford, in 1630," Holbrook, p. 56.

    9   "the main point," Furnas, *Americans*, p. 142.

    9   "only prayer," quoted in Fleming, p. 51.

    9   "What wasn't consumed," Hamilton, p. 15.

    9   "As the first president," ibid., p. 16.

    9   "the colony's elite," Rorabaugh, p. 28

    9   "Drunkenness, Swearing," quoted in Burnham, p. 52.

   10   "want his people," Holbrook, p. 56.

10   "in a certain degree," quoted in Rorabaugh, p. 7.

10   "An average American," Lender and Martin, p. 14

10   "The custom," Furnas, *Life and Times*, p. 17.

11   "the consumption of strong drink," quoted in Ackroyd, pp. 344–45.

11   "liquid fire," quoted in ibid., p. 346.

11   "the thickness," quoted in Haller, p. 208.

11   "drink, like gambling," ibid., p. 208.

11   "anything from cherry brandy," Fleming, p. 61.

11   "I have frequently seen," quoted in Rorabaugh, p. 14.

11   "after he has eaten," quoted in Haller, p. 67.

13   "If barley be wanting," quoted in Getz, p. 11.

14   "In Charleston," Gelb, p. 138.

14   "when people were baffled," and "that the Devil entered," Fleming, pp. 30–31.

14   "was particularly good," Handlin, p. 101.

15   "Farmers, equally solicitous," Fleming, pp. 61–62.

15   "a good creature," quoted in Barr, p. 366.

16   "The benefits arising," quoted in Getz, p. 39.

16   "showed more interest," Forbes, p. 44.

17   "when kisses and drams," quoted in ibid., p. 55.

17   "the debauched drinking," quoted in Kobler, p. 28.

18   "the Excesses,' quoted in Furnas, *Life and Times*, p. 32.

18   "If the foreman," Rorabaugh, p. 20.

19   "a brewer's wagon," Randall, p. 353.

19   "straight as an Indian," quoted in Flexner, pp. 191–92.

21   "Washington then went," ibid., pp. 140–41.

21   "stare them down," ibid., p. 141.

22   "too sparing a hand," quoted in Rorabaugh, p. 152.

22   "For his 144 gallons," ibid., p. 152.

22   "swilling the planters," quoted in Troy, p. 9.

22   "manner and style," and "The favored aspirant," Rorabaugh, p. 152.

22   "good nature and congeniality," ibid., p. 154.

23   "that voters deserved," and "the beneficial effect," and "expressed dismay," Schlesinger, p. 14.

23   "the candidates offer drunkenness," Dinkin, p. 13.

23   "with a couple of tin cups," ibid., p. 13.

23   "An election in Kentucky," quoted in Simmons, p. 10.

24   "the corrupting influence," Dinkin, p. 3.

24   "I guess Mr. A.," quoted in Rorabaugh, p. 153.

24   "Montana's peerless Senator," Beebe, p. xxi.

25   "a generous allotment," Asinof, p. 231.

25   "who persuaded Washington," Grimes, p. 51.

25   "light held together by moisture," quoted in Sobel, Dava (*Galileo's Daughter*. New York: Walker & Company, 1999), p. 266.

26   "emptied a large tankard," Kobler, p. 31.

26 "I shall never forget," quoted in McCullough, p. 36.
26 "found no inconvenience," quoted in ibid., p. 85.
26 "I know not why," quoted in Schlesinger, p. 50.
26 "fired with a zeal," quoted in Holbrook, p. 58.
26 "All his life," Brookhiser, *Adamses*, p. 65.
27 "had a big eloquent mouth," Forbes, p. 62.
27 "to have stopped at the home," Fleming, p. 51.
27 "a hearty, gregarious fellow," Simon, pp. 24–25.
27 "gaudy legend," Davis, Kenneth S., *A Sense of History: The Best Writing from the Pages of American Heritage* (New York: Heritage, 1985), p. 84.
27 "When the drinks began to wear off," ibid., pp. 84–85.
28 "All the better," quoted in Rorabaugh, p. 103.
28 "The chief was brought up," and "The best Madeira," quoted in Kobler, p. 26.
28 "preserve my small-beer," quoted in Shenkman, Richard and Kurt Reiger, *One-Night Stands with American History* (New York, William Morrow, 1980), p. 28.
29 "Nothing more like a Fool," and "he that drinks fast," quoted in Morgan, p. 24.
29 "'Tis true, drinking does not improve," quoted in Van Doren, p. 29.
29 "a passable spruce beer," Lender and Martin, p. 6.
29 "'Twas honest old Noah," quoted in Kobler, p. 34.
29 "we are enabled," quoted in Isaacson, p. 375.
29 "he is Addled," quoted in Getz, pp. 21–22.
30 "the most remarkable generation," Schlesinger, p. 245.
30 "It sloweth age," quoted in Furnas, *Life and Times*, p. 18.
31 "from the moment," and "to keep up," Waller, p. 46.
31 "the trembles, the slows," quoted in Furnas, *Americans*, p. 336.
31 "horse doses of brandy or rum," ibid., p. 336.
31 "in the northern colonies," Barr, pp. 202–3.
32 "lie down, and extending their legs," quoted in Robicsek, Francis. *The Smoking Gods* (Norman, Oklahoma, University of Oklahoma Press, 1978), p. 23.
32 "thin and watery," quoted in Kobler, p. 26.
33 "shallow brackish wells," Rorabaugh, p. 96.
33 "an excuse to many persons," quoted in Barr, p. 206.
34 "lowly and common," quoted in Rorabaugh, p. 96.
34 "a drink very generally used," quoted in Barr, p. 312.
35 "the Stomachs of the Populace," quoted in Ackroyd, p. 347.
35 "hot bread," Forbes, p. 123.
35 "Many of the pressing issues," Liell, p. 67–8.
36 "Since neither the cows' rear ends," quoted in Furnas, *Americans*, p. 163.
36 "extraordinary rivers of butter," quoted in Rorabaugh, p. 117.
37 "I could reckon," quoted in Kobler, p. 28.
37 "six and one half barrels," ibid., p. 26.

37 "even if he had wanted to do so," Asbury, p. 16.

38 "Add brandy to the amount," quoted in Lowenkopf, Anne, "How Our Ancestors Got Their Likker," *The American Legion Magazine*, August 1967, p. 31.

38 "half the preachers round Albany," Furnas, *Life and Times*, p. 23.

39 "Without molasses," Miller, pp. 576–77.

39 "Far from being considered a crime," Fleming, pp. 49–50.

40 "Some of them boycotted," Barr, p. 311.

40 "every five miles," quoted in Rorabaugh, p. 18.

41 "The Industrial Revolution," Getz, p. 81.

42 "Even if the farmer," Rorabaugh, p. 74.

43 "The consumption of ardent spirits," quoted in Brookhiser, *Hamilton*, p. 85.

43 "an infernal one," quoted in Lee, p. 24.

43 "appears unequal," and "the powers necessarily vested," quoted in Barr, p. 227.

44 "It allowed collectors," Weisberger, p. 112.

44 "a federal marshal," Fleming, p. 53.

45 "They formed an army," Barr, p. 321.

45 "To his disappointment," Tindall, p. 303.

45 "to a light chaise," Getz, p. 14.

Chapter 2

page 47 "infamy [that] hath spread itself," and "speedie redress," quoted in Krout, p. 3.

47 "Drink is in itself," quoted in Barr, p. 366.

47 "in 1693," Getz, p. 13.

48 "holding on to the gate," Silverman, Kenneth, *The Life and Times of Cotton Mather* (New York: Harper & Row, 1984), p. 46.

48 "was aggressive," and "a finely honed conception," and "thought highly of," Spalding, p. 3

49 "expressed his approval," *A Brief Biography*, Ettinger, p. 97.

50 "presented to the House of Commons," ibid., p. 92.

50 "If given an opportunity," Spalding, pp. 3–4.

51 "serve as a military buffer," Schlesinger, p. 125.

51 "on a tract," Ettinger, *A Brief Biography*, p. 131.

51 "10 tons of Alderman Parson's best beer," quoted in ibid., p. 130.

51 "a fatal Liquor," quoted in Spalding, p. 5.

51 "keep up their Courage," quoted in Boorstin, p. 91.

52 "honestly believed that the presence," Spalding, p. 20.

53 "Whereas it is found," quoted in Lowenkopf, Anne, "How Our Ancestors Got Their Likker," *The American Legion Magazine*, August, 1967, p. 33.

53 "that rum added to water," Barr, p. 205.

54 "as it is the nature of mankind," quoted in Miller, pp. 629–30.

55   "The ultimate proof," Boorstin, p. 214.

55   "embarked on his lifelong campaign," Schlesinger, p. 117.

55   "In folly, it causes him," quoted in Kobler, p. 23.

56   "Punch, Idleness, Sickness, Debt," quoted in Behr, pp. 15–16.

56   "as uncommon as a drink," quoted in Holbrook, p. 62.

56   For the transition period," Asbury, p. 27.

57   "anti-federal," quoted in Furnas, *Americans*, p. 315.

57   "a moderate quantity of spirits," quoted in Kobler, p. 44.

57   "mild foretaste," Asbury, p. 43.

58   "gone to bed sober," "hardly burned," and "She died," Harrison, p. 15.

58   "suddenly destroyed," quoted in Furnas, *Life and Times*, p. 189.

58   "In the fall of 1867," quoted in Asbury, p. 44.

58   "roasted from the crown," quoted in Ward, Geoffrey C., *Before the Trumpet: Young Franklin Roosevelt, 1882–1905* (New York: Harper & Row, 1985), p. 29.

Chapter 3

page 61   "the heart of a rich timberland," Kobler, p. 48.

62   "afforded exceptional advantages," Durkee, ed., p. 10.

62   "a three-miles journey," Kobler, p. 49.

62   "*Mr. Armstrong,*" quoted in Armstrong, p. 18.

63   "ARTICLE IV," quoted in Asbury, pp. 29–30.

64   "One man, for example," Rorabaugh, pp. 171–72.

64   "Finally, the victim falls," ibid., p. 170.

65   "Americans of all ages," and "What is a man born for," quoted in Tindall, p. 494.

65   "took a fairly lenient approach," Fleming, p. 63.

65   "has, after devout and deliberate attention," quoted in Krout, p. 111.

66   "A pyrrhic victory," Tindall, p. 496.

67   "like the Egyptian angel of death," quoted in Mitgang, p. 30.

67   "flabby and undone," quoted in Oates, p. 47.

67   "According to the near-mythic account," Pegram, p. 27.

67   "When all such of us," and "It is true," quoted in Getz, p. 91.

68   "Prohibition will work great injury," quoted in Kobler, pp. 63–64.

68   "pass laws the most effectual," quoted in Lee, p. 2.

68   "The moderate drinker," Furnas, *Life and Times*, p. 88.

69   "the cultivated Boston classicist," ibid., p. 71.

69   "and take the burden," ibid., p. 79.

69   "badly needed," Furnas, *Americans*, p. 509.

70   "From a high of just over," Lender and Martin, pp. 71–72.

70   "would at least be more innocent," quoted in Fleming, p. 106.

70   "No nation is drunken," quoted in Starr, Kevin, *Inventing the Dream: California Through the Progressive Era* (New York: Oxford University Press, 1985), p. 157.

71 "I wish to see this beverage," quoted in Fleming, p. 106.
71 "dared not bar the recruitment," Rorabaugh, p. 15.
71 "Instance the murder," Armstrong, pp. 139–40.
71 "extraordinary number of capital offenses," ibid., p. 219.
72 "As I was riding," quoted in Rorabaugh, p. 199.
72 "Give me whiskey," quoted in Bettmann, p. 133.
73 "permits little alcohol in the body," Karlen, Arno, *Napoleon's Glands and Other Ventures in Biohistory* (New York: Little, Brown, 1984), p. 93.
73 "another European-based ailment," Marriott and Rachlin, p. 224.
74 "Alcohol also offered," Alan Taylor, p. 96.
74 "the island of general intoxication," quoted in Milton, p. 186.
75 "After a burst of wild hilarity," Kobler, pp. 366–67.
75 "a hail of arrows," Milton, p. 181.
75 "This was not done," ibid., 181.
75 "a lifelong passion," Kobler, p. 37.
75 "Hearts and tongues," quoted in ibid., p. 37.
76 "fuddle [the natives] with rum," quoted in Furnas, *Americans*, p. 40.
76 "take advantage of," Barr, p. 7.
76 "Rum will kill us," quoted in Marks, p. 36.
76 "liquor addiction," and "extraordinarily lyric poems," Behr, p. 18.
76 "I am afraid to drink," quoted in ibid., p. 18.
77 "Is it to be wondered at," quoted in Barr, p. 7.
77 "forbade sale of drink," Furnas, *Life and Times*, p. 121.
78 "in all their frolicks," quoted in Furnas, *Americans*, p. 38.
78 "to labour for a Reformation," quoted in Boorstin, p. 62.
78 "Who hath woe," quoted in Kobler, p. 54.
79 "has been among the more constant," quoted in Behr, p. 24.
79 "temperance seemed," quoted in Seldes, p. 251.
79 "come hot from Ireland," Furnas, *Life and Times*, p. 98.
79 "The president of the United States," ibid., p. 99.
80 "resolved in the strength of the Lord," quoted in Krout, p. 111.
80 "took on the attributes," quoted in Seldes, p. 250.
80 "gave prominence to one particular vice," quoted in Holbrook, p. 65.
80 "The outward reformation," quoted in ibid., p. 65.
82 "Rum did that," quoted in Kobler, p. 80.
83 "succeeded in preventing," ibid., p. 284.
83 "a most brilliant," Neal Dow, p. 112.
83 "This was no easy task," ibid., p. 109.
83 "Mr. Chief," ibid., p. 111.
83 "the moral Columbus," and "the invention of printing," quoted in Kobler, p. 87.
84 "Eighty-four per cent," quoted in Frederick Neal Dow, p. 11.
84 "an infamous crime," quoted in Holbrook, p. 78.
85 "the law of Heaven Americanized," quoted in Bailey and Kennedy, p. 317.
85 "prohibited the sale," quoted in Asbury, p. 59.

85   "After the enactment," Neal Dow, p. 393.

86   "The trouble with the drink places," Ade, p. 23.

89   "inescapable irony," and "[The war] was fought," Winchester, Simon. *The Professor and the Madman* (New York: HarperCollins, 1998), p. 52.

90   "the American national debt," Gordon, James Steele, *A Thread Across the Ocean: The Heroic Story of the Transatlantic Cable* (New York: Walker & Company, 2002), p. 163.

91   "Doctor, can you tell me," quoted in Kobler, p. 65.

92   "including a thousand dollars," Rugoff, Milton. *America's Gilded Age.* New York: Henry Holt, p. 34.

92   "tediously truthful," and "scrupulously truthful," quoted in Perret, *Grant*, p. 443.

92   "sixteen-year-old soldier," Barr, p. 204.

93   "great inconvenience," Neal Dow, p. 677.

93   "Napoleon of temperance," quoted in Pegram, p. 40.

93   "One of them," Neal Dow, p. 677.

93   "welcomed the alcoholic traffic," Schlesinger, p. 116.

94   "furnished the wets," Kobler, p. 91.

94   "the soul-searing moans," and "motionless forms," Cullen, Joseph P. *The Image of War, 1861–1865, Volume I: Shadows of the Storm* (Garden City, New York: Doubleday, 1981), p. 177.

94   "1. It is not sinful," Asbury, p. 61.

Chapter 4

page 97   "Who can be independent," quoted in Pegram, p. 28.

98   "Outraged, the two women," Murdock, p. 26.

98   "Instances of female influence," Armstrong, p. 167.

98   "You might say it's a disgrace," Furnas, *Life and Times*, p. 236.

98   "Let women's motto be," quoted in Seldes, p. 280.

99   "beautiful, bran-eating Dio," quoted in Furnas, *Life and Times*, p. 261.

00   "large, rotund body," quoted in Asbury, p. 69.

100   "A clean tooth never decays," quoted in ibid., p. 69.

100   "Visitation Bands," quoted in Holbrook, p. 87.

102   "Carrying their knitting," Seldes, p. 262.

102   "the mother of a promising son," Pegram, p. 61.

102   "family cares," quoted in Ward, p. 6.

102   "with tearful eyes," quoted in ibid., p. 6.

102   "This is the way," quoted in ibid., p. 6.

102   "was properly alarmed," Holbrook, p. 87.

103   "We will sing," quoted in ibid., p. 87.

103   "I came unexpectedly upon," quoted in Kobler, p. 119.

104   "Ach, vimmins," quoted in Behr, p. 37.

104   "The saloonkeeper," Furnas, *Americans*, p. 640.

105   "vowed to Heaven," quoted in Asbury, p. 75.

105 "And where are the hands," quoted in Holbrook, p. 89.
106 "In Cincinnati," ibid., p. 80.
106 "line of praying crusaders," Asbury, p. 80.
106 "blocked up their chimneys," Kobler, p. 122.
108 "This little band," quoted in Krout, p. 151.
108 "Father, dear father," quoted in Getz, p. 113.
108 "the assessors and gaugers," quoted in Asbury, p. 85.
109 "Drunkenness is a disease," quoted in Holbrook, p. 92.
109 "Dr. Keeley responded," ibid., p. 92.
109 "one of the large," Larson, p. 161.
110 "roomed in the sanitarium," Holbrook, p. 92.
110 "if there is a single village," ibid., p. 92.
110 "so frequent as to cast doubt," ibid., p. 93.

Chapter 5

page 111 "because they felt," and "we would shut out," and "the moderate use," and "women extended their hands," quoted in Ward, p. 10.
112 "the most formidable woman," Furnas, *Americans*, p. 448.
112 "The Uncrowned Queen," quoted in Furnas, *Life and Times*, p. 277.
112 "Help me, God," quoted in Beer, p. 115.
112 "a rarely endowed home," and "a home sheltered," Gordon, p. 5.
113 "a great pity," Willard, p. 12.
113 "the flame of the ideal," quoted in Kobler, p. 133.
113 "I love you," and "Oh, Frank!' quoted in Seldes, pp. 270–71.
114 "man of brilliant gifts," Willard, p. 226.
114 "In 1861–62," quoted in Kobler, pp. 135–36.
114 "good and gracious," Willard, p. 612.
115 "the sober second thought," quoted in Seldes, p. 263.
115 "harried state and territorial legislatures," Kobler, pp. 137–38.
115 "a colorless liquid poison," and the quotes that follow are from educational materials provided to the author either through the mail by, or at the headquarters of, the Woman's Christian Temperance Union in Evanston, Illinois.
116 "We'll See to You," quoted in Furnas, *Life and Times*, p. 252.
118 "Germans, Indians," Ward, p. 22.
119 "newest, tallest Chicago skyscrapers," Larson, p. 57.
119 "great without arrogance," Willard, p. 109.
120 "Licensed," quoted in Lee, pp. 34–35.
121 "subsidized newspapers," Kobler, p. 162.
122 "In the early days," quoted in Seldes, p. 280.
122 "They put pressure," Gurko, p. 264.
122 "At the White House," quoted in Furnas, *Life and Times*, p. 252.
123 "I have young sons," quoted in ibid., p. 219.

123 "Life Saving Station," quoted in Fleming, p. 75.
124 "In the early 1870s," Pegram, p. 53.
124 "such relationships," Rose, Phyllis. *Parallel Lives: Five Victorian Marriages* (New York: Alfred A. Knopf, 1983), p. 12.
124 "There is a creature," quoted in Willard, p. x.
125 "There came an intent upward gaze," quoted in Seldes, p. 269.
125 "there were a few tired sighs," Gordon, pp. 271–72.

Chapter 6

page 127 "a thoughtful but restless Irishman," Robert Lewis Taylor, p. 18.
128 "put in a glass," quoted in ibid., p. 17.
128 "went for a rather aimless ride," ibid., p. 17.
129 "choicest slave," and "a scarlet hunting coat," and " a brass hunting horn," and "set off to call," ibid., p. 19.
129 "I have met many men," quoted in ibid., p. 19.
129 "was as much scholar," and "she issued a royal ban," ibid., p. 50.
131 "a wretched girl," ibid., p. 58.
131 "reveals what on first glance," ibid., p. 59.
133 "Touch not, taste not," quoted in Seldes, p. 274.
134 "Rum-soaked rummy!" and "Ally of Satan!" and "Makers of drunkards and widows!" quoted in Kobler, p. 150.
134 "Sullivan retreated to the rear," Robert Lewis Taylor, p. 21.
135 "the harmless, half-asleep town," ibid., p. 94.
135 "Go to Kiowa," quoted in Getz, p. 118.
136 "ran out of armament," Robert Lewis Taylor, p. 117.
136 "Men of Kiowa," Nation, p. 118.
136 "was not allowed a pillow," ibid., p. 82.
137 "Peace on earth," quoted in Kobler, p. 151.
137 "The first smashing," ibid., p. 112.
137 "Forty-odd joints," Holbrook, p. 100.
138 "was more than fifty feet long," Robert Lewis Taylor, p. 130.
138 "Smash! Smash!" quoted in Kobler, p. 151.
138 "however effective," Seldes, p. 274.
138 "God gave Samson," quoted in Asinof, p. 237.
139 "The first thing," quoted in Sinclair, p. 56.
139 "The three raiders," Holbrook, p. 102.
140 "Say, Billy, git ten two-by-four," quoted in Nation, p. 193.
141 "If she comes," and "Tell her I'm sick," quoted in Kobler, p. 153.
143 "she has a method," quoted in ibid., p. 146.
143 "bulldog, running along," quoted in ibid., p. 147.
144 "In the first years," Robert Lewis Taylor, p. 347.
145 "My life has been made miserable," quoted in ibid., p. 309.
146 "with the avowed intention," Holbrook, p. 104.
146 "nervous trouble," quoted in Asbury, p. 120.

Chapter 7

page 149   "to stay the tide," quoted in Furnas, *Life and Times*, p. 301.
  149   "exactly where one," Seldes, p. 268.
  149   "the division between church," Link and Catton, p. 38.
  149   "conjure up an image," Lender and Martin, p. 99.
  150   "where men come together," quoted in Behr, p. 75.
  150   "It was in the saloon," quoted in Sinclair, p. 75.
  150   "the common lavatory," quoted in Pegram, p. 103.
  150   "the church of the poor," Barr, p. 378.
  150   "the acme of evil," quoted in Pegram, p. 91.
  151   "the patience of driver ants," Kobler, p. 194.
  152   "The League took its blackjack," Furnas, *Americans*, p. 919.
  152   "Propaganda fell thicker," Sinclair, p. 112.
  152   "You can't drink liquor, et al.," quoted in ibid., p. 113.
  152   "Many a frock-coated," Furnas, *Life and Times*, p. 305.
  153   "Neat-mustached," ibid., p. 307.
  153   "doesn't have anything to do," quoted in ibid., p. 308.
  154   "I hope that someday," quoted in Kobler, p. 181.
  154   "I could never understand," quoted in ibid., p. 181.
  154   "My father once owned," Neal Dow, p. 37.
  155   "locomotive in trousers," quoted in Asinof, p. 227.
  155   "We wouldn't mind," quoted in ibid., p. 228
  156   "The simplicity," quoted in Steuart, pp. 38–39.
  156   "The new David," quoted in Kobler, p. 182.
  156   "He persuaded the ASL," Behr, p. 55.
  156   "Wheeler on his wheel," quoted in Asinof, p. 229.
  157   "was dissuaded from appointing," Cashman, p. 135.
  157   "controlled six Congresses," Steuart, p. 11.
  158   "I do it the way," quoted in Mordden, p. 142.
  160   "There is no easier way," quoted in Engelmann, p. 7.
  160   "from all the unending horror," quoted in ibid., p. 7.
  160   "found that the workers," Ciulla, p. 198.
  160   "apprentices and servants," Krout, p. 17.
  161   "The speed at which we run," quoted in Cashman, p. 167.
  161   "the use of liquor," quoted in Birmingham, *Our Crowd*, p. 142.
  161   "a well-meant burst," quoted in Lord, p. 218.
  162   "Gentlemen, there is a liquor shop," quoted in Sinclair, p. 256.
  162   "never enter a bar-room," quoted in Lender and Martin, p. 108.
  163   "Start a saloon," quoted in Asinof, p. 249.
  163   "When the laboring man," quoted in Engelmann, p. 30.
  163   "the momentous event," Kobler, p. 206.
  164   "Brewery products," quoted in Sinclair, p. 122.
  165   "January 9," Sullivan, pp. 637–38.
  166   "the bill carrying this provision," Merz, p. 41.
  166   "the finest, the cleanest," quoted in Kobler, p. 206.

166 "Kaiser kultur," quoted in Sinclair, p. 264.

167 "German language instruction," Bradshaw, Jon. *Dreams That Money Can Buy: The Tragic Life of Libby Holman* (New York: William Morrow, 1985), p. 27.

167 "Strauss was changed to Stratford," Barr, p. 33.

168 "informed that there are," quoted in Behr, p. 69.

168 "engaging in pro-German activities," Kyvig, *Repealing*, p. 36.

168 "gross greed," Kobler, pp. 204–5.

169 "With pride and gratification," quoted in ibid., p. 158.

169 "Dubois will surely be," quoted in Asinof, p. 241.

170 "most zealous spy," quoted in Kobler, pp. 186–87.

170 "I have told," quoted in ibid., p. 187.

171 "real hell-fire," and "Johnson whipped out," ibid., p. 189.

171 "Ethics be hanged," quoted in ibid., p. 191.

171 "We must create," quoted in Asinof, p. 242.

172 "We can put on your desk," quoted in Kobler, p. 194.

172 "The Anti-Saloon League," quoted in Asinof, p. 251.

172 "went dry because," Ade, p. 20.

173 "whereas we believe," quoted in Barr, p. 212.

173 "in cases of fainting," Sinclair, p. 61.

173 "attributed the success," quoted in Engelmann, p. 17.

173 "his last shot of whiskey," Asinof, p. 242.

174 "want high returns," Durant, *Greece*, p. 268.

174 "the money people were there," Asinof, pp. 232–33.

175 "Brochures showed," Morton, Frederic. *A Nervous Splendor: Vienna, 1888–1889.* Boston: Little, Brown, 1979, p. 51.

175 "found himself, dazed," Lerner, p. 86.

176 "unfit for horses," quoted in Bettmann, p. 129.

177 "The mother of ignorance," quoted in Kobler, p. 185.

177 "It was among country Methodists," quoted in Fecher, p. 106.

178 "among the hardest drinking," Kobler, p. 243.

178 "sexual hyenas," quoted in Sinclair, p. 32.

178 "the only way," quoted in Furnas, *Life and Times*, p. 312.

179 "was the main cause," Kobler, p. 199.

179 "Liquor will actually make," quoted in Barr, p. 253, n.

179 "Of the 197 members," Sinclair, p. 163.

180 "laid down such a barrage," quoted in Dabney, p. 123.

181 "It was the trade," Cashman, p. 18.

181 "In New York State," ibid., p. 19.

181 "entered into a holy conspiracy," and "We blocked the telegraph," quoted in Lee, p. 40.

181 "if the ballot," quoted in Mordden, p. 144.

182 "a congressman is a man," quoted in Asinof, p. 255.

183 "In Michigan," Cashman, p. 19.

184 "I am in favor," quoted in Sinclair, p. 147.

184 "you have to take," quoted in Cashman, p. 40.

184 "The penalties for violation," quoted in Kobler, pp. 13–14.

185 "The Prohibition Law," quoted in Cashman, p. 29.

185 "that if prohibition came," Cooper, Robert. *Around the World with Mark Twain* (New York: Arcade, 2000), p. 147.

Chapter 8

page 187 "This is a big moment," quoted in Kobler, p. 17.

187 "The reign of tears," quoted in ibid., p. 12.

187 "the longest and most effective step," quoted in Blumenthal, p. 84.

188 "You shall not bury," quoted in Kobler, p. 12.

188 "will last as long," quoted in ibid., p. 13.

188 "God's present," quoted in ibid., p. 11.

188 "Public sentiment," quoted in Lender and Martin, p. 95.

188 "Goodbye forever," quoted in Engelmann, p. 30.

188 "In New York City," Kobler, p. 16.

189 "strong drink," ibid., p. 17.

190 "Mother's in the kitchen," quoted in ibid., p. 238.

191 "After I've had," quoted in ibid., p. 239.

191 "Last Sunday I manufactured," quoted in Mordden, p. 147.

192 "A brewmaster," Perrett, *Twenties*, p. 176.

192 "Newspapers all over America," Behr, p. 171.

192 "hops, yeast, malt," Asbury, p. 157.

193 "If a fellow feels like," Lewis, Sinclair. *The Man Who Knew Coolidge* (London: Jonathan Cape, 1928), pp. 19–20.

193 "In southern Florida," Perrett, *Twenties*, p. 175.

194 "apples, oats, bananas," Abels, p. 92.

194 "The illicit liquor traffic," Asbury, p. 228.

194 "Mother makes brandy," quoted in *This Fabulous Century*, p. 105.

196 "The spectacle of immigrants," Sinclair, p. 207.

196 "Manufacturers capitalized," Murdock, p. 98.

197 "It's too much trouble," quoted in Cashman, p. 37.

197 "once walked the north and south lengths," Mordden, p. 134.

198 "Door fitters," Lee, pp. 55–56.

199 "One afternoon," Abels, p. 96.

200 "it took money," *This Fabulous Century*, p. 160.

200 "there were four alarm buttons," ibid., p. 160.

200 "used its hearses," Furnas, *Great Times*, pp. 353–54.

201 "Take this away," quoted in Cashman, p. 45.

202 "Distillers were required," Fleming, p. 34.

203 "In small towns," Birmingham, *The Rest of Us*, p. 148.

203 "Peg's new bootlegger," quoted in Kramer, Dale (*Ross and the New Yorker*. New York: Doubleday, 1951), p. 129.

203 "When I sell liquor," quoted in Asbury, p. 291.

203 "Add the cost of corruption," Furnas, *Great Times*, p. 355.

204 "costs associated," Lender and Martin, p. 145.

204 "In Northern cities," ibid., p. 145.

204 "the passion of the prohibitionists," quoted in Cashman, p. 29.

205 "talkative, energetic, a book lover," quoted in Behr, p. 93.

205 "short, stout, bald man," Kobler, p. 316.

205 "I was prominent enough," quoted in Behr, p. 94.

205 "As compared to," Coffey, p. 30.

206 "took more than routine wifely interest," ibid., p. 90.

207 "made wine," Murdock, p. 91.

207 "trays with bottles," quoted in Coffey, p. 95.

208 "in front of each couple," ibid., p. 103.

209 "Daddy, don't do it!" quoted in ibid., p. 216.

210 "She who dances," quoted in ibid., p. 218.

210 "temporary maniacal insanity," quoted in Kobler, p. 321.

211 "booze and bribery," Coffey, p. 224.

211 "When he walked," and "as nattily as," quoted in Kessler, p. 141.

212 "Frank Costello would later say," Kessler, p. 36.

212 "The best Scotch," ibid., p. 37.

212 "intimate familiarity," ibid., p. 37.

213 "kicked holes in the laws," quoted in Coffey, p. 41.

213 "might stand as the patron saint," quoted in ibid., p. 41.

214 "a pyramid-shaped package," Fleming, p. 85.

214 "Three days later," Kobler, p. 256.

215 "a floating liquor store," Behr, p. 137.

216 "When the Canadian vessel," Morris, p. 41.

217 "Canadian smugglers," Kobler, p. 268.

219 "The person who drinks," quoted in Barr, p. 241.

219 "seemed a notice," Holbrook, p. 105.

220 "a distillation of alcohol," ibid., p. 284.

220 "The experienced drinker," Morris, p. 36.

221 "supposedly made from peaches," Asbury, p. 283.

221 "Farm hands in the Middle West," ibid., p. 282.

223 "Floating around on top," quoted in ibid., p. 283.

223 "In 1927," Mordden, p. 135.

223 "governments used to murder," quoted in Leinwand, p. 83.

225 "Recipes were invented," Birmingham, *The Right People*, pp. 241–42.

225 "the citizenry would be assured," Mordden, p. 146.

225 "Partly it was his snobbish nature," Birmingham, *The Rest of Us*, p. 145.

225 "I never poisoned anybody," quoted in Kobler, p. 315.

226 "over-competition," Sinclair, p. 199.

Chapter 9

page 227   "brutalized the Church," Riding, Alan. *Distant Neighbors: A Portrait of the Mexicans* (New York: Knopf, 1985), p. 51.

227   "I blew up," and "executive firmness," quoted in Engelmann, p. 149.

228   "If necessary," quoted in Kobler, p. 288.

229   "It is not the individual poisoning," quoted in Barr, p. 162.

230   "very much like that," Lerner, p. 662.

230   "The Untouchables located," Perrett, *Twenties*, p. 396.

230   "the inadequate," quoted in Engelmann, p. 82.

231   "This is to certify," quoted in Asbury, p. 175.

232   "as devoid of honesty," quoted in Kobler, pp. 272–73.

232   "few New Yorkers," ibid., p. 322.

233   "debauched," quoted in ibid., p. 323.

233   "one inspector," Lee, p. 6.

233   "in time wearied," Asbury, p. 176.

233   "Every son of a bitch," quoted in ibid., p. 176.

234   "Barely two months," Asinof, p. 276.

234   "One of the most shocking," Lee, p. 171.

235   "Some days," quoted in Asbury, p. 177.

235   "The prohibition service," quoted in Kobler, pp. 274–75.

235   "police the police," quoted in *This Fabulous Century*, p. 154.

236   "sixty percent of my police," quoted in Coffey, p. 88.

236   "An alleged dry law violator," quoted in ibid., pp. 63–64.

237   "his noble paunch," Asbury in Leighton, ed., p. 36.

238   "master hooch hound," quoted in Cashman, p. 47.

238   "probably made the front pages," Asbury in Leighton, ed., p. 40.

239   "sewed into his breast pocket," Kobler, p. 295.

240   "You're not the type," quoted in Coffey, p. 15.

241   "There's sad news here," quoted in Kobler, p. 295.

241   "Hundreds of actual Harlem residents," Coffey, p. 185.

241   "Hanging around there," Einstein, pp. 33–34.

242   "three quarters," Asinof, p. 264.

242   "Once he shot out a lock," Asbury in Leighton, ed., p. 46.

243   "was three times larger," Engelmann, p. 125.

243   "the bartender refused," quoted in ibid., p. 127.

244   "Izzy Einstein . . . holds the record," quoted in Einstein, p. 74.

244   "Izzy does not sleep," quoted in Asbury in Leighton, ed., p. 40.

244   "[Izzy Einstein is] the master mind," quoted in Kobler, p. 297.

245   "[Izzy Einstein has] become as famous," quoted in ibid., p. 297.

245   "The bootlegger who gets away," quoted in Einstein, p. 86.

245   "The service must be dignified," quoted in ibid., p. 298.

246   "the 4,932 persons," ibid., p. v.

246   "In my work," ibid., pp. 260–61.

246   "But Mr. Einstein," quoted in Coffey, p. 307.

247   "I don't get you," quoted in ibid., p. 307.

248 "Wheeler's puppet," Kobler, p. 274.
248 "The Amendment," and "[The] home brew fad," and "Bootleg patronage," and "There is little," quoted in ibid., p. 274.
249 "It is very easy," and "Most of the present prosperity," quoted in Abels,
p. 88.
250 "Closed for One Year," quoted in Perrett, *America in the Twenties*, p. 171.
250 "boots expansible at the ankles," Kobler, p. 235.
250 "At the Buffalo end," ibid., p. 254.
250 "One Detroit mechanic," Engelmann, p. 34.
251 "I shall make dandelion wine," quoted in Mordden, p. 147.
251 "he had a bottle of gin," Taylor, Robert Lewis, *W.C. Fields: His Follies and
Fortunes* (New York: Doubleday, 1949), p. 163.
251 "had a card pushed," Jenkins, p. 130.
251 "The Prohibition Bureau," Abels, p. 91.
252 "In 1928 and 1929," Kyvig, *Repealing*, p. 108.
252 "the fifth floor," ibid., p. 109.
253 "This is unmitigated bunk," quoted in Kobler, p. 339.
253 "His incessant activity," Steuart, p. 262.
253 "loved the limelight," ibid., p. 12.
254 "engulfed in flame," Coffey, p. 212.
254 "his voice was so weak," and "after recovering sufficiently," ibid., p. 213.

Chapter 10

page 257 "There is as much chance," quoted in Engelmann, p. 189.
258 "were drinking," Allen, p. 90.
258 "the feminist journalist," Murdock, p. 137.
259 "*alcohol inflames the passions*," quoted in ibid., p. 78.
259 "been infected by," Allen, p. 90.
259 "her grace and delicate beauty," Kyvig, *Repealing*, p. 119.
259 "a world without liquor," quoted in Barr, p. 152.
260 "By the beginning," Leinwand, p. 81.
260 "growing up," quoted in ibid., p. 152.
260 "a great social and economic experiment," quoted in Coffey, p. 247.
260 "At an earlier meeting," Kyvig, *Repealing*, p. 121.
261 "Because I believe," quoted in Cashman, p. 160.
261 "prohibition's criminal offspring," quoted in Dabney, p. 301.
261 "the scum of the earth," quoted in Sinclair, p. 343.
261 "Mrs. Sabin and her cocktail-drinking women," quoted in ibid., p. 343.
261 "that the women of America," quoted in Carter, p. 96.
262 "was evading the law," quoted in Mordden, p. 143.
262 "The WCTU has always been," quoted in Ward, p. 55.
262 "unless only the dry position," quoted in Murdock, p. 146.
262 "When I said," quoted in Kobler, p. 342.
263 "not trying to make it easier," quoted in Engelmann, p. 210.

264 "Mrs. Sabin," Carter, p. 97.

264 "individuals of irreproachable reputation," quoted in Murdock, p. 135.

264 "Beer and Light Wine," quoted in Barr, p. 183.

265 "watched with growing alarm," Kyvig, *Repealing*, p. 39.

265 "a symptom of a disease," quoted in Lender and Martin, p. 156.

265 "scattered fairly evenly," Kyvig, *Repealing*, p. 46.

266 "The Association used," Sinclair, p. 338.

266 "the great error," quoted in Kyvig, *Repealing*, p. 81.

267 "It is a perplexing and unpleasant truth," Hoffer, Eric. *The True Believer* (New York: Harper & Row, 1951), p. 75.

267 "inconsistent with the spirit," quoted in Kobler, p. 336.

268 "No one who is intellectually honest," quoted in Bergreen, p. 300.

269 "which was available," Coffey, p. 265.

269 "a fine, true-to-type," quoted in Cashman, p. 213.

270 "I am against Prohibition," quoted in Barr, p. 239.

270 "Have [we] not come," quoted in Murdock, p. 137.

270 "Neither my father," quoted in Kobler, pp. 350–51.

271 "generally supported," and "That this has not been the result," quoted in ibid., p. 351.

271 "where a tough on the rise," quoted in Mordden, p. 137.

272 "The Prohibition experiment," Lacey, p. 363.

273 "crime had been steadily rising," Dobyns, pp. 372–73.

274 "Every available index," Kyvig, *Repealing*, p. 29.

274 "the billions of pounds," Getz, p. 158.

276 "Billions Spent," and "Prohibition and Poverty," and "Bring Back Beer," quoted in Engelmann, p. 201.

276 "not just a blow," Cooke, Alistair, *Alistair Cooke's America* (New York: Knopf, 1973), p. 327.

276 "if the production," Englemann, p. 198.

277 "The Procession," quoted in ibid., p. 201.

277 "The plot of the first," Burnham, p. 37.

277 "motion pictures should depict," quoted in ibid., p. 37.

279 "probably the greatest expert," Johnson, Paul, *Modern Times: The World from the Twenties to the Eighties* (New York: Harper & Row, 1983), p. 211.

279 "a truck load," and "there is considerably more," ibid., p. 211.

279 "During the period," Kyvig, *Revealing*, p. 24.

279 "reviewed the literature," Lender and Martin, p. 139.

280 "In 1943," ibid., p. 138.

280 "The Welch Grape Juice Company," ibid., p. 146.

281 "Prohibition was a condition," quoted in Thomas and Morgan-Witts, p. 115.

282 "There are so few patients," quoted in Sullivan, *The Twenties*, p. 535.

282 "There is less drinking," quoted in Churchill, Sir Winston, *The Great Republic: A History of America* (New York: Random House, 1999), p. 271.

282 "the Eighteenth Amendment," quoted in Cashman, pp. 231–32.

283   "Congressional voting districts," Murdock, p. 152.
284   "Happily for the welfare," Frederick Neal Dow, pp. 77–78.
284   "Most speakeasies," Kobler, p. 354.
285   "waiters wheeled in," Kyvig, *Repealing*, p. 183.
285   "To Captain William Henry Stayton," quoted in ibid., p. 183.
285   "My first in thirteen years," quoted in Kobler, p. 354.
285   "A day after repeal," Blumenthal, p. 121.

Epilogue

page 290   "It has even been suggested," Barr, p. 22.
293   "the issue of drunk driving," Glassner, Barry, *The Culture of Fear* (New York: Basic Books, 1999), p. 9.
293   "poured $5,000 worth," Murdock, p. 116.
295   "Even relatively modest amounts," quoted in Emery, Gene. "Alcohol Can Cut Heart Attack Risk in Men—Study," *World News Digest*, January 8, 2003.
299   "It never was difficult," Rogan, Carl A., "Story of Whisky In Oklahoma Is Lengthy and Spirited One," *Muskogee* [Oklahoma] *Sunday Phoenix & Times-Democrat*, August 14, 1966, p. 3, Section III.
299   "A newcomer to the state," ibid., p. 3, Section III.
299   "Oklahoma will be dry," quoted in ibid., p. 3, Section III.

Select Bibliography

Abels, Jules. *In the Time of Silent Cal.* New York: G.P. Putnam's Sons, 1969.

Ackroyd, Peter. *London: The Biography.* New York: Doubleday, 2000.

Ade, George. *The Old-Time Saloon.* Detroit: Gale Research Company, 1975.

Allen, Frederick Lewis. *Only Yesterday: An Informal History of the Nineteen-Twenties.* New York: Harper Brothers, 1957.

Armstrong, Rev. Lebbeus. *The Temperance Reformation.* New York: Fowler and Wells, 1853.

Asbury, Herbert. *The Great Illusion.* New York: Doubleday, 1950.

Asinof, Eliot. *1919: America's Loss of Innocence.* New York: Donald I. Fine, 1990.

Bailey, Thomas A, and David M. Kennedy. *The American Pageant, 7th Edition.* Lexington, Massachusetts: D.C. Heath and Company, 1983.

Barr, Andrew. *Drink: A Social History of America.* New York: Carroll & Graf, 1999.

Barzun, Jacques. *From Dawn to Decadence: 1500 to the Present.* New York: HarperCollins, 2000.

Beebe, Lucius. *The Big Spenders.* Garden City, New York: Doubleday, 1966.

Beer, Thomas. *The Mauve Decade: American Life at the End of the Nineteenth Century.* New York: Alfred A. Knopf, 1926.

Behr, Edward. *Prohibition: Thirteen Years That Changed America.* New York: Arcade, 1995.

Bergreen, Laurence. *Capone: The Man and the Era.* New York: Simon and Schuster, 1994.

Bettmann, Otto L. *The Good Old Days—They Were Terrible.* New York: Random House, 1974.

Birmingham, Stephen. *Our Crowd: The Great Jewish Families of New York.* Harper & Row, 1967.

———. *The Rest of Us: The Rise of America's Eastern European Jews.* Boston: Little, Brown, 1984.

———. *The Right People: The Social Establishment in America.* Boston, Little, Brown, 1968.

Blumenthal, Ralph. *Stork Club: American's Most Famous Nightspot and the Lost World of Café Society.* Boston: Little, Brown, 2000.

Boorstin, Daniel. *The Americans: The Colonial Experience.* Norwalk, Connecticut: Easton Press, 1987.

Brookhiser, Richard. *Alexander Hamilton, American.* New York: Free Press, 1999.

———. *America's First Dynasty: The Adamses, 1735–1918.* New York: Free Press, 2002.

———. *Gentleman Revolutionary: Gouverneur Morris—The Rake Who Wrote the Constitution.* New York: Free Press, 2003.

Burnham, John C. *Bad Habits: Drinking, Smoking, taking Drugs, Gambling, Sexual Misbehavior, and Swearing in American History* New York: New York University Press, 1993.

Carter, Paul A. *Another Part of the Twenties.* New York: Columbia University Press, 1977.

Cashman, Sean Dennis. *Prohibition: The Lie of the Land.* New York: Free Press, 1981.

Ciulla, Joanne B. *The Working Life: The Promise and Betrayal of Modern Work.* New York: Times Books, 2000.

Coffey, Thomas M. *The Long Thirst: Prohibition in America, 1920–1933.* New York: Norton, 1975.

Dabney, Virginius. *Dry Messiah: The Life of Bishop Cannon.* Westport, Connecticut: Greenwood Press, 1949.

Dinkin, Robert J. *Campaigning in America: A History of Election Practices.* Westport, Connecticut: Greenwood Press, 1989.

Dobyns, Fletcher. *The Amazing Story of Repeal.* Evanston, Illinois: Signal Press, 1974.

Dow, Frederick Neal. *Prohibition: Why-How-Then-Now.* Portland, Maine: Maine Woman's Christian Temperance Union, 1931.

Dow, Neal. *The Reminiscences of Neal Dow: Recollections of Eighty Years.* Portland, Maine: Express Publishing Company, 1898.

Duis, Percy R. *The Saloon: Public Drinking in Chicago and Boston, 1880–1920.* Urbana: University of Illinois Press, 1983.

Durant, Will. *Caesar and Christ: The Story of Civilization: 3.* New York: Simon and Schuster, 1944.

———. *The Life of Greece: The Story of Civilization: 2.* New York: Simon and Schuster, 1939.

Durkee, Rev. J. H., ed. *History of the World's Temperance Centennial Congress.* Rochester, New York: 1908.

Einstein, Isidor. *Prohibition Agent No. 1.* New York: Frederick A. Stokes Company, 1932.

Englemann, Larry. *Intemperance: The Lost War Against Liquor.* New York: Free Press, 1979.

Ettinger, Amos Aschbach. *James Edward Oglethorpe: Imperial Idealist.* New York: Archon Books, 1968.

———. *Oglethorpe: A Brief Biography.* Macon, Georgia: Mercer University Press, 1984.

Fecher, Charles A. *Mencken: A Study of His Thought.* New York: Alfred A. Knopf, 1978.

Fernández-Armesto, Felipe. *Near A Thousand Tables: A History of Food.* New York: Free Press, 2002.

Fleming, Alice. *Alcohol: The Delightful Poison*. New York: Delacorte Press, 1979.

Flexner, James Thomas. *George Washington: The Forge of Experience (1732–1775)*. Boston: Little, Brown, 1965.

Forbes, Esther. *Paul Revere and the World He Lived In*. New York: Book-of-the-Month Club, 1983.

Franklin, Jimmie Lewis. *Born Sober: Prohibition in Oklahoma, 1907–1959*. Norman: University of Oklahoma Press, 1971.

Furnas, J.C. *The Americans: A Social History of the United States, 1587–1914*. New York: G.P. Putnam's Sons, 1969.

————. *Great Times: An Informal Social History of the United States, 1914–1929*. New York: G.P. Putnam's Sons, 1974.

————. *The Life and Times of the Late Demon Rum*. London: W.H. Allen, 1965.

Gelb, Norman. *Less Than Glory: A Revisionist's View of the American Revolution*. New York: G.P. Putnam's Sons, 1984.

Getz, Oscar. *Whiskey: An American Pictorial History*. New York: David McKay Company, 1978.

Goodwin, Doris Kearns. *The Fitzgeralds and the Kennedys: An American Saga*. New York: Simon and Schuster, 1987.

Gordon, Anna A. *The Beautiful Life of Frances E. Willard*. Chicago: Woman's Temperance Publishing Association, 1898.

Grimes, William. *Straight Up or On the Rocks: A Cultural History of American Drink*. New York: Simon and Schuster, 1993.

Gurko, Miriam. *The Ladies of Seneca Falls: The Birth of the Women's Rights Movement*. Norwalk, Connecticut: Easton Press, 1990.

Hallahan, William H. *The Day the American Revolution Began*. New York: William Morrow, 2000.

Halliday, E. M. *Understanding Thomas Jefferson*. New York: HarperCollins, 2001.

Hamilton, Edward. *Rums of the Eastern Caribbean*. Culebra, Puerto Rico: Tafia Publishing, 1997.

Handlin, Oscar and Lillian. *A Restless People: Americans in Rebellion, 1770–1787*. Garden City, New York: Anchor Press/Doubleday, 1982.

Harrison, Michael. *Fire from Heaven: A Study of Spontaneous Combustion in Human Beings*. New York: Metheun, 1977.

Hartigan, Francis. *Bill W.: A Biography of Alcoholics Anonymous Co-Founder Bill Wilson*. New York: St. Martin's Press, 2000.

Holbrook, Stewart H. *Dreamers of the American Dream*. Garden City, New York: Doubleday, 1957.

Isaacson, Walter. *Benjamin Franklin: An American Life*. New York: Simon & Schuster, 2003.

Jenkins, Alan. *The Twenties*. New York: Universe Books, 1974.

Kessler, Ronald. *Sins of the Father: Joseph P. Kennedy and the Dynasty He Founded*. New York: Warner Books, 1996.

Kobler, John. *Ardent Spirits: The Rise and Fall of Prohibition*. New York: G.P. Putnam's Sons, 1973.

Krout, John Allen. *The Origins of Prohibition*. New York: Alfred A. Knopf, 1925.

Kyvig, David, ed. *Law, Alcohol, and Order: Perspectives on National Prohibition*. Westport, Connecticut: Greenwood Press, 1985.

————. *Repealing National Prohibition.* Chicago: University of Chicago Press, 1979.

Lacey, Robert. *Ford: The Men and the Machine.* Boston: Little, Brown, 1986.

Larson, Erik. *The Devil in the White City: Murder, Magic and Madness at the Fair That Changed America.* New York: Crown, 2003.

Lee, Henry. *How Dry We Were: Prohibition Revisited.* Englewood Cliffs, New Jersey: Prentice-Hall, 1963.

Leighton, Isabel, ed. *The Aspirin Age, 1919–1941.* New York: Simon and Schuster, 1949.

Leinwand, Gerald. *1927: High Tide of the Twenties.* New York: Four Walls Eight Windows, 2001.

Lender, Mark Edward, and James Kirby Martin. *Drinking in America: A History.* New York: Free Press, 1982.

Lerner, Max. *America As A Civilization.* New York: Simon and Schuster, 1957.

Liell, Scott. *46 pages: Thomas Paine, Common Sense, and the Turning Point to American Independence.* Philadelphia: Running Press, 2003.

Link, Arthur S., and William B. Catton. *American Epoch: A History of the United States Since the 1890s.* New York: Alfred A. Knopf, 1967.

Lord, Walter. *The Good Years: From 1900 to the First World War.* New York: Harper & Brothers, 1960.

Lucia, Salvatore Pablo, M.D., ed. *Alcohol and Civilization.* New York: McGraw-Hill, 1963.

Marks, Paula Mitchell. *In A Barren Land: American Indian Dispossession and Survival.* New York: William Morrow, 1998.

Marriott, Alice, and Carol K. Rachlin. *American Epic: The Story of the American Indian.* New York: G.P. Putnam's Sons, 1969.

McCullough, David. *John Adams.* New York: Simon and Schuster, 2001.

Merz, Charles. *The Dry Decade.* Garden City, New York: Doubleday, Doran & Company, 1931.

Miller, John C. *This New Man, the American: The Beginnings of the American People.* New York: McGraw-Hill, 1974.

Milton, Giles. *Nathaniel's Nutmeg or, The True and Incredible Adventures of the Spice Trader Who Changed the Course of History.* New York: Farrar, Straus and Giroux, 1999.

Mitgang, Herbert. *Once Upon A Time in New York: Jimmy Walker, Franklin Roosevelt, and the Last Great Battle of the Jazz Age.* New York: Free Press, 2000.

Mordden, Ethan. *That Jazz: An Idiosyncratic Social History of the American Twenties.* New York: G.P. Putnam's Sons, 1978.

Morgan, Edmund S. *Benjamin Franklin.* New Haven, Connecticut: Yale University Press, 2002.

Morris, Joe Alex. *What A Year!* New York: Harper Brothers, 1956.

Murdock, Catherine Gilbert. *Domesticating Drink: Women, Men, and Alcohol in America, 1870–1940.* Baltimore: The Johns Hopkins University Press, 1998.

Nation, Carry. *The Use and Need of the Life of Carry A. Nation*. Topeka, Kansas: F.M. Steves and Sons, 1905.

Oates, Stephen B. *Abraham Lincoln: The Man Behind the Myths*. New York: Harper & Row, 1984.

Pegram, Thomas R. *Battling Demon Rum: The Struggle for a Dry America, 1800–1933*. Chicago: Ivan R. Dee, 1998.

Perrett, Geoffrey. *America in the Twenties*. New York, Simon and Schuster, 1982.

———. *Ulysses S. Grant: Soldier & President*. New York: Random House, 1997.

Phillips, Kevin. *Wealth and Democracy: A Political History of the American Rich*. New York: Broadway Books, 2002.

Pickering, Clarence R. *The Early Days of Prohibition*. New York: Vantage Press, 1964.

Porter, Roy. *The Greatest Benefit to Mankind: A Medical History of Humanity*. New York, W.W. Norton, 1998.

Randall, Willard Sterne. *Alexander Hamilton: A Life*. New York: HarperCollins, 2003.

Rorabaugh, W. J. *The Alcoholic Republic: An American Tradition*. New York: Oxford University Press, 1979.

Schlesinger, Arthur, M. *The Birth of the Nation: A Portrait of the American People on the Eve of Independence*. New York: Knopf, 1969.

Seldes, Gilbert. *The Stammering Century*. Gloucester, Massachusetts: Peter Smith, 1972.

Simmons, James C. *Star-Spangled Eden: 19th Century America Through the Eyes of Dickens, Wilde, Frances Trollope, Frank Harris, and Other British Travelers*. New York: Carroll & Graf, 2000.

Simon, James F. *What Kind of Nation: Thomas Jefferson, John Marshall, and the Epic Struggle to Create a United States*. New York: Simon and Schuster, 2002.

Sinclair, Andrew. *Prohibition: The Era of Excess*. New York: Atlantic–Little, Brown, 1962.

Spalding, Phinizy. *Oglethorpe in America*. Chicago: University of Chicago Press, 1977.

Steuart, Justin. *Wayne Wheeler, Dry Boss*. Chicago: Revell Publishers, 1928.

Sullivan, Mark. *Our Times: The United States, 1900–1925, Volume V: Over Here, 1914–1918*. New York: Charles Scribner's Sons, 1933.

———. *Our Times: The United States, 1900–1925, Volume VI: The Twenties*. New York: Charles Scribner's Sons, 1935.

Tannehill, Reay. *Food in History*. New York: Stein and Day, 1973.

Taylor, Alan. *American Colonies*. New York: Viking, 2001.

Taylor, Robert Lewis. *Vessel of Wrath: The Life and Times of Carry Nation*. New York: New American Library, 1966.

This Fabulous Century, Volume III: 1920–1930. New York: Time-Life Books, 1969.

Thomas, Gordon, and Max Morgan-Witts. *The Day the Bubble Burst: A Social History of the Wall Street Crash of 1929*. Garden City, New York: Doubleday Company, 1979.

Tindall, George Brown. *America: A Narrative History, Volume I*. New York, W.W. Norton, 1984.

Troy, Gil. *See How They Ran: The Changing Role of the Presidential Candidate*. New York: Free Press, 1991.

Van Doren, Carl. *Benjamin Franklin*. New York: Book-of-the-Month Club, 1980.

Waller, Maureen. *1700: Scenes from London Life*. New York: Four Walls Eight Windows, 2000.

Ward, Sarah F. *The White Ribbon Story: 125 Years of Service to Humanity*. Evanston, Illinois: Signal Press, 1999.

Weisberger, Bernard A. *America Afire: Jefferson, Adams, and the Revolutionary Election of 1800*. William Morrow, 2000.

Willard, Frances E. *The Autobiography of An American Woman: Glimpses of Fifty Years*. Evanston, Illinois: National Woman's Christian Temperance Union, 1889.

Index